THE TRAGEDY OF OTHELLO
THE MOOR OF VENICE

The Tragedy of Othello the Moor of Venice

WILLIAM SHAKESPEARE

EDITED BY LAWRENCE J. ROSS

THE BOBBS-MERRILL COMPANY, INC.

INDIANAPOLIS · NEW YORK

First Printing

Copyright © 1974 by The Bobbs-Merrill Company, Inc.

Printed in the United States of America

Cover and Title Page Illustrations by Edward Gorey

The Bobbs-Merrill Shakespeare Series

is under the General Editorship of

Ian Watt, Stanford University

Library of Congress Cataloging in Publication Data

Shakespeare, William, 1564–1616.
　　The tragedy of Othello.

　　(The Bobbs-Merrill Shakespeare series)
　　Bibliography: p.
　　I. Ross, Lawrence J., ed.　II. Title.　III. Title: Othello.
PR2829.A2R64　　　822.3'3　　　73–14771
ISBN 0–672–51483–4
ISBN 0–672–61106–6 (pbk.)

CONTENTS

vi   *Contents*

Introduction

When he wrote *The Tragedy of Othello*, Shakespeare was at the height of his powers and was intensively devoting them, more exclusively than during any other period of his career, to the creation of one kind of play—tragedy. In six years he produced all the tragedies generally thought his greatest. *Othello*, probably written about 1603–4, was the second of these, following *Hamlet* and preceding *King Lear* and *Macbeth*. Although very often considered the most perfectly structured of these great tragedies, this play frequently has been regarded also as something of an anomaly. Certain features have tended not only to set it apart from these other supreme achievements of Shakespeare's tragic genius, but even to obscure its close participation with them in a continuity of profound tragic concerns. *Othello* clearly is unlike them in its dependence on a fictional source, in its tightly plotted action, and in its concentration on a narrower central cast of characters. But it is because of its emphasis on domestic and psychological situation and its Renaissance setting that it seems strikingly to differ. As a result, the play can seem less unlike a dramatized story of mere private life than the other great tragedies; by comparison with them it can appear, as it has to many, a delimited drama imaginatively confined to a wholly mundane subject. Indeed, because of its ostensibly narrow focus, contemporaneity, and intense verisimilitude, the play can even tempt us to associate it with realistic "domestic tragedy"—a kind of play, little practiced by the Elizabethans, which *Othello* in fact very slenderly resembles. Ironically, to try to apprehend the play in this limiting way is to reverse the imaginative process by which Shakespeare transcended the narrow, realistic story with which he began.

The primary narrative source for the play, a *novella* in Giraldi

Cinthio's *Hecatommithi*, is a straightforward, rather sordid, story of jealousy, intrigue, revenge, and murder. Shakespeare, although he managed to use a remarkable amount from this source, utterly transformed it into a profoundly disturbing and symbolically resonant tragedy of the thwarting of ideal-aspiring human virtue. A translation of the bulk of Cinthio's *novella*, and some consideration of models and sources of inspiration for the changes Shakespeare wrought on it, can be found in Appendix C. The present discussion must limit itself simply to some of the crucial ways in which this transformation was effected.

Most obviously, Shakespeare ennobled the Moor of the source. Gross differences separate Othello from the Moor of the prose *novella*, who shows no concern for his wife's soul, brutally murders her in a manner calculated to keep himself free from suspicion, and never confesses or judges his own guilt. His Moor Shakespeare made a creation of poetry, and he gave him not only a more impressive passionate love but also a moral stature, and a capacity for vision and suffering, equal to the immensely greater size of what he tragically loses. Above all, the playwright endowed Othello, initially, with that "visage in his mind" which Desdemona has seen and for which she loves him. That such an inner "visage" should have been supposed for a Moor itself indicates the difference and greater complexity of Shakespeare's intentions. Cinthio's story can be viewed, very much as his ill-fated heroine fears, as an example to Italian ladies "not to go with a man whom nature, heaven, and way of life separates from us." We readily detect here the same prejudiced view that Iago expounds with such poisonous effect (e.g. III. iii. 225–35). It was one to which most Elizabethans (to whom Moors were in fact exotic) would easily have assented. Moors were thought typically to be passionate, hot-tempered, and quick to vengeance. The Moor was associated with the barbaric, with savage intemperance, with the bond-slavery appropriate to the sons of Cham (the divinely rejected son of Noah thought the ancestor of dark races). Indeed, their very color, blackness, was that of the devil, sin, and the reprobate; it was the badge of hell itself. The Moor of these prejudices—the very one (apart from the many hints to the contrary) which Roderigo's, Iago's, and Brabantio's slandering, envious, and vengeful testimonies in the first scene prepare us to see—sets in startling relief the nobly disciplined and lofty-minded Christian commander who appears at the start of I. ii. Shakespeare makes it tragically ironic that *this* Moor, so different in his essential being, should, as a result of temptation, come to correspond in any way with the Moor of Elizabethan prejudice.

Shakespeare further shaped his ennobled Moor into a tragic figure by making him a proven hero who becomes ensnared "body and soul" not simply by an intrigue but by temptations which test, with profoundly representative force, the stability of the very exemplary virtues which comprise his heroic identity. For the Renaissance, Virtue could be seen (as in the medal reproduced here, p. x; fig. a) to manifest itself in its mastering of "Cupid" and "Fortune." Though the age variously conceived of Fortune and Virtue, the relationship between them most frequently posited was radical antagonism. The same was often true for Virtue and Love: Cupid (as in the medal, where his bow is at his feet) must be disarmed to be mastered. Fortune is here represented by the figure known to the Renaissance as "Occasion" (or "Opportunity")—a personification of the idea of life as made up of moments of decisive choice which may declare what a man essentially is. It symbolizes that instability of life at the mercy of the vicissitudes of Fortune which Virtue must master to be and remain itself. Men's weakness in virtue makes the chances most often into occasions to evil; thus Spenser calls Occasion "the roote of all wrath and despight" (*Faerie Queene*, II. iv. x) and Shakespeare himself indicts Opportunity as "an accessary by . . . inclination/ To all sins" (*Lucrece*, lines 922–3). Cupid may stand here not merely for the "young and sweating devil" in us "That commonly rebels," but for a whole potentially dangerous side of our passional life. Traditionally, the irrational appetites were divided into the irascible (whose types are wrath and grief) and the concupiscent. Jealousy—a passion of love also typically involving grief, wrathful vengefulness, and despair—was an attractive subject for a Renaissance tragedian because it involved both appetitive faculties of the soul. It permitted consideration in one hero of the chaos man can make of his higher rational nature and its purposes through appetite if he does not remain strong in virtue.

Patience,
ouercōmeth all
thinges.

Wrath,
deuoureth it
selfe.

b

(a) Virtue mastering Love and Chance. Niccolò
Fiorentino, Medal of Stefano Taverna. Made in
Florence about 1495. *(Courtesy of the Royal Scottish
Museum.)* (b) Patience over Wrath. Woodcut border
illustration from *A Booke of Christian Prayers*,
compiled by Richard Day (London, 1579), fol. 63ᵛ.
(Courtesy of the Pierpont Morgan Library, New York.)

Latet anguis in herba.

The adder lurketh priuilie in the grasse.

c

(c) "Latet anguis in herba." Device from *The Heroicall Devises of M. Claudius Paradin* (London, 1591), p. 83. *(Courtesy of the Folger Shakespeare Library.)* (d) "He, that his Course directly Steeres." Engraved emblem by Crispin Van der Passe (1601), with portion of accompanying poem, from George Wither, *A Collection of Emblemes* (London, 1635), p. 37. *(Courtesy of the Princeton University Library.)*

He, *that his* Course *directly Steeres,* Nor Stormes, *nor* Windy-Censures *feares.*

ILLVSTR. XXXVII.   Book. I.

Ee to the *Sea,* this *World* may well compare;
For, ev'ry Man which liveth in the same,
Is as a *Pilot,* to some *Vessell* there,
Of little size, or else of larger frame.

Even the trial in I. iii which forbodingly challenges his virtuous identity serves largely to attest that Othello is a heroic exemplar of such strength. It reveals him not only an important battle-tried general but a man as yet unvanquished by "the battles, sieges, fortunes" of life, one as undaunted by hardship and vicissitude as he is unruled by passions, "the vices of [the] blood." By this "quality" as much as his literal valorous soldiership is Desdemona's heart "subdued." And much in the trial scene further establishes the bond between his deserved estimation as a man of such "perfect soul," government, and fortitude and his fitness to lead "the serious and great business" of the state. Hence the profound justness, once he has succumbed to temptation, of the arrival of orders from Venice removing him from his post as governor and, as well, the exact propriety of the terms of the ducal emissary's shocked disappointment in the character of the Othello he now finds.

> Is this the noble Moor whom our full senate
> Call all in all sufficient? Is this the nature
> Whom passion could not shake? whose solid virtue
> The shot of accident nor dart of chance
> Could neither graze nor pierce?
>
> (IV. i. 247–51)

For the tragic fall of this "Othello that [was] once so good" Shakespeare provided an accordant background of dramatically significant conflict not found in his source: the "present wars against the Ottomites." The long struggle with the Turks in the Renaissance was regarded not as a power contest or war of nations but as nothing less than a spiritual antagonism between Christendom and the infidel, between the powers of light and those of darkness. That Othello is sent by Christian Venice to a far distant and weakly defended outpost as the leader of the defense against the Turk is a stunning testimony of his stature as a champion of Christendom. Nor is the force of this point blunted when the providential storm lames the Turkish designs against Cyprus; this background, of a particular embodiment of spiritual conflict, helps to define and color the nature of the challenge Othello actually encounters on Cyprus after the merely military threat by the literal Turkish forces has been eliminated.

For the Turks function in the play very much as do the monstrous "Anthropophagi, and men whose heads/Do grow beneath their shoulders" of the dangerous far-off lands Othello has traversed: they serve to point up the fact that in the world of Christian society itself can equally be found "monstrous" men and deeds, barbarous impulses, infidel threats. In the "barbarous brawl" in II. iii, the rioting officers who violate "Christian shame" have acted, says Othello, as though they had "turned Turk": they do that to each other which heaven had prevented the Turks from doing (lines 149–50). Earlier, Iago jokingly admits he is "a Turk" if his grossly denigrative comments on womankind are slanders (II. i. 114–15). And the central action plainly turns on various infidelities, real and imagined, literal and spiritual. The climax of this motif comes when Othello attempts to wreak judgment on his "infidel" self by killing himself as he once had slain "a malignant and a turbaned Turk" in Aleppo (V. ii. 348–52).

In various other ways Shakespeare gave the issues of the drama philosophical, moral, and social, as well as merely psychological, depth. He depicted the pride-stung, value-corroding villain as a pseudo-Machiavellian Renaissance "new man," who professes a self-loving "service" and amoral *virtù* scornful of the older sanctions of identity and action associated with the hero and heroine. In announcing his belief in the primacy of Will in man, and the subservience of Reason to it in human choice and action, Iago the ensign shows the standard which those he leads will follow. Shakespeare thematically characterized the central personages in other ways as well. Thus, for example, Othello's belief in the slander creates for both Desdemona and himself tests not only of faith and love, but also of patience in adversity. The idea of Patience, so sharply defined for Shakespeare by his Elizabethan Christian culture (e.g., p. x, fig. b), reflected first of all upon vengeance for injuries "which patience could not pass." The play assumes that (in an instance like Othello's) the high importance the Renaissance attributed to personal honor will complicate reaction to the idea of private revenge (as distinguished from public revenge justly performed by a true magistrate). But it insists that such vengeance be more fundamentally regarded as blind error, forbidden sin, terrible hybris; the biblical dictum, "Vengeance is mine, . . . saith the Lord" (Rom. 12: 19), was deeply inculcated. In a larger sense, patience was also understood to concern the proper human response to fortune, particularly adversity, affliction, and loss, in a world supposedly governed by divine providence. All the major characters will be found to construe themselves for us by reference to this inclusive and richly implicative Christian standard. This applies most centrally to Othello, who climactically articulates the theme in the Brothel Scene (IV. ii).

> Had it pleased heaven
> To try me with affliction, had they rained
> All kinds of sores and shames on my bare head,
> Steeped me in poverty to the very lips,
> Given to captivity me and my utmost hopes,
> I should have found in some place of my soul
> A drop of patience . . .
>
> (lines 48–54)

But even Patience herself, he says, could not but turn color and "look grim as hell" confronting the adversity he suffers.

Shakespeare also suggests in the characters and their interplay a sophisticated version of the earlier morality play's dynamics and issues. Of course *Othello* is a symbolic tragedy of moral choice, not an allegory or morality play. And Desdemona and Iago, for instance, cannot accurately be described as Virtue and Vice, or good and bad angel, debating for domination of the hero's soul. Nevertheless, a clear dramatic tradition does lead from the earlier moralities to Shakespeare's conception of this kind of tragic action. We do not find in Shakespeare's play a hero attended by a Satan-prompted Pride, Wrath, and Envy whose debate with godly-instigated Meekness, Patience, and Charity serves to externalize the interior war within him. The moral conflict has become more internal and psychological as well as more complex. Nevertheless, what we do find is not only the persisting sense of an evil adversary to man's good, but also resurgent dramatic functions, exactly analogous to those of earlier personification, being assumed by largely realistic and individualized characters, who exemplify these virtues and vices by explicitly professing them and acting upon them as principles of conduct. The significance of the hero's decisive choices is then clarified partly by his changing relationships to these figures as these are defined by the dramatic poetry. This again is seen most readily in Iago whose characterization clearly goes beyond its frightening particularity. It is anchored conventionally in the figure of the Vice, who declares, in what he is and what he tells us he will do, the concupiscence by which his representative victim will be made to succumb.

It is important to appreciate that the poetry which is one of the glories of the play, so far from being mere splendid embellishment, is a principal means of enlarging the significance of its action. Everywhere it serves to discover the import in the literal and reveal the implicit representativeness and symbolic dimensions of what is being incarnated upon the stage. A fine illustration of this is afforded by Othello's speech, as he adoringly watches Desdemona's exit, just before the temptation scene with Iago begins.

> Excellent wretch! Perdition catch my soul
> But I do love thee! and when I love thee not,
> Chaos is come again.
>
> (III. iii. 89–91)

The very lines by which he declares the power and permanence of his love, and its likeness with the force that keeps the universe in order, also imply the idolatry in his love, and the chaos, and the personal fate, it will bring about. The poetry of the speech, in other words, fully informs the poignancy and tragic irony of its placement in the action.

As the passage itself suggests, moreover, much of the enlargement of significance in the action is dependent on the symbolic capacities of literal theme. The proper order of marriage could itself symbolize the idea of concord everywhere in the universe. Much more, therefore, could poetically be suggested to be at stake in the challenges to this particular marital relationship— challenges from malice and envy without, and from the limited human capacity within to achieve the ideal ends of actions.

OTHELLO

If it were now to die,
'Twere now to be most happy; for I fear
My soul hath her content so absolute
That not another comfort like to this
Succeeds in unknown fate.

DESDEMONA

The heavens forbid
But that our loves and comforts should increase
Even as our days do grow.

OTHELLO

Amen to that, sweet powers!
I cannot speak enough of this content:
It stops me here; it is too much of joy.
And this, and this, the greatest discords be   *They kiss.*
That e'er our hearts shall make!

IAGO

[*Aside*] O, you are well tuned now!
But I'll set down the pegs that make this music,
As honest as I am.   (II. i. 183–95)

Traditionally, the devil is the principal agent for discord in the universe, society, and the order of marriage, and this passage illustrates how other analogical perspectives on the literal action turn upon Shakespeare's daring and subtle use of "ideal referents"—in this case allusion to the very spirit of spiritual disorder. The diabolic references and imagery, by no means exclusively associated with Iago, are found throughout this play more abundantly than in any other Shakespeare wrote. The implicit basic rationale of these is the conventional Christian division of mankind into "children" of the two spiritual "fathers" they may in their actions resemble: sin turns man from "being in the image of God" to acting in the image of Satan. The explicative and evocative powers of such an idea are enormous, but here they are always used, not to displace the primary human drama enacted before us, but rather to enrich and give resonance to it.

The possibilities of discovering the import in the literal were greatly enhanced for Shakespeare by the abundance of commonplace symbolic ideas and conventional imagery which his tradition made available to him. Unhappily, much of this now requires annotation. For example, the fact that the embroidered "spots" on the fatal handkerchief in the play happen to be "strawberries" is a realistic touch, as this actually was a favorite subject for ornamentation in English domestic needlework. We need to know this just as we need to know that a handkerchief was often a troth-plight gift in Elizabethan times. But we also need to know that strawberries could have special significance as referring by emblematic convention to the attractions of apparent goodness beneath which dangerous evil may lurk (see p. xi, fig. c). Much of what looks, and indeed is, literal in the play enjoys further significance by virtue of the controlled poetic evocation of such conventions. Thus, the awaiting of Othello's ship in II. i is throughout informed by the common-place figure of Everyman as spiritual sailor on the stormy seas of life in this world (p. xi, fig. d), the very figure Othello will invoke—ironically before his suicide—in referring to his having reached "the very sea-mark of my utmost sail" (V. ii. 265). In the context of such a conception, the anxious discussion about the strength and seaworthiness of Othello's ship and the reputed sufficiency of its pilot (II. i. 44–9) is symbolic. It is as loaded with an expository significance as Cassio's saying "The great contention of the sea and skies/ Parted our fellowship" (92–3) is weighted with a preparative one.

The analogical habits of thought so strikingly evidenced in the backgrounds of the play, and in Shakespeare's use of them, were native to the mind of the English Renaissance, and they are also manifested in the structure of this play. Some eighteenth-century critics supposed that, had the tragedy's action begun in Cyprus, and the matter of Act I been reported, the drama would have wanted little of being "regular," which is to say neoclassic, in form. Actually, the play fully exhibits the characteristic Elizabethan taste for multiplicity. Points along the narrative line not strictly essential to such a tight and condensed design are more separably developed into effective scenes and groupings. These are important for their contribution, not primarily to plot, but rather to emotive range or progression (e.g. the "trance" scene, IV. i), intensified expression of theme or conflict (the Brothel Scene, IV. ii), and above all, elaborative enrichment through reflective characters and situations (as in the interviews between Cassio and Bianca). In V. i, for example, the action is vigorously direct; at least the main event (the attempt on Cassio's life) is important to the plot; and nothing in the rest of the scene is really irrelevant to the full story. But analysis will show that much in the scene deserves its place in the design of the drama by virtue of illuminating parallelism with other matter and actions, particularly those of the next, concluding, scene. Of course, as suggested earlier, the characters and their relationships themselves are ordered and placed throughout the tragedy by means of various and complex patterns of analogy. Thus, for instance, Brabantio's impatience at Desdemona's "revolt" and loss foreshadows Othello's, and the seduction and ruination of Roderigo illuminates, at a remove, those of Iago's much greater dupe. At the center of this design, in the most schematic view, we watch Othello, by virtue of his belief that Desdemona is a "fair devil" (III. iii. 475), move from a contrast in parallel with Desdemona (fair face/ fair soul) to one with Iago (fair face/evil soul) in a way which underscores the tragic shift in the meaning of his blackness. It is the progression from the Duke's conditional assertion,

> If virtue no delighted beauty lack,
> Your son-in-law is far more fair than black.
> (I. iii. 285–6)

to Emilia's insistent unmasking of the hero's delusion of righteousness after the murder:

OTHELLO

> She's like a liar gone to burning hell!
> 'Twas I that killed her.

EMILIA

> O, the more angel she,
> And you the blacker devil!
> (V. ii. 128–30)

The above discussion of the play has been primarily concerned to suggest some of the essential ways and means by which Shakespeare transmuted what might otherwise have been simply a domestic intrigue plot into a tragic action built upon one. In consequence, the drama realizes with a rare and suspenseful immediacy our condition in a world of treacherous appearances, capable of deceiving the highminded and the low-intentioned, the idealistic and the pragmatic, alike. It is a condition between the ennobling human goals our nature might seek and the fallible and corruptible human resources we must rely upon in trying to attain them. Only *King Lear* perhaps is more painfully beautiful in tragic paradox, affirming and refining our sense of the humanly valuable by making us vicariously undergo the costly suffering caused by human limitation and failure.

OTHELLO ON SHAKESPEARE'S STAGE

The Elizabethan public theater for which most of Shakespeare's plays were primarily intended was a remarkably flexible expressive instrument. It was also basically a very simple one so that its plays were readily adaptable to production on other stages where virtually the same conventions could obtain. During its first decade on the boards (see Appendix F) we know that *Othello* was played not only at the Globe, but also before the Court at Whitehall Palace, at Oxford (presumably in a college hall), and in the King's Men's second playhouse, Blackfriars, the roofed "private" theater acquired by the company in 1608–9.

The permanent open-air theaters like the Globe were among the colorful sights of Elizabethan London. With its flag flying to announce a performance, a typical public playhouse might boast an ornate stage façade with tapestried hangings, painted cloths, and carved posts; and, extending from this above a large platform stage, a "heavens" (or stage-cover), elaborately decorated with celestial or zodiacal symbols, supported by columns painted to resemble marble. These were vivid and festive showplaces for professional entertainment, and they attracted a large and varied audience of avid playgoers. This audience, drawn from all classes, comprised a rough cross-section of the London populace—a circumstance partly responsible for the extraordinary variety of appeals built into the plays as well as for the range of accommodations offered the theater patrons. For the entrance fee to the theater (probably a penny) a good part of the audience—the so-called "groundlings"—stood throughout the performance, exposed to the weather, crowded about three sides of the platform stage in the "pit" (what we would now call the orchestra). For additional sums admission might be gained to the three circling tiers of roofed seats, and to the most expensive accommodations in the house, the "Lords' Rooms." Thus, although an audience much huger than those of the present-day legitimate playhouses could be accommodated—perhaps one as large as 3000—its disposition was such that a much greater proportion of the auditors than can be the case in any proscenium arch theater was close to the action. Indeed, frequently in the course of a play an actor might be much nearer to members of his audience than to other on-stage performers in the cast.

This proximity enabled that emphasis on the actors and their relation to the audience essential to an open platform stage which, paradoxically, must build its imaginative power upon its ever being inescapably what it fundamentally is—a place afforded actors to perform amidst their auditors. On such a stage, forms of utterance that assume, with varying degrees of candor, the presence of the theater audience could be highly effective, whereas they are scarcely viable on the picture-frame stage of the proscenium arch theater. Thus, for example, soliloquy, aside, and direct address, instead of being embarrassments, afforded opportunity for brilliant economies of dramatic statement and focus. In this play the role most patently dependent upon such conventions is that of Iago, who at points (as in his mock-denial of evil in his advice to the disgraced Cassio) even exhibits that jocular familiarity with the audience which was a trademark of the Vice in the older morality play.

> And what's he then that says I play the villain,
> When this advice is free I give, and honest . . . ?
> (II. iii. 305–6)

The Elizabethan audience would have understood Iago's soliloquies to be sophisticated versions of the stage-villain's conventional self-revelation of motive and intention—here so developed as to suggest for them the psychological, moral, and social dimensions of the conflicts which his testing villainy exploits. In these speeches, the actor's proximity to the audience vitalized the convention so that the listeners could be drawn by his confidences, disclosures, and self-exhibition into intimate relation with the unmasked springs of the action. Again, Iago's contrapuntal aside at the ecstatic reunion of Othello and Desdemona at Cyprus—"O you are well tuned now . . ." (II. i. 193ff.)—assumes a nearness to the audience that can enforce its awareness of the dramatic ironies implicit in his very inclusion in the grouping onstage. Such modulation of audience engagement with the action, and perspective upon it, is well exemplified in Othello's soliloquy after the first scene of temptation, when his disturbed musings on Iago's honesty and worldly knowledge panic him into anticipatory reactions to Desdemona's supposed guilt. In the Elizabethan playhouse the audience was physically near enough to share immediately in the hero's disturbed emotion. At the same time, their superior knowledge of character and situation compelled them to be critically detached. This made ironic Othello's direction of their attention to the stage reality: at the start of the soliloquy it is to the door where Iago has just made his exit ("This fellow's of exceeding honesty . . ."), and, at its close, to Desdemona's entrance from the other door.

> . . . Even then this forkèd plague is fated to us
> When we do quicken.
>> *Enter* DESDEMONA *and* EMILIA.
>>> Look where she comes:
> If she be false, O then heaven mocks itself!
> I'll not believe't.
>>>> (III. iii. 273–6)

In this theater entrances from the side were not possible, and this passage illustrates dramatically purposeful use of the short speech to "cover" entrances and exits—in this case the movement downstage of actors entering from one of the stage doors in the façade of the "tiring house" (the backstage area where the actors prepared themselves). This immediately suggests something of the character and size of the principal acting area of the playhouse, the open platform stage. First, it was very large. That in the Fortune Theater, erected a year after the Globe and patterned in many respects upon it, was (according to the builder's contract) 43 feet wide by 27 feet 6 inches deep.

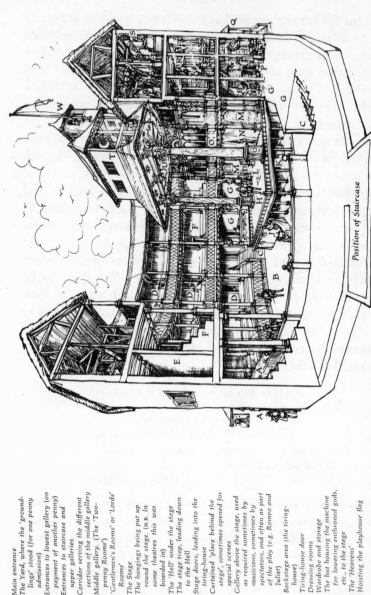

AA   Main entrance
B   The Yard, where the 'ground-
     lings' stood (for one penny
     admission)
CC   Entrances to lowest gallery (on
     payment of another penny)
D   Entrances to staircase and
     upper galleries
E   Corridor serving the different
     sections of the middle gallery
F   Middle gallery. (The 'Two-
     penny Rooms')
G   'Gentlemen's Rooms' or 'Lords'
     Rooms'
H   The Stage
J   The hangings being put up
     round the stage. (N.B. In
     some theatres this was
     boarded in)
K   The 'Hell' under the stage
L   The stage trap, leading down
     to the Hell
MM   Stage doors, leading into the
     tiring-house
N   Curtained 'place behind the
     stage', sometimes opened for
     special scenes
O   Gallery above the stage, used
     as required sometimes by
     musicians, sometimes by
     spectators, and often as part
     of the play (e.g. Romeo and
     Juliet)
P   Backstage area (the tiring-
     house)
Q   Tiring-house door
R   Dressing rooms
S   Wardrobe and storage
T   The hut housing the machine
     for lowering enthroned gods,
     etc., to the stage
U   The 'Heavens'
W   Hoisting the playhouse flag

A conjectural reconstruction of the Globe theater, by C. Walter Hodges (1958). This lively cut-away view, which represents the fruit of much modern research, of course remains quite hypothetical in many details (e.g., the position of the "Lords' rooms" and the nature of the "discovery-space"). *Courtesy of Ernest Benn, Ltd.*

Such generous dimensions invited processional movements and made possible impressive entries, such as those of Desdemona and Othello in II. i, and Lodovico in IV. i. They also permitted strikingly effective groupings of the actors, whether in opposed parties, as at the confrontation of Othello and Brabantio in I. ii, or in arrangements spaced upstage and down, as perhaps in V. i, where Lodovico and Gratiano hesitate to "come in to the cry" of the wounded Cassio and Roderigo. On a stage this wide and deep actions assuming a credible representation of distance are feasible. Thus, Cassio can mistake the irate Brabantio and his armed company in I. ii for one of the "three several quests" for Othello sent by the Duke, and in IV. i Othello can be placed where he can see Iago and Cassio's conversation but supposedly not hear them. This potential of the stage is tellingly used just before the temptation begins in III. iii, when Othello and Iago's entrance provokes Cassio's embarrassed departure.

OTHELLO

Was not that Cassio parted from my wife?

IAGO

Cassio, my lord? No sure, I cannot think it,
That he would steal away so guilty-like,
Seeing your coming.

(lines 36–9)

The other playing areas of the public theater were so generally used in conjunction with this main platform stage that they should be considered with it. Evidently unemployed in this play was the hidden space beneath the platform (sometimes called the "hell") to which a stage trap, worked by a winch below, provided one access; it was here that the Ghost in *Hamlet* moved about with such mysterious ease, crying "swear!" to those above. At the rear of the platform, and above it, a narrow upper gallery (reached by inner stairs connecting the floors of the tiring house with the stage doors) provided the possibility of elevation. Such scenes "above" are infrequent, and, as the space afforded limited movement or visibility in depth, tended to be uncomplicated and brief. They usually relate to action on the platform below. Brabantio's appearance "above" ("at a window" according to the Quarto text), when aroused from sleep by Iago and Roderigo's cries in I. i, illustrates its use. After verbal confrontation with those below confirms his fearful dreams, dialogue between Iago and Roderigo covers his descent within, and he reenters below in his "nightgown" (a warm Elizabethan dressing gown) through a stage door now easily imagined the entrance of his residence. The two main platform doors, it will have been noted, have a crucial importance for staging in this theater, and various kinds of business involve them. Most often they simply are conventional means of getting on and off the platform; but of course they can be used literally to represent the door of a building (as here), or a hall (I. iii), or room (V. ii). It seems to have been conventional for actors entering by one door to exit by the other. The placement of the doors, moreover, encouraged contrasting use of them to underscore characters' differing origins (I. ii), destination (III. ii), intention, or attitude (IV. iii).

Some scenes would seem to have required a third access to the platform, and it may be that certain public theaters had another, central, door or alcove. Although it would be misleading to think of this as an "inner stage" (a term never used by Elizabethans), this opening, either itself curtained or with a curtained scaffolding or booth before it, may have served as the discovery-space required in those directions which call for the sudden disclosure of a pre-arranged group with properties. Once disclosed, this discovery-space either absorbs, or is absorbed into, the platform stage. In this play, the emergency ducal council revealed in progress, "behind the scene" as it were, at the start of I. iii provides a probable example of such a "discovery": "*Enter* DUKE *and Senators, set at a table, with lights and Attendants.*"

Much of the character of Elizabethan staging is consequent on the basic fact that the main platform stage itself was open and uncurtained. Hence the careful attention given to getting characters on and off stage, a notable awkwardness being that bodies have to be carried off in full view of the audience (V. i) unless a convenient property, like the curtained bed in V. ii, is called for which permits them to be "hid." On the open platform there could be no disclosure of an already arranged grouping of the actors, and of scenery, in our sense of the term, there was none whatever. In such a theater the imaginative reality depends, not upon a consistent and detailed representational illusion, but emphatically upon the histrionic coherence created by the actors, upon the poetry, and upon the "imaginary forces" of the audience. A distinctive dramaturgy too was native to this theater where, but for momentary clearings of the stage, scene could follow scene in rapid and unbroken continuity. The crucial unit in this dramaturgy is the scene, not the act. It follows that in the ordering and relation of the scenes, and the groupings of which they are composed, are to be found the most fundamental clues to the meaning of the action.

It is important to keep in mind that the platform and tiring house façade do not, and need not, represent any place in particular. The stage fundamentally is neutral as regards locale, and many Shakespearean scenes in fact are nowhere specifically localized. This gave locale, where the dramatist chose to make it explicit, especial dramatic import. In the first scene in this play, for instance, even the general locale, Venice, is at first only in the barest way implicit, and it is a full seventy-five lines into the scene before a particular locale is insisted upon, at the point where Iago urges Roderigo to "call up her father." When Roderigo says "Here is her father's house," the tiring house façade imaginatively becomes, for the remainder of the scene, Brabantio's residence, and the platform where Iago and Roderigo stand, the street before it.

The neutral Elizabethan stage importantly differs from modern unlocalized stages with which the reader may be familiar, such as the television "limbo," because its very structure had symbolic associations which could be evoked to "place" actors and actions in terms of Elizabethan world views. Shakespeare's playhouse was called the Globe, after all, since its stage presumed to mirror that of the world theater (*theatrum mundi*) where Everyman plays his part. The physical "heavens" over the stage implicitly symbolized the cosmic order, and the façade the properly analogous political and social order, within which man acts. It is tremendously important for the scope and significance of Elizabethan drama that such symbolic values were available for a playright to invoke, and latent and general enough for him to poetically define, as the context for a particular play's action. *Othello* was written to be performed in a theater where "heaven" and "hell" literally were parts of the stage, as we have particular cause to remember in the temptation scene (III. iii. 441–59), when the hero blows all his "fond love . . . to heaven," summons vengeance to arise "from the hollow hell," and finally kneels to swear "by yond marble heaven" his "capable and wide revenge." The emphasis of this scene is intensely upon the play of mind upon mind and no specific locale is ever insisted upon; but we know, at least by its climax, that the significance of the action is profoundly enlarged by where it "takes place": it is on a stage of human choice between heaven and hell.

The Elizabethan dramatist enjoyed a similar imaginative freedom as regards time, which he could manipulate for dramatic purposes virtually at will. He could "o'erleap" time (as between I. iii and II. i), create the impression of partly overlapping events (as in I. iii, III. ii, and V. ii), and even handle an action from more than one temporal perspective. In II. iii for example, the hour is carefully indicated near the start of the scene as "not yet ten" at night; and the exciting scene of drinking and riot which ensues is continuous, giving the impression that stage time and actual elapsed time are identical. Yet, near the end of the scene Iago amusedly announces, "By th' mass, 'tis morning!/Pleasure and action make the hours seem short" (346–7)—and the entire night is thus, in a stroke, convincingly compressed. *Othello* has fascinated students because examination in the study has revealed it to be of all Shakespeare's plays the one in which he most audaciously dared to enjoy the advantages of two quite contradictory time-schemes for the central action itself. The primary temporal references establish an urgently precipitate duration, a "short time" according with the violent passions that rush the action headlong toward catastrophe. Cassio's arrival with his music before Othello's residence in III. i, initiating the central action, is noted to occur on the very morning following the arrival in Cyprus, celebration of the Turkish fleet's disaster, consummation of the hero's marriage, and the riot of the watch. From this point, all the rest of the play's events are represented as occurring during the remainder of this same day and the early morning hours of the next. By this "short time" Desdemona in fact has no opportunity to commit adultery let alone be guilty of the "oft"-repeated infidelities (IV. i. 84), "stol'n hours of lust"

(III. iii. 335), and "act of shame/A thousand times committed" (V. ii. 208–9) of which she stands accused. As these references suggest, however, a number of speeches and situations variously imply a much longer duration of time on Cyprus, and a few— like Bianca's thrice-iterated complaint that Cassio has ignored her for a week (III. iv. 163–6)—are quite explicit. So consummate and subtle is Shakespeare's skill in managing these contradictory temporal references that both sorts of impressions about the time of the action have imaginative validity for the untroubled audience in the theater; and in fact it was not until two hundred and fifty years after the play was written that even a close analysis of the text discovered the artifice.

Lacking the movable painted scenery and other representational resources of later theaters, the Elizabethan playwright had to rely on verbal description for many effects of setting. But this limitation had its positive side in that setting could be more tightly disciplined to dramatic purpose: the imagination of the audience can the more readily be engaged (as by the powerful lines about the "molestation/On the enchafed flood" in II. i) with the poetic significance, rather than the mere literal reality, of scene and atmosphere. As performances in this open-air theater began about two in the afternoon, the unmalleable condition of a daylit stage made night scenes a particular imaginative challenge. Yet, in this regard so confident was Shakespeare of his theater's conventions, his performers and the means he gave them, that he actually structured this play around the exciting events of three nights (I. i–iii; II. iii; IV. iii–V. ii). In these scenes the emphasized torches, tapers, and lights (climaxed in Othello's entrance "with a light" in V. ii) have a conventional as well as a literal force; and they cooperate with language, situation, action, other properties (like the bed in V. ii), and costumes (Brabantio's "nightgown," Desdemona's "nightly wearing") in establishing the dramatic illusion of night settings. As these are purely imaginative constructs they actually are better able than a literally darkened stage precisely to body forth the metaphoric, symbolic, and ironic implications of darkness, night, and light assumed or developed in the poetry.

Representation in this theater necessarily tends to be synecdochic (so that three or four actors with weapons must stand for an army), and it is one hallmark of Shakespeare's art that he makes imaginative power out of such necessity. This is remarkably exemplified in his use of sound effects, a point easily illustrated in *Othello*, as a repeated insistence on the audience's awareness of offstage presences and action is a notable feature of the play. Sounds—including voices "within" (as in the cries for help in II. iii and the speeches of Emilia and Gratiano "at the door" in V. ii)—are particularly important in giving the impression of a larger world off-stage impinging on the stage reality or affected by it. Thus, in I. iii, the off-stage hail of the sailor, immediately announced by an officer at the door as "A messenger from the galleys," has in context an effect which carries our imaginations out to the busied warships off Venice and thence far to sea where the Turkish fleet's movements near Rhodes and Cyprus are being shadowed and reported. Sound effects wonderfully create the spatial dimensions of the expectant scene near the harbor in II. i, where the safe arrival of Governor Othello's ship is anxiously awaited on endangered Cyprus. Off-stage cries of "A sail!" immediately are identified, and located, as those of the entire populace looking out from "the brow of the sea"; this is instantly followed by a sound from the still-distant ship itself: the report of its cannon-salute identifying it (in a world of deceptive appearances and dangerous enemies) as "a friend" (51–7). This shot was fired, perhaps from the "hut" above the stage-cover, from the theater's "chamber" by a small cannon (no doubt the very one whose firing during a performance of *Henry VIII* was to burn the Globe to the ground in 1613). Another off-stage sound in this same scene, the identifying trumpet flourish preceding Othello's entrance, has a still sharper significance as announcing the arrival of a figure in authority. The same implication of superior public authority informs the complete surprise effected when the trumpet preceding the appearance of the Duke's emissary Lodovico ironically intrudes upon Othello's pleasure in the "justice" of Iago's plan for Desdemona's death (IV. i. 194–200). Other juxtapositions of public and private worlds are accomplished by the trumpets which summon the weeping Desdemona to dinner with the noble messengers of Venice (IV. ii), and also by the "dreadful bell" whose clamors in II. iii sound the public menace of the "private and domestic quarrel" of the watch. A stroke of particular imaginative power here is the continued clanging of this frightening alarm all through the outraged Othello's first full speech of rebuke to his disgraced subordinates (148–57).

To one aspect of physical production the Elizabethans paid great attention; this was the costuming, which seems often to have constituted a company's largest single expense in mounting a play. Costume and make-up had an obvious importance, of course, in supporting the illusion created by the highly skilled boy-actors who played the female roles. More generally, the bareness of the stage and its emphasis upon the actors underscored costumes and heightened their opportunity to register dramatically significant distinctions, such as the contrast between Roderigo as wealthy young Venetian in Act I and the same character's appearance as soldier with "usurped beard" in Cyprus. Costume would certainly have been contemporary in *Othello*, and indeed was predominantly so in this theater. This practice tended to underscore for the audience the immediate relevance of the issues of a play, and in historical, legendary, and fanciful actions produced the possibility of multiple audience perspectives upon them. It offered the further advantage of exploiting the great capacity of Renaissance dress to manifest distinctions in social position (the Duke and Lodovico), occupation (Bianca, the Clown), and locale and nationality (Italy, Venice). Renaissance clothing also gave remarkable opportunity for individual self-display and expression; we may suppose, for example, that Cassio's costume was a visual counterpart of his rather elaborate, courtly-mannered speech. The Elizabethan inclination toward symbolism in treatment of the visual also affects the impact of make-up and costume on the dramatic significance of character and action. *Othello* provides varied illustration of the point in Cassio's "privy coat" and Desdemona's white smock in Act V and, most impressively, through the entire action, in the centrally ambiguous blackness of the hero.

The same is true of properties, which tend to be few, simple, and highly functional. They often focus the action of a scene, and serve in a synecdochic way to establish its place, time, and subject (e.g. the lighted council table in I. iii). Because of the carefully prepared associations, the bed and light in V. ii powerfully condense even further kinds of dramatic meaning. Apart from the lights in the night scenes, the wine in II. iii, Cassio's "chair" in Act V, and the bodies on the bed in V. ii, the most important properties in *Othello* are the weapons which figure so prominently in I. ii, the Watch Scene, and the climactic actions in Act V for which these earlier scenes involving improper swordplay prepare. (Such sword combats, incidentally, were not the tame and awkward affairs which so often embarrass modern productions. The Elizabethan audience, familiar with weapons in daily life, brought a critical eye to the theater, and one of the miscellaneous accomplishments required of actors was expertise in fencing.)

Established traditions, which associated particular objects, events, and actions with the attributive representation of important abstractions and concepts, could enrich properties with conventional significance requiring elucidation for modern readers. A crucial example in this play is the knife or dagger with which Othello commits suicide at the catastrophe. Notable earlier in the final scene are the potently iterated references and actions associating Othello with swords: the rejection of his blade as the instrument of Desdemona's death, the reference to the sword of Justice, Othello's threat to draw against Emilia, and most stunning, the successive disarmings of the hero, after two unsuccessful attacks on Iago, of two swords carefully connected with his former valor, honor, and soldiership. These emphatically contrast with the secreted suicide weapon when it appears, and give it the force of a substitution: for the sword— primarily associated with justice, legitimate magistracy, public retribution, valorous manhood, and true spiritual struggle— the knife—associated with treachery, private vengeance, carving for one's own rage, "carnal strife," and suicidal desperation. What the virtue Patience characteristically "overcomes" (as in her depiction in fig. b) is the self-destructive Wrath conventionally represented by the desperate suicide with knife at breast— an action often used to symbolize spiritual Despair itself. In an earlier conventionally charged action (we recall) Othello "falls" in an "ecstasy" at Iago's feet (IV. i), presenting a grouping reminiscent of the "Image of Prostration" in the morality play, where (by way of obversion of the common visual formula for representing spiritual victory) a fallen figure once associated with virtue is triumphed over by vice.

Othello's death, because it crowns the many earlier references to "happiness to die" and "killing oneself for grief" (going as far back in the tragedy as the lovesick Roderigo's threats to do away with himself in I. iii), reminds us how readily upon this stage actions are given prominence and definition through repetition and parallelism. The incrementally iterated actions in this play, even apart from the changes rung on deliberate and undeliberate deception, envious slander, false accusations, misdeeming of character, and jealous suspicion, are remarkably numerous and central. Among such repetitive actions which will repay careful critical attention are the kisses, instances of kneeling, the inquests and trials, entrances with a light, awakenings to strife, and the confrontations of violence by Othello. In addition to these, the vivid parallel situations (such as Iago as deceiver-tempter with Roderigo in I. i, and then with Othello in I. ii) and rhythmic or patterned actions (such as the alternation of temptations of Othello with scenes showing him with Desdemona) also should be noted. To heighten our reader's awareness of such iterative actions can serve to approximate the relief-like clarity they would have enjoyed under the conditions of continuous performance on the open-platform Elizabethan stage.

The attempt to read a Shakespearean play in terms of the Elizabethan theater and staging assumed in its making can give a reader's experience of it a vital authenticity not otherwise to be attained. But the reader must be prepared to do a great deal for himself in the way of scrupulously making explicit hints that are only implicit in the text. Characteristically, stage directions in Elizabethan play-texts tend to be very sparse, and it is largely in the speeches themselves that indications for action, movement, gesture, and expression are to be found. In this respect as in so many others Shakespeare is extraordinary. The lines he gave the actors are instinct with impersonation appro-

priate to part, situation, and play; they seem to speak themselves with remarkable clarity of intonation; and they appear
to ask of us, even as readers, the physical motion and relationship, gesture and facial expression required of actors to realize
them upon his stage.

SHAKESPEARE'S TEXTS AND THE PRESENT EDITION

Shakespeare was a principal actor-sharer of the King's Men and also one of the part-landlords in theaters they used, but the plays he wrote for them became the property of the company itself. The Elizabethan playwright customarily sold the manuscript of his play, and all his rights in it, directly to the players for cash. The company might hope at some time to recover part of this expense by publication. And various circumstances could hasten the appearance of the play in print. The company might fall into financial straits, as during suspensions of playing due to the plague; again, the surreptitious publication of a "pirated" text by an unscrupulous printer might make sale of their text to an authorized printer desirable. Normally, however, until the play's appeal in the theater considerably diminished, the actors would have little interest in publishing it. Thus, many plays were not published at all, and others, like *Othello*, first appeared in print long after they were written.

At least eighteen years elapsed between Shakespeare's original penning of this play and its first publication in 1622, six years after his death. During that time the author's manuscript had been in the hands of actors. It had either itself been prepared for theatrical use or been transcribed to make such prompt copy; the text had been exposed to censorship to permit its performance; and, especially in the case of a play many times revived, the players might have made various later alterations for theatrical purposes. Finally, the play, whatever manuscript of it at last came into the printing house, might then have suffered further change through editing and typesetting. Since none of the manuscripts of Shakespeare's plays has survived, the modern editor is obliged to try to establish their texts through study of the early printed editions. In the case of *Othello* there are two such editions.

The edition of *Othello* in 1622 is called the First Quarto (Q1) after its publishing format, the one most commonly used for single plays. In quarto (Latin "in four") sheets of the standard size (roughly 20 by 15 inches) are folded twice; thus, each sheet, when it has been printed on both sides, yields eight pages measuring 10 by 7½ inches. The usual format for large books, appropriate for a collection of plays (after the precedent of Ben Jonson's *Works* in 1616), was folio (Latin "by the leaf"); in this form each sheet is folded once, yielding four printed pages measuring 15 by 10 inches. The First Folio (F1), the only authoritative collection of Shakespeare's plays, gathered by his friends among the King's Men, was published in 1623. It contains all the plays now generally ascribed to Shakespeare with the exception of *Pericles* and the collaboration *The Two Noble Kinsmen*.

Although the publishers of the Folio advertise the plays as "printed according to the true originall copies," we know the texts used were not invariably those originally provided by the author. The Folio in fact depends on a wide variety of sources, including prompt books, rewritten versions, and earlier printed texts. Eighteen of the thirty-six plays in the Folio had already been published in quarto versions, all of them, with the exception of *Othello*, during Shakespeare's lifetime. Unfortunately, but by no means unusually, none of these appeared under his supervision. The existence of parallel quarto and Folio texts of fourteen of these plays, including *Othello*, has afforded our closest insight into the nature of the copy provided the printers whose texts the modern editor must use.

The texts of *Othello* in the First Quarto and the Folio are the only ones which can lay claim to substantive authority. A Second Quarto edition (Q2), which alters the text of the First with readings from the Folio, was published in 1630 and reprinted in 1655 (Q3); it rests upon no independent manuscript source and therefore is unauthoritative. The Folio was reprinted, with minor changes that have no authority, in 1632 (F2), 1663–4 (F3), and 1685 (F4). With the first edition in the modern sense, the work of Nicholas Rowe in 1709, begins the long history of accretions to the received texts by generations of editors. Rowe regularized the act and scene divisions, provided lists of characters and scene locations, attempted emendation of unintelligible passages, and generally cleaned up the text according to the taste of his time, which inclined toward a stricter metrical regularity than was usual a century earlier. Subsequent editors followed Rowe's example, "correcting" and adding to one another's work, until it became obvious in the present century that a fresh start must be made with the original texts.

Unhappily, study of these in the case of *Othello* reveals a complex problem sufficiently puzzling to frustrate hopes of establishing a fully authoritative text for the play. The Quarto and Folio offer distinct texts; neither is dismissably "bad"; and an editor must use both of them. The Quarto, a cut text, lacks 160 lines found in the Folio, which itself lacks sixteen short passages supplied by the Quarto. The texts further differ in more than a thousand substantive readings, and also in such other matters as stage directions and lineation. An editor must determine on what grounds, and with what admission of eclecticism and conflation, he will deal with these variations.

The text in the present edition is a new one grounded on a theory of these early editions that attempts, by assessing their nature, authority, and relationship, to account for their differences. A brief sketch of this theory (further illustrated in Appendix B) will serve immediately to clarify editorial practices in the text of the play which follows.

Although the Quarto and Folio texts of *Othello* are distinct, they clearly also are related, for both ultimately reflect, though at different removes, a common original. This original, which contained the longer F-only as well as the Q-only passages, must have been the author's "foul papers," or draft preceding fair copy. At some time (or times) cuts were made in these "foul papers"—presumably in the preparation of prompt copy for abridged performance. Still later, a none too careful transcript was made of this cut, and no doubt confusing and partly illegible, authorial draft. The transcriber (possibly there were two) appears to have been neither closely familiar with the play nor professionally knowledgeable about it. This transcript provided the copy from which the Quarto text was printed.

The manuscript underlying the Folio text also derived from the "foul papers," but before they were cut; it therefore had the passages omitted in the Quarto. Moreover, this manuscript also contained authorial revisions, second thoughts, and substitutions. As the spare stage directions in the Folio text do not suggest a text prepared for the theater, this manuscript may have been an intermediate fair copy from which the company's promptbook itself was made. In any case, Heminge and Condell evidently considered it more authoritative than either the "foul papers" or the transcript that served as copy for the Quarto. Unfortunately, many evidences of expurgation, sophistication, substitution, and regularizing show that this authoritative manuscript underwent considerable alteration before being printed in the Folio. If (as some scholars suppose, but have by no means yet proved) the Folio text was printed not from the manuscript itself but rather from an example of the Quarto hand-corrected by reference to it, then a still further ground of undependability in this text must be reckoned with.

In sum, the Quarto's text is adjudged on the whole more reliably to represent a less authoritative manuscript of the play, and the Folio's less reliably to represent a more authoritative one. On this theory, then, an editor is obliged to follow the Folio, but only where his analysis of its various probable kinds of corruption does not lead him to distrust it. Wherever he has cause to suspect its readings, and he cannot plausibly recover those of the underlying authoritative manuscript, he must attempt to reconstruct those of the original draft through the printed evidence of the transcript used as copy for the Quarto. This complex, difficult, and (given our ignorance) by no means infallible procedure has been used in arriving at the text in this edition. The decisions made in the course of it are reflected in the textual notes, at the foot of each page, which record all rejected readings affecting substantive meaning or meter.* Although considerations of space forbid the noting of all differences in lineation, every instance in which one text presents a passage as verse and the other as prose has also been recorded.

The present text further differs from many commercial modern editions in that it clears away all accretions to the text by editors since Rowe, except where modern scholarship has vindicated them. A new list of characters replaces those built

---

* These include substantive variants from uncorrected states of the texts, the authoritative work on which has been done by Charlton Hinman ("The Printing of the First Quarto of *Othello*," Ph.D. Diss., University of Virginia, 1941; *Printing and Proof-Reading of the First Folio of Shakespeare*, I [Oxford, 1963]: 226–334.)

upon Rowe's. The stage directions (abbreviated to "S. D." in the notes) have been redone, those in the early texts being preserved, but reordered or expanded where necessary; where required some new directions have been added to clarify the action. Anything not found in the Quarto or Folio has been placed in square brackets. Also in brackets are the indications of act and scene division, even though these already appear in the First Folio, because they are undoubtedly literary or editorial in origin. Preserved here only to facilitate reference, they almost certainly have no bearing on the play's original unbroken performance, and, if wrongly taken, inevitably distort dramatic values dependent upon the continuity of action.

A similar consideration has eliminated scene locations, conventionally added since eighteenth-century editions first catered to readers' tastes in accordance with the increasingly elaborate theatrical practice of representing scenes on the stage. Such headings (as Rowe's "The Garden of the Castle" preceding III. iii), implying a change of representational scenery, although they conformed to stage practices until this century, have no relevance whatever to staging in Shakespeare's theater, where the staged characters and their speech alone set the scene. To give such scene locations prominence is false to the original texts and misleading in relation to the nature of the Shakespearean theater, which left the playwright imaginatively free to localize only when, and then only to the precise degree, he wished. To help the reader, scene locations are discussed in the notes to this edition, together with questions of time, which Shakespeare handles with similar poetic freedom.

In this edition spelling and punctuation have been modernized. In particular, where it proved possible to do so without altering phrasing or emphasis, I have reduced the heavy pointing encountered in the early texts (especially the Folio) to a lighter modern punctuation rather more rhetorical than syntactical. Punctuation variants in the early texts, or alterations of their pointing, are recorded in the textual notes only when they decisively affect the meaning.

All references to and quotations from other works of Shakespeare, with the exception of plays already published in this series, follow the text and lineation of the *Tudor Shakespeare,*

edited by Peter Alexander (London, 1951). Editors who have
contributed to our knowledge of the play are referred to in the
commentary and elsewhere by name only, as Rowe, Pope,
Capell, etc. (see Appendix H). A full dated list of major editions
may be found in recent volumes of the *New Variorum Shakespeare*, among the appendixes to each play; or see E. K.
Chambers, *William Shakespeare* (Oxford, 1930), I, 275–7. These
lists do not include such important recent one-volume editions
as those of G. L. Kittredge (1936), Alexander (1951), and C. J.
Sisson (1954).

CHARACTERS*

DUKE OF VENICE

BRABANTIO *a Venetian senator, father to Desdemona.*

GRATIANO *brother to Brabantio.*

LODOVICO *Brabantio's kinsman, emissary from the Duke.*

OTHELLO *a noble Moor, general in the service of the Venetian state.*

CASSIO *Othello's recently appointed lieutenant, a Florentine.*

IAGO *Othello's ancient or standard-bearer, his aide-de-camp.*

MONTANO *predecessor of Othello as Governor of Cyprus.*

RODERIGO *a Venetian gentleman, Iago's gull, a rejected suitor of Desdemona.*

CLOWN *a servant in Othello's household on Cyprus.*

OTHELLO'S HERALD

DESDEMONA *Brabantio's daughter, wife to Othello.*

EMILIA *wife to Iago, attending Desdemona on Cyprus.*

BIANCA *a courtesan, enamored of Cassio.*

Sailor, messenger, senators, gentlemen, officers, musicians, servants, and attendants.

---

* By the present editor. A list of "The Names of the Actors," of questionable authority, immediately follows the text of the play in the First Folio. This labels Cassio "an Honourable Lieutenant," Iago "a Villain," Roderigo "a gull'd Gentleman," Montano "Gouernor of Cyprus," and Bianca "a Curtezan."

The Tragedy of Othello
the Moor of Venice

[*Act I, scene i.*] *Enter* IAGO *and* RODERIGO.

RODERIGO

Tush, never tell me. I take it much unkindly
That thou, Iago, who hast had my purse
As if the strings were thine, shouldst know of this.

IAGO

'Sblood, but you will not hear me!
5 If ever I did dream of such a matter,
Abhor me.

RODERIGO

Thou told'st me thou didst hold him in thy hate.

I. i **S.D.** Q. F has *Enter Rodorigo, and Iago.*
  1. **Tush** Q. Not in F.
  2. **thou . . . hast** F. Q has 'you . . has'.
  4. **'Sblood, but you will** Q. F has 'But you'l'.

Act I, scene i The play begins most unusually, with the audience required to balance inferences not only about the characters on-stage but also about the subject and central character they allude to. To the development and clarification of these, in both their retrospective and preparatory aspects, the remainder of the Act is devoted.

The general locale of the scene, Venice, gradually established by implication, is first made explicit at line 106. The setting becomes particularized as before Brabantio's house, and late at night, from line 75.

3. *this* i.e., as later clarified, Desdemona's elopement with Othello.

4. *'Sblood* by God's blood—a powerful oath expurgated in the Folio text.

7, 10. *him* i.e., as gradually defined, the Moorish general of Venice, Othello.

IAGO

Despise me if I do not. Three great ones of the city,
In personal suit to make me his lieutenant,
10   Off-capped to him; and by the faith of man
I know my price: I am worth no worse a place.
But he, as loving his own pride and purposes,
Evades them with a bombast circumstance
Horribly stuffed with epithets of war;
15   And, in conclusion,
Non-suits my mediators; for, "Certes," says he,
"I have already chose my officer."
And what was he?
Forsooth, a great arithmetician,
20   One Michael Cassio, a Florentine
(A fellow almost damned in a fair wife),

---

10.   **Off-capped** F (off-capt).   Q has 'Oft capt'.
15.   Q. Not in F.
17.   **chose** F.   Q has 'chosen'.

10. *Off-capped* i.e. approached him with respect due a superior.
11. *price* value.
13. *bombast circumstance* pompous padded circumlocution, "bombast" being cotton used for stuffing or lining, hence figuratively applied to styles padded with big-sounding words.
14. *epithets* phrases—here, I think, "technical terms."
16. *Non-suits* throws their suit out of court, refuses their petition. *Certes* certainly.
19. *arithmetician* a veteran's sneer at the theoretician who knows the mathematics of warfare instead of the actualities of soldiering. (Contemporary military manuals, however, concur in Othello's choice.)
21. *almost . . . wife* a slur on Cassio (and indirectly on the just-married General who appointed him) as a soft ladies' man more suited to the boudoir than the battlefield. This much debated line is often held a crux because Cassio turns out not to have a wife. But the audience does not know that here, and Iago's cagey insinuation does not make clear whether Cassio is already or just recently a husband, or just about to be one, or whether he is a bachelor with a general adulterous (and therefore damnable) interest in anyone's "fair wife." Cynical Renaissance proverbs say a man with a beautiful wife is "damned"—because he is bound to suffer jealous suspicion, endure "the hell of having a false woman" (*Merry Wives* II. ii. 260), or condemn himself by idolatrously loving her.

That never set a squadron in the field,
Nor the division of a battle knows
More than a spinster—unless the bookish theoric,
25   Wherein the togèd consuls can propose
As masterly as he. Mere prattle without practice
Is all his soldiership. But he, sir, had th' election;
And I (of whom his eyes had seen the proof
At Rhodes, at Cyprus, and on other grounds
30   Christen and heathen) must be belee'd and calmed
By debitor-and-creditor, this counter-caster:

---

23.   **division** Q2.   QF have 'deuision'.
25.   **togèd** Q.   F has 'Tongued'.
27.   **th'** F.   Q has 'the'.
29.   **other** Q.   F has 'others'.
30.   **Christen** Wilson conj.   F reads 'Christen'd'; Q has 'Christian'.
       belee'd F (be-leed).   Q has 'be led'.
31.   **debitor-and-creditor** QF.   Hyphens Staunton.

22. *squadron*   i.e. even a squadron, a mere troop of twenty-five men led by a corporal.

23. *the division of a battle*   how an army should be drawn up "in . . . right form of war" (*Julius Caesar* II. ii. 20).

24. *bookish theoric*   pedantic theorizing.

25. *togèd consuls*   the gowned counsellors, senators of Venice, regarded as wearing the toga, the garb of peace of Roman senators. So far as sense is concerned, the Q and F readings differently place the emphasis on "mere prattle without practice." However, I think F's "Tongued" a suspect substitution for Q's more richly significant word, not elsewhere found, and that it may result from misconstrual of a spelling such as "togued." In *Coriolanus* II. iii. 112, F reads "tongue" for "toge."   *propose*   hold forth.

30. *belee'd and calmed*   A ship is *belee'd* when an adversary comes between her and the wind, taking the wind out of her sails and leaving her *calmed* and losing headway. Such a nautical metaphor is appropriate for a soldier of Venice, used as he would be to fighting at sea as well as on land.

31. *debitor-and-creditor*   Mister accountbook.   *counter-caster* one who computes petty accounts by means of counters or an abacus, with scornful glance back at "arithmetician" (line 19).

He, in good time, must his lieutenant be,
And I—God bless the mark!—his Moorship's ancient.

RODERIGO

By heaven, I rather would have been his hangman.

IAGO

35 Why, there's no remedy; 'tis the curse of service.
Preferment goes by letter and affection,
Not by the old gradation, where each second
Stood heir to th' first. Now sir, be judge yourself
Whether I in any just term am affined
40 To love the Moor.

RODERIGO

I would not follow him then.

IAGO

O sir, content you.
I follow him to serve my turn upon him.

---

33. **God** Q. Not in F. **Moorship's** F. Q has 'Worships'.
35. **Why** F. Q has 'But'.
37. **Not by the** Q. F has 'And not by'.
38. **th'** F. Q has 'the'.

32. *in good time* a common ironic phrase, literally meaning "opportunely"—"a fine thing!"

33. *God bless the mark!* God avert the evil omen! A common interjection used in expressing scorn or at the mention of something or someone terrible. The latter sense is brought into play by buried allusion to the proverb, "It is an ill army, where the Devil carries the colors" (Tilley, P596). *ancient* ensign—literally, standard-bearer. Actually, Iago's post in the play seems to be that of Othello's aide-de-camp.

34. *I . . . hangman* "I'd have seen him hanged first!"—with a play on *his:* "rather than accept so low a post as ensign, I would have served as executioner in his army—so I could hang him."

35. *there's no remedy* a common colloquialism, like our "There's nothing for it," but a popular proverb possibly points to a deeper drift of suggestion: "There is no remedy but patience" (Tilley, R71).

36. *Preferment* advancement. *letter and affection* influence (literally, "letter of recommendation") and favoritism.

37. *old gradation* regular promotion by seniority, as the good old way was.

39. *in . . . affined* am related in such manner as obliges me.

We cannot all be masters, nor all masters
Cannot be truly followed. You shall mark
45   Many a duteous and knee-crooking knave
That, doting on his own obsequious bondage,
Wears out his time, much like his master's ass,
For naught but provender; and when he's old, cashiered.
Whip me such honest knaves! Others there are
50   Who, trimmed in forms and visages of duty,
Keep yet their hearts attending on themselves;
And, throwing but shows of service on their lords,
Do well thrive by 'em; and when they have lined their coats,
Do themselves homage. These fellows have some soul;
55   And such a one do I profess myself.
For, sir,
It is as sure as you are Roderigo,
Were I the Moor, I would not be Iago.
In following him, I follow but myself.
60   Heaven is my judge, not I for love and duty,
But seeming so for my peculiar end;
For when my outward action doth demonstrate

---

43. **all be** F. Q has 'be all'.
44. **followed. You . . . mark** F. Q has 'followed, you . . . marke.'
48. **naught** F. Q has 'noughe'.
53. **'em** Q. F has 'them'.
54. **These** F. Q has 'Those'.
62. **doth** F. Q has 'does'.

45. *knee-crooking* bowing (cf. *Hamlet* III. ii. 59). *knave* fellow.

48. *cashiered* turned off, dismissed from service.

49. *Whip . . . knaves!* The "ethical dative" *me* marks the offhand, contemptuous tone: "Such honorable fellows want whipping, say I!"

50. *trimmed . . . visages* dressed up in the outward behavior and masks.

51–2. *hearts . . . service* The emphasis on *hearts* and *shows* points up the explicit inversion of the conventional attitude toward service inculcated by the Elizabethans. Cf. Ephesians 6: 6, "Not with service to the eye, as men pleasers, but as the servants of Christ, doing the will of God from the heart . . ."

61. *peculiar* personal, private.

The native act and figure of my heart
In complement extern, 'tis not long after
65 But I will wear my heart upon my sleeve
For daws to peck at: I am not what I am.

RODERIGO

What a full fortune does the thick-lips owe
If he can carry't thus!

IAGO

Call up her father,
Rouse him. Make after him, poison his delight,
70 Proclaim him in the streets. Incense her kinsmen,
And though he in a fertile climate dwell,
Plague him with flies; though that his joy be joy,
Yet throw such changes of vexation on't
As it may lose some color.

---

66. **daws** F. Q has 'Doues'.
67. **full** Q. F has 'fall'. **thick-lips** Q. F has 'Thicks-lips'.
70. **streets** F. Q has 'streete'.
73. **changes** Q. F has 'chances'. **on't** F. Q has 'out'.

63. *The . . . heart* i.e. its innate action and shape, what I really think and intend.

64. *complement extern* outward appearance.

65. *upon my sleeve* where Elizabethan servingmen often wore a badge.

66. *daws* fools, the jack-daw being a proverbially stupid bird. The Q reading, "Doues," contemptuously referring to mild and harmless innocents, may be a first thought and not an error. *I . . . am* a self-defining reminiscence of God's self-assertion: "I am that I am" (Exodus 3: 14).

67. *thick-lips* The Elizabethans often blurred or ignored the distinction between dark Moors and Negroes ("blackamoors"). Thus, Aaron the Moor in *Titus Andronicus* calls his child "you thick-lipp'd slave" (IV. ii. 176). *owe* own.

68. *carry't* have things his own way.

69. *Rouse him* i.e. her father. The pronoun is emphatic. *Make after him* i.e. Othello.

71. *in . . . dwell* i.e. may be enjoying abundant fortune.

72. *though that* although.

73. *throw . . . vexation* inflict on it such vexing vicissitudes.

74. *As it may* that may cause it to.

RODERIGO

75   Here is her father's house. I'll call aloud.

IAGO

Do, with like timorous accent and dire yell
As when, by night and negligence, the fire
Is spied in populous cities.

RODERIGO

What ho, Brabantio! Signior Brabantio, ho!

IAGO

80   Awake! what ho, Brabantio! thieves! thieves! thieves!
Look to your house, your daughter, and your bags!
Thieves! thieves!

BRABANTIO [*appears*] *above, at a window.*

BRABANTIO

What is the reason of this terrible summons?
What is the matter there?

RODERIGO

85   Signior, is all your family within?

IAGO

Are your doors locked?

BRABANTIO

Why, wherefore ask you this?

IAGO

'Zounds sir, you're robbed! for shame, put on your gown!
Your heart is burst; you have lost half your soul.

---

80.   **thieves** Q (thrice). F has it twice.
81.   **your daughter** F. Q has 'you Daughter'.
82.   **S.D.** Q reads 'Brabantio *at a window.*' F prefixes line 83 'Aboue.'
86.   **your doors locked** F. Q has 'all doore lockts'.
87.   **'Zounds** Q. Not in F. **you're** F (y'are). Q has 'you are'.
88.   **soul.** Q (soule;). F has 'soule'.

76. *like timorous*   such terrifying.
77. *by night and negligence*   through negligence at night.
84. *What . . . there*   What is your business?
87. *'Zounds*   by God's wounds (i.e. those suffered by Christ on the Cross)—a tremendous oath.

Even now, now, very now, an old black ram
90 Is tupping your white ewe. Arise, arise!
Awake the snorting citizens with the bell,
Or else the devil will make a grandsire of you.
Arise, I say!

BRABANTIO

What, have you lost your wits?

RODERIGO

Most reverend signior, do you know my voice?

BRABANTIO

95 Not I. What are you?

RODERIGO

My name is Roderigo.

BRABANTIO

The worser welcome!
I have charged thee not to haunt about my doors;
In honest plainness thou hast heard me say
My daughter is not for thee; and now, in madness,
100 Being full of supper and distempering draughts,
Upon malicious bravery dost thou come
To start my quiet?

RODERIGO

Sir, sir, sir—

---

89. **now, now, very** F. Q has 'now, very'.
96. **worser** F. Q has 'worse'.
101. **bravery** Q. F has 'knauerie'.
102. **quiet?** Q. F has 'quiet.'

91. *snorting* snoring. *the bell* the alarm bell.
92. *the devil* associating the black Othello with the traditional blackness of the devil and invoking the idea, still terrifying in the Renaissance, of the incubus or demon lover.
100. *distempering* mind-disturbing.
101. *Upon malicious bravery* on account of a malicious wish to make a show of defiance. F's reading "knauerie" makes rather redundant sense but seriously weakens the point. The reverend signior's fury here is at the outrageous insolence of what he takes to be vengefully defiant intrusion on his peace.
102. *start* disturb.

BRABANTIO

But thou must needs be sure
My spirit and my place have in them power
105   To make this bitter to thee.

RODERIGO

Patience, good sir.

BRABANTIO

What tell'st thou me of robbing? This is Venice:
My house is not a grange.

RODERIGO

Most grave Brabantio,
In simple and pure soul I come to you.

IAGO

'Zounds, sir, you are one of those that will not serve God if
110   the devil bid you. Because we come to do you service, and you
think we are ruffians, you'll have your daughter covered with
a Barbary horse; you'll have your nephews neigh to you;
you'll have coursers for cousins, and gennets for germans.

BRABANTIO

What profane wretch art thou?

---

104.   **spirit . . . them** Q. F has 'spirits . . . their'.
106.   **What tell'st** F. Q has 'What, tell'st'.
109.   **'Zounds** Q. Not in F.
110.   **and** F. Not in Q.

107.   *grange*   isolated farmhouse.
108.   *simple*   sincere, not with duplicity.
111.   *covered*   the proper term for equine copulation.
112.   *Barbary horse*   The horse, often considered the most libi-
dinous of animals, was a widely used symbol of unbridled lust.
The match with a "barb" or Arab—a horse much prized for its running—suggests the not uncommon Elizabethan cross between a
stallion of this breed and an English mare (*Shakespeare's England*).
nephews grandsons.
113.   *gennets for germans*   Spanish horses for near kinsmen.
114.   *profane*   foul-mouthed.

IAGO

115   I am one, sir, that comes to tell you your daughter and the
          Moor are now making the beast with two backs.

BRABANTIO

Thou art a villain.

IAGO

You are a senator.

BRABANTIO

This thou shalt answer. —I know thee, Roderigo.

RODERIGO

Sir, I will answer anything. But I beseech you,
120   If't be your pleasure and most wise consent,
          As partly I find it is, that your fair daughter,
          At this odd-even and dull watch o' th' night
          Transported, with no worse nor better guard
          But with a knave of common hire, a gondolier,
125   To the gross clasps of a lascivious Moor—
          If this be known to you, and your allowance,
          We then have done you bold and saucy wrongs.
          But if you know not this, my manners tell me
          We have your wrong rebuke. Do not believe
130   That, from the sense of all civility,
          I thus would play and trifle with your reverence.
          Your daughter, if you have not given her leave,

---

115.   **comes** F.   Q has 'come'.
116.   **now** Q.   Not in F.
120–36.   F.   Not in Q.
122.   **odd-even** Hyphen Malone.

118.   *thou*   using the contemptuous *thou* instead of the respectful
"you."   *thee*   emphatic.
120.   *wise*   fully aware.
122.   *odd-even*   between   night   and   morning.   *dull*   lifeless,
sleepy.
126.   *your allowance*   approved by you.
127.   *saucy*   insolent (stronger than our word).
128.   *manners*   knowledge of proper behavior.
130.   *from the sense*   contrary to every feeling.

I say again, hath made a gross revolt,
Tying her duty, beauty, wit, and fortunes
135 In an extravagant and wheeling stranger
Of here and everywhere. Straight satisfy yourself.
If she be in her chamber, or your house,
Let loose on me the justice of the state
For thus deluding you.

BRABANTIO

[*To those within*] Strike on the tinder, ho!
140 Give me a taper! call up all my people!—
This accident is not unlike my dream;
Belief of it oppresses me already.—
Light, I say! light!   *Exit* [*above*].

IAGO

Farewell, for I must leave you.
It seems not meet, nor wholesome to my place,
145 To be produced—as, if I stay, I shall—
Against the Moor. For I do know the state,
However this may gall him with some check,
Cannot with safety cast him; for he's embarked
With such loud reason to the Cyprus wars,
150 Which even now stands in act, that for their souls

---

139. **thus deluding you** F. Q has 'this delusion'.
143. **S.D.** *Exit*. F. Not in Q.
144. **place** F. Q has 'pate'.
145. **produced** Q (produc'd). F has 'producted'.
147. **However** Q uncorr. and F (How euer). Mistakenly altered to 'Now euer' in Q corr.

134. *wit* intellect.
135. *extravagant and wheeling stranger* expatriate and ever-roving foreigner.
136. *Straight satisfy yourself* straightway inform yourself.
140. *taper* candle (more substantial than the modern taper).
141. *accident* occurrence.
144. *my place* i.e. as Othello's ensign.
147. *gall . . . check* annoy him with some reprimand. The terms sustain the horse imagery; cf. *Hamlet* III. ii. 237.
148. *cast* discharge (from his office as general).
150. *stands in act* are going on.

Another of his fathom they have none
To lead their business. In which regard,
Though I do hate him as I do hell pains,
Yet, for necessity of present life
155 I must show out a flag and sign of love,
Which is indeed but sign. That you shall surely find him,
Lead to the Sagittary the raisèd search,
And there will I be with him. So farewell.   *Exit.*

[Re-]enter, [below,] BRABANTIO *in
his nightgown, and Servants with torches.*

BRABANTIO

It is too true an evil: gone she is;
160 And what's to come of my despisèd time

---

151. **none** F. Q has 'not'.
153. **hell pains** F has 'hell apines'. Q has 'hells paines'.
157. **Sagittary** F. Q has 'Sagittar'.
158. **S.D.** Q. F has '*Enter Brabantio, with Seruants and Torches.*'

151. *fathom* capacity.
152. *business* trisyllabic.
154. *life* livelihood.
155. *flag . . . love* This remark, appropriate to a seemer and an ensign, alludes to "the sign of blind Cupid" which was put "up at the door of a brothel house" *Much Ado* I. i. 218–19.
157. *Sagittary* presumably an inn the sign of which was the Sagittary, the figure of a Centaur, half man-half horse, with bent bow and drawn arrow. The significances of this symbol—which makes ironic the place where the newly-eloped Othello is to be "surely" found by a "raised search"—were based on those of the centaur. For the Renaissance the centaur was a symbol of human life emphasizing man's need of rational control over the inferior irrational part of his nature. It most often denoted man made bestial by unbridled carnal concupiscence. Classical references to Centaurs as woman-ravishers made it a figure associated—as by Shakespeare—particularly with lust, violent disregard of law, and disruption of the proper order of marriage (cf. *All's Well* IV. iii. 281; *Midsummer Night's Dream* V. i. 44–5; *King Lear* IV. vi. 120). Under the influence of its infernal associations in antiquity, the Sagittary since the Middle Ages also was connected with the diabolic hunter of souls and with treacherously deceiving men in the image of the Satanic "deceiver of the world."
158. S.D. *nightgown* dressing-gown.

Is naught but bitterness. Now, Roderigo,
Where didst thou see her? —O unhappy girl!—
With the Moor saist thou? —Who would be a father?—
How didst thou know 'twas she? —O she deceives me
165   Past thought!— What said she to you? —[*To Servants*] Get
    moe tapers!
Raise all my kindred!—Are they married, think you?

RODERIGO

Truly I think they are.

BRABANTIO

O heaven! How got she out? O treason of the blood!—
Fathers, from hence trust not your daughters' minds
170   By what you see them act! —Is there not charms
By which the property of youth and maidhood
May be abused? Have you not read, Roderigo,
Of some such thing?

RODERIGO

Yes sir, I have indeed.

BRABANTIO

[*To Servants*] Call up my brother. —[*To* RODERIGO] O would
    you had had her!—

---

161. **bitterness. Now** F. Q has 'bitternesse now'.
164. **she deceives** F. Q has 'thou deceiuest'.
165. **moe** F. Q has 'more'.
169. **Fathers, from** F. Q has 'Fathers from'.
171. **maidhood** F. Q has 'manhood'.
173. **Yes . . . indeed.** F. Q has 'I haue sir.'
174. **would** F. Q has 'that'.

165. *moe*   more (of number).

168. *of the blood*   against her high birth. But the phrase may also
mean: "by the passions"; cf. Iago's reference to "the blood and baseness of our natures" (I. iii. 320–1).

170. *charms*   magical means, including love philtres, which
irresistibly turn the affections. The existence of these was widely
believed in Shakespeare's time.

171. *property*   normal nature.   *youth and maidhood*   hendiadys:
young maidenhood.

172. *abused*   led astray, deceived, deluded.

175   Some one way, some another. —Do you know
       Where we may apprehend her and the Moor?

RODERIGO

I think I can discover him, if you please
To get good guard and go along with me.

BRABANTIO

Pray you lead on. At every house I'll call;
180   I may command at most. —Get weapons, ho!
       And raise some special officers of night. —
       On, good Roderigo; I'll deserve your pains.   *Exeunt.*

[*Scene ii.*] *Enter* OTHELLO, IAGO, *and Attendants with
torches.*

IAGO

Though in the trade of war I have slain men,
Yet do I hold it very stuff o' th' conscience
To do no contrived murder. I lack iniquity

---

175. **you** F.   Q has 'yon'.
179. **you lead** F.   Q has 'leade me'.
181. **night** Q.   F has 'might'.
182. **I'll** Q (Ile).   F has 'I will'.
I. ii 2.   **stuff o'th'** F.   Q has 'stuft of'.

177. *discover*   uncover (not merely "find").
180. *at most*   i.e. at most of their houses.
181. *officers of night*   On the rejection of F's variant, see Appendix B, p. 254.
182. *deserve*   i.e. by showing gratitude for them.
I. ii   Iago's "there will I be with him" (i. 158) implicitly localizes this scene as before the Sagittary (for which the stage façade now stands). The off-stage presence "within the house" of Brabantio's eloped daughter is dramatically emphasized at lines 48, 52, 62.
2. *very . . . conscience*   a scruple essential in conscience.
3. *contrived*   deliberate. Here, accented on the first syllable: "cóntrived."

Sometimes to do me service. Nine or ten times
5   I had thought t'have yerked him here under the ribs.

OTHELLO

'Tis better as it is.

IAGO

Nay, but he prated,
And spoke such scurvy and provoking terms
Against your honor
That, with the little godliness I have,
10   I did full hard forbear him. But I pray you, sir,
Are you fast married? Be assured of this,
That the magnifico is much beloved,
And hath in his effect a voice potential
As double as the Duke's. He will divorce you,
15   Or put upon you what restraint or grievance
The law, with all his might to enforce it on,
Will give him cable.

---

4.   **Sometimes** Q. F has 'Sometime'.
5.   **t'have** F. Q has 'to haue'.
10. **you** F. Not in Q.
11. **Be assur'd** F. Q has 'For be sure'.
15. **or** F. Q has 'and'.
16. **The** F. Q has 'That'.
17. **Will** F. Q has 'Weele'.

5. *yerked*   stabbed.
7. *scurvy*   vilely insulting.
9–10. *with . . . him* alluding to Colossians 3: 13, "Forbearing one another, if any man have a quarrel to another: even as Christ forgave, even so do ye."
11. *fast*   securely.
12. *magnifico*   grandee, one of the chief men of Venice (Brabantio).
13. *hath . . . potential* has, in its capacity to work his will, a powerful voice.
14. *As double* as doubly influential. Shakespeare seems (erroneously) to have assumed that in a tightly contested issue the Doge would have two votes; thus Iago says the well-beloved Brabantio could be virtually as influential.
15. *grievance*   what causes annoyance.
16. *enforce it on*   make it exercise its rigor.
17. *cable*   scope (another nautical metaphor).

OTHELLO

Let him do his spite.
My services which I have done the signiory
Shall out-tongue his complaints. 'Tis yet to know—
20 Which, when I know that boasting is an honor,
I shall provulgate—I fetch my life and being
From men of royal siege; and my demerits
May speak unbonetted to as proud a fortune
As this that I have reached. For know, Iago,
25 But that I love the gentle Desdemona,
I would not my unhousèd free condition
Put into circumscription and confine
For the sea's worth.

Enter CASSIO *and Officers with torches.*

But look, what lights come yond?

---

20. **Which . . . know** F. Not in Q.
21. **provulgate** Q. F has 'promulgate'.
22. **siege** F. Q has 'height'.
28. **S.D.** Q (. . . *with lights, Officers, and torches*). F has '. . .
     with torches' after 'yond?' **yond** F. Q has 'yonder'.

18. *signiory*   Venetian government—literally, the entire Venetian
oligarchy.

19. *yet to know*   not yet commonly known.

21. *provulgate*   make common knowledge. Either variant could
have resulted from misreading. But it seems to me that F substitutes a
commoner word with inappropriate connotations of publication by
authority.

22. *siege*   rank—literally, "seat." *demerits* deservings, deserts.
The word at this time could mean good or ill deserts strictly depend-
ing upon context.

23. *unbonetted*   It is not clear (and perhaps ambiguous) whether
this word (not found elsewhere in Shakespeare) means "with the hat
off" (by way of respect) or not; the tonal difference is considerable.
With the latter meaning, Othello appears to say his deservings may
speak on equal terms even with so honorable a fortune as this alliance
with Brabantio's family.

26. *unhousèd*   unconfined, unrestrained.

28. *sea's worth*.   The sea traditionally was regarded as a hoard
of wealth, "rich . . . as is the ooze and bottom of the sea/ With
sunken wrack and sumless treasuries" (*Henry V* I. ii. 163–5).

IAGO

Those are the raisèd father and his friends.
30   You were best go in.

OTHELLO

                Not I; I must be found.
My parts, my title, and my perfect soul
Shall manifest me rightly. Is it they?

IAGO

By Janus, I think no.

OTHELLO

The servants of the Duke, and my lieutenant!
35   The goodness of the night upon you, friends!
What is the news?

CASSIO

                The Duke does greet you, General,
And he requires your haste-post-haste appearance
Even on the instant.

OTHELLO

                What's the matter, think you?

---

29. **Those** F. Q has 'These'.
32. **Is it** F. Q has 'It is'.
34. **Duke** Q. F has 'Dukes'.
35. **you** F. Q has 'your'.
38. **Even** Q. F has 'Enen'. **What's** Q. F has 'What is'.

31. *parts* past deeds.   *perfect soul* By this Othello means his
"absolutely unblemished conscience" and signifies his certainty that
he has in no way violated his sanctification as a Christian. Cf.
Hebrews 10: 14, "For by one offering he hath perfected forever them
that are sanctified." The Christian's "perfection of soul" of course is
an imputed one, posited on Christ's.

33. *By Janus* the appropriate oath for a seemer, and for these
circumstances. The god Janus was pictured as two-faced and was
associated with peace and war since his temple's gates were open in
war, closed in peace.

35. *The . . . you* an instance of blessing used as the form of
greeting.

38. *matter* business.

CASSIO

Something from Cyprus, as I may divine.
40 It is a business of some heat: the galleys
Have sent a dozen sequent messengers
This very night at one another's heels,
And many of the consuls, raised and met,
Are at the Duke's already. You have been hotly called for;
45 When, being not at your lodging to be found,
The senate sent about three several quests
To search you out.

OTHELLO

'Tis well I am found by you.
I will but spend a word here in the house,
And go with you.   [*Exit.*]

CASSIO

Ancient, what makes he here?

IAGO

50 Faith, he tonight hath boarded a land carrack;
If it prove lawful prize, he's made forever.

CASSIO

I do not understand.

IAGO

He's married.

CASSIO

To who?

[*Re-enter* OTHELLO.]

---

41. **sequent** F. Q has 'frequent'.
46. **sent** Q. F has 'hath sent'. **about** F. Q has 'aboue'.
48. **I will but** F. Q has 'Ile'.
49. **S.D.** Rowe.
50. **carrack** Q (Carrick). F has 'Carract'.
51. **he's** Q. F has 'he'.
52. **S.D.** Capell.

40. *galleys* warships.
41. *sequent* consecutive.
43. *consuls* counsellors (i.e., actually, some forty of the three hundred comprising the signiory).
50. *carrack* treasure ship (from the name of the Spanish and Portuguese vessel used for this purpose).

IAGO

Marry, to— Come, captain, will you go?

OTHELLO

Ha' with you.

Enter BRABANTIO, RODERIGO, *and Officers*
with torches and weapons.

CASSIO

Here comes another troop to seek for you.

IAGO

55   It is Brabantio. General, be advised:
He comes to bad intent.

OTHELLO

Holla! stand there!

RODERIGO

Signior, it is the Moor.

BRABANTIO

Down with him, thief!

[*They draw on both sides.*]

IAGO

You, Roderigo! come, sir, I am for you.

---

53. **Ha' with you.** Q2.   F has 'Haue with you.'   Q has 'Ha, with who?'
S.D. *and . . . weapons.*   F has '*with Officers, and Torches*' (after
'for you' line 54).   Q has '*and others with lights and weapons*'
(after 'To who?' line 52).
57. **S.D.** Rowe.

53. *Marry*   why, indeed—an oath by the Virgin Mary, in common use as an interjection. (Wordplays on marry-Mary-merry are
frequent.)   *captain*   general.   *Ha' with you*   an idiom indicating
readiness to accompany another, like our "come on."

54. *another troop*   The arms, torches, and "officers of night" of
Brabantio's company lead Cassio to mistake it for one of the "three
several quests" sent by the Duke to "search . . . out" Othello. This
mistake—like its counterpart by Iago at line 29—emphasizes the
contrast between the two matters of importance whose focal point is
the character of the hero.

58. *I am for you*   I'll be your adversary. "This is to prevent harm
to Roderigo, for whose purse Iago has a tender regard" (Booth).

OTHELLO

Keep up your bright swords, for the dew will rust 'em. —
60 Good signior, you shall more command with years
Than with your weapons.

BRABANTIO

O thou foul thief, where hast thou stowed my daughter?
Damned as thou art, thou hast enchanted her!
For I'll refer me to all things of sense,
65 If she in chains of magic were not bound,
Whether a maid so tender, fair, and happy,
So opposite to marriage that she shunned
The wealthy curlèd darlings of our nation,
Would ever have, t' incur a general mock,
70 Run from her guardage to the sooty bosom
Of such a thing as thou—to fear, not to delight.
Judge me the world if 'tis not gross in sense
That thou hast practiced on her with foul charms,
Abused her delicate youth with drugs or minerals
75 That weaken motion. I'll have't disputed on!
'Tis probable, and palpable to thinking.
I therefore apprehend and do attach thee

59–61. Q. As prose in F.
59. **'em** Q. F has 'them'.
64. **things** F. Q has 'thing'.
65. F. Not in Q.
68. **darlings** Q. F has 'Deareling'.
72–7. **Judge . . . thee** F. Not in Q.

59. *Keep up* sheathe.
64. *refer me* appeal for judgment. *all things of sense* all creatures of normal perception.
69. *a general mock* universal ridicule (by Venetian society).
70. *her guardage* (my) guardianship of her.
71. *to fear* to frighten (transitive, picking up from "such a thing").
72. *Judge me the world* let the world judge for me. *gross in sense* obvious to perception.
73. *practiced* schemingly worked evil arts.
75. *motion* normal perception and impulse. *disputed on* discussed (by experts).
77. *attach* arrest.

For an abuser of the world, a practicer
Of arts inhibited and out of warrant.

80   Lay hold upon him! If he do resist,
Subdue him at his peril.

OTHELLO

Hold your hands,
Both you of my inclining and the rest.
Were it my cue to fight, I should have known it
Without a prompter. —Where will you that I go

85   To answer this your charge?

BRABANTIO

To prison, till fit time
Of law and course of direct session
Call thee to answer.

OTHELLO

What if I do obey?
How may the Duke be therewith satisfied,
Whose messengers are here about my side,

90   Upon some present business of the state,
To bring me to him?

OFFICER

'Tis true, most worthy signior:
The Duke's in council, and your noble self
I am sure is sent for.

---

78. **For** F. Q has 'Such'.
83. **cue** F. Q has 'Qu.'
84. **Where** Q. F has 'Whether'.
85. **To answer** F. Q has 'And answer'.
87. **I** Q. Not in F.
91. **bring** F. Q has 'beare'.

78. *abuser*   deceiver. "Abuser of the world" was a common epithet for the Devil.

79. *inhibited . . . warrant*   prohibited and illegal.

82. *my inclining*   my party, my side.

85–6. *till . . . session*   until the time of the next regular court session and by normal legal process. Brabantio means Othello is to be imprisoned as a common criminal awaiting trial according to the court calendar.

90. *present*   immediate, urgent.

91. *worthy*   honorable.

BRABANTIO

How! the Duke in council?

In this time of the night! Bring him away.

95   Mine's not an idle cause. The Duke himself,

Or any of my brothers of the state,

Cannot but feel this wrong as 'twere their own;

For if such actions may have passage free,

Bondslaves and pagans shall our statesmen be!   *Exeunt.*

[*Scene iii.*] *Enter* DUKE *and Senators, set at a table,
with lights and Attendants.*

DUKE

There is no composition in these news

That gives them credit.

1 SENATOR

        Indeed they are disproportioned.

My letters say a hundred and seven galleys.

DUKE

And mine a hundred forty.

2 SENATOR

        And mine two hundred.

I. iii **S.D.** Q. F has '*Enter Duke, Senators, and Officers.*'
  1. **There is . . . these** Q. F has 'There's . . . this'.
  4. **forty** F. Q has 'and forty'.

95. *idle* trifling.
98–9. I.e. they would be "bondslaves and pagans" instead of Christian statesmen if they permitted such a wrong. However, Brabantio is thinking also of what will surely happen (*shall be*) to the noble blood of the Venetian oligarchy if they do allow such a marriage.
  I. iii S.D. This scene probably begins with a "discovery," the curtains of the discovery-space being drawn to reveal the Duke and Senators in council—an effective method for suggesting temporally overlapping action at another locale.
  1. *composition* consistency. *these news* these reports. "News" was a plural: new things.
  2. *disproportioned* in disagreement.
  3. *my letters* the dispatch I received.

5 But though they jump not on a just account—
  As in these cases where the aim reports
  'Tis oft with difference—yet do they all confirm
  A Turkish fleet, and bearing up to Cyprus.

DUKE

  Nay, it is possible enough to judgment.
10 I do not so secure me in the error
  But the main article I do approve
  In fearful sense.

SAILOR (*within*)
What ho! what ho! what ho!

OFFICER

A messenger from the galleys.

Enter Sailor.

DUKE

                     Now, what's the business?

SAILOR

  The Turkish preparation makes for Rhodes.
15 So was I bid report here to the state
  By Signior Angelo.

---

   6. **the aim** F. Q has 'They aym'd'.
 10. **in** F. Q has 'to'.
 11. **article** F. Q has 'Articles'.
 12. **S.P.** F. Q has '*One within.*' following '*Enter a Messenger.*' (line
      12).
 13. **S.P. OFFICER** F. Q has '*Sailor.*'
      galleys F (Gallies). Q has 'Galley'.
      S.D. F (after 'what ho!' line 12). Q has '*Enter a Messenger.*'
      (after 'fearful sense.' line 12).
      Now, Q. F has 'Now?' **what's** F (What's). Not in Q.
 16. F. Not in Q.

  5. *jump* agree. *just* exact.
  6. *the aim* conjecture.
  7. *difference* discrepancy.
  10. *so . . . error* so allow the discrepancy (as to numbers) to
free me from anxiety (by leading me to discredit the whole report).
  11. *the . . . approve* I believe the main item, i.e. that confirmed
by all the dispatches: a Turkish fleet bearing toward Cyprus.
  12. *In fearful sense* with alarm.

DUKE

How say you by this change?

1 SENATOR

This cannot be
By no assay of reason. 'Tis a pageant
To keep us in false gaze. When we consider
20 Th' importancy of Cyprus to the Turk,
And let ourselves again but understand
That, as it more concerns the Turk than Rhodes,
So may he with more facile question bear it,
For that it stands not in such warlike brace,
25 But altogether lacks th' abilities
That Rhodes is dressed in—if we make thought of this,
We must not think the Turk is so unskillful
To leave that latest which concerns him first,
Neglecting an attempt of ease and gain
30 To wake and wage a danger profitless.

DUKE

Nay, in all confidence he's not for Rhodes.

OFFICER

Here is more news.

Enter a Second Messenger.

MESSENGER

The Ottomites, reverend and gracious,

---

20. **Th'** F. Q has 'The'.
24–30. **For . . . profitless.** F. Not in Q.
31. **Nay,** F. Q has 'And'.
32. **S.D.** *Second* Q (2.). Not in F.

18. *assay* test. *pageant* a show, a feint.
19. *in false gaze* looking the wrong way.
20. *the Turk* This can mean the whole Turkish force or the Sultan guiding it.
23. *with . . . it* capture it in an easier contest. *Question* literally means "discussion" or "debate."
24. *brace* state of defiant readiness.
25. *abilities* defensive means.
26. *dressed in* fitted out with.
30. *wake and wage* rouse and risk.

Steering with due course toward the isle of Rhodes,
35   Have there injointed with an after fleet—

1 SENATOR

Ay, so I thought. How many, as you guess?

MESSENGER

Of thirty sail; and now they do restem
Their backward course, bearing with frank appearance
Their purposes toward Cyprus. Signior Montano,
40   Your trusty and most valiant servitor,
With his free duty recommends you thus,
And prays you to believe him.

DUKE

'Tis certain then for Cyprus.
Marcus Luccicos—is not he in town?

1 SENATOR

45   He's now in Florence.

DUKE

Write from us: wish him post, post-haste dispatch.

Enter BRABANTIO, OTHELLO, CASSIO, IAGO,
RODERIGO, *and Officers.*

---

35.   **injointed** Q.   F has 'injointed them'.
36–7.   **1 SENATOR . . . guess? MESSENGER** F.   Not in Q.
37.   **restem** F.   Q has 'resterine'.
39.   **toward** F.   Q has 'towards'.
44.   **he in town?** F.   Q has 'here in Towne.'
46.   **wish him post** Q.   F has 'To him, Post'.
   S.D. F (after 'valiant Moor' line 47).   Q erroneously adds 'Desdemona'.

35. *injointed*   joined themselves.
37–8. *restem/Their backward course*   steer their course back
again.
   41. *free duty*   unqualified respects.   *recommends*   informs.
   44. *Marcus Luccicos*   The identity and point of this strangely
named figure (much more than those of the ironically named
"signior Angelo," line 16) are obscure. He apparently is a foreigner
in the service of Venice, and the suggestion is of a government
suddenly faced with a military crisis and calling upon all its resources
of intelligence.

1 SENATOR

Here comes Brabantio and the valiant Moor.

DUKE

Valiant Othello, we must straight employ you
Against the general enemy Ottoman.

50 [*To* BRABANTIO] I did not see you. Welcome, gentle signior.
We lacked your counsel and your help tonight.

BRABANTIO

So did I yours. Good your grace, pardon me.
Neither my place nor aught I heard of business
Hath raised me from my bed; nor doth the general care
55 Take hold on me; for my particular grief
Is of so floodgate and o'erbearing nature
That it engluts and swallows other sorrows,
And it is still itself.

DUKE

Why, what's the matter?

BRABANTIO

My daughter! O, my daughter!

1 SENATOR

Dead?

BRABANTIO

Ay, to me.
60 She is abused, stol'n from me, and corrupted
By spells and medicines bought of mountebanks;

---

51. **lacked** F (lack't).   Q has 'lacke'.
55. **hold on** F.   Q has 'any hold of'. **grief** F.   Q has 'griefes'.
58. **Why,** Q.   F has 'Why?'
59. **S.P. 1 SENATOR** F.   Q has '*All*'.

48. *straight*   straightway.
49. *the general enemy*   the common enemy of all Christendom.
This and like phrases often were used of the Devil; cf. *Macbeth* III. i.
67–8: "mine eternal jewel/ Given to the common enemy of man."
55. *particular*   personal, individual.
56. *floodgate*   torrential, overwhelming, like the stream when a
sluice-gate is opened.
57. *engluts*   devours.
61. *mountebanks*   strolling quacks, known to deal in such wares.

For nature so prepost'rously to err,
Being not deficient, blind, or lame of sense,
Sans witchcraft could not.

DUKE

65   Whoe'er he be that in this foul proceeding
Hath thus beguiled your daughter of herself,
And you of her, the bloody book of law
You shall yourself read in the bitter letter
After its own sense; yea, though our proper son
70   Stood in your action.

BRABANTIO

               Humbly I thank your grace.
Here is the man—this Moor, whom now, it seems,
Your special mandate for the state affairs
Hath hither brought.

ALL

             We are very sorry for't.

DUKE

[*To* OTHELLO] What in your own part can you say to this?

BRABANTIO

75   Nothing, but this is so.

OTHELLO

Most potent, grave, and reverend signiors,
My very noble and approved good masters:

---

63.   F. Not in Q.
64.   **Sans** F.   Q corr. has 'Saunce'; Q uncorr. has 'Since'.
69.   **its** Q. F has 'your'. **yea** F. Not in Q.

62. *err*   go wrong, become abnormal.
63. *deficient*   feeble-minded.   *lame of sense*   crippled in physical perceptivity.
64. *Sans*   without. Pronounced as spelled in Q, "saunce."
69. *its*   F s reading, "your," generally preferred by editors, appears a sophistication in view of the fact, obviously shown in *Merchant of Venice* to be known to Shakespeare, that Venice's pride in the impartiality of its justice was a byword. The letter of the law would be harsh enough: the punishment for "arts inhibited" (witchcraft) was death.   *our proper son*   my own son.
70. *Stood in your action*   were the defendent in your suit.
77. *approved*   proved by experience to be.

That I have ta'en away this old man's daughter,
It is most true; true I have married her.
80 The very head and front of my offending
Hath this extent, no more. Rude am I in my speech,
And little blessed with the soft phrase of peace;
For since these arms of mine had seven years' pith,
Till now some nine moons wasted, they have used
85 Their dearest action in the tented field;
And little of this great world can I speak
More than pertains to feats of broil and battle;
And therefore little shall I grace my cause
In speaking for myself. Yet, by your gracious patience,
90 I will a round unvarnished tale deliver
Of my whole course of love—what drugs, what charms,
What conjurations, and what mighty magic
(For such proceedings am I charged withal)

---

82. **soft** F. Q has 'set'.
87. **feats** F. Q has 'feate'. **broil** Q (broyle). F has 'broiles'.
93. **proceedings am I** Q. F has 'proceeding I am'.

80. *front of my offending* This literally renders the legal term *frons causae*, "the features of the case which immediately meet the eye" (*front* literally means "forehead"). When such features are "discreditable" (says Quintilian, whom Shakespeare studied in school), one should "insinuate into the minds of his judges" (*Institutio oratoria*, IV. i. 42)—as Othello does with reference to his honorable "services," his "approved good masters," and his true warrior's blunt simplicity.

81. *Rude* oratorically unpolished, unpracticed. "Rude am I in my speech" (for a biblically knowledgeable audience) inevitably recalls 2 Corinthians 11: 6: "And though I be rude in speaking, yet I am not so in knowledge, but among you we have been made manifest to the uttermost, in all things."

82. *soft* Q's reading, "set" (= "elegant," "polished"), I consider a first thought.

83. *pith* strength. It should be noted that "the strength of the arm" was a commonplace symbol of spiritual fortitude.

84. *Till . . . wasted* until about nine months ago: i.e. the only period of peace the warrior Othello has known since his childhood.

85. *dearest* in the Elizabethan sense, that which concerned them most closely.

90. *round* plain.

I won his daughter.

BRABANTIO

A maiden never bold
95   Of spirit, so still and quiet that her motion
Blushed at her self; and she—in spite of nature,
Of years, of country, credit, everything—
To fall in love with what she feared to look on!
It is a judgment maimed and most imperfect
100 That will confess perfection so could err
Against all rules of nature, and must be driven
To find out practices of cunning hell
Why this should be. I therefore vouch again
That with some mixtures pow'rful o'er the blood,
105 Or with some dram conjured to this effect,
He wrought upon her.

DUKE

To vouch this is no proof,
Without more wider and more overt test
Than these thin habits and poor likelihoods
Of modern seeming do prefer against him.

94–5. **bold/Of spirit, so** Q (bold of spirit,/So). F has 'bold:/Of spirit so'.
98. **on!** Q has 'on?' F has 'on.'
99. **maimed** Q (maimd). F has 'main'd'.
100. **could** F. Q has 'would'.
104. **pow'rful** F (powrefull). Q has 'powerfull'.
106. **S.P. DUKE** Q. Not in F. **vouch** F. Q has 'youth'.
107. **wider** F. Q has 'certaine'. **overt** Q. F has 'ouer'.
108–9. **Than these . . . seeming do** F (Then). Q has 'These are . . . seemings, you'.

95–6. *her . . . self* i.e. her own (normal) emotions made her blush.
102. *practices* plots, evil machinations. *cunning* underhandedly knowledgeable.
103. *vouch* assert.
104. *blood* passions.
105. *conjured* made efficacious by magic spells.
107. *more . . . test* more extensive evidence and manifest testimony.
108. *thin habits* a clothing figure for "insubstantial semblances." *poor likelihoods* i.e. shabby support for inferences.
109. *modern* commonplace.

1 SENATOR

110　But, Othello, speak:
　　　Did you by indirect and forcèd courses
　　　Subdue and poison this young maid's affections?
　　　Or came it by request, and such fair question
　　　As soul to soul affordeth?

OTHELLO

　　　　　　　　　　　I do beseech you,
115　Send for the lady to the Sagittary
　　　And let her speak of me before her father.
　　　If you do find me foul in her report,
　　　The trust, the office, I do hold of you
　　　Not only take away, but let your sentence
120　Even fall upon my life.

DUKE

　　　[*To Attendants*]　Fetch Desdemona hither.

OTHELLO

　　　Ancient, conduct them; you best know the place.
　　　　　　　　　　　　Exit [IAGO, *with Attendants*].
　　　And till she come, as truly as to heaven
　　　I do confess the vices of my blood,
　　　So justly to your grave ears I'll present
125　How I did thrive in this fair lady's love,
　　　And she in mine.

DUKE

　　　Say it, Othello.

115.　**Sagittary** F.　Q has 'Sagittar'.
118.　F.　Not in Q.
121.　**S.D.** Q has '*Exit two or three.*' (after 'hither' line 120).　Not in F.
122.　**till** Q.　F has 'tell'.　**truly** F.　Q has 'faithfull'.
123.　F.　Not in Q.

111.　*forcèd*　brought about by constraint.
113.　*question*　conversation.
117.　*foul*　blameworthy, wicked, with an implication, here, of "impure."
124.　*justly*　exactly.

Her father loved me, oft invited me,
Still questioned me the story of my life
From year to year—the battles, sieges, fortunes
130   That I have passed.
I ran it through, even from my boyish days
To th' very moment that he bade me tell it:
Wherein I spake of most disastrous chances,
Of moving accidents by flood and field,
135   Of hairbreadth scapes i'th' imminent deadly breach;
Of being taken by the insolent foe,
And sold to slavery; of my redemption thence,
And portance in my travels' history;
Wherein of anters vast and deserts idle,
140   Rough quarries, rocks, and hills whose heads touch heaven,
It was my hint to speak—such was the process;

---

129.   **battles . . . fortunes** Q. F has 'Battaile . . . Fortune'.
133.   **spake** Q. F has 'spoke'.
134.   **accidents by** F. Q has 'accident of'.
137.   **of** F. Q has 'and'.
138.   **portance** F. Q has 'with it all'. **travels'** Q. F has 'Trauellours'.
139.   **anters** F (Antars). Q has 'Antrces'.
140.   **and** Q. Not in F. **heads** Q. F has 'head'.
141.   **hint** F. Q has 'hent'. **the** Q. F has 'my'.

128.   *Still*   continually.

134.   *moving accidents*   stirring events.

135.   *i'th' imminent deadly breach*   in the death-threatening breach
(of the wall of an attacked city or fortress).

138.   *portance in*   behavior, conduct, how I bore myself, throughout.

139–40. Othello's wanderings are reminiscent of those undergone
by those who (in a much cited passage) "were strangers and pilgrims
on the earth" before the new dispensation and "obtained a good
report through faith": "Whom the world was not worthy of: they
wandered in wildernesses and mountains, and dens, and caves of the
earth" (Hebrews 11: 13, 38–9).

139.   *anters*   caves.   *deserts idle*   desolate and uninhabited lands.
Idle   literally means "empty."

141.   *It was my hint*   I had occasion.   *process*   narrative, course
of my story.

And of the Cannibals that each other eat,
The Anthropophagi, and men whose heads
Do grow beneath their shoulders. These things to hear
145 Would Desdemona seriously incline;
But still the house affairs would draw her thence,
Which ever as she could with haste dispatch,
She'd come again, and with a greedy ear
Devour up my discourse; which I observing,
150 Took once a pliant hour, and found good means
To draw from her a prayer of earnest heart
That I would all my pilgrimage dilate,
Whereof by parcels she had something heard,
But not intentively. I did consent,
155 And often did beguile her of her tears
When I did speak of some distressful stroke
That my youth suffered. My story being done,
She gave me for my pains a world of sighs.

---

142. **other** Q. F has 'others'.
143. **Anthropophagi** Q (*Anthropophagie*). F has '*Anthropophague*'.
144. **Do grow** Q. F has 'Grew'. **These things** F. Q has 'this'.
146. **thence** Q. F has 'hence'.
147. **Which** F. Q has 'And'.
153. **parcels** F. Q has 'parcell'.
154. **intentively** Q. F has 'instinctiuely'.
156. **distressful** F. Q has 'distressed'.
158. **sighs** Q. F has 'kisses'.

143. *Anthropophagi* a race of man-eating Scythians, particularly supposed to prey on strangers, noted by old geographers. Their name was virtually synonymous with cannibal—often applied figuratively, as in Jonson, *Staple of Newes* (III. ii. 179)—and became in the popular drama a symbol of mercilessly cruel barbarity.

143–4. *men . . . shoulders* another marvellous race commonplace in travellers' tales and even found in illustrated maps (see App. C). These too were considered "monsters"—but in form, not, as those "that each other eat," in manners contrary to "nature."

150. *pliant* propitious, suitable.

152. *pilgrimage* drawn from the traditional image of the life of the Christian as a hard pilgrimage. *dilate* narrate in full (not "enlarge").

153. *by parcels* piecemeal.

154. *intentively* with fully continuous attention.

She swore, i' faith, 'twas strange, 'twas passing strange;
160 'Twas pitiful, 'twas wondrous pitiful.
She wished she had not heard it; yet she wished
That heaven had made her such a man. She thanked me;
And bade me, if I had a friend that loved her,
I should but teach him how to tell my story,
165 And that would woo her. Upon this hint I spake.
She loved me for the dangers I had passed,
And I loved her that she did pity them.
This only is the witchcraft I have used.

Enter DESDEMONA, IAGO *and Attendants.*

Here comes the lady; let her witness it.

DUKE

170 I think this tale would win my daughter too.
Good Brabantio, take up this mangled matter at the best;
Men do their broken weapons rather use
Than their bare hands.

BRABANTIO

I pray you hear her speak.
If she confess that she was half the wooer,
175 Destruction on my head if my bad blame
Light on the man. —Come hither, gentle mistress.

---

159. **i'faith** Q.   F has 'in faith'.
165. **hint.** F.   Q has 'heate'.
168. **S.D.** *Attendants.* F.   Q has *'and the rest.'*
175. **on my head** F.   Q has 'lite on me'.

159. *passing* surpassingly.

162. *That . . . man* i.e. that heaven's will had been for her to have been such a valorous man of fortitude and adventure. The pronoun *her* is accusative.

165. *hint* opportunity, i.e. the occasion afforded by her remark. Not (though I think moving toward) the modern sense: a suggestion deliberately made.

175. *bad* since he would then be wrong to blame him.

176. *mistress* madam—a ceremonious vocative which, with the complimentary epithet, *gentle* (a reminder of her noble birth), might be expected to recall to Desdemona her social identity and responsibility.

Do you perceive in all this noble company
Where most you owe obedience?

DESDEMONA

My noble father,
I do perceive here a divided duty.
180 To you I am bound for life and education;
My life and education both do learn me
How to respect you: you are the lord of duty;
I am hitherto your daughter. But here's my husband;
And so much duty as my mother showed
185 To you, preferring you before her father,
So much I challenge that I may profess
Due to the Moor my lord.

BRABANTIO

God bu'y! I ha' done.
Please it your grace, on to the state affairs.
I had rather to adopt a child than get it. —
190 Come hither, Moor.
I here do give thee that, withal my heart,

---

182. **the lord of duty** F. (Lord). Q has 'Lord of all my duty'.
187. **bu'y . . . ha'** Q. F has 'be with you . . . haue'.
191. **that, withal my heart,** This edition. F has 'that with all my heart,'. Q has 'that, with all my heart'.

180. *education* upbringing.
181. *learn* teach.
182. *respect you* The commandment, "Honor thy father and thy mother . . ." (Exodus 20: 12), underlying this phrase very definitely included for the Elizabethans the "consent of parents" in the marriage of a child. *the lord* i.e. the lord by natural right.
186. *challenge . . . profess* claim the right to declare.
187. *God bu'y* a contracted form of "God be with you."
188. *Please it* if it be pleasing to—literally, "let it please."
189. *get* beget—Brabantio's embittered point being that an adopted child could scarcely be less dutiful and would cause less parental pain even if it were.
191. *that, withal my heart,* This emendation is required to allow F, which has line 192, to make sense (and meaningful word play). The word *withal* is spelled "*withall*" in both texts, e.g. above at line 93 and at V. ii. 56.

Which, but thou hast already, with all my heart
I would keep from thee. —For your sake, jewel,
I am glad at soul I have no other child;
195   For thy escape would teach me tyranny,
To hang clogs on 'em. —I have done, my lord.

DUKE

Let me speak like yourself, and lay a sentence
Which like a grise or step may help these lovers
Into your favor.
200   When remedies are past, the griefs are ended
By seeing the worst, which late on hopes depended.
To mourn a mischief that is past and gone
Is the next way to draw new mischief on.
What cannot be preserved when Fortune takes,
205   Patience her injury a mock'ry makes.
The robbed that smiles steals something from the thief;
He robs himself that spends a bootless grief.

BRABANTIO

So let the Turk of Cyprus us beguile:
We lose it not so long as we can smile.
210   He bears the sentence well that nothing bears

---

192.   F. Not in Q.
196.   **'em** Q. F has 'them'.
198.   **grise** F. Q has 'greese'.
199.   Q. Not in F.
203.   **new** F. Q has 'more'.
204.   **preserved** Q (preseru'd). F has 'presern'd'.
205.   **mock'ry** F. Q has 'mockery'.

193. *For your sake*   because of you, on your account.
195. *escape*   in a double sense: (1) getaway and (2) transgression.
196. *clogs*   *Clog* is a word for anything hung on an animal to hinder its movement.
197. *like yourself*   as you would (if you were not furious).   *lay a sentence*   set down a proposition in the form of a maxim or gnomic saying (Latin "sententia").
198. *grise or step*   synonymous.
201. *hopes*   expectations of good or ill.
205. *Patience . . . makes*   Patiently bearing the malice of Fortune makes a mockery of injuries by her that we cannot avoid.

But the free comfort which from thence he hears;
But he bears both the sentence and the sorrow
That to pay grief must of poor patience borrow.
These sentences, to sugar, or to gall,
215   Being strong on both sides, are equivocal.
But words are words: I never yet did hear
That the bruisèd heart was pierced through the ear.
Beseech you now, to the affairs of the state.

DUKE

The Turk with a most mighty preparation makes for Cyprus.
220   — Othello, the fortitude of the place is best known to you.
And though we have there a substitute of most allowed suffi-

---

217.   **bruisèd . . . pierced** F (bruized . . . pierc'd).   Q has 'bruis'd
. . . pierced'. **ear** Q.   F has 'eares'.
218.   **Beseech you now, to** Q.   F has 'I humbly beseech you proceed to'.
the affairs of the Q.   F has 'th'Affaires of'.
219.   **a** F.   Not in Q.

211.   *free*   free of care and grief.
214.   *gall*   embitter—with a play on the verb in its more usual
sense—"to rub the skin off" and thus "to irritate."
215.   *equivocal*   I.e. your sentences can embitter misfortune as well
as sweeten it.
217.   *bruisèd . . . ear*   Considered a crux, and often emended
"piecèd" (i.e. "made whole") after Warburton, since "piercing" a
bruised heart seemed an odd way to cure or relieve it. I think that
the line's emphasis falls on *bruisèd heart* and that there is word-play
in the QF reading *pierced* (in the senses "penetrate" and "deeply
move"). Words often "pierce" the ear in Shakespeare; cf. *Love's
Labour's Lost* V. ii. 741: "Honest plain words best pierce the ear of
grief." I believe Brabantio sarcastically means: "Words may, as they
say, 'pierce' the ear; but I've yet to hear that they ever moved (to
consolation) a heart as bruised as mine."
220.   *fortitude*   strength, fortification. But this very unusual use
of a spiritual term for an inanimate object calls attention to itself, and
to an important theme: it is "fortitude" for which Othello is known
and because of which Desdemona married him.
221.   *substitute*   for myself, one commanding in my name (i.e.
Montano).   *allowed*   acknowledged.

ciency, yet opinion, a sovereign mistress of effects, throws a
more safer voice on you. You must therefore be content to
slubber the gloss of your new fortunes with this more stub-
225 born and boist'rous expedition.

OTHELLO

The tyrant, custom, most grave senators,
Hath made the flinty and steel couch of war
My thrice-driven bed of down. I do agnize
A natural and prompt alacrity
230 I find in hardness; and do undertake
This present wars against the Ottomites.
Most humbly, therefore, bending to your state,
I crave fit disposition for my wife,
Due reference of place, and exhibition,
235 With such accommodation and besort
As levels with her breeding.

---

222. **a sovereign** Q. F has 'a more soueraigne'.
225. **boist'rous** F (boystrous).   Q has 'boisterous'.
226. **grave** F.   Q has 'great'.
227. **couch** Pope.   Q has 'Cooch'; F reads 'Coach'.
230. **do** F.   Q has 'would'.
234. **reference** F.   Q has 'reuerence'.

222. *opinion . . . effects* general opinion, which determines
what gets to be done.
224. *slubber* besmear.
224–5. *stubborn and boist'rous* rough and harshly violent.
228. *thrice-driven* i.e. softest, only the finest and lightest feathers
being used after three winnowings with currents of air. *agnize*
recognize in myself.
229–30. *A . . . hardness* a natural and ready response to hardship.
234. *Due . . . exhibition* assignment to some appropriate residence and allowance of money for maintenance.
235. *accommodation and besort* such befitting arrangements (for
her)—the figure of speech, hendiadys.
236. *As . . . breeding* as corresponds with her upbringing.

DUKE

If you please,

Be't at her father's.

BRABANTIO

I'll not have it so.

OTHELLO

Nor I.

DESDEMONA

Nor I. I would not there reside,
To put my father in impatient thoughts
240 By being in his eye. Most gracious Duke,
To my unfolding lend your prosperous ear,
And let me find a charter in your voice
T'assist my simpleness.

DUKE

What would you, Desdemona?

DESDEMONA

That I did love the Moor to live with him,
245 My downright violence and storm of fortunes

236–7. **If . . . /Be't** Capell.   Q has 'If you please, bee't'; F has 'Why
        at her Fathers?'
237. **I'll** Q. (Ile). F has 'I will'.
238. **Nor I. I would not** Q. F has 'Nor would I'.
241. **your prosperous** F. Q has 'a gracious'.
243. **T'assist my simpleness.** F.   Q has 'And if my simpleness. - - - -'.
      you, Desdemona? F (you *Desdemona?*). Q has 'you - - - -
      speake.'
244. **did** Q. Not in F.
245. **storm** F. Q has 'scorne'.

241. *To . . . your prosperous ear* to what I have to say give
your favorable attention.

242. *charter in your voice* authority in your assent.

243. *simpleness* lack of skill (in petitioning).

244. *live* emphatic: i.e. in the fullest sense "as his wife," sharing
his life as a soldier.

245. *storm of fortunes* a military figure: my taking my fortunes
by storm. The preparative thought of "stormy fortunes" is inevitably
present. Either the F reading or the Q could have been read for the
other; but Q's "scorne," though it makes textually adequate sense,
does not accord as well with "trumpet" and "quality."

May trumpet to the world. My heart's subdued
Even to the very quality of my lord:
I saw Othello's visage in his mind,
And to his honours and his valiant parts
250 Did I my soul and fortunes consecrate.
So that, dear lords, if I be left behind,
A moth of peace, and he go to the war,
The rites for which I love him are bereft me,
And I a heavy interim shall support
255 By his dear absence. Let me go with him.

OTHELLO

Let her have your voice.
Vouch with me, heaven, I therefore beg it not
To please the palate of my appetite,

---

247. **very quality** F. Q has 'utmost pleasure'.
253. **which** Q. F has 'why'.
256–7. **Let . . . heaven** F. Q has 'Your voyces Lords: beseech you
        let her will/Haue a free way'.

246. *trumpet to the world* This phrase, besides its militant flavor,
recalls the figure of Fame as usually depicted.

247. *very quality* his profession (of soldiering) itself (which she
identifies with his essential character).

249. *parts* deeds.

253. *rites* i.e., picking up "consecrate" (line 250), the "amorous
rites" of marriage (*Romeo and Juliet* III. ii. 8), and even, in this
context, the "rite of war" (*Hamlet* V. ii. 391). I think the word when
spoken also involves a play on "rights" (i.e. those of a wife to be
with her husband); cf. "the great prerogative and rite of love" (*All's
Well* II. iv. 39).

255. *dear* i.e. in the Elizabethan sense: his absence would be *dear*
because it would touch her with personal pain.

256–7. I regard these lines as evidently revised.

256. *voice* your vote, agreement.

257. *Vouch with me, heaven* God witness my assertion.

Nor to comply with heat the young affects
260 (In me defunct), and proper satisfaction;
But to be free and bounteous to her mind.
And heaven defend your good souls that you think
I will your serious and great business scant
For she is with me. No, when light-winged toys

---

259. **heat** F.   Q has 'heate,'.
260. **me** Upton conj. Capell.   Q and F have 'my'.
261. **bounteous to** F.   Q has 'bounteous of'.
263. **great** F.   Q has 'good'.
264. **For** Q.   F has 'When'.

259–60. *Nor . . . satisfaction*   A famous and most difficult crux which has been variously emended and interpreted. In the present version, the point of the lines is to give his denial that indulgence of sensual appetite is his motive a more general reference, inclusive of Desdemona, and to set it in an important conceptual context. The *young affects* refer to "the lusts of youth" "which St. Paul admonishes Timothy to flee from and the Romans to mortify" (Henley): i.e. "the lusts of the flesh" which the Christian is commanded not to "fulfil" (Galatians 5: 16). His parenthetic claim that these are *defunct* in him means they are "deadened" or "mortified"—as in the Book of Common Prayer Baptismal Service, "Grant that all carnal affections may die in them . . ." Thus, having denied a simply selfish sexual motive for his request (line 258), Othello now disclaims also (*Nor*), as a man who has mortified the "flesh," any purpose to fulfil (*comply*) *the* (not, "my") *young affects* with the passionate deeds (*heat*) and gratification proper to them (*and proper satisfaction*). It is preparatively important that the theological term "lusts of youth" can refer not only to sexual lust, but also to such other passions as vengeful wrath. "Flee also from the lusts of youth, and follow after righteousness, faith, love and peace, with them that call on the Lord with pure heart" (2 Timothy 2: 22).

261. *mind*   wishes—but the context also gives the word a force often found in Shakespeare, "the soul, the mental power; opposed to the body" (Schmidt).

264. *For*   because.

264–5. *light-winged . . . Cupid*   frivolous trifles of amorous dallying.

265   Of feathered Cupid seel with wanton dullness
      My speculative and officed instrument,
      That my disports corrupt and taint my business,
      Let housewives make a skillet of my helm,
      And all indign and base adversities
270   Make head against my estimation!

DUKE

Be it as you shall privately determine
Either for her stay or going. Th' affair cries haste,
And speed must answer it.

---

265. **Of** F. Q has 'And'.
265–6. **seel . . . officed instrument** F. Q has 'foyles . . . actiue in-
      struments'.
270. **estimation** F. Q has 'reputation'.
272. **her stay . . . Th'affair cries** F. Q has 'stay . . . the affaires
      cry'.
273–4. **answer it./1 SENATOR/You must away tonight.** F. Q has
      'answer, you must hence to night,/*Desd.* To night my
      Lord?/*Du.* This night.'

265. *seel with wanton dullness* blind with lascivious stupidity. To
seel is, literally, to sew up the eyelids of a hawk in the process of
taming him. I think lines 265–6 revised. Q's version is more inclusive:
the "toys" and Cupid "foyles" his "speculatiue and actiue instruments"—i.e. all his mental, sensory, and physical powers. F's emphasizes what Hooker called "the eye of understanding" capable of dis-
cerning rightly the "goodness" one should choose.

266. *My . . . instrument* the responsible sight of my mind:
officed means "provided with duties" (Latin *officia*).

267. *That* so that. *disports* pastime, sport, frequently with
sexual implication.

268. *skillet* saucepan. *helm* helmet—the protection of his
head and reason ("My speculative and officed instrument") as the
symbol of his untainted soldiership.

269. *indign* shameful, disgraceful (Latin *indignus*).

270. *Make head against* a military image: gather as troops in a
combined body to make a concerted attack against. *estimation*
generally acknowledged worth, reputation.

273–4. Evidently revised, presumably by Shakespeare, to eliminate
Desdemona's protesting question "To night my Lord?" (Q), very
human under the circumstances but implicitly undermining of her
dramatically central assertion that her "heart's subdued/ Even to
the very quality of my lord" (lines 246–7).

1 SENATOR

You must away tonight.

OTHELLO

With all my heart.

DUKE

275 At nine i'th' morning here we'll meet again.
Othello, leave some officer behind,
And he shall our commission bring to you,
With such things else of quality and respect
As doth import you.

OTHELLO

So please your grace, my ancient:
280 A man he is of honesty and trust.
To his conveyance I assign my wife,
With what else needful your good grace shall think
To be sent after me.

DUKE

Let it be so.
Goodnight to everyone. [*To* BRABANTIO] And noble signior,
285 If virtue no delighted beauty lack,
Your son-in-law is far more fair than black.

1 SENATOR

Adieu, brave Moor; use Desdemona well.

---

275. **nine i' th'** F. Q has 'ten i' the'.
278. **With** Q. F has 'And'. **and** F. Q has 'or'.
279. **import** F. Q has 'concerne'. **So** F. Not in Q.

278. *of quality and respect* pertaining to your position and honor.
279. *As doth import you* as concern you, as are important for you to have.
281. *conveyance* escort, convoy. But other Shakespearean meanings of this word support the audience's anticipatory qualms about the meaning of this plan—particularly: (1) removal; (2) document by which transference of property is effected; (3) underhand dealing.
285. *delighted* delightful.
286. *more fair than black* an attempt to palliate the implication of Othello's blackness to Brabantio by affirming that the hero's inner virtue makes him *fair*—with a play on the senses "beautiful," "white or fair complexioned," "pure, honorable," "good, accomplished."

BRABANTIO

Look to her, Moor, if thou hast eyes to see;
She has deceived her father, and may thee.

OTHELLO

290   My life upon her faith!
                    Exeunt [DUKE, BRABANTIO, *Senators, and Officers*].
                    Honest Iago,
My Desdemona must I leave to thee.
I prithee let thy wife attend on her,
And bring them after in the best advantage. —
Come, Desdemona, I have but an hour
295   Of love, of worldly matters and direction,
To spend with thee. We must obey the time.
                            Exit [OTHELLO *with*] DESDEMONA.

RODERIGO

Iago—

IAGO

What say'st thou, noble heart?

RODERIGO

What will I do, think'st thou?

IAGO

300   Why, go to bed and sleep.

RODERIGO

I will incontinently drown myself.

---

288.   **if . . . see** F.   Q has 'haue a quicke eye to see'.
289.   **and may** F.   Q has 'may doe'.
290.   **S.D.** Q.   F has *'Exit'*.
293.   **them** F.   Q has 'her'.
295.   **worldly matters** Q.   F has 'wordly matter'.
296.   **the** Q.   F has 'the the'.
        S.D.   Q has *'Exit* Moore *and* Desdemona.'   F has *'Exit'*.
299.   **think'st** F.   Q has 'thinkest'.

293. *in the best advantage*   at the earliest favorable opportunity.
301. *incontinently*   forthwith.

IAGO

If thou dost, I shall never love thee after. Why, thou silly gentleman!

RODERIGO

305 It is silliness to live when to live is torment; and then have we a prescription to die when death is our physician.

IAGO

O villainous! I ha' looked upon the world for four times seven years; and since I could distinguish betwixt a benefit and an injury, I never found man that knew how to love himself. Ere I would say I would drown myself for the love of a guineahen,
310 I would change my humanity with a baboon.

RODERIGO

What should I do? I confess it is my shame to be so fond, but it is not in my virtue to amend it.

---

302. **If thou do'st** F. Q has 'Well, if thou doest'.
     after F. Q has 'after it'.
302–3. **Why, . . . gentleman!** Q has 'Why, . . . Gentleman.' F has
     'Why . . . Gentleman?'
304. **torment** F. Q has 'a torment'. **have we** F. Q has 'we haue'.
306. **O villainous** F. Not in Q. **ha'** Q. F has 'haue'.
307. **betwixt** F. Q has 'betweene'.
308. **man** F. Q has 'a man'.

305. *prescription* prescriptive right, with a pun on "doctor's orders."
306. *villainous* a general term of scornful abuse or reproof, but in this context more specifically "base and servile."
308. *love himself* Iago in effect resumes the exposition (I. i. 60-1) of his amorality of masked, strong-willed self-interest. In placing self-love and self-sufficiency at its foundation, Iago implicitly rejects the love of God and the spiritual grace of traditional received belief.
309. *guineahen* a contemptuous term for woman—a skirt, a broad.
310. *baboon* like other simians, noted for their sexuality, and commonplace as symbols for the sub-humanity of man's enslavement to appetite.
311. *fond* infatuated.
312. *virtue* power, strength of character—as though it were a given trait over which one had no control.

IAGO

Virtue? a fig! 'Tis in ourselves that we are thus or thus. Our
bodies are our gardens to the which our wills are gardeners: so
315   that if we will plant nettles or sow lettuce, set hyssop and
weed up thyme, supply it with one gender of herbs or distract
it with many, either to have it sterile with idleness or manured
with industry—why, the power and corrigible authority of

---

314. **our gardens** F.   Q has 'gardens'.

313–24. *Virtue . . . scion*   Iago explains the traditional distinction between Appetite ("inferior natural desire") and the Appetite's
controller, Will ("desire . . . where Reason and Understanding, or
the show of Reason, prescribeth the thing desired" [Hooker]). The
forms of Appetite are "Affections, as joy, and grief, and fear, and
anger" and "it is not altogether in our power, whether we will be
stirred by affections or no: whereas actions which issue from the disposition of the Will are in the power thereof to be performed or
stayed." The gradually revealed Iagoan perversion of this conventional moral psychology is that Reason, instead of governing Will,
"panders" to it (*Hamlet* III. iv. 88): thus it becomes, instead of the
lord of the Will, its servant in the willed pursuit of the objects of
Appetite.

313. *a fig!   Fig* is a type of valuelessness: "nonsense!"

314. *gardens*   This image (man's will as gardener responsible for
the fruits and herbs he brings forth of himself) is one conventionally
associated with Iago's subject.

315–16. *plant . . . thyme*   A hurtful stinging herb, *nettles* (symbolizing depraved affections, particularly lechery), is contrasted with
lettuce, a beneficial bitter one (symbolizing what purifies the blood
and acts as a bridle on acts of lust)—(Bersuire, *De proprietatibus
rerum*, XII, cxc, lxxxvii). The humble herb *hyssop* traditionally symbolizes the instrument of true spiritual purification (Psalm 51: 7).
Thyme was associated with the virtue of drawing benefit from
adversity (Plutarch, *Moralia*, VI, 180–3). And Elizabethan gardeners
in fact grew hyssop and thyme together "as ayders the one to the
growth of the other" (Lyly). The structure of the references is
chiasmic: "weeding up thyme" is a folly paralleled with "planting
nettles."

316. *supply*   satisfy.   *gender*   kind, species.

317. *manured*   well cultivated.

318. *corrigible authority*   the power able to correct or control.

this lies in our wills. If the beam of our lives had not one scale
320   of reason to poise another of sensuality, the blood and baseness of our natures would conduct us to most preposterous
conclusions. But we have reason to cool our raging motions,
our carnal stings, our unbitted lusts; whereof I take this that
you call love to be a sect or scion.

RODERIGO

325   It cannot be.

IAGO

It is merely a lust of the blood and a permission of the will.
Come, be a man. Drown thyself? Drown cats and blind
puppies! I have professed me thy friend, and I confess me
knit to thy deserving with cables of perdurable toughness. I
330   could never better stead thee than now. Put money in thy
purse; follow thou these wars; defeat thy favor with an
usurped beard. I say, put money in thy purse. It cannot be that

---

319.   **beam** Theobald.   F has 'braine'.   Q has 'ballance'.
323.   **our unbitted** Q.   F has 'or unbitted'.
324.   **scion** Steevens.   Q has 'syen';   F has 'seyen'.
328.   **have professed** F.   Q has 'professe'.
331.   **thou** F.   Not in Q. **these** Q.   F has 'the'.
332-3.   **be that . . . should long** Q (be,).   F has 'be long that . . .
          should'.

319.   *beam*   F's variant "braine" no doubt is a compositor's mis-
reading of "beame," a more precise word for the context than Q's
"ballance" as it is Shakespeare's term for the cross-bar of the
apparatus without the scales.   *poise*   counterbalance.
320-1.   *blood and baseness*   hendiadys: base appetitive passions.
322.   *motions*   impulses, compelling desires.
323.   *carnal stings*   sexual urges. "The wanton stings and motions
of the sense" (*Measure for Measure* I. iv. 59).   *unbitted lusts*   unbridled desires (returning to the horse image).
324.   *sect or scion*   cutting or graft.
329.   *knit to thy deserving*   bound to your merit, but also,
ironically, bound to that for which you deserve well—the favors
received of you.   *perdurable*   everlasting, eternal.
331-2.   *defeat . . . beard*   change your appearance for the worse
by growing a soldier's beard as your disguise. But there is a scornful
sense lurking in other meanings of *defeat* and *usurped*: "overcome
that pretty face by growing a manly beard to which it has no right."

Desdemona should long continue her love to the Moor—put
money in thy purse—nor he his to her. It was a violent com-
335 mencement, and thou shalt see an answerable sequestration—
put but money in thy purse. These Moors are changeable in
their wills—fill thy purse with money. The food that to him
now is as luscious as locusts shall be to him shortly as acerbe
as the coloquintida. She must change for youth: when she is
340 sated with his body, she will find the error of her choice. She
must have change, she must; therefore put money in thy
purse. If thou wilt needs damn thyself, do it a more delicate
way than drowning. Make all the money thou canst. If sanctimony and a frail vow betwixt an erring barbarian and a super-
345 subtle Venetian be not too hard for my wits and all the tribe
of hell, thou shalt enjoy her; therefore make money. A pox o'
drowning! 'Tis clean out of the way. Seek thou rather to be

---

333. **love to** F.   Q has 'loue vnto'.
334. **his** F.   Not in Q.
334–5. **commencement** Q.   F has 'Commencement in her'.
338–9. **acerbe as the** Q.   F has 'bitter as'.
339. **She . . . youth** F.   Not in Q.
340. **error** Q.   F has 'errors'.
340–1. **She . . . must** Q.   Not in F.
344. **and a** Q.   F has 'and'.
346–7. **o'drowning** Q.   F has 'of drowning thy selfe.'

335. *answerable sequestration*   corresponding estrangement and
termination.

338. *locusts*   evidently a delicacy, probably the carob, a kind of
sweet locust fruit called "St. John's bread"; cf. "locusts and honey"
(Matthew 3: 4).   *acerbe*   bitter.

339. *coloquintida*   a bitter medicine, a purgative derived from
the colocynth or bitter-apple. Noted as one of the products from
Cyprus in Hakluyt.

343. *Make*   raise.

343–4. *sanctimony*   holiness, sanctity, of the marriage rite.

344. *erring*   wandering, vagabond.

344–5. *supersubtle*   hyper-refined (and therefore an odd match for
a "barbarian").

347. *clean . . . way*   quite off the track.

hanged in compassing thy joy than to be drowned and go
without her.

RODERIGO

350 Wilt thou be fast to my hopes if I depend on the issue?

IAGO

Thou art sure of me. Go, make money. I have told thee often,
and I retell thee again and again, I hate the Moor. My cause is
hearted; thine hath no less reason. Let us be conjunctive in
our revenge against him. If thou canst cuckold him, thou dost
355 thyself a pleasure, me a sport. There are many events in the
womb of time which will be delivered. Traverse, go, provide
thy money! We will have more of this tomorrow. Adieu.

RODERIGO

Where shall we meet i'th' morning?

IAGO

At my lodging.

RODERIGO

360 I'll be with thee betimes.   [*Going.*]

IAGO

Go to; farewell. —Do you hear, Roderigo?

---

350. **hopes if . . . issue?** F (hopes,).   Q has 'hopes?'
352. **retell** F.   Q has 'tell'.
353. **hath** F.   Q has 'has'. **conjunctive** F (coniunctiue).   Q has 'com-
        municatiue'.
355. **me** F.   Q has 'and me'.

348–9. *hanged . . . her*   This pairing of *hanged* and *drowned* is
perhaps suggested by the proverb, "He that is born to be hanged shall
never be drowned" (Tilley, B139). "If you're so bent on self-destruc-
tion, it would be better to have what you want, though you hang for
it, than to be a frustrate suicide."

353. *hearted*   my heart is in it.

356. *Traverse*   a military command (recalling "follow thou these
wars" line 331); but the exact meaning is in debate. Perhaps (with
"go") = "Port arms! march!"

361. *Go to*   a colloquial formula in dismissing a subject as settled:
"Enough said."

RODERIGO

What say you?

IAGO

No more of drowning, do you hear?

RODERIGO

I am changed.

IAGO

365   Go to; farewell. Put money enough in your purse!

RODERIGO

I'll sell all my land.   *Exit* RODERIGO.

IAGO

Thus do I ever make my fool my purse;
For I mine own gained knowledge should profane
If I would time expend with such a snipe
370   But for my sport and profit. I hate the Moor;
And it is thought abroad that 'twixt my sheets
H'as done my office. I know not if't be true,
But I, for mere suspicion in that kind,
Will do as if for surety. He holds me well;
375   The better shall my purpose work on him.
Cassio's a proper man. Let me see now:
To get his place, and to plume up my will

362–5. Q. Not in F.
366. F. Not in Q.
369. **a snipe** Q. F has 'Snpe'.
372. **H'as** Q (Ha's). F has 'She ha's'.
373. **But** F. Q has 'Yet'.
377. **his** F. Q has 'this'. **plume** F. Q has 'make'.

367ff. Iago's soliloquy is an instance of the villain's self-explana-
tion to the audience, conventional in the Elizabethan drama, which
still discernibly shows its derivation from the homiletic self-display
of "quality" and intent by the Vice of the earlier morality play.

369. *snipe*   dupe, contemptible fool—a bird proverbially so stupid
it would put its own head in the noose.

373. *in that kind*   in that regard.

374. *as if for surety*   as though I were certain of it.   *well*   in
high regard.

376. *proper*   handsome.

377. *plume up*   gratify—literally, "proudly deck with plumes."

In double knavery—how? how? Let me see:

After some time to abuse Othello's ear

380   That he is too familiar with his wife.

He hath a person and a smooth dispose

To be suspected—framed to make women false.

The Moor is of a free and open nature

That thinks men honest that but seem to be so;

385   And will as tenderly be led by th' nose

As asses are.

I have't! It is engendered! Hell and night

Must bring this monstrous birth to the world's light.   *Exit.*

[*Act II, scene i.*] Enter MONTANO *and two Gentlemen.*

MONTANO

What from the cape can you discern at sea?

---

378. **In** F.   Q has 'A'. **Let me** Q.   F has 'Let's'.
379. **ear** Q.   F has 'eares'.
381. **hath** F.   Q has 'has'.
383. **is of a free . . . nature** F.   Q has 'a free . . . nature too'.
384. **seem** F.   Q has 'seemes'.
387. **have't** F.   Q has 'ha't'.
388. **S.D.** Q.   Not in F.
II. i **S.D.** F.   Q has '*Enter* Montanio, *Gouernor of Cypres, with two other Gentlemen.*'

381. *dispose*   manner.
383. *free*   frank.
385. *tenderly*   easily, docilely.   *led by th' nose*   made a fool of.
387–8. *Hell . . . light*   virtually an invocation to the powers of evil appropriately to assist in bringing the morally "unnatural" plot he has conceived (*engendered*) into the light of actuality. The apparent contradiction between the rhyme-paired *night* and *light* is resolved by the theological sense of *world*—one of the triad of the Christian's enemies, whose "light" proverbially is "darkness" (Ephesians 6: 12)—i.e. the darkness over which Satan, its Prince, rules and in which men make their evil choices. Traditionally, it is contrasted with "the light of the world" (John 8: 12) and the illumined "children of light" (Ephesians 5: 8).
II. i   The scene is quickly localized as near the harbor of a seaport on Cyprus, apprehensive of the Turkish threat to the island and awaiting the arrival of its new governor, Othello, who is still at sea (lines 28–9).

1 GENTLEMAN

Nothing at all: it is a high-wrought flood;
I cannot 'twixt the heaven and the main
Descry a sail.

MONTANO

5   Methinks the wind hath spoke aloud at land;
A fuller blast ne'er shook our battlements.
If it hath ruffianed so upon the sea,
What ribs of oak, when mountains melt on them,
Can hold the mortise? What shall we hear of this?

2 GENTLEMAN

10   A segregation of the Turkish fleet.
For do but stand upon the banning shore,
The chidden billow seems to pelt the clouds;
The wind-shaked surge, with high and monstrous mane,
Seems to cast water on the burning Bear
15   And quench the Guards of th'ever-fixèd Pole.

---

3. **heaven** F.   Q has 'hauen'.
5. **hath spoke** F.   Q has 'does speake'.
7. **hath** F.   Q has 'ha'.
8. **mountains melt on them** F.   Q has 'the huge mountaine mes lt'.
9. **mortise** QF have 'morties'.
11. **banning** Q.   F has 'foaming'.
12. **chidden** F.   Q has 'chiding'.
13. **mane** Knight.   Q has 'mayne';   F has 'Maine'.
15. **-fixèd** F.   Q has 'fired'.

2. *high-wrought*   made or roused high; with a secondary sense: "made from on high."

9. *hold the mortise*   keep their joints held together.

10. *segregation*   separation, dispersal.

11. *banning*   a daring implied personification in parallel to "the wind hath spoke aloud at land" (line 5): i.e. the shore as it were announces a prohibition (or curse) to prevent the encroachment of the waves. F's too-easy "foaming" appears to me a simplifying substitution.

13. *mane*   Besides the vivid figure for the wild crest of the "wind-shaked surge," there may be play on "main" in the sense "full might."

15. *the Guards*   two stars of the Little Bear used in navigation. *th'ever-fixèd Pole*   the pole star.

I never did like molestation view
On the enchafèd flood.

MONTANO

If that the Turkish fleet
Be not ensheltered and embayed, they are drowned;
It is impossible they bear it out.

Enter a third Gentleman.

3 GENTLEMAN

20   News, lads! our wars are done:
The desperate tempest hath so banged the Turks
That their designment halts. A noble ship of Venice
Hath seen a grievous wrack and sufferance
On most part of their fleet.

MONTANO

25   How! is this true?

3 GENTLEMAN

The ship is here put in,
A verinessa; Michael Cassio,
Lieutenant to the warlike Moor Othello,

---

19. **they** Q. F has 'to'. **S.D.** Q. F has '*Enter a Gentleman.*'
20. **lads! our** F (Laddes: our). Q has 'Lords, your'.
21. **Turks** F. Q has 'Turke'.
22. **A noble** F. Q has 'Another'.
24. **their** F. Q has 'the'.
25–6. **in,/A verinessa; Michael** Elze conj. Q has 'in: A Veronessa,
      Michael'; F has 'in: A *Verennessa, Michael*'.

16. *molestation* tumult, disturbance.
22. *their designment halts* their plan (to invade Cyprus) is
crippled—literally, "limps."
23. *sufferance* disastrous damage.
26. *verinessa* cutter. The reading is little more than a good guess,
assuming a noun derived from the Italian nautical term "verrinare" =
to cut through. This makes sense (as explaining the speed of Cassio's
ship's arrival) whereas to identify the ship as "A Veronesa" (one
supplied by Verona, an inland city) just after it has been identified as
"A noble ship of Venice" (line 22) does not. The QF pointing, identifying Cassio as the "Veronessa," certainly is wrong since much has
already and is yet to be made of his being a Florentine (I. i. 20, III.
i. 38).

Is come ashore; the Moor himself at sea,
And is in full commission here for Cyprus.

MONTANO

30   I am glad on't: 'tis a worthy governor.

3 GENTLEMAN

But this same Cassio, though he speak of comfort
Touching the Turkish loss, yet he looks sadly
And prays the Moor be safe; for they were parted
With foul and violent tempest.

MONTANO

                          Pray heaven he be!

35   For I have served him, and the man commands
Like a full soldier. Let's to the seaside, ho!
As well to see the vessel that's come in
As to throw out our eyes for brave Othello,
Even till we make the main and th'aerial blue

40   An indistinct regard.

3 GENTLEMAN

                Come, let's do so;

For every minute is expectancy
Of more arrivance.

                Enter CASSIO.

CASSIO

Thanks, you, the valiant of this warlike isle,
That so approve the Moor! O, let the heavens

---

28.   **ashore** Q.   F has 'on shore'.
33.   **prays** Q.   F has 'praye'.
34.   **heaven** Q.   F has 'Heauens'.
39–40. F. Not in Q.
39.   **th'aerial blue** Pope. F reads 'th'Eriall blew'.
42.   **arrivance** Q. F has 'Arriuancie'.
43.   **Thanks, you,** F (Thankes you,). Q has 'Thankes to'.
      this Q. F has 'the'. **warlike** F.   Q has 'worthy'.
44.   **Moor! O, let** F (Moor: Oh let).   Q has 'Moore, and let'.

29. *in . . . Cyprus* on his way hither to Cyprus commissioned
to bear full powers as governor.
32. *sadly* grave.
40. *An indistinct regard* i.e. even till we cannot distinguish sea
from sky.

45   Give him defense against the elements,
    For I have lost him on a dangerous sea.

MONTANO

Is he well shipped?

CASSIO

His bark is stoutly timbered, and his pilot
Of very expert and approved allowance;
50   Therefore my hopes, not surfeited to death,
Stand in bold cure.

VOICES (*within*)
A sail, a sail, a sail!
[*Enter a fourth Gentleman.*]

CASSIO

What noise?

4 GENTLEMAN

The town is empty; on the brow o' th' sea
Stand ranks of people, and they cry "A sail!"

CASSIO

55   My hopes do shape him for the governor.   *A shot* [*offstage*].

---

45. **the** F. Q has 'their'.
48. **pilot** F (Pylot). Q has 'Pilate'.
50. **hopes, not . . . death** F3 (hopes). F1 has 'hope's (not . . . death)'; Q has 'hope's not . . . death'.
51. **S.P.** F has '*Within.*' Q has '*Mess.*'
    S.D. Q has '*Enter a Messenger.*' (after 'bold cure' line 51). Not in F.
53. **S.P. 4 GENTLEMAN** F (Gent.). Q has '*Mess.*'
54. **Stand** F. Q has 'otand'.
55. **governor** F. Q has 'guernement'.
    S.D. Q (after 'least' line 57). Not in F.

49. *Of . . . allowance* admitted on good evidence to be proved by experience.

50–1. *my hopes . . . cure* a strained figurative expression for "though anxious, I yet hope for a happy outcome." Literally: "my hopes, though fed to excess (with unfulfilled expectation), are yet not mortally so (i.e. turned to despair), and still are confident of their curability (by fulfilment)."

2 GENTLEMAN

They do discharge the shot of courtesy:
Our friends at least.

CASSIO

I pray you, sir, go forth,
And give us truth who 'tis that is arrived.

2 GENTLEMAN

I shall.   *Exit.*

MONTANO

60   But, good lieutenant, is your general wived?

CASSIO

Most fortunately: he hath achieved a maid
That paragons description and wild fame;
One that excels the quirks of blazoning pens,
And in th'essential vesture of creation
65   Does tire the ingener.

[Re-] *enter 2 Gentleman.*

How now! who has put in?

---

56.   **the** Q. F has 'their'.
57.   **friends** F. Q has 'friend'.
63.   **quirks of** F. Not in Q.
64.   **th'essential** F. Q has 'the essentiall'.
65.   **tire the ingener** Knight. F has 'tyre the Ingeniuer.' Q has 'beare
          all excellency.' **S.D.** Q (but placed after 'put in?'). F has
          'Enter Gentleman.' (after 'Ingeniuer.') **How** F. Not in Q.

62. *paragons . . . fame* surpasses what rumor when most given
to exaggeration might compare with her. A "paragon" is a "pattern"
and thus a "non-pareil."

63. *excels . . . pens* uniquely surpasses the extravagant flour-
ishes of writers who set out the praises (of lovely ladies).

64–5. *in . . . ingener* Because of the real adornments God gave
her in creating her, she exhausts the most skillful inventor of compli-
ments who would praise her. There possibly is a strained play on
tire in the meaning "attire" (alluding to the "clothing of style" and
picking up *vesture*): "in her God-given real adornments she decks
the contriver of invented praise." Cf. Sonnet 84: "Let him but copy
what in you is writ,/ Not making worse what nature made so clear,/
And such a counterpart shall fame his wit,/ Making his style
admired every where."

2 GENTLEMAN

'Tis one Iago, ancient to the general.

CASSIO

H'as had most favorable and happy speed:
Tempests themselves, high seas, and howling winds,
The guttered rocks and congregated sands,
70 Traitors ensteeped to clog the guiltless keel,
As having sense of beauty, do omit
Their mortal natures, letting go safely by
The divine Desdemona.

MONTANO

What is she?

CASSIO

She that I spake of, our great captain's captain,
75 Left in the conduct of the bold Iago,
Whose footing here anticipates our thoughts
A se'ennight's speed.—Great Jove, Othello guard,
And swell his sail with thine own powerful breath,
That he may bless this bay with his tall ship,
80 Make love's quick pants in Desdemona's arms,
Give renewed fire to our extinct spirits,

---

67. **S.P.** CASSIO F. Not in Q (which prints speech as 2 GENTLE-MAN's). **H'as** F (Ha's). Q has 'He has'.
68. **high** F. Q has 'by'.
70. **ensteeped** F. Q has 'enscerped'. **clog** Q. F has 'enclogge'.
72. **mortal** F. Q has 'common'.
74. **spake** F. Q has 'spoke'.
80. **Make . . . in** F. Q has 'And swiftly come to'.

69. *guttered* here, apparently, "submerged," out of the sense "indented."

70. *ensteeped* concealed by submergence. Ridley suggests a hint of "double-dyed." Q's reading, "enscerped," is not yet explained; it possibly stands for "enscarped" or "escarped," but could be a mis-reading of the word preserved in F. *clog* prevent the motion of.

72. *mortal* deadly.
73. *divine* accented on first syllable.
76. *footing* landing.
77. *se'ennight's* week's.
81. *renewed* accented on first syllable.

And bring all Cyprus comfort.

    Enter DESDEMONA, IAGO, EMILIA, *and* RODERIGO.

                O, behold!

The riches of the ship is come ashore!

Ye men of Cyprus, let her have your knees.—

              [They "courtesy" to DESDEMONA.*]*

85 Hail to thee, lady! and the grace of heaven,

Before, behind thee, and on every hand,

Enwheel thee round!

DESDEMONA

       I thank you, valiant Cassio.

What tidings can you tell me of my lord?

CASSIO

He is not yet arrived; nor know I aught

90 But that he's well and will be shortly here.

DESDEMONA

O, but I fear! How lost you company?

CASSIO

The great contention of the sea and skies

Parted our fellowship.

VOICES (*within*)

A sail, a sail!

---

82. **And . . . comfort** Q. Not in F.
    S.D. Q (but placed after 'arms' line 80). F ('. . . *Rodorigo, and*
    Æmilia.') places after 'spirits' line 81.

83. **ashore** Q. F has 'on shore'.

84. **Ye** Q. F has 'You'.

88. **me** Q. Not in F.

92. **the sea** Q. F has 'Sea'.

93. (*within*) **A . . . sail!** Q places after 'company' line 91;   F after
    'a sail' line 94.

84. S.D., *courtesy* "bow in the knees, a kind of reverence made
by men as well as women" (Schmidt).

87. *Enwheel thee round* encompass thee. The image, in context,
evokes the scriptural figure of the good "mystical woman" espoused
to God (Revelation 12: 1), often depicted in Elizabethan illustration
as described in the popular Genevan-Tomson Bible—"compassed
about" with "the Son of Righteousness" and "with glory given of
God."

CASSIO

But hark! a sail!   [*A shot offstage.*]

2 GENTLEMAN

95   They give their greeting to the citadel:
This likewise is a friend.

CASSIO

See for the news.

[*Exit Gentleman.*]

Good ancient, you are welcome. [*To* EMILIA] Welcome,
mistress.—

Let it not gall your patience, good Iago,
That I extend my manners; 'tis my breeding
100   That gives me this bold show of courtesy.   [*Kisses* EMILIA.]

IAGO

Sir, would she give you so much of her lips
As of her tongue she oft bestows on me,
You'd have enough.

DESDEMONA

Alas, she has no speech!

IAGO

In faith, too much.

---

94.   **S.D.** Capell (*Guns*).   Not in QF.
95.   **their** Q.   F has 'this'.
96.   **See for the news** F.   Q has 'So speakes this voyce'.
      S.D.   Not in QF.
97.   **S.D.**   Rowe.
101. **Sir** F.   Q has 'For'.
102. **oft bestows** F.   Q has 'has bestowed'.
103. **You'd** Q.   F has 'You would'.
104. **In faith** F (Infaith).   Q has 'I know'.

97. *mistress*   madam.
98. *gall*   irritate.
99. *extend*   give   scope   to.   *manners*   forms   of   politeness.
breeding   upbringing, training in etiquette.
100. *this . . . courtesy*   Cassio's kiss of greeting is normal
Elizabethan social courtesy; *bold show* is merely persiflage—at least
as he intends it.

105 I find it still when I have leave to sleep.
    Marry, before your ladyship, I grant,
    She puts her tongue a little in her heart
    And chides with thinking.

EMILIA

You ha' little cause to say so.

IAGO

    Come on, come on! You are pictures out o' doors, bells in your
110 parlors, wildcats in your kitchens, saints in your injuries,
    devils being offended, players in your housewifery, and
    housewives in your beds.

DESDEMONA

O, fie upon thee, slanderer!

IAGO

    Nay, it is true, or else I am a Turk:
115 You rise to play, and go to bed to work.

---

105. **it still . . . have leave** F.   Q has 'it, I; for . . . ha list'.
108. **ha'** Q.   F has 'haue'.
109–12. F.   As verse in Q.
109. **o' doors** Q (adores).   F has 'of doore'.
113. **S.P.** F.   Not in Q.

109. *pictures* pretty as pictures—idealized images with painted faces. Cf. Hamlet's jibe: "I have heard of your paintings too, well enough; God hath given you one face, and you make yourselves another" (*Hamlet* III. i. 142). *bells* as sweet-voiced as bells, but perhaps with the implication that their clappers (tongues) are ever in motion.
110. *wildcats in your kitchens* presumably to the servants behind the scenes. *saints in your injuries* "When you have a mind to do injuries, you put on an air of sanctity" (Johnson).
111. *players* Three meanings are possible: (1) "play-actors" or "deceivers," (2) "spendthrifts" (literally, "gamblers"), and (3) "triflers." *housewifery* skillful housekeeping.
112. *housewives* (1) hussies, (2) "there you really pay attention to skillful housekeeping!"
113. *O . . . slanderer* a smiling protest to this stock satire on women.
114. *Turk* infidel—with a deeper sense for the audience than for those engaged in this slight but time-beguiling badinage.

EMILIA

You shall not write my praise.

IAGO

No, let me not.

DESDEMONA

What wouldst thou write of me, if thou shouldst praise me?

IAGO

O gentle lady, do not put me to't;
For I am nothing, if not critical.

DESDEMONA

120   Come on, assay. —There's one gone to the harbor?

IAGO

Ay, madam.

DESDEMONA

I am not merry; but I do beguile
The thing I am by seeming otherwise. —
Come, how wouldst thou praise me?

IAGO

125   I am about it; but indeed my invention comes from my pate as
birdlime does from frieze—it plucks out brains and all. But
my muse labors, and thus she is delivered.

If she be fair and wise, fairness and wit,
The one's for use, the other useth it.

---

117. **wouldst thou** Q. F has 'would'st'.
118. **to't** Q. F has 'too₍t'.
125–7. F. As verse in Q.
126. **brains** F. Q has 'braine'.
129. **useth** F. Q has 'vsing'.

119. *critical* censorious.
120. *assay* try, make an attempt.
122–3. *I . . . otherwise* a half-aside: "I distract myself from
what I am (anxiety itself: *The thing I am*) by appearing carelessly
merry."
126. *birdlime* a sticky viscous substance used to catch birds.
frieze coarse woolen material.
128. *wit* quickness of apprehension.

DESDEMONA

130 Well praised! How if she be black and witty?

IAGO

If she be black, and thereto have a wit,
She'll find a white that shall her blackness fit.

DESDEMONA

Worse and worse!

EMILIA

How if fair and foolish?

IAGO

135   She never yet was foolish that was fair;
For even her folly helped her to an heir.

DESDEMONA

These are old fond paradoxes to make fools laugh i'th' ale-
house. What miserable praise hast thou for her that's foul
and foolish?

IAGO

140   There's none so foul, and foolish thereunto,
But does foul pranks which fair and wise ones do.

---

132. **fit** F. Q has 'hit'.
136. **an heir** F (*heire*). Q has 'a haire'.
137-8. F. As verse in Q.
137. **fond** F. Not in Q.

130. *black* dark—an inviting question since conventionally the
Elizabethans preferred blondes.
131. *thereto* besides.
132. *white . . . fit* with a pun on "wight" and moral "blackness." Since Desdemona has asked Iago to "praise" her, the "fitness"
of black and white in his view has covertly nasty application; but
this is for the audience, not for Desdemona, playing as she is a casual
game of wit.
136. *folly* (1) foolishness and (2) wantonness, unchastity.
137. *old fond* stale and silly. *paradoxes* views contrary to
received opinion.
138. *foul* ugly.
140. *thereunto* besides.
141. *pranks* malicious or mischievous tricks, infidelities.

DESDEMONA

O heavy ignorance! that praises the worst best. But what
praise couldst thou bestow on a deserving woman indeed—
one that in the authority of her merit did justly put on the
145   vouch of very malice itself?

IAGO

She that was ever fair, and never proud;
Had tongue at will, and yet was never loud;
Never lacked gold, and yet went never gay;
Fled from her wish, and yet said "Now I may";
150   She that, being angered, her revenge being nigh,
Bade her wrong stay, and her displeasure fly;
She that in wisdom never was so frail
To change the cod's head for the salmon's tail;
She that could think, and ne'er disclose her mind;
155   See suitors following, and not look behind:
She was a wight (if ever such wight were)—

DESDEMONA

To do what?

IAGO

To suckle fools and chronicle small beer.

---

142.   **ignorance! that praises** Q (ignorance,).   F has 'ignorance: thou
       praisest'.
144.   **merit** F.   Q has 'merrits'.
155.   F.   Not in Q.
156.   **such wight** Q.   F has 'such wightes'.

142.   *heavy*   stupid.
143.   *deserving woman indeed*   really praiseworthy woman.
144-5.   *put on the vouch*   compel the approval.
153.   *To . . . tail*   I think this means "to exchange the best part
of a cheap fish for the worst part of an expensive one"—with a clear
undertone of bawdry in *cod's head* and *tail*. However, *change* can
mean "accept in exchange for" as well as "exchange," and such evidence as we have of the way Elizabethans would have comparatively
valued cod's heads and salmon tails is indecisive. Thus, the line could
possibly mean "to exchange a delicacy for coarser fare" (Steevens).
158.   *chronicle small beer*   keep petty household accounts.

DESDEMONA

O most lame and impotent conclusion! Do not learn of him,
160 Emilia, though he be thy husband. —How say you, Cassio? Is
he not a most profane and liberal counsellor?

CASSIO

He speaks home, madam. You may relish him more in the
soldier than in the scholar.

IAGO

[*Aside*] He takes her by the palm. [*Aloud*] Ay, well said,
165 [*Aside*] whisper! With as little a web as this will I ensnare as
great a fly as Cassio. Ay, smile upon her, do! I will gyve thee
in thine own courtship. [*Aloud*] You say true; 'tis so indeed!
[*Aside*] If such tricks as these strip you out of your lieuten-
antry, it had been better you had not kissed your three fingers
170 so oft—which now again you are most apt to play the sir in.
Very good! well kissed! an excellent curtsy! [*Aloud*] 'Tis so

---

159–63. F. As verse in Q.
164. **S.D.** *Aside* Rowe. **S.D.** *Aloud* This edition.
165. **With as . . . this will I** F (this,). Q has 'As . . . this will'.
166. **fly** F. Q has 'Flee'. **gyve** F2. F has 'giue'; Q has 'catch'.
166–7. **thee in thine** F. Q has 'you in your'.
167. **courtship** F. Q has 'courtesies'.
169. **kissed** F. Q has 'rist'.
171. **Very** F. Not in Q. **an** Q. F has 'and'. **curtsy** F. Q has
'courtesie'.

161. *profane and liberal* indelicately outspoken and licentious.

162. *He speaks home* his words are home thrusts, i.e. find their
mark and go deep: "He speaks bluntly."   *in the* in the character of.

163. *scholar* man of letters.

164. *well said* double in sense: (1) "that's right!" and, ironically, (2) "well done!"

166. *gyve* manacle.

167. *courtship* courtly manners. *You . . . indeed!* to Cassio's
easily supposed compliment.

169. *kissed your three fingers* a courtly gesture.

170. *now again* The effect depends on Iago's predicting Cassio's
behavior so the latter appears almost his marionette.   *sir* the fine
gentleman.

171. *curtsy* courtesy—recalling "this bold show of courtesy,"
line 100.

indeed! [*Aside*] Yet again your fingers to your lips? Would they were clyster pipes for your sake!

Trumpets within.

[*Aloud*] The Moor! I know his trumpet.

CASSIO

'Tis truly so.

DESDEMONA

175   Let's meet him and receive him.

Enter OTHELLO *and Attendants.*

CASSIO

Lo, where he comes.

OTHELLO

O my fair warrior!

DESDEMONA

My dear Othello!

OTHELLO

It gives me wonder great as my content
To see you here before me. O my soul's joy!
If after every tempest come such calms,
180   May the winds blow till they have wakened death;

---

172. **to** F.   Q has 'at'.
173. **clyster pipes** Q (Clisterpipes).   F has 'Cluster-pipes'.
     S.D. Q (after 'trumpet' line 174).   Not in F.
175. **S.D.** F places after 'comes' line 175, Q after 'trumpet' line 174.
179. **calms** F.   Q has 'calmenesse'.

173. *clyster pipes*   syringes for enemas and douches.
174. *his trumpet*   Given Iago's tone in this context, this may very well involve a sly wordplay shared with the audience (based on elision: "his strumpet"; cf. *Troilus and Cressida* IV.v.64). In the obvious sense: Iago yet competes with Cassio, for distinguished people were announced by recognizably individualized trumpet calls, and he is the one who knows the Moor's *trumpet*.
176. *O my fair warrior*   recalling her wish "that heaven had made her such a man" (I.iii.162) and her assertion that her "heart's subdued/ Even to the very quality of my lord" (lines 246–7).
177. *content*   happiness.

And let the laboring bark climb hills of seas
Olympus-high and duck again as low
As hell's from heaven. If it were now to die,
'Twere now to be most happy; for I fear

185   My soul hath her content so absolute
That not another comfort like to this
Succeeds in unknown fate.

DESDEMONA

The heavens forbid
But that our loves and comforts should increase
Even as our days do grow.

OTHELLO

Amen to that, sweet powers!

190   I cannot speak enough of this content:
It stops me here; it is too much of joy.
And this, and this, the greatest discords be   *They kiss.*
That e're our hearts shall make!

---

189.   **that, sweet powers** Q2.   F has 'that (sweet Powers)'; Q1 has
       'that sweet power'.
192.   **discords** F.   Q has 'discord'. **S.D.** Q.   Not in F.

181–3. The entire passage, and these lines particularly, are in-
debted to Psalm 107: 23–9 (Prayer Book version): "They that go
down to the sea in ships: and occupy their business in great waters./
These men see the works of the Lord: and his wonders in the deep./
For at his word the stormy wind ariseth: which lifteth up the waves
thereof./ They are carried up to the heaven, and down again to the
deep: their soul melteth away because of the trouble./ They reel to
and fro, and stagger like a drunken man: and are at their wits' end./
So when they cry unto the Lord in their trouble: he delivereth them
out of their distress./ For he maketh the storm to cease: so that the
waves thereof are still."

192. *discords*   The application of this term to the kisses involves a
deeper irony than the obvious one Othello smilingly intends. Technically, a *discord* is "A combination of two or more notes not in harmony with each other; a chord which by itself is unpleasing or un-
satisfactory to the ear, and requires to be 'resolved' or followed by
some other chord" (*Shakespeare's England*).

IAGO

               [*Aside*] O, you are well tuned now!
But I'll set down the pegs that make this music,
195   As honest as I am.

OTHELLO

         Come, let us to the castle.
News, friends! our wars are done; the Turks are drowned.
How does my old acquaintance of this isle? —
Honey, you shall be well desired in Cyprus;
I have found great love amongst them. O my sweet,
200   I prattle out of fashion, and I dote
In mine own comforts. —I prithee, good Iago,
Go to the bay and disembark my coffers.
Bring thou the master to the citadel;
He is a good one, and his worthiness
205   Does challenge much respect. —Come, Desdemona:
Once more well met in Cyprus.

              Exit OTHELLO [*with all but* IAGO *and* RODERIGO].

---

193. **S.D.** Rowe.
193–5. **O . . . am** Q. As prose in F.
197. **does my** F. Q has 'doe our'. **this** F. Q has 'the'.
201. **own** F. Q has 'one'.
206. **S.D.** F has 'Exit Othello and Desdemona.' Q has 'Exit.'

194. *set down the pegs* i.e. loosen them, in order to put the string instrument out of tune. The well-tuned string instrument was a common symbol for concord in the universe, in society, and in marriage. It is pertinent that the Devil, and those "in his image," were regarded as inciters of "discord," and particularly in marriage.

198. *well desired* warmly received, welcomed.

199. *I . . . them* Othello means, "they have always been very kind to me"; those in the audience who knew Cyprus' broadcast reputation as the "blessedly" fertile island, sacred to Venus and dedicated to lechery and pleasure, the place where prostitution supposedly was invented, would hear another meaning. This inevitably casts shadows on line 198 as well.

200. *out of fashion* unbecomingly, unlike me, and irrelevantly: when I ought to be thinking of other things.

203. *master* the ship's captain.

205. *challenge* deservedly claim.

IAGO

[*To an Attendant going out*] Do thou meet me presently at
the harbor. [*To* RODERIGO] Come hither. If thou be'st valiant
(as they say base men being in love have then a nobility in
210 their natures more than is native to them), list me. The lieutenant tonight watches on the court of guard. First, I must tell
thee this: Desdemona is directly in love with him.

RODERIGO

With him! why, 'tis not possible.

IAGO

Lay thy fingers thus, and let thy soul be instructed. Mark me
215 with what violence she first loved the Moor but for bragging
and telling her fantastical lies. And will she love him still for
prating? —let not thy discreet heart think it. Her eye must
be fed; and what delight shall she have to look on the devil?
When the blood is made dull with the act of sport, there

---

207. **S.D.** Delius conj.
208. **hither** Q.   F has 'thither'.
211. **must** F.   Q has 'will'.
212. **thee this: Desdemona** F.   Q has 'thee, this Desdemona'.
216. **And will she** Q.   F has 'To'.
217. **thy . . . it.** F.   Q has 'the . . . so.'

207. *presently*   immediately.
211. *court of guard*   headquarters of the guard.
214. *thus*   i.e. on your lips: be silent.
215. *but for*   for no more than.
216. *still*   forever.
219. *act of sport*   coitus.

220 should be, again to inflame it and give satiety a fresh appetite,
     loveliness in favor, sympathy in years, manners, and beauties;
     all which the Moor is defective in. Now, for want of these
     required conveniences, her delicate tenderness will find itself
     abused, begin to heave the gorge, disrelish and abhor the
225 Moor. Very nature will instruct her in it and compel her to
     some second choice. Now, sir, this granted—as it is a most
     pregnant and unforced position—who stands so eminent in
     the degree of this fortune as Cassio does? —a knave very
     voluble; no further conscionable than in putting on the mere

---

220. **again . . . give** Q. F has 'a game . . . to giue'.
      satiety F. Q has 'saciety'.
220–1. **appetite, loveliness** Theobald. F has 'appetite. Louelinesse'; Q
      has 'appetite. Loue lines'.
225. **in** F. Q has 'to'.
227. **eminent** F. Q has 'eminently'.

220–1. *again . . . favor* an interesting crux which I think, on
balance, requires the traditional conflation and emendation here used.
Ridley brilliantly proposes reading "a game to inflame it . . .
appetite. Love lives in favor etc." This retains F's "game" (i.e. sexual
sport, which sounds like Iago; cf. II.iii.18); explains the period and
capital after *appetite;* and corrects Q's "Loue lines" in a justifiable
way different from F's. But I think the odds are against it. "Game"
and "gain" are easily misread for one another; F makes the same
mistake, the other way round, at V.i.14. The indefinite article before
"game" is quite awkward; and Iago does not go on to talk of "a
game" at all. The period and capital "L" are most likely shared errors
stemming from a transcriber's blunder preserved in Q. All the blatant
errors shared by Q and F (like "hope's" at II.i.50) occur in Act II,
which is also the only Act without any longer F-only passages. This
means the theory that the copy for F was an exemplar of Q corrected
by reference to the authoritative manuscript has most chance of being
true for Act II, but perhaps for that Act only.
  221. *favor* features.
  223. *conveniences* advantages apt for the purpose.
  224. *abused* deceived, cheated. *heave the gorge* become nau-
seated.
  227. *pregnant* obvious. *position* hypothesis.
  227–8. *so . . . of* so high on the ladder of advancement to.
  229. *conscionable* This word, not used elsewhere by Shakespeare,
appears to mean "concerned with or restrained by scruples of
conscience."

230 form of civil and humane seeming for the better compassing
of his salt and most hidden loose affection? Why, none! why,
none!—a slipper and subtle knave, a finder-out of occasions;
that has an eye can stamp and counterfeit advantages, though
true advantage never present itself; a devilish knave! Besides,

235 the knave is handsome, young, and hath all those requisites
in him that folly and green minds look after. A pestilent
complete knave! and the woman hath found him already.

RODERIGO

I cannot believe that in her; she's full of most blessed condition.

IAGO

240 Blessed fig's-end! The wine she drinks is made of grapes. If
she had been blessed, she would never have loved the Moor.
Blessed pudding! Didst thou not see her paddle with the palm
of his hand? Didst not mark that?

---

230. **humane seeming** F.   Q has 'hand-seeming'.
    compassing Q.   F has 'compasse'.
231. **most hidden loose affection** F.   Q has 'hidden affections'.
231–2. **Why . . . none** F.   Not in Q.
232. **slipper and subtle** F.   Q has 'subtle slippery'.
    finder-out of occasions Q.   F has 'finder of occasion'.
233. **has** Q.   F has 'he's'.
233–4. **advantages, though true advantage . . . itself** F.   Q has 'the
    true aduantages . . . themselues'.
234. **a devilish knave** F.   Not in Q.
235. **hath** F.   Q has 'has'.
242. **Blessed pudding** F. (Bless'd).   Not in Q.
243. **Didst . . . that?** F.   Not in Q.

230. *humane*   polite.
231. *salt*   lecherous.
232. *slipper*   slippery, tricky.   *occasions*   opportunities.
233. *stamp and counterfeit advantages*   mint and contrive advantageous opportunities.
236. *green*   unripe, inexperienced.   *pestilent*   plaguy.
237. *found him*   got his message.
238–9. *condition*   character.
240. *fig's-end*   nonsense!   my foot!   *The . . . grapes* i.e.
"There's no 'condition of a saint' (*Merchant of Venice* I.ii.116) in
her—she's only a human being with appetites like the rest of us in
this non-spiritual nature." I think the force of the expression comes
from scornful skepticism about the Eucharist.
242. *pudding*   sausage.

RODERIGO

Yes, that I did; but that was but courtesy.

IAGO

245 Lechery, by this hand! an index and obscure prologue to the history of lust and foul thoughts. They met so near with their lips that their breaths embraced together. Villainous thoughts, Roderigo! When these mutualities so marshal the way, hard at hand comes the master and main exercise, th'incorporate

250 conclusion. Pish! But sir, be you ruled by me; I have brought you from Venice. Watch you tonight; for the command, I'll lay't upon you. Cassio knows you not; I'll not be far from you. Do you find some occasion to anger Cassio, either by speaking too loud, or tainting his discipline, or from what other

255 course you please which the time shall more favorably minister.

RODERIGO

Well.

---

244. **that I did** F. Not in Q.
245. **obscure** F. Not in Q.
247–8. **Villainous . . . Roderigo** F. Not in Q.
248. **mutualities** Q. F has 'mutabilities'.
249. **master and** F. Not in Q.
     th'incorporate F. Q has 'the incorporate'.
250. **Pish** F. Not in Q.
251. **the** F. Q has 'your'.
255. **course** F. Q has 'cause'.

245. *by this hand* a common light oath. *index* table of contents.

248. *mutualities* intimacies. *marshal* lead.

248–9. *hard at hand* almost immediately.

249–50. *incorporate conclusion* i.e. the conclusion in which bodies are united into one.

254. *tainting* casting a slur on.

256. *minister* afford.

IAGO

Sir, he's rash and very sudden in choler, and haply with his
truncheon may strike at you. Provoke him that he may; for
260 even out of that will I cause these of Cyprus to mutiny, whose
qualification shall come into no true taste again but by the dis-
planting of Cassio. So shall you have a shorter journey to your
desires by the means I shall then have to prefer them, and the
impediment most profitably removed without the which there
265 were no expectation of our prosperity.

RODERIGO

I will do this, if you can bring it to any opportunity.

IAGO

I warrant thee. Meet me by and by at the citadel. I must fetch
his necessaries ashore. Farewell.

RODERIGO

Adieu.   *Exit.*

---

258. **he's** F. Q has 'he is'.
258–9. **with his truncheon** Q. Not in F.
261. **taste again** F. Q has 'trust again't'.
264. **the** F. Not in Q.
266. **you** F. Q has 'I'.

258. *sudden in choler* "precipitately violent" (Johnson) in
anger. *haply* perhaps.
258–9. *with his truncheon* baton of office. F may (as Ridley
suggests) omit the phrase because someone saw a discrepancy with
Iago's later account, before witnesses, of Cassio following Roderigo
"with determined sword/ To execute upon him" (iii. 206–7). But
Cassio does "beat" Roderigo and at first only threatens to knock
the interfering Montano "o'er the mazzard" (lines 132–4). For Iago to
say "with the flat of his sword" here could hardly help to make the
prospects more attractive to Roderigo. I think F's omission very
suspect.
261. *qualification* appeasement, pacification. *come . . . again*
shall not resume its proper flavor—i.e. won't be achieved. This curi-
ous expression possibly is generated by picking up *qualification*
in the sense "dilution."
263. *prefer* advance, further.
267. *I warrant thee* I'll guarantee you the opportunity. *by and
by* presently.
268. *his* Othello's.

IAGO

270   That Cassio loves her, I do well believe it.

      That she loves him, 'tis apt and of great credit.

      The Moor, howbe't that I endure him not,

      Is of a constant, loving, noble nature;

      And I dare think he'll prove to Desdemona

275   A most dear husband. Now I do love her too,

      Not out of absolute lust, though peradventure

      I stand accountant for as great a sin,

      But partly led to diet my revenge,

      For that I do suspect the lusty Moor

280   Hath leaped into my seat; the thought whereof

      Doth like a poisonous mineral gnaw my inwards;

      And nothing can nor shall content my soul

      Till I am evened with him, wife for wife;

      Or failing so, yet that I put the Moor

285   At least into a jealousy so strong

      That judgment cannot cure. Which thing to do,

      If this poor trash of Venice, whom I trash

---

270. **believe it** Q. F has 'beleeu't'.
272. **howbe't** Q. F has 'how beit'.
273. **loving, noble** F. Q has 'noble, louing'.
277. **accountant** Q. F has 'accomptant'.
278. **led** F. Q has 'lead'.
279. **lusty** F. Q has 'lustfull'.
282. **nor** Q. F has 'or'.
283. **evened** F. Q has 'euen'. **for wife** Q. F has 'for wift'.
287. **I trash** Steevens. Q has 'I crush'; F has 'I trace'.

271. *apt . . . credit*   likely and very credible.
272. *howbe't that*   although.
277. *accountant*   accountable.
278. *led to diet*   led on by the desire to feed, to glut.
279. *For that*   because.

287–8. *trash . . . hunting* Trash, the usual emendation of this corrupt passage (for the "crush" and "trace" of Q and F seem hopeless) means "to hang weights on a hound's collar to slow him so he won't outrun the pack." This makes *for his quick hunting* mean "because of (and, therefore, to prevent) his quick hunting after his quarry, Desdemona." What makes one skeptical is the abrupt switch from restraining Roderigo to the need to incite him. I adopt this emendation because others seem weaker and I do not have anything else to propose.

For his quick hunting, stand the putting on,
I'll have our Michael Cassio on the hip,
290   Abuse him to the Moor in the rank garb—
For I fear Cassio with my nightcap too—
Make the Moor thank me, love me, and reward me
For making him egregiously an ass
And practicing upon his peace and quiet
295   Even to madness. 'Tis here, but yet confused:
Knavery's plain face is never seen till used.   *Exit.*

[*Scene ii.*] *Enter* OTHELLO's *Herald with a proclamation.*

HERALD

It is Othello's pleasure, our noble and valiant general, that,
upon certain tidings now arrived importing the mere perdition
of the Turkish fleet, every man put himself into triumph: some

---

290.   **rank** Q.   F has 'right'.
291.   **nightcap** Q.   F has 'Night-Cape'. **too** F.   Q has 'to'.
II. ii   **S.D. OTHELLO**'s *Herald with* F.   Q has *'a Gentleman reading'.*
  1.   **S.P.** F.   Not in Q.
  3.   **every** F.   Q has 'that every'.

288.   *putting on*   inciting.
289.   *on the hip*   in my power—a term from wrestling.
290.   *Abuse*   slander.   *rank garb*   gross manner—with a sexual
undertone. Shakespeare does not use "garb" of dress, but of fashion
or manner. The Folio's "right" (= "in a manner suited to the purpose") seems (after lines 284–6) much too suspiciously weak to be a
second thought. It does not seem a likely error, but there are other
odd readings hereabout in F ("wift," "Iealouzie," "trace," "Night-
Cape").
294.   *practicing upon*   plotting against.
II. ii   The Herald reads his proclamation directly to the audience,
thereby conveniently announcing both the time and the circumstances
of the ensuing action. (We should note that F gives no scene indication at the start of II. iii.) This conventional effect frequently is
spoiled by "realistic" staging and editorial directions which give him
an unwarranted audience on-stage.
  2.   *upon*   in consequence of.   *importing*   the import of which is.
mere perdition   utter destruction.
  3.   *triumph*   joyous celebration, revelry.

to dance, some to make bonfires, each man to what sport and
5　revels his addiction leads him; for, besides these beneficial
news, it is the celebration of his nuptial. So much was his
pleasure should be proclaimed. All offices are open, and there
is full liberty of feasting from this present hour of five till the
bell have told eleven. Heaven bless the isle of Cyprus and our
10　noble general Othello!　　　　　　　　　　　　　　　　*Exit.*

[*Scene iii.*] *Enter* OTHELLO, DESDEMONA, CASSIO, *and
Attendants.*

OTHELLO

Good Michael, look you to the guard tonight.
Let's teach ourselves that honorable stop,
Not to outsport discretion.

CASSIO

Iago hath direction what to do;
5　But notwithstanding, with my personal eye
Will I look to't.

OTHELLO

　　　　Iago is most honest.
Michael, good night; tomorrow with your earliest

4.　**to make** F.　Q has 'make'.
5.　**addiction** Q2.　F has 'addition'.　Q has 'minde'.
6.　**nuptial** F.　Q has 'Nuptialls'.
8.　**of feasting** F.　Not in Q.
9.　**have** F.　Q has 'hath'.　**Heaven** Q.　Not in F.
10.　S.D. F.　Not in Q.
II. iii　**S.D.** *and Attendants.* F.　Not in Q.
2.　**that** F.　Q has 'the'.
4.　**direction** F.　Q has 'directed'.
6.　**to't** F.　Q has 'to it'.

5. *addiction*　inclination. F's "addition" (literally = "title") could
be taken to mean, in context, "to such pastime as is suitable for
his rank and station." But Q's reading, "minde," suggests that Q2's
fancier word for the same idea is the correct emendation.

7. *offices*　kitchens, butteries, storerooms, etc.　*open* i.e. to
everyone for free food and drink.

9. *told*　numbered.

II. iii　The locale, implicit from the first line, is specified as the
headquarters of the watch at line 195. The time is marked at line 13
as four hours after the proclamation in II. ii.

Let me have speech with you. [*To* DESDEMONA] Come, my dear
   love,

The purchase made, the fruits are to ensue:

10 That profit's yet to come 'tween me and you. —

Good night. *Exit* OTHELLO *and* DESDEMONA [*with Attendants*].

Enter IAGO.

CASSIO

Welcome, Iago. We must to the watch.

IAGO

Not this hour, lieutenant; 'tis not yet ten o'clock. Our general
cast us thus early for the love of his Desdemona; who let us

15 not therefore blame. He hath not yet made wanton the night
with her, and she is sport for Jove.

---

10. **That profit's** F.   Q has 'The profit'. **'tween** F.   Q has 'twixt'.
11. **S.D.** Q.   F has *'Exit.'*
13. **o'clock** Q (aclock).   F has 'o'th'clocke'.

12. *watch* viz. the "guard" (line 1) kept for military purposes.
But this obviously key word in the scene will importantly reappear
in action, wordplay, and ironies invoking other meanings besides
that of the attention of a group of soldiers set for sentinel duty:
staying awake (line 114) or keeping from sleep for "business" (line
97), indulging in sexual pleasure (line 15) or revelling and carousing
("watch tonight, pray tomorrow," *Henry IV, Part I* II. iv. 237); waiting
expectantly or observantly (line 46); being vigilant. This last sense
permits the crucial symbolic meanings developed from the central
conception of the Christian's "watch" against temptation by his ever-
wakeful and vigilant spiritual enemies. For basic texts underlying
the homiletic commonplaces Shakespeare takes for granted here, see,
e.g., Matthew 26: 40–1 ("Watch, and pray, that ye enter not into
tentation"), 1 Thessalonians 5: 3–8 ("Ye are the children of light
. . . we are not of the night, neither of darknesse./ Therefore let
vs not sleepe as do other, but let vs watch and be sober." [5–6]),
and Romans 13: 11–14 (". . . *it is* nowe time that we should arise
from sleepe: . . ./ The night is past, and the day is at hand, let vs
therefore cast away the workes of darkenesse . . ./ So that we
walke honestly, as in the day: not in gluttonie and drunkennesse,
neither in chambering and wantonesse, nor in strife and enuying."
[11–13]).

13. *not this hour* not for an hour yet.

14. *cast* dismissed.

CASSIO

She's a most exquisite lady.

IAGO

And, I'll warrant her, full of game.

CASSIO

Indeed, she's a most fresh and delicate creature.

IAGO

20 What an eye she has! methinks it sounds a parley to provocation.

CASSIO

An inviting eye; and yet methinks right modest.

IAGO

And when she speaks, is it not an alarum to love?

CASSIO

She is indeed perfection.

IAGO

25 Well, happiness to their sheets! Come, lieutenant, I have a stoup of wine, and here without are a brace of Cyprus gallants that would fain have a measure to the health of black Othello.

CASSIO

Not tonight, good Iago. I have very poor and unhappy brains for drinking. I could well wish courtesy would invent some
30 other custom of entertainment.

---

17. **She's** F. Q has 'She is'.
19. **she's** F. Q has 'she is'.
20–1. Pope. QF divide as verse.
20. **to** F. Q has 'of'.
23. Q. Divided as verse in F. **is it not** F. Q has 'tis'.
24. **She** F. Q has 'It'.
27. **of** F. Q has 'of the'.

18. *game*   amorous sport.
19. *fresh*   with the bloom of youth.
20. *parley*   a military term: a conference with a view to an expected agreement.
23. *alarum*   another military metaphor: summons to the encounter—literally, a call to arms.
26. *stoup*   two quart tankard.

IAGO

O, they are our friends. But one cup! I'll drink for you.

CASSIO

I have drunk but one cup tonight, and that was craftily qualified too; and behold what innovation it makes here. I am unfortunate in the infirmity and dare not task my weakness with
35   any more.

IAGO

What, man! 'Tis a night of revels; the gallants desire it.

CASSIO

Where are they?

IAGO

Here at the door; I pray you call them in.

CASSIO

I'll do't, but it dislikes me.   *Exit.*

IAGO

40   If I can fasten but one cup upon him
With that which he hath drunk tonight already,
He'll be as full of quarrel and offense
As my young mistress' dog. Now my sick fool Roderigo,
Whom love hath turned almost the wrong side out,

---

32.   **have** F.   Q has 'ha'.
33.   **too** F.   Q has 'to'.
33–4.   **unfortunate** Q.   F has 'infortunate'.
44.   **hath** F.   Q has 'has'. **out** F.   Q has 'outward'.

31. *I'll drink for you*   Custom obliged a drinker to drain his cup
whenever anyone had drunk to him. Another could, however, chari-
tably relieve him of the obligation by drinking in his place ("to drink
alms-drink").

32–3. *craftily qualified*   diluted on the sly. Diluting wine with
water was the identifying symbolic action associated, through depiction, with the personifications of "Measure" and "Temperance."

33. *innovation*   revolution.   *here*   pointing to his head.

39. *dislikes*   displeases.

42. *offense*   readiness to take offense.

43. *As . . . dog*   The *my* is generalizing ("any young lady's
dog") and gives the likeness a proverbial air; but the proverb is unknown and the phrase has not really been satisfactorily explained.

45 To Desdemona hath tonight carroused
Potations pottle-deep; and he's to watch.
Three else of Cyprus, noble swelling spirits
That hold their honors in a wary distance—
The very elements of this warlike isle—
50 Have I tonight flustered with flowing cups;
And they watch too. Now, 'mongst this flock of drunkards
Am I to put our Cassio in some action
That may offend the isle.

      [Re-enter] CASSIO, *[with]* MONTANO *and Gentlemen;*
           [Servants with wine following].
                But here they come.
If consequence do but approve my dream,
55 My boat sails freely, both with wind and stream.

CASSIO

'Fore God, they have given me a rouse already.

MONTANO

Good faith, a little one; not past a pint, as I am a soldier.

---

47. **else** F. Q has 'lads'.
48. **honors** F. Q has 'honour'.
51. **they** F. Q has 'the'.
52. **Am I** F. Q has 'I am'. **to put** Q. F has 'put to'.
53. **S.D.** F has '*Enter Cassio, Montano, and Gentlemen.*' after 'come.'
    Q has '*Enter* Montanio, Cassio, *and others.*' after 'isle.'
56. **God** Q. F has 'heauen'.
57–8. F. As verse in Q.

46. *pottle-deep* bottoms up—literally, to the bottom of the two-quart tankard.
47. *swelling spirits* arrogant men of spirit.
48. *hold . . . distance* i.e. hold them out of the reach of any slur, and thus: who are very sensitive about their personal honor.
49. *very elements* the essential constituents, just what it's made of.
52. *Am I to put* I must put.
54. *If . . . dream* If succeeding events confirm my expectations.
55. *stream* sea current.
56. *rouse* bumper, draught.

IAGO

Some wine, ho!   [*Servants pour.*]

[*Sings*]   And let me the canakin clink, clink;
60   And let me the canakin clink:
                    A soldier's a man;
                    O, man's life's but a span—
                  Why then, let a soldier drink!

Some wine, boys!   [*Servants pour.*]

CASSIO

65   'Fore God, an excellent song!

IAGO

I learned it in England, where indeed they are most potent in
potting. Your Dane, your German, and your swag-bellied
Hollander—Drink, ho!—are nothing to your English.

CASSIO

Is your Englishman so exquisite in his drinking?

IAGO

70   Why, he drinks you with facility your Dane dead drunk; he
sweats not to overthrow your Almain; he gives your
Hollander a vomit ere the next pottle can be filled.

CASSIO

To the health of our general!

---

60. **clink** F.   Q has 'clinke, clinke'.
62. **O, man's** F.   Q has 'a'.
65. **God** Q.   F has 'Heauen'.
69. **Englishman** Q.   F has 'Englishmen'. **exquisite** F.   Q has 'expert'.

59. *let me   Me* is the ethical dative; we should say "let's have."
canakin   little can.

62. *span*   Cf. Psalm 39: 6 (Prayer Book version): "thou hast made
my days as it were a span long."

67. *Your*   a colloquial "generalizing" usage, like our "these
Danes."   *swag-bellied*   pendulous-paunched.

71. *Almain*   German.

72. *a vomit*   In Renaissance emblematic depiction attacking riot-
ous excess, intemperance, and gluttony, the figure of the vomiting
man was a familiar symbolic fixture.

MONTANO

I am for it, lieutenant, and I'll do you justice.   [*They drink.*]

IAGO

75   O sweet England!

[*Sings*]   King Stephen was and-a worthy peer;
                    His breeches cost him but a crown.
                  He held 'em sixpence all too dear;
                    With that he called the tailor lown.
80   He was a wight of high renown,
                    And thou art but of low degree.
                  'Tis pride that pulls the country down;
                    Then take thine o'd cloak about thee.

Some wine, ho!   [*Servants pour.*]

CASSIO

85   'Fore God, this is a more exquisite song than the other.

IAGO

Will you hear't again?

---

74. **I'll** F (Ile).   Q has 'I will'.
76. **and-a** F.   Q has 'a'.
78. **'em** Q.   F has 'them'. **too** Q.   F has 'to'.
83. **Then** Q.   F has '*And*'. **thine o'd** Q (*owd*).   F has '*thy awl'd*'.
85. **'Fore God** Q.   F has 'Why'.

74. *I'll do you justice*   drink as deep a draught to that health as
you do: a point of manners in drinking.

76–83. A stanza of an old popular song entitled "Bell my Wife,"
doubtless familiar to all in the original audience.

76. *and*   introduced merely to carry a note. It has no meaning.

79. *lown*   rascal.

82. *'Tis . . . down*   The theme: it's pride (in the song—extrav-
agance in dress) that causes hard times.

83. *o'd*   old. The reading modernizes Q's "*owd*"—a dialectical
form which correctly implies a northern English origin for the song,
whereas F's "awl'd" and Q2's "auld" imply a Scottish one.

CASSIO

No, for I hold him to be unworthy of his place that does those things. Well, God's above all; and there be souls must be saved, and there be souls must not be saved.

IAGO

90 It's true, good lieutenant.

CASSIO

For mine own part—no offence to the general, nor any man of quality—I hope to be saved.

IAGO

And so do I too, lieutenant.

CASSIO

Ay, but by your leave, not before me. The lieutenant is to be
95 saved before the ancient. Let's ha' no more of this; let's to our affairs. —God forgive us our sins!—Gentlemen, let's look to our business. Do not think, gentlemen, I am drunk. This is my ancient; this is my right hand; and this is my left hand. I am not drunk now: I can stand well enough, and I speak well
100 enough.

ALL

Excellent well!

---

87. **to be** F.   Not in Q.
88. **God's** Q.   F has 'heau'ns'. **must** F.   Q has 'that must'.
89. **and . . . not be saved** F.   Not in Q.
90. **It's** F.   Q has 'It is'.
93. **too** F.   Not in Q.
95. **ha'** Q.   F has 'haue'.
96. **God** Q.   Not in F.
98. **left hand** Q.   F has 'left'.
99. **I speak** F.   Q has 'speake'.

87–8. *No . . . things* spoken with the intoxicated man's maudlin solemnity and vagueness.

88–9. *there . . . saved* the doctrine of divine preordination. Cassio's tipsy concern about what is or is not worthy "of his place" has led him to think of the place each man will be judged worthy of. The two kinds of "place" become thoroughly blurred by lines 94–5. The verb *be* is an old plural.

92. *I hope to be saved* recalling Romans 8: 24 "For we are saved by hope."

CASSIO

Why, very well then; you must not think then that I am
drunk.   *Exit.*

MONTANO

To th' platform, masters. Come, let's set the watch.

IAGO

105   [*Apart to* MONTANO] You see this fellow that is gone before:
He is a soldier fit to stand by Caesar
And give direction; and do but see his vice.
'Tis to his virtue a just equinox,
The one as long as th'other. 'Tis pity of him.

110   I fear the trust Othello puts him in,
On some odd time of his infirmity,
Will shake this island.

MONTANO

But is he often thus?

---

102.   **Why** F.   Not in Q. **then that** F.   Q has 'that'.
104.   **th' platform** F.   Q has 'the plotforme'.
         masters. Come Q.   F has '(Masters) come,'.
106.   **He is** Q.   F has 'He's'.
110.   **puts** F.   Q has 'put'.

104. *platform*   a level gun-platform where the guard is to be
mustered.   *set the watch*   mount the guard.

106–7. *stand . . . direction*   This could mean that "he" could
give orders as Caesar's right-hand man or that he is worthy enough
to give orders to Caesar.

108. *a just equinox*   an exact equivalent, as day and night are
equal at the equinox.

110. *trust . . . in*   The construction makes the pronoun *him*
ambiguous in reference, as I think it was meant to be. "To put in
trust" means "to entrust with important business," thus referring to
Cassio. But the phrase can also be construed to mean "the state of
confidence Othello puts himself in."

111. *On . . . infirmity*   some time or other when he's overcome
by his weakness.

IAGO

'Tis evermore the prologue to his sleep:
He'll watch the horologe a double set
115   If drink rock not his cradle.

MONTANO
It were well
The general were put in mind of it.
Perhaps he sees it not, or his good nature
Prizes the virtue that appears in Cassio
And looks not on his evils. Is not this true?
Enter RODERIGO.
120   [*Aside to* RODERIGO] How now, Roderigo.
I pray you after the lieutenant, go!   *Exit* RODERIGO.

MONTANO

And 'tis great pity that the noble Moor
Should hazard such a place as his own second
With one of an ingraft infirmity.
125   It were an honest action to say
So to the Moor.

IAGO

Not I, for this fair island!
I do love Cassio well, and would do much

---

113.   **the** Q.   F has 'his'.
115.   **It were** F.   Q has 'Twere'.
118.   **Prizes the virtue** F.   Q has 'Praises the vertues'.
119.   **looks** F.   Q has 'looke'. **S.D.** F.   Q places after line 120.
120.   **S.D.** Capell.
125–6. Malone.   F divides at 'so'; lines 125–6ª as one line in Q.
126.   **Not** F.   Q has 'Nor'.

114. *watch . . . set*   stay up twice around the clock, i.e. all night as well as all day.
115. *rock not his cradle*   doesn't put him to sleep.
123. *hazard . . . second*   risk (take a chance on) such a position as his own next in command. The action of the scene, however, brings *his own second* into play in other senses—"his supporter," "the one who acts as his own deputy."
124. *ingraft*   ingrained.

To cure him of this evil.   (*Within*) Help! help!
                    But hark! what noise?

[*Re-*]*enter* CASSIO, *driving in* RODERIGO.

CASSIO

'Zounds, you rogue! you rascal!

MONTANO

130   What's the matter, lieutenant?

CASSIO

                              A knave teach me my duty!
I'll beat the knave into a twiggen bottle.

RODERIGO

Beat me?

CASSIO

    Dost thou prate, rogue?   [*Strikes* RODERIGO.]

MONTANO

                        Nay, good lieutenant!
Pray sir, hold your hand.   [*Tries to stay* CASSIO.]

CASSIO

                  Let me go, sir,
Or I'll knock you o'er the mazzard.

MONTANO

                        Come, come, you're drunk!

CASSIO

135   Drunk!   *They fight.*

---

128. (*Within*) **Help! help!** Q (*Helpe helpe, within*) after 'much' line
        127. Not in F. **S.D.** *driving in* Q. F has '*pursuing*'.
129. **'Zounds** Q. Not in F.
130–1. As verse. F raggedly divides (at 'the'). Q treats as prose.
131. **I'll** F. Q has 'but I'le'. **twiggen** F. Q has 'wicker'.
132. **S.D.** Capell (*Beats Rod.*). **Nay** F. Not in Q.
132–4. F. As prose in Q.
133. **Pray** Q. F has 'I pray you'.
134. **you're** F. Q has 'you are'.
135. **S.D.** Q. Not in F.

131. *into a twiggen bottle* so he'll be glad to hide in a large wine
bottle covered with wicker-work (like a Chianti flask).
134. *mazzard* old slang for "head."

IAGO

[*Aside to* RODERIGO] Away I say! go out and cry a mutiny. —

[*Exit* RODERIGO.]

Nay, good lieutenant. God's will, gentlemen!—

Help, ho! —lieutenant, sir!—Montano, sir!—

Help, masters! —Here's a goodly watch indeed! *A bell rung.*

140   Who's that that rings the bell? Diablo, ho!

The town will rise. —God's will, lieutenant, hold!

You will be shamed for ever.

Enter OTHELLO *and Gentlemen with weapons.*

OTHELLO

What is the matter here?

MONTANO

'Zounds, I bleed still;

I am hurt to th' death. He dies!   [*Attacks* CASSIO *again.*]

OTHELLO

Hold for your lives!

IAGO

145   Hold, hold! lieutenant—sir—Montano—gentlemen!

Have you forgot all sense of place and duty?

Hold! the general speaks to you. Hold, hold, for shame!

---

136.   **S.D.** *Aside* Capell. *Exit* **RODERIGO.** Q2.   Not in QF.
137.   **God's will** Q.   F has 'Alas'.
138.   **lieutenant, sir!—Montano, sir!** Q2 (Leiutenant: Sir, Montanio, sir,).   Q1 has 'Leiutenant: Sir *Montanio*, sir'; F has 'Lieutenant, Sir *Montano*'.
139.   **S.D.** Q (after 'mutiny' line 136).   Not in F.
140.   **that that** Q.   F has 'that which'.
141.   **God's will** Q.   F has 'Fie, fie'.   **hold** Q.   Not in F.
142.   **You will be shamed** Q.   F has 'You'l be asham'd'.
          S.D. *with weapons.* Q.   Not in F.
143.   **'Zounds** Q.   Not in F.
144.   **th' death. He dies!** F (dies:).   Q has 'the death:'.   **S.D.** Capell.
145.   **Hold, hold** Q.   F has 'hold, hoa'.
          sir—Montano most eds.   Q has 'sir *Montanio*'; F has 'Sir *Montano*'.
146.   **sense of place** Hanmer.   QF have 'place of sense'.
147.   **Hold, hold** Q.   F has 'hold'.

136.   *mutiny*   riot.
137.   *God's will*   a common oath, here used protestingly, like (but much stronger than) our "for God's sake!"
139.   *masters*   gentlemen.   S.D. *bell*   the alarum bell.

OTHELLO

Why, how now, ho! from whence ariseth this?
Are we turned Turks, and to ourselves do that
150 Which heaven hath forbid the Ottomites?
For Christian shame put by this barbarous brawl!
He that stirs next to carve for his own rage
Holds his soul light; he dies upon his motion.
Silence that dreadful bell! It frights the isle
155 From her propriety. What's the matter, masters?
—Honest Iago, that looks dead with grieving,
Speak who began this; on thy love I charge thee.

[*The bell is silenced.*]

IAGO

I do not know. Friends all but now, even now,
In quarter, and in terms like bride and groom
160 Divesting them for bed; and then, but now,
As if some planet had unwitted men—
Swords out, and tilting one at other's breast
In opposition bloody. I cannot speak
Any beginning to this peevish odds,

---

148. **ariseth** F. Q has 'arises'.
150. **hath** F. Q has 'has'.
152. **for** F. Q has 'forth'.
155. **What's** Q. F has 'What is'.
160. **for** F. Q has 'to'.
162. **breast** Q. F has 'breastes'.

149–50. "Are we, by our unchristian behavior to one another, now to do to ourselves what God (by destroying their fleet) has forbidden the declared unfaithful from doing to us?"

152. *carve for* indulge. The metaphor derives from the idea of "choosing for oneself the best cut."

153. *holds his soul light* values his soul lightly—because he will be struck dead while in a state of mortal sin. *upon his motion* the instant he moves.

155. *From her propriety* i.e. out of its identity (a town kept peaceful by their protection). *What's the matter, masters?* What goes on here, gentlemen?

159. *In quarter* in their assigned places—a military term (cf. *King John* V. v. 20 and *Antony and Cleopatra* IV. iii. 22).

164. *peevish odds* silly quarrel.

165 And would in action glorious I had lost
These legs that brought me to a part of it.

OTHELLO

How comes it, Michael, you are thus forgot?

CASSIO

I pray you pardon me; I cannot speak.

OTHELLO

Worthy Montano, you were wont be civil;
170 The gravity and stillness of your youth
The world hath noted, and your name is great
In mouths of wisest censure. What's the matter
That you unlace your reputation thus,
And spend your rich opinion for the name
175 Of a night-brawler? Give me answer to't.

MONTANO

Worthy Othello, I am hurt to danger.
Your officer, Iago, can inform you—
While I spare speech which something now offends me—
Of all that I do know; nor know I aught
180 By me that's said or done amiss this night—
Unless self-charity be sometimes a vice,
And to defend ourselves it be a sin
When violence assails us.

---

166. **These** Q. F has 'Those'.
167. **comes ... are** F. Q has 'came ... were'.
169. **be** Q. F has 'to be'.
172. **mouths** F. Q has 'men'.
175. **to't** Q. F has 'to it'.
181. **sometimes** F. Q has 'sometime'.

169. *Worthy* noble. *civil* quiet and well-behaved.
170. *gravity and stillness* decorum and sobriety.
172. *wisest censure* most acute judgment.
173. *unlace* carve up—i.e. utterly disgrace.
174. *spend your rich opinion* squander your valuable reputation.
178. *something* somewhat. *offends* hurts.
181. *self-charity* "care of one's self" (Johnson). However, the expression is ironically self-condemning since "to carve for" one's "own rage" is by definition to violate the law of charity—hence Othello's appeal to their sense of "Christian shame" (line 151).

OTHELLO

Now, by heaven,
My blood begins my safer guides to rule,
185   And passion, having my best judgment collied,
Assays to lead the way. 'Zounds, if I stir,
Or do but lift this arm, the best of you
Shall sink in my rebuke! Give me to know
How this foul rout began, who set it on;
190   And he that is approved in this offense,
Though he had twinned with me, both at a birth,
Shall lose me. What! in a town of war,
Yet wild, the people's hearts brimful of fear,
To manage private and domestic quarrel?
195   In night, and on the court and guard of safety!
'Tis monstrous. Iago, who began't?

---

185.   **collied** F.   Q has 'coold'.
186.   **'Zounds, if I** Q.   F has 'If I once'.
194.   **quarrel** F.   Q has 'quarrels'.
195.   **and guard of** QF.   Theobald and many eds. emend 'of guard, and'.
196.   **began't** F.   Q has 'began'.

184. *My . . . rule* i.e. my base passions—here, particularly, anger—begin to rule those *safer guides* of action, my rational powers, which should be in charge of them.
185. *collied* blackened, obscured.
186. *Assays* attempts.
189. *rout* brawl.
190. *approved in* proved guilty of.
192. *of war* still in a state of war.
194. *manage* engage in. *domestic* intestine, with people of your own nation.
195. *on . . . safety* in the headquarters of the watch and while on duty as the watch responsible for the safety of the town.

MONTANO

[*To* IAGO] If partially affined, or leagued in office,
Thou dost deliver more or less than truth,
Thou art no soldier.

IAGO

Touch me not so near.
200   I had rather have this tongue cut from my mouth
Than it should do offense to Michael Cassio;
Yet I persuade myself, to speak the truth
Shall nothing wrong him. —This it is, general:
Montano and myself being in speech,
205   There comes a fellow crying out for help,
And Cassio following him with determined sword
To execute upon him. Sir, this gentleman
Steps in to Cassio and entreats his pause;
Myself the crying fellow did pursue,
210   Lest by his clamor—as it so fell out—
The town might fall in fright. He, swift of foot,
Outran my purpose; and I returned the rather
For that I heard the clink and fall of swords,
And Cassio high in oath; which till tonight
215   I ne'er might say before. When I came back—
For this was brief—I found them close together

---

197.   **partially** F.   Q has 'partiality'.
      leagued Pope.   QF have 'league'.
200.   **have . . . cut** F.   Q has 'ha . . . out'.
203.   **This** F.   Q has 'Thus'.
212.   **the** Q.   F has 'then'.
214.   **oath** F.   Q has 'oaths'.
215.   **say** F.   Q has 'see'.

197. *partially affined* bound by ties of partiality.   *leagued in office* ties of association as fellow officers.

199. *Touch me not so near* hurt me not so intimately (by supposing I would "deliver more or less than truth"). But (for the audience) the line may also mean: "Don't hit so close to home about me."

201. *offense* an injury.

207. *execute* work his will, carry out his purpose.   *this gentleman* with a gesture indicating Montano.

212–13. *the rather/ For that* especially because.

At blow and thrust, even as again they were
When you yourself did part them.
More of this matter cannot I report.
220   But men are men; the best sometimes forget:
Though Cassio did some little wrong to him,
As men in rage strike those that wish them best,
Yet surely Cassio I believe received
From him that fled some strange indignity,
225   Which patience could not pass.

OTHELLO

I know, Iago,
Thy honesty and love doth mince this matter,
Making it light to Cassio.—Cassio, I love thee;
But never more be officer of mine.

[*Re-*]*enter* DESDEMONA, *attended.*

Look if my gentle love be not raised up!
230   I'll make thee an example.

DESDEMONA

What is the matter, dear?

OTHELLO

All's well now, sweeting;
Come away to bed. —[*To* MONTANO] Sir, for your hurts,
Myself will be your surgeon. —Lead him off.

[MONTANO *is led off.*]

Iago, look with care about the town,
235   And silence those whom this vile brawl distracted.—
Come, Desdemona: 'tis the soldiers' life

---

219. **cannot** I F.   Q has 'Can I not'.
228. **S.D.** *attended.* F.   Q has '*with others.*'
231. **dear** F.   Not in Q. **now** Q.   Not in F.
235. **vile** Q.   F has 'vil'd'.

224. *indignity*   insult.
225. *pass*   disregard (by controlling his resentment).
226. *mince*   tone down, minimize.
231. *sweeting*   a term of endearment (from the name of a sweet apple)—Othello's such expressions being notably saccharine in contrast to Desdemona's. Cf. "Honey," above II. i. 198.

To have their balmy slumbers waked with strife.

                           Exit [all but IAGO *and* CASSIO.]

IAGO

What, are you hurt, lieutenant?

CASSIO

Ay, past all surgery.

IAGO

240 Marry, God forbid!

CASSIO

Reputation, reputation, reputation! O, I ha' lost my reputation!
I ha' lost the immortal part of myself, and what remains is
bestial. My reputation, Iago, my reputation!

IAGO

As I am an honest man, I thought you had received some bodily
245 wound. There is more sense in that than in reputation. Reputation is an idle and most false imposition, oft got without
merit and lost without deserving. You have lost no reputation
at all unless you repute yourself such a loser. What, man!
there are ways to recover the general again. You are but now
250 cast in his mood—a punishment more in policy than in malice;

---

237. **S.D.** F.   Q has 'Exit Moore, Desdemona, *and attendants.*' after
          'Leiutenant' line 238.
240. **God** Q.   F has 'Heauen'.
240–3. F.   Verse in Q.
241. **Reputation** (thrice) F.   Q has it twice. **O** F.   Not in Q.
          ha' Q.   F has 'haue'.
242. **ha'** Q.   F has 'haue'. **part** F.   Q has 'part sir'.
244. **thought** Q.   F has 'had thought'.
245. **sense** F.   Q has 'offence'.
249. **ways** Q.   F has 'more wayes'.

245. *sense* feeling.
246. *idle* vain, empty, unsubstantial.   *imposition* put upon one
from without.
249. *recover* win back (the favor of).
250. *cast in his mood* dismissed on account of his anger.   *malice*
enmity, ill-will (not spitefulness).

even so as one would beat his offenseless dog to affright an imperious lion. Sue to him again, and he's yours.

CASSIO

I will rather sue to be despised than to deceive so good a commander with so slight, so drunken, and so indiscrete an officer.
255 Drunk! and speak parrot! and squabble! swagger? swear? and discourse fustian with one's own shadow? O thou invisible spirit of wine, if thou hast no name to be known by, let us call thee devil!

IAGO

What was he that you followed with your sword? What had
260 he done to you?

CASSIO

I know not.

IAGO

Is't possible?

CASSIO

I remember a mass of things, but nothing distinctly: a quarrel, but nothing wherefore. O God, that men should put an enemy
265 in their mouths to steal away their brains! that we should with joy, pleasance, revel, and applause transform ourselves into beasts!

---

254. **slight** F. Q has 'light'. **and so** F. Q has 'and'.
255–6. **Drunk . . . shadow?** F. Not in Q.
264. **God** Q. Not in F.
265. **their** F. Q has 'there'.
266. **pleasance, revel** F. Q has 'Reuell, pleasure'.

251–2. *as . . . lion* explaining "a punishment more in policy" by citing the proverb "to beat the dog before [i.e. in the presence of] the lion" (Tilley, D443)—to punish a mean person as warning example to an important one. Cassio is being punished as an example so as to maintain discipline in the whole army.

254. *slight* insignificant, worthless. Q's "light" means, rather, "irresponsible," "full of levity."

255. *speak parrot* talk without understanding what you are saying.

256. *fustian* nonsense—from a generic name for coarse cotton materials used as bombast; see note at I. i. 13.

266. *pleasance* delight. *applause* approbation.

IAGO

Why, but you are now well enough. How came you thus
recovered?

CASSIO

270   It hath pleased the devil drunkenness to give place to the devil
wrath. One unperfectness shows me another, to make me
frankly despise myself.

IAGO

Come, you are too severe a moraller. As the time, the place,
and the condition of this country stands, I could heartily wish
275   this had not befall'n; but since it is as it is, mend it for your
own good.

CASSIO

I will ask him for my place again; he shall tell me I am a
drunkard! Had I as many mouths as Hydra, such an answer
would stop 'em all. To be now a sensible man, by and by a
280   fool, and presently a beast! O strange! Every inordinate cup
is unblest, and the ingredience is a devil.

---

274.   **and** F.   Not in Q.
275.   **befall'n** F (befalne).   Q has 'so befalne'.
279.   **'em** Q.   F has 'them'.
280.   **O strange!** F.   Not in Q. **inordinate** F.   Q has 'vnordinate'.
281.   **ingredience** Q.   F has 'ingredient'.

270–1. *give . . . wrath*   based on Ephesians 4: 26–7 "Be angry
but sin not: let not the sun go down upon your wrath,/ Neither give
place to the devil." Cassio's apostrophe on wine and drunkenness
(lines 255 ff.) contains many scriptural echoes common in Elizabethan
discussions of intemperance; cf. Ephesians 5: 18, 1 Corinthians 10:
21, Ecclesiastes 31: 25–31.
271. *unperfectness*   defect of character.
272. *frankly*   without reserve.
273. *moraller*   moralizer.
278. *Hydra*   the many-headed monstrous snake of Greek mythol-
ogy the destruction of which was one of the labors of Hercules. As
each head was cut off, two others grew in its place.
279. *sensible man*   one in full possession of his faculties.   *by and
by*   in a moment.
280. *presently*   immediately.   *inordinate*   beyond moderation.
281. *ingredience*   contents.

IAGO

Come, come, wine is a good familiar creature if it be well used;
exclaim no more against it. And, good lieutenant, I think you
think I love you.

CASSIO

285   I have well approved it, sir. —I drunk!

IAGO

You or any man living may be drunk at a time, man. I'll tell
you what you shall do. Our general's wife is now the general.
I may say so in this respect, for that he hath devoted and given
up himself to the contemplation, mark, and denotement of her
290   parts and graces. Confess yourself freely to her; importune
her help to put you in your place again. She is of so free, so
kind, so apt, so blessed a disposition, she holds it a vice in her
goodness not to do more than she is requested. This broken
joint between you and her husband entreat her to splinter.

---

282. **wine** Walker.   QF have 'good wine'.
286. **a time, man** F.   Q has 'some time'. **I'll** Q.   F has 'I'.
288. **hath** F.   Q has 'has'.
289. **mark, and** Q (marke and).   F has 'mark: and'.
        denotement Q2.   QF have 'deuotement'.
291. **her help** F.   Q has 'her shee'll helpe'. **of** F.   Not in Q.
292. **she** F.   Q has 'that she'.
293-4. **broken joint** F.   Q has 'braule'.

282. *wine . . . used* alluding to the Christian doctrine of "use
and abuse of the creatures": "For every creature of God is good, and
nothing ought to be refused, if it be received with   thanksgiving."
(1 Timothy 4: 4); on drunkenness specifically, cf. Ecclesiasticus 31:
28. There is wordplay on *familiar* (here, literally, "friendly") in the
sense "familiar spirit," i.e. a demon in association with a man and
at his call: "you've exclaimed against the 'invisible spirit of wine'
(lines 256–8); well, if well used it's a *good familiar*."
285. *approved it* found it true by experience.
288. *for that* because.
290. *parts* accomplishments.
291. *free* bounteous.
292. *apt* ready (to do kindnesses). *vice* defect.
293-4. *broken joint* I suppose this an inferior second thought
since a joint is properly dislocated, not broken; but it may be an F
sophistication. Q's "braule" would mean "quarrel."
294. *splinter* put in splints.

295 And my fortunes against any lay worth naming, this crack of
     your love shall grow stronger than 'twas before.

CASSIO

You advise me well.

IAGO

I protest, in the sincerity of love and honest kindness.

CASSIO

     I think it freely; and betimes in the morning will I beseech the
300 virtuous Desdemona to undertake for me. I am desperate of
     my fortunes if they check me here.

IAGO

You are in the right. Good night, lieutenant; I must to the
watch.

CASSIO

Good night, honest Iago.   *Exit* CASSIO.

IAGO

305 And what's he then that says I play the villain,
     When this advice is free I give, and honest,
     Probal to thinking, and indeed the course
     To win the Moor again? For 'tis most easy
     Th'inclining Desdemona to subdue
310 In any honest suit; she's framed as fruitful
     As the free elements. And then for her

---

296. **'twas** Q. F has 'it was'.
299. **will I** Q. F has 'I will'.
301. **here** Q. Not in F.
302–3. F. Divided as verse in Q.
309. **Th'inclining** F. Q has 'The inclining'.

295. *lay*   wager.
299. *betimes*   early.
300. *undertake*   normally with an object: undertake my business.
306. *free*   (1) generous and (2) innocent.
307. *Probal to*   such as surely would be approved by.
309. *inclining*   favorably disposed. *subdue*   persuade.
310. *fruitful*   generous.
311. *elements*   i.e. fire, air, earth, and water which are free to all.

To win the Moor again—were't to renounce his baptism,
All seals and symbols of redeemèd sin—
His soul is so enfettered to her love
315   That she may make, unmake, do what she list,
Even as her appetite shall play the god
With his weak function. How am I then a villain
To counsel Cassio to this parallel course,
Directly to his good? Divinity of hell!
320   When devils will the blackest sins put on,
They do suggest at first with heavenly shows,
As I do now. For whiles this honest fool
Plies Desdemona to repair his fortune,
And she for him pleads strongly to the Moor,

---

312.   **were't** Q.   F has 'were'.
314.   **enfettered** F (enfetter'd).   Q has 'infetter'd'.
320.   **the** F.   Q has 'their'.
322.   **whiles** F.   Q has 'while'.
323.   **fortune** F.   Q has 'fortunes'.

313. *All . . . sin* reference to the Anglican doctrine of the Remission of sins and the gift of the Spirit through the sacrament of Baptism. *Seals* and *symbols* are technical terms. The sacraments were considered "testimonies, signs, and seals of God's grace" (Becon); Baptism was regularly termed "A seal of our entrance into Christianity." The word "symbol" was applied to the sacraments "because they represent and shew unto us the exceeding great and deep mysteries of God" (Bullinger).

316–17. *Even . . . function* according as her inferior natural desire shall hold god-like sway over his pliantly feeble intellectual and moral powers. The husband was supposed to be the "head" to the wife. Iago claims Othello's bondage to love has made him idolatrously place his entire being, all his senses and faculties, at the whim even of her appetitive desires.

318. *parallel* conformable, in complete accordance (with his "good").

319. *Divinity of hell* diabolic theology—which takes evil as its good and makes black look like white.

320–1. *When . . . shows* "Devils soonest tempt, resembling spirits of light" (*Love's Labour's Lost* IV. iii. 253). Cf. 2 Corinthians 11:4 and the proverb "The Devil can transform himself into an angel of light" (Tilley, D231).

320. *put on* instigate.

321. *suggest* tempt.

323. *Plies* urges.

325 I'll pour this pestilence into his ear,
     That she repeals him for her body's lust;
     And by how much she strives to do him good,
     She shall undo her credit with the Moor.
     So will I turn her virtue into pitch,
330 And out of her own goodness make the net
     That shall enmesh 'em all.

                    [*Re-*]*enter* RODERIGO.
                    How now, Roderigo?

                         RODERIGO

     I do follow here in the chase, not like a hound that hunts, but
     one that fills up the cry. My money is almost spent; I have
     been tonight exceedingly well cudgelled; and I think the issue
335 will be, I shall have so much experience for my pains; and so,
     with no money at all, and a little more wit, return again to
     Venice.

                         IAGO

     How poor are they that have not patience!
     What wound did ever heal but by degrees?
340 Thou know'st we work by wit, and not by witchcraft,
     And wit depends on dilatory time.
     Does't not go well? Cassio hath beaten thee,

---

331. **enmesh 'em** Q.   F has 'en-mash them'.
     S.D. As in Q.   F places after 'Roderigo?'
333. **have** F.   Q has 'ha'.
334. **and** F.   Not in Q.
335. **pains** F.   Q has 'paines, as that comes to'.
335–6. **so, with** F.   Not in Q.
336. **a . . . again** F.   Q has 'with that wit returne'.
338. **have** F.   Q has 'ha'.
340. **know'st** F.   Q has 'knowest'.
342. **hath** F.   Q has 'has'.

325. *pestilence*   poisonous suggestion (to infect his mind).
326. *repeals him*   tries to procure his recall.
329. *pitch*   referring to its blackness, foulness, and ensnaring stickiness.
333. *that fills up the cry*   included in the pack to give voice as he follows those actually running the scent.
338. *poor . . . patience*   because, according to the Elizabethan proverb, "He that has no patience has nothing" (Tilley, P103).
340. *wit*   clever apprehension and planning.

And thou by that small hurt hast cashiered Cassio.

Though other things grow fair against the sun,

345   Yet fruits that blossom first will first be ripe.

Content thyself awhile. —By th' mass, 'tis morning!

Pleasure and action make the hours seem short.—

Retire thee: go where thou are billeted.

Away, I say! thou shalt know more hereafter.

350   Nay, get thee gone.   *Exit* RODERIGO.

                    Two things are to be done:

My wife must move for Cassio to her mistress—

I'll set her on—

Myself the while to draw the Moor apart

And bring him jump when he may Cassio find

355   Soliciting his wife. Ay, that's the way!

Dull not device by coldness and delay.   *Exit.*

---

343.   **hast** Q.   F has 'hath'.

345.   **Yet** F.   Q has 'But'.

346.   **By th' mass** Q (bi'the).   F has 'Introth'.

350.   **S.D.** F.   Not in Q.   **Two** F.   Q has 'Some'.

352–3.   Q.   As one line in F.

          on—/ Myself Q (on.).   F has 'on my selfe,'.

353.   **the while** Theobald.   QF have 'a while'.

356.   **device** F.   Q has 'deuise'.   **S.D.** F.   Q has *'Exeunt.'*

343. *cashiered Cassio*   got Cassio dismissed—with contemptuous wordplay in the choice of the verb.

344–5. A bit of mollifying sententiousness: "our plans (for you to get Desdemona, me the lieutenancy, and both of us revenge) are maturing nicely, but we must expect their fruition in the order set by nature; first things (the dismissal of Cassio) first." *Against* here means "in," "facing."

347. As does Shakespeare's staging: the time represented in this scene is thus indicated to be from ten in the evening until the following dawn.

348. *where thou art billeted*   to the house where you've been assigned quarters—a reminder that Roderigo appears as a soldier in Cyprus.

349. *thou . . . hereafter*   an ironic reminiscence of John 13: 7, "Jesus answered, and said unto him, What I do thou knowest not now: but thou shalt know it hereafter."

350. *Nay*   rebuffing Roderigo, whose expression indicates he wants to continue his protest.

354. *jump*   at the exact moment.

356. *coldness*   lack of push, sluggishness.

[*Act III, scene i.*] *Enter* CASSIO, *with Musicians.*

CASSIO

Masters, play here; I will content your pains:
Something that's brief; and bid "Good morrow, general."

[*The Musicians play.*]

[*Enter the Clown.*]

CLOWN

Why, masters, ha' your instruments been in Naples, that they
speak i'th' nose thus?

MUSICIAN

5 How, sir, how?

III. i **S.D.** QF add '*Clowne.*'
2. **S.D.** Q2. Not in QF.
3. **ha'** Q. F has 'haue'. **in** F. Q has 'at'.
4. **i'th'** F. Q has 'i'the'.
5. **S.P.** F. Q has '*Boy.*' (as throughout this dialogue).

III. i 1–2. *Masters . . . general."* Cassio gracefully would put
to use the courteous custom of greeting a newly married couple with
music. The scene (*here*) is thus set as before the general's residence
in the citadel (which the theater's façade now represents) and early
the same morning that dawned at the end of Act II. This point will
be carefully emphasized in lines 29–30.

1. *content your pains* reward you to your satisfaction for your
trouble.

2. S.D. *The Musicians play.* The ensuing dialogue emphasizes
that they play wind instruments, with the bagpipes predominant.
Ancient tradition, going back to the Greeks and reinforced by early
Christianity, pejoratively compared wind with string instruments.
From the time of the Middle Ages, the bagpipe (increasingly associated with rude and rural use) was connotative of irrationality and
intemperate appetite, and frequently served as a symbol of the folly
of carnal man led by vain and carnal reason. *Enter the Clown*
the stock comic servant, not a jester or professional fool.

3–4. *your . . . thus* identifying the musicians with their instruments, and alluding to the genital-like shape of the bagpipes, their
nasal tone, and the "Neopolitan" (i.e. venereal) disease. "Speaking
in the nose" was associated with the latter because of the breakdown
of nasal cartilage thought consequent upon it. Cf. Timon's address to
the whores (*Tim.* IV. iii. 156–7): "down with the nose, / Down with
it flat; take the bridge quite away."

CLOWN

Are these, I pray you, wind instruments?

MUSICIAN

Ay, marry are they, sir.

CLOWN

O, thereby hangs a tail.

MUSICIAN

Whereby hangs a tale, sir?

CLOWN

10 Marry, sir, by many a wind instrument that I know. But, masters, here's money for you; and the general so likes your music that he desires you, for love's sake, to make no more noise with it.

MUSICIAN

Well, sir, we will not.

---

6. **pray you,** F. Q has 'pray, cald'.
8–9. **tail . . . tale** Q has 'tayle . . . tayle'; F has 'tale . . . tale'.
12. **for love's sake** F. Q has 'of all loues'.

6. *these* with a gesture including the players as well as their instruments.
7. *marry are they* indeed they are.
8. *tail* common Elizabethan for "penis."
10. *wind instrument* i.e. the "wind-breaker."
13. *noise* This could mean "music" and "musical band" as well as "din."

CLOWN

15 If you have any music that may not be heard, to't again; but
as they say, to hear music the general does not greatly care.

MUSICIAN

We ha' none such, sir.

CLOWN

Then put up your pipes in your bag, for I'll away. Go, vanish
into air, away!   *Exit Musicians.*

CASSIO

20 Dost thou hear, my honest friend?

CLOWN

No, I hear not your honest friend; I hear you.

---

17. **ha'** Q. F has 'haue'.
18. **up** F. Not in Q.
19. **into air, away.** F. Q has 'away.' **S.D.** F. Not in Q.
20. **hear, my** Q (heare my). F has 'heare me, mine'.

15. *music . . . heard* i.e. music that cannot be heard—comically
alluding to the music of the spheres, product and symbol of the
ordered universe, a harmony in which immortal souls share, and
which society, marriage, and friendship should imitate. "Such harmony is in immortal souls;/ But whilst this muddy vesture of decay/
Doth grossly close it in, we cannot hear it" (*Merchant of Venice*
V. i. 63–5). The Clown's inquiry makes sense first because General
Othello wants silence. But it is also meaningful in view of the wide-
spread Renaissance idea that instrumental music was supposed
properly to imitate heavenly harmony; it thereby could induce in
hearers reminiscence of that concord useful for the ordering of the
analogous "music of men's lives" (*Richard II* V. v. 44). Thus the
ironic point of his next, generalizing, comment and the musicians'
answer, "We ha' none such, sir." (line 17).
    16. *general* with a play on the sense, "the public."
    18. *put . . . bag* "put up your pipes" is proverbial for "desist,"
"pack it up" (as we should say). The comically literal pertinence
which the Clown opportunistically seizes is elaborated by using the
less common form of the expression, which adds *in your bag*, here
alluding to the bagpipes and also to the codpiece (codd = bag), the
article of Renaissance clothing worn over a man's genitals.
    18–19. *vanish into air* implying they ought to be as unsubstantial
as the air of the wind music with which they have been identified.

CASSIO

Prithee keep up thy quillets. There's a poor piece of gold for
thee. If the gentlewoman that attends the general's wife be
stirring, tell her there's one Cassio entreats her a little favor
25 of speech. Wilt thou do this?

CLOWN

She is stirring, sir. If she will stir hither, I shall seem to
notify unto her.

CASSIO

Do, good my friend.   *Exit Clown.*
                    Enter IAGO.
            In happy time, Iago.

IAGO

You ha' not been abed then?

CASSIO

                              Why no, the day had broke
30 Before we parted. I have made bold, Iago,
To send in to your wife: my suit to her
Is that she will to virtuous Desdemona
Procure me some access.

IAGO

                              I'll send her to you presently;
And I'll devise a mean to draw the Moor

---

23. **general's wife** Q. F has 'Generall'.
28. **Do . . . friend** Q. Not in F.
     S.D. *Exit Clown.* Q2. F places after line 27. Not in Q1.
29. **ha'** Q. F has 'haue'.
30. **have** F. Q has 'ha'.

22. *keep up thy quillets* keep your verbal tricks to yourself—
referring to the Clown's little joke (spoiled by the Folio) made by
ignoring the pause after "hear" (line 20): a simple conventional
pointer to the questionableness of Cassio's way of seeking reinstatement.
28. *good my friend* a vocative phrase, such as "my friend," often
was treated as a single word and modified by an adjective. *In
happy time* opportunely met.
33. *access* accented on the second syllable. *presently* instantly.
34. *mean* means.

35   Out of the way, that your converse and business
       May be more free.

                         CASSIO

       I humbly thank you for't.   *Exit* [IAGO].
                         I never knew
       A Florentine more kind and honest.
                     Enter EMILIA.

                         EMILIA

       Good morrow, good lieutenant. I am sorry
40   For your displeasure; but all will sure be well.
       The general and his wife are talking of it,
       And she speaks for you stoutly. The Moor replies
       That he you hurt is of great fame in Cyprus
       And great affinity, and that in wholesome wisdom
45   He might not but refuse you; but he protests he loves you,
       And needs no other suitor but his likings
       To take the safest occasion by the front
       To bring you in again.

                         CASSIO
                         Yet I beseech you,
       If you think fit, or that it may be done,

       _____

       37. **for't** F. Q has 'for it'. **S.D.** QF place after 'free' line 36.
       40. **sure** F. Q has 'soon'.
       47. Q. Not in F.

       35. *converse* conversation.
       38. *A Florentine* emphatic—"even a Florentine, one of my own
       native city."
       40. *your displeasure* the disfavor you are in.
       44. *great affinity* with kinsmen of high degree.
       45. *might* could.
       47. *To . . . front* to take the earliest politic opportunity. Oc-
       casion (Opportunity) was proverbially described and represented in
       the Renaissance as a bald, nude, winged female with a single fore-
       lock which had to be seized before she flew away (see above, p. x,
       fig. a). Opportunity is an iterated idea of this part of the scene: see
       lines 28, 47, 50, 52.
       49. *that* if.

50 Give me advantage of some brief discourse
With Desdemon alone.

EMILIA

Pray you come in.
I will bestow you where you shall have time
To speak your bosom freely.

CASSIO

I am much bound to you. *Exeunt.*

[*Scene ii.*] *Enter* OTHELLO, IAGO, *and Gentlemen.*

OTHELLO

These letters give, Iago, to the pilot,
And by him do my duties to the state.
That done, I will be walking on the works;
Repair there to me.

IAGO

Well, my good lord, I'll do't.

OTHELLO

5 This fortification, gentlemen, shall we see't?

GENTLEMEN

We wait upon your lordship. *Exeunt.*

---

51. **Desdemon** F. Q has '*Desdemona*'.
53. **CASSIO I . . . you.** F. Not in Q. **S.D.** Q. Not in F.
III. ii 1. **pilot** F (Pylot). Q has 'Pilate'.
2. **state** Q. F has 'Senate'.
6. **We** Q. F has 'Well'.

50. *advantage* opportunity.
52. *bestow* place. *time* opportunity.
53. *your bosom* whatever you have on your mind.
III. ii This scene, although not specifically localized, implicitly takes place of course elsewhere than the action of III. i. Its primary function is to indicate Othello's absence during Cassio's interview with Desdemona, and to explain Iago's being with the hero when he enters "jump when he may Cassio find/ Soliciting his wife."
1. *pilot* i.e. the "master" or navigating officer of the ship (not "pilot" in the modern restricted seaman's sense).
3. *works* fortifications.

[Scene iii.] Enter DESDEMONA, CASSIO, *and* EMILIA.

DESDEMONA

Be thou assured, good Cassio, I will do
All my abilities in thy behalf.

EMILIA

Good madam, do. I warrant it grieves my husband
As if the cause were his.

DESDEMONA

5   O, that's an honest fellow. Do not doubt, Cassio,
But I will have my lord and you again
As friendly as you were.

CASSIO

Bounteous madame,
Whatever shall become of Michael Cassio,
He's never anything but your true servant.

DESDEMONA

10   I know't; I thank you. You do love my lord;
You have known him long, and be you well assured

III. iii   3.   **warrant** F.   Q has 'know'.
   4.   **cause** F.   Q has 'case'.
   7.   **madame** Q.   F has 'madam'.
  10.   **I know't** F.   Q has 'O sir'.

III. iii The scene opens in the midst of conversation following
Cassio's private interview with Desdemona. Implicitly, the locale is
the same as that in III. i, but it is not specified, so the groupings
comprising the scene are unlocalized before the symbolic façade. Convention, however, supported the idea that performance in front of a
scenic castle or fort could represent actions understood as within it.
   4. *cause*   the charge against the accused, the case before Othello
as the legal authority—with an unknowing double under-meaning.
The variants here both make nice, but different, ironies. I think F's
reading a later Shakespearean thought, not necessarily a better one.
   7. *madame*   Q's spelling (here and at IV. iii. 3 below) preserves, I
think, the more formal expression of respect (like "Madonna") suited
both to Cassio's courtliness and also to her present function in
relation to him.

He shall in strangeness stand no farther off
Than in a politic distance.

CASSIO

Ay, but lady,
That policy may either last so long,
15 Or feed upon such nice and wat'rish diet,
Or breed itself so out of circumstance,
That, I being absent and my place supplied,
My general will forget my love and service.

DESDEMONA

Do not doubt that; before Emilia here,
20 I give thee warrant of thy place. Assure thee,
If I do vow a friendship, I'll perform it
To the last article. My lord shall never rest:
I'll watch him tame, and talk him out of patience;
His bed shall seem a school, his board a shrift;
25 I'll intermingle everything he does
With Cassio's suit. Therefore be merry, Cassio,
For thy solicitor shall rather die
Than give thy cause away.

Enter OTHELLO *and* IAGO.

---

12. **strangeness** F.   Q has 'strangest'.
14. **That** F.   Q has 'The'.
16. **circumstance** Q.   F has 'Circumstances'.
28. **thy cause away.** F.   Q has 'thee cause: away.'
    S.D. F.   Q adds '*and Gentlemen.*'

12. *strangeness*   aloofness, his estrangement.
13. *in a politic distance*   as policy requires.
15. *feed . . . diet*   be continued for such trivial and inconsequential reasons.
16. *breed . . . circumstance*   be so perpetuated from new circumstances.
17. *supplied*   filled up.
19. *doubt*   expect, fear.
20. *Assure thee*   assure thyself.
23. *watch him tame*   tame him to obedience (until he gives in) by keeping him awake (as a hawk is tamed).
24. *school*   where you must sit and be taught by the master. *shrift*   where you must be penitent to receive absolution.
27. *solicitor*   the one who solicits for you.
28. *give thy cause away*   abandon your case.

EMILIA

Madam, here comes my lord.

CASSIO

30   Madam, I'll take my leave.

DESDEMONA

Why, stay, and hear me speak.

CASSIO

I am very ill at ease, unfit for mine own purposes.

DESDEMONA

Well, do your discretion.   *Exit* CASSIO.

IAGO

[*with* OTHELLO, *yet at a distance*]

Ha! I like not that.

OTHELLO

What dost thou say?

IAGO

35   Nothing, my lord; or if—I know not what.

OTHELLO

Was not that Cassio parted from my wife?

IAGO

Cassio, my lord? No sure, I cannot think it,
That he would steal away so guilty-like,
Seeing your coming.

OTHELLO

I do believe 'twas he.

DESDEMONA

40   How now, my lord!
I have been talking with a suitor here,
A man that languishes in your displeasure.

OTHELLO

Who is't you mean?

---

32.   **purposes** F.   Q has 'purpose'.
38.   **steal** F.   Q has 'sneake'.
39.   **your** F.   Q has 'you'.

DESDEMONA

Why, your lieutenant, Cassio. Good my lord,
45 If I have any grace or power to move you,
His present reconciliation take;
For if he be not one that truly loves you,
That errs in ignorance, and not in cunning,
I have no judgment in an honest face.
50 I prithee call him back.

OTHELLO

Went he hence now?

DESDEMONA

Yes, faith; so humblèd,
That he hath left part of his grief with me
To suffer with him. Good love, call him back.

OTHELLO

Not now, sweet Desdemon; some other time.

DESDEMONA

55 But shall't be shortly?

OTHELLO

The sooner, sweet, for you.

DESDEMONA

Shall't be tonight at supper?

OTHELLO

No, not tonight.

DESDEMONA

Tomorrow dinner then?

---

51. **Yes, faith** Q. F has 'I sooth'.
52. **hath** F. Q has 'has'. **grief** F. Q has 'griefes'.
53. **To** F. Q has 'I'.
54. **Desdemon** F. Q has '*Desdemona*'.

45. *grace* favor in your eyes.
46. *present* immediate. *reconciliation* a theological term: repentance with a view to reconcilement (with God).
48. *in cunning* on purpose—literally, "wittingly."
51. *humblèd* trisyllabic: "hum bl ed."
57. *dinner* the mid-day meal.

OTHELLO

I shall not dine at home:
I meet the captains at the citadel.

DESDEMONA

Why then, tomorrow night; or Tuesday morn?
60 On Tuesday noon, or night; on Wednesday morn?
I prithee name the time, but let it not
Exceed three days. I' faith, he's penitent;
And yet his trespass, in our common reason—
Save that they say the wars must make examples
65 Out of her best—is not almost a fault
T'incur a private check. When shall he come?
Tell me, Othello. I wonder in my soul
What you could ask me that I should deny
Or stand so mamm'ring on. What? Michael Cassio,
70 That came a-wooing with you, and so many a time
When I have spoke of you dispraisingly
Hath ta'en your part—to have so much to do
To bring him in? By'r Lady, I could do much—

OTHELLO

Prithee no more: let him come when he will;
75 I will deny thee nothing.

DESDEMONA

Why, this is not a boon;
'Tis as I should entreat you wear your gloves,

---

59. **or** Q. F has 'on'.
60. **noon** F. Q has 'morne'. **night; on** F. Q has 'night, or'.
62. **I' faith** Q. F has 'Infaith'.
64. **examples** Q. F has 'example'.
66. **T'incur** Q. F has 'To incurre'.
68. **could** Q. F has 'would'. **deny** F (deny,). Q has 'deny?'
69. **mamm'ring** F. Q has 'muttering'.
73. **By'r Lady** Q (Birlady). F has 'Trust me'.

63. *in our common reason*   as we ordinarily judge (such a fault).
65. *not almost*   hardly.
66. *a private check*   (even) a rebuke in private.
69. *mamm'ring on*   hesitating about.
74. *Prithee no more*   not spoken angrily or impatiently (as mis-interpreting actors sometimes do): a smiling, "your petition is granted."

Or feed on nourishing dishes, or keep you warm,
Or sue to you to do a peculiar profit
To your own person. Nay, when I have a suit
80　Wherein I mean to touch your love indeed,
It shall be full of poise and difficult weight,
And fearful to be granted.

OTHELLO

　　　　　　　I will deny thee nothing.
Whereon I do beseech thee grant me this,
To leave me but a little to myself.

DESDEMONA

85　Shall I deny you? no. Farewell, my lord.

OTHELLO

Farewell, my Desdemona; I'll come to thee straight.

DESDEMONA

Emilia, come. —[*To* OTHELLO] Be as your fancies teach you;
Whate'er you be, I am obedient. 　　　*Exit* [*with* EMILIA].

81.　**difficult weight** F.　Q has 'difficulty'.
87.　**Be** F.　Q has 'be it'.
88.　**S.D.** Q (*Exit* Desd. *and* Em.).　F has '*Exit.*'

78.　*peculiar*　special to yourself. The point is made emphatic by
"To your own person" in the next line.
80.　*touch*　try, test—as the quality of gold is tested by a touch-
stone.
81.　*poise*　weight, with a suggestion of its being carefully meas-
ured.
85.　*Shall I deny you?*　i.e. after saying "I wonder in my soul/
What you could ask me that I should deny" (lines 67–8)—spoken
with a smile.
86.　*straight*　straightway.

OTHELLO

Excellent wretch! Perdition catch my soul
90 But I do love thee! and when I love thee not,
Chaos is come again.

IAGO

My noble lord—

OTHELLO

What dost thou say, Iago?

IAGO

Did Michael Cassio,
When you wooed my lady, know of your love?

OTHELLO

He did, from first to last. Why dost thou ask?

IAGO

95 But for a satisfaction of my thought;
No further harm.

OTHELLO

Why of thy thought, Iago?

---

93. **you** Q. F has 'he'.
95. **thought** F. Q has 'thoughts'.

89. *Excellent wretch Wretch* is often used as an affectionate term of endearment; *excellent* has a much stronger sense than our word, not just "very good" but "surpassing all." *Perdition* damnation.

90. *But I do* if I do not. However, *But* can also pertinently be understood as the particle of objection, signifying "yet," "nevertheless"—thus making "Perdition . . . thee" depend for its meaning on reference to the idea that to love a mortal idolatrously is a sin against God.

90–1. *when . . . again* The verbs are futurative in force. In Othello's sense, this means: "When I stop loving you, the primal darkness and confusion will have returned," i.e. "I will love you as long as the universe lasts." But it can also be understood to mean "When I cease loving you, chaos will come again"—a sense supported by the Renaissance commonplace that it is love which holds together the universe, and, analogously, society, friendship, marriage, and prevents their return to primal disorder.

96. *no further harm* already implying there is some harm which he is hiding.

IAGO

I did not think he had been acquainted with her.

OTHELLO

O yes, and went between us very oft.

IAGO

Indeed?

OTHELLO

100   Indeed? ay indeed. Discern'st thou aught in that?
Is he not honest?

IAGO

Honest, my lord?

OTHELLO

Honest. Ay, honest.

IAGO

My lord, for aught I know.

OTHELLO

What dost thou think?

IAGO

Think, my lord?

OTHELLO

"Think, my lord?"

By heaven he echoes me,
105   As if there were some monster in his thought
Too hideous to be shown. Thou dost mean something:
I heard thee say but now, thou lik'st not that,
When Cassio left my wife. What didst not like?
And when I told thee he was of my counsel
110   In my whole course of wooing, thou cried'st "Indeed?"

---

98.   **oft** F.   Q has 'often'.
100. **Indeed? ay indeed.** F (I).   Q has 'Indeed? Indeed,'.
104. **By . . . echoes** Q.   F has 'Alas, thou ecchos't'.
105. **his** Q.   F has 'thy'.
106. **dost** F.   Q has 'didst'.
107. **but** Q.   F has 'euen'.
110. **In** Q.   F has 'Of'.

109. *of my counsel*   in my confidence.

And didst contract and purse thy brow together,
As if thou then hadst shut up in thy brain
Some horrible conceit. If thou dost love me,
Show me thy thought.

IAGO

115   My lord, you know I love you.

OTHELLO

I think thou dost;
And for I know thou'rt full of love and honesty,
And weigh'st thy words before thou giv'st 'em breath,
Therefore these stops of thine fright me the more:
For such things in a false disloyal knave
120   Are tricks of custom; but in a man that's just
They're close dilations, working from the heart
That passion cannot rule.

---

113.   **conceit** F.   Q has 'counsell'.
116.   **thou'rt** F.   Q has 'thou art'.
117.   **weigh'st** F.   Q has 'weighest'.
         giv'st 'em Q2.   F has 'giu'st them'; Q has 'giue em'.
118.   **fright** F.   Q has 'affright'.
121.   **They're . . . dilations** F.   Q has 'They are . . . denotements'.

111.   *purse*   close up, i.e. knit.
113.   *conceit*   conception, idea.
115.   *My . . . you*   echoing with horrid irony Peter's response to Jesus' thrice-asked "Lovest thou me?": "Lord, thou knowest all things: thou knowest that I love thee. Jesus said unto him, Feed my sheep" (John 21: 17).   *I think thou dost   Dost* is emphatic, not *think.*
118.   *stops*   breakings off.
120.   *tricks of custom*   customary tricks.
121–2.   *close . . . rule*   secret, confined swellings originating in the heart of a man who can rule his passions but not these mute symptoms of his emotion ("these stops of thine" line 118). Q's "close denotements"—meaning, "indications of something secret"—gives a simple version of the same sense, but F's reading, though difficult, daringly fusing the idea of confinement with that of uncontrollable "swelling," is (I think) the more powerful.

IAGO

For Michael Cassio,
I dare be sworn I think that he is honest.

OTHELLO

I think so too.

IAGO

Men should be what they seem;
125 Or those that be not, would they might seem none!

OTHELLO

Certain, men should be what they seem.

IAGO

Why then I think Cassio's an honest man.

OTHELLO

Nay, yet there's more in this.
I prithee speak to me as to thy thinkings,
130 As thou dost ruminate, and give thy worst of thoughts
The worst of words.

IAGO

Good my lord, pardon me:

---

123. **be sworn** F. Q has 'presume'.
124. **what** F. Q has 'that'.
129. **as** F. Not in Q.
130–1. **thy . . . thoughts / . . . words.** F. Q has 'the . . . thought, /
        . . . word.'

123. *I think* Iago has already forced Othello to traverse the distinction between "thinking" and "knowing" (lines 102–3). Thus, now,
a "thought" that Cassio is "honest," seemingly meant as reassurance,
can sound quite as hollow and tainted with reservation as it is meant
to be.

124–7. *Men . . . man* Because he seems one; and only because
we are prepared to think men are what they seem since, really to be
men, they should be. But men can and do seem men—and not the
monsters they are (*seem none*)—even when they are not what they
seem. Thus Iago displays the possible insubstantiality of the
"thought" of Cassio's honesty which he pretends to share with
Othello, hinting there are other opinions—more accurate ones
precisely because not based on such fine expectations—which might
be held about the now almost discredited Cassio.

Though I am bound to every act of duty,
I am not bound to that all slaves are free to.
Utter my thoughts! Why, say they are vile and false?

135   As where's that palace whereinto foul things
Sometimes intrude not? Who has a breast so pure
But some uncleanly apprehensions
Keep leets and law-days, and in session sit
With meditations lawful?

OTHELLO

140   Thou dost conspire against thy friend, Iago,
If thou but think'st him wrong'd and mak'st his ear
A stranger to thy thoughts.

IAGO

I do beseech you—

---

133.   **that all . . . to.** Q.   F has 'that: All . . . free:'.
134.   **vile** Q.   F has 'vild'.
136.   **a** Q.   F has "that".
137.   **But some** Q.   F has 'Wherein'.
138.   **session** Q.   F has 'Sessions'. **sit** F.   Q has 'fit'.
141.   **think'st . . . mak'st** F.   Q has 'thinkest . . . makest'.

133. *bound . . . to*   bound to do that with reference to which all slaves are free: viz. "utter my thoughts" (line 134). *Slaves* is emphatic. The punctuation and omission of *to* in F show how carefully it carried through its misconstruction of the sense: for Iago by no means is calling himself a "slave."

137. *uncleanly apprehensions*   dirty thoughts, unchaste ways of interpreting.

138. *leets*   sessions of the district court.   *in session sit*   i.e. on the bench.

140. *conspire*   practise.

142–52 *I . . . thoughts*   A remarkably subtle speech in which the too scrupulous elaboration of reasons for distrusting his thoughts is made to appear a way to evade telling what he knows: "I beseech you—notwithstanding that I perhaps am mistaken (as, knowing my compulsively mistrustful nature, I have cause to suspect)—that your wisest course still would be not to disturb yourself with the haphazard observations of one so given to imperfect conjecture." *Though* means "even if"; the force of the indicative *am* (suggesting something founded on fact) is blunted by *perchance;* accordingly, *yet* ambiguously can mean "nevertheless" (in spite of my unreliable suspiciousness) or "as yet" (till some future time). Thus, the reticent "honest Iago" implies he protects his friend because the truth would disturb him and not because a probably erroneous suspicion might.

Though I perchance am vicious in my guess
(As I confess it is my nature's plague
145 To spy into abuses, and oft my jealousy
Shapes faults that are not)—that your wisdom yet,
From one that so imperfectly conjects,
Would take no notice, nor build yourself a trouble
Out of his scattering and unsure observance.
150 It were not for your quiet nor your good,
Nor for my manhood, honesty, or wisdom,
To let you know my thoughts.

OTHELLO

What dost thou mean?

IAGO

Good name in man and woman, dear my lord,
Is the immediate jewel of our souls.
155 Who steals my purse, steals trash: 'tis something, nothing;

---

145. **oft** Q. F has 'of'.
146. **that your wisdom yet** Q2. F has 'that your wisedome'; Q1 has
      'I intreate you then'.
147. **conjects** Q (coniects). F has 'conceits'.
148. **Would** F. Q has 'You'd'.
149. **his** F. Q has 'my'.
151. **or** Q. F has 'and'.
152. **What . . . mean** F. Q has 'Zouns'.
153. **woman, dear my lord** F [woman (deere my Lord)]. Q has
      'woman's deere my Lord'.
154. **our** Q. F has 'their'.

143. *vicious* mistaken, faulty—but also capable of meaning
"blameworthy."

145. *jealousy* aptitude for mistrustful scrutiny. (No sense of
personal injury is implied).

147. *conjects* conjectures.

149. *scattering* haphazard. *observance* observation.

152. *What dost thou mean?* An instance, I believe, where F's
elimination of an oath (Q: "Zouns.") is due to revision rather than
expurgation.

154. *immediate jewel of* jewel closest to.

155. *trash* rubbish, also a scornful term for money.

'Twas mine, 'tis his, and has been slave to thousands;
But he that filches from me my good name
Robs me of that which not enriches him
And makes me poor indeed.

OTHELLO

By heaven, I'll know thy thoughts!

IAGO

160   You cannot, if my heart were in your hand;
Nor shall not whil'st 'tis in my custody.

OTHELLO

Ha!

IAGO

O beware, my lord, of jealousy!
It is the green-eye'd monster which doth mock
The meat it feeds on. That cuckold lives in bliss
165   Who, certain of his fate, loves not his wronger;
But O, what damnèd minutes tells he o'er
Who dotes, yet doubts, suspects, yet fondly loves!

---

159. **By heaven** Q. Not in F. **thoughts** F. Q has 'thought'.
162. **OTHELLO Ha!** F. Not in Q. **my lord, of** F. Not in Q.
164. **The** F. Q has 'That'.
166. **he** F. Q has 'be'.
167. **fondly** Knight. F has 'soundly'; Q has 'strongly'.

160. *if* even if.

163–4. *the . . . on* the jealous man's suspiciousness external-
ized and personified as a monster that plays with and mocks its prey,
releasing him only to seize him again.

164. *cuckold* husband of an adulteress. Iago, by way of illustrating suspiciousness ("jealousy," line 162), for the first time specifically refers to sexual jealousy. *in bliss* a wry irony: as though
in an eternity of heavenly contentment (because his certainty affords
him relief in hate) in contrast to the "damnèd minutes" of tormented
uncertainty suffered by the foolish husband who excessively loves yet
suspects (lines 166–7).

165. *loves not his wronger* ironic, particularly for the Elizabethan
audience, since (given a different sense of *loves*) loving one's *wronger*
is precisely what is expected of a Christian.

167. *fondly* with a strong sense of "foolishly."

OTHELLO

O misery!

IAGO

Poor and content is rich, and rich enough;
170   But riches fineless is as poor as winter
To him that ever fears he shall be poor.
Good God, the souls of all my tribe defend
From jealousy!

OTHELLO

Why, why is this?
Think'st thou I'd make a life of jealousy,
175   To follow still the changes of the moon
With fresh suspicions? No; to be once in doubt
Is once to be resolved. Exchange me for a goat
When I shall turn the business of my soul
To such exsufflicate and blown surmises

---

172.   **God** Q. F has 'Heauen'.
177.   **once** Q. Not in F.
179.   **exsufflicate** Capell. QF have 'exufflicate'.
        blown Q. F has 'blow'd'.

168. *O misery!*   a response to an imagined state, not to one he must now positively assume to be his own.

169–71. *Poor . . . poor*   The strong implication, in context, is that (now) one best bewares of jealousy by actively acknowledging that he no longer possesses what he fears to lose.

170. *fineless*   boundless, endless.

175–6. *follow . . . suspicions*   ever wax and wane, like the ever-changing moon, in suspicion.

177. *once to be resolved*   once for all to have my doubt cleared up. *goat* traditionally representing the vice of lechery. It is an Elizabethan commonplace that the root of a man's jealousy most often was to be found in his own illicit lusts or intemperate or imperfect love. Thus, Spenser's personification of Lechery rides "Upon a bearded Goat, whose rugged haire,/ And whally eyes (the signe of gelosy)/ Was like the person selfe, whome he did beare." (*Faerie Queene* I. iv. 24).

179. *exsufflicate and blown*   The tone of contempt is clear but the exact meaning is in doubt. *Exsufflicate* is a nonce word meaning either "contemptibly odious" (after low Latin "exsufflare") or perhaps "swollen, puffed up." *Blown* probably means "fly-blown"—i.e. covered with fly excrement or eggs—but might here signify "blown up, inflated, unsubstantial."

180   Matching thy inference. 'Tis not to make me jealous
      To say my wife is fair, feeds well, loves company;
      Is free of speech, sings, plays, and dances well.
      Where virtue is, these are more virtuous.
      Nor from mine own weak merits will I draw
185   The smallest fear or doubt of her revolt;
      For she had eyes, and chose me. No, Iago:
      I'll see before I doubt; when I doubt, prove;
      And on the proof there is no more but this—
      Away at once with love or jealousy!

                        IAGO

190   I am glad of it; for now I shall have reason
      To show the love and duty that I bear you
      With franker spirit. Therefore, as I am bound,
      Receive it from me. I speak not yet of proof.
      Look to your wife; observe her well with Cassio;
195   Wear your eye thus: not jealous, nor secure;
      I would not have your free and noble nature
      Out of self-bounty be abused. Look to't.

---

182. **well** Q. Not in F.
190. **it** Q. F has 'this'.
195. **eye** Q. F has 'eyes'.

180. *Matching thy inference*   according with what you allege (of the suspicions of the jealous man).

181. *feeds well*   This belongs in a list of points that might make him jealous because rich diet was supposed provocative of sensual appetite.

183. *virtuous*   besides the moral meaning, also "full of excellence, merit, accomplishment."

184. *from . . . merits*   on the assumption that my merits are weak.

185. *doubt of her revolt*   suspicion of her falling off from love, faithfulness, or allegiance.

187. *prove*   test.

188. *on*   as a result of.

195. *not jealous, nor secure*   neither suspicious, nor (blindly) free from care and suspicion.

196. *free*   open and generous.

197. *self-bounty*   its very natural goodness. But this compound, unique in Shakespeare, might (to the audience) very well also mean, with dramatic irony, "bounty to yourself." *abused*   deceived.

I know our country disposition well:
In Venice they do let God see the pranks
200 They dare not show their husbands; their best conscience
Is not to leave't undone, but kept unknown.

OTHELLO

Dost thou say so?

IAGO

She did deceive her father, marrying you;
And when she seemed to shake and fear your looks,
205 She loved them most.

OTHELLO

And so she did.

IAGO

Why, go to then!
She that, so young, could give out such a seeming
To seal her father's eyes up close as oak—
He thought 'twas witchcraft—but I am much to blame.
I humbly do beseech you of your pardon
210 For too much loving you.

OTHELLO

I am bound to thee for ever.

IAGO

I see this hath a little dashed your spirits.

---

199. **God** Q. F has 'Heauen'.
200. **not** F. Not in Q.
201. **leave't . . . kept** F. Q has 'leaue . . . keepe'.
207. **seal** Q. F has 'seele'.

198. Implying: as you, a foreigner, do not, and I, a so generally acknowledged honest and observant native, must know absolutely.
199. *pranks*   mischievous, or malicious, deeds, infidelities.
205. *Why, go to then!*   Iago dares suddenly to shift into a further level of familiarity with the colloquialism, "go to." Here it almost means, "Why, there now, what more could you require!"
207. *seal . . . oak*   close them up as tight as the grain of oak. F's variant "seele" I think a substitution, perhaps memorially induced by the more precisely appropriate use of that word at I. iii. 265.
208. *to blame*   at fault.
209. *of*   for.

OTHELLO

Not a jot, not a jot.

IAGO

I'faith I fear it has.
I hope you will consider what is spoke
Comes from your love. But I do see y'are moved.
215   I am to pray you not to strain my speech
To grosser issues, nor to larger reach
Than to suspicion.

OTHELLO

I will not.

IAGO

Should you do so, my lord,
My speech should fall into such vile success
220   As my thoughts aim not at. Cassio's my worthy friend—
My lord, I see y'are moved.

OTHELLO

No, not much moved:
I do not think but Desdemona's honest.

IAGO

Long live she so! and long live you to think so!

---

212. **I'faith** Q. F has 'Trust me'.
214. **your** F. Q has 'my'. **y'are** F. Q has 'you are'.
219. **vile** Q. F has 'vilde'.
220. **As . . . aim not at** Q. F has 'Which . . . aym'd not'.
      worthy F. Q has 'trusty'.
221. **y'are** F. Q has 'you are'.

214. *from your love* from my love for you—but also, from your love, i.e. Desdemona: which is what makes Othello "moved."
215. *I am to pray you* I must beg you.
216. *grosser issues* i.e. more palpable, more manifest, consequences. But I think the context invites or tempts the hearer to interpret *grosser* in the sense, "more brutally shocking." *reach* scope.
219. *fall into such vile success* have such an odious consequence.
221. *moved* because Othello thought Cassio was his "worthy friend" too.
222. *I . . . honest* A quite uncertain way to say "I can't believe that Desdemona's unchaste."

OTHELLO

And yet, how nature erring from itself—

IAGO

225   Ay, there's the point! as (to be bold with you)
Not to affect many proposèd matches
Of her own clime, complexion, and degree,
Whereto we see in all things nature tends—
Foh! one may smell in such a will most rank,
230   Foul disproportion, thoughts unnatural.—
But pardon me: I do not in position
Distinctly speak of her; though I may fear

---

229. **Foh! one** F.   Q has 'Fie we'.
229-30. **such a will most rank, / Foul** Q2.   F has 'such, a will most
        rank, / Foule'; Q has 'such a will, most ranke / Foule'.
230.   **disproportion** Q.   F has 'disporportions'.

224. *how . . . itself* This thought assumes man's corruptible
fallen nature; i.e. "I think her nature pure, yet given our natural
propensity to err from what our nature should be, she might indeed . . ."

225-35. *Ay . . . repent* Othello has just considered the improb-
able possibility that Desdemona's nature might have erred "from
itself" in adultery. Iago cleverly shifts the point, implying that Desdemona most clearly violated nature in marrying someone of another
nation, race, and degree—an action usually indicative (he says) of
abnormal lust. He then slyly concedes she might be the exception to
the rule: her choice of Othello might indicate only an error of
judgment and not *a will most rank*—an error which comparison of
him with *her country forms* may lead her to repent. He thus retreats
into the hardly less telling insinuation that her possible adultery with
Cassio would mark the return of her will *to her better judgment*, a
more "natural" one than she had followed in marrying someone so
alien as a Moorish "stranger" beneath her.

226. *affect*   care for, like, look with favor on.

227. *complexion*   color.   *degree*   rank (by birth).

229. *in . . . rank*   in such women (who act thus) a lust most hot
—*rank* literally meaning, "overly luxuriant."

230. *Foul disproportion*   filthy abnormality.

231-2. *in . . . her*   lay down a proposition meant particularly to
apply to her.

Her will, recoiling to her better judgment,

May fall to match you with her country forms,

235   And happily repent.

OTHELLO

Farewell, farewell!

If more thou dost perceive, let me know more;

Set on thy wife to observe.

Leave me, Iago.

IAGO

My lord, I take my leave.   [*Going.*]

OTHELLO

Why did I marry? This honest creature doubtless

240   Sees and knows more, much more, than he unfolds.

IAGO [*returning*]

My lord, I would I might entreat your honor

To scan this thing no further: leave it to time.

Although 'tis fit that Cassio have his place—

---

235.   **farewell** F. Not in Q.

238.   **S.D.** Rowe.

241.   **S.P.** F. Q corr. (state 3) places at head of line 242.   Not in Q
          uncorr. (states 1 and 2). **S.D.** Capell (*Returns*).
          As in F. Q prints as part of Oth.'s previous speech.

242.   **further** Q.   F has 'farther'.

243.   **Although 'tis** F. Q has 'Though it be'.

233. *will* here, virtually "carnal desire."   *recoiling* going back
to, reverting to.   *better* i.e. now no longer disproportioned.

234. *fall to match* (thereby) chance to compare.   *her country
forms* i.e. the external appearance of those of her own native
country.

235. *And happily repent* and so perhaps feel regret. But *happily*
of course can mean "fortunately," and *repent* can have the sense "be
repentant for that done against God's law." Ironically, an essential
part of repentance is "amendment of life."

243. *Although 'tis* The difference between the texts is a real one
in sense. Q's "Though it be" implicitly challenges the fitness of
Cassio's having his lieutenancy. The F reading, by assuming the
"fitness," shifts the ironic emphasis to the possible ambiguity in
"place." Honest Iago can argue the appropriateness of Cassio's
having his lieutenancy, and his undermeaning can applaud Cassio's
fitness and sufficiency as Desdemona's lover. The *double entendres*
which follow assume this undermeaning.

For sure he fills it up with great ability—
245   Yet if you please to hold him off awhile,
        You shall by that perceive him and his means.
        Note if your lady strain his entertainment
        With any strong or vehement importunity:
        Much will be seen in that. In the mean time,
250   Let me be thought too busy in my fears
        (As worthy cause I have to fear I am)
        And hold her free, I do beseech your honor.

OTHELLO

Fear not my government.

IAGO

I once more take my leave.   *Exit.*

OTHELLO

255   This fellow's of exceeding honesty,
        And knows all qualities, with a learned spirit
        Of human dealings. If I do prove her haggard,
        Though that her jesses were my dear heart-strings,

---

245. **hold** Q. Not in F.
247. **his** F. Q has 'her'.
254. **S.D.** F and Q corr. (states 2 and 3). Not in Q uncorr. (state 1).
256. **qualities** Q. F has 'Quantities'.
      learned F (learn'd). Q has 'learned'.
257. **dealings** F. Q has 'dealing'.

244–5. *fills it up . . . hold him off* straight-faced *double entendres.*

246. *his means* i.e. the methods he uses to achieve his reinstatement.

247. *strain his entertainment* press for his welcome, his recall to service.

250. *busy* busy-bodying.

252. *free* i.e. of guilt, innocent.

253. *government* discreet conduct—but the audience also hears in the Governor's word the ironic meaning, "self-control."

256. *qualities* natures.

257. *haggard* a wild hawk—i.e. an unfaithful woman.

258. *jesses* leather thongs for attaching a falcon's legs to its leash.

I'd whistle her off and let her down the wind

260   To prey at fortune. Haply, for I am black,

And have not those soft parts of conversation

That chamberers have, or for I am declined

Into the vale of years—yet that's not much—

She's gone; I am abused, and my relief

265   Must be to loathe her. O curse of marriage,

That we can call these delicate creatures ours,

And not their appetites! I had rather be a toad

And live upon the vapor of a dungeon

Than keep a corner in the thing I love

270   For others' uses. Yet 'tis the plague of great ones;

Prerogatived are they less than the base.

'Tis destiny unshunnable, like death:

Even then this forkèd plague is fated to us

When we do quicken.

---

260. **Haply** F. Q has 'Happily'.
262. **chamberers** F and Q corr. (state 3). Q uncorr. (states 1 and 2) has 'Chamlerers'.
263. **vale** F. Q has 'valt'.
268. **of** F. Q has 'in'.
269. **keep** F and Q corr. (states 2 and 3). Q uncorr. (state 1) has 'leepe'. **the** F. Q has 'a'.
270. **of** Q. F has 'to'.

259. *whistle her off* give her the falconer's signal of dismissal back to the wild—viz. divorce her.

259–60. *down . . . fortune* fly away and take such prey as fortune affords—(continuing the falcon metaphor). *Haply, for* perhaps, because.

261. *soft parts of conversation* facile and ingratiating manners in social intercourse.

262. *chamberers* bedroom-gallants.

264. *abused* deceived.

267. *toad* a type of the detestable.

270. *'tis . . . ones* i.e. wifely fidelity is not to be expected in high life.

271. *Prerogatived* exempt by privilege (from marital infidelity). *base* lowly.

273. *this forkèd plague* this plague of horns, alluding to those said to grow on the forehead of the husband of an unfaithful wife.

274. *do quicken* are born.

Enter DESDEMONA *and* EMILIA.

Look where she comes:

275 If she be false, O then heaven mocks itself!
I'll not believe't.

DESDEMONA

How now, my dear Othello?
Your dinner, and the generous islanders
By you invited, do attend your presence.

OTHELLO

I am to blame.

DESDEMONA

Why do you speak so faintly?

280 Are you not well?

OTHELLO

I have a pain upon my forehead, here.

DESDEMONA

Faith, that's with watching; 'twill away again.
Let me but bind it hard, within this hour
It will be well.

OTHELLO

Your napkin is too little;

---

274. **S.D.** F places after 'comes'; Q after 'believe't' line 276.
Look where she F. Q has '*Desdemona.*'
275. **O then heaven mocks** Q. F has 'Heauen mock'd.'
276. **believe't.** F. Q has 'beleeue it.'
277. **islanders** F. Q has 'Ilander'.
279. **to** Q. F has 'too'.
do . . . faintly? F. Q has 'is your speech so faint?'
282. **Faith** Q. F has 'Why'.
283. **it hard** F. Q has 'your head'.
284. **well** F. Q has 'well againe'.

275. *heaven mocks itself* by laughing to scorn its own beauty, purity, and truth, so convincingly represented in her fair appearance: "heaven must make a mockery of the heavenly if her inner nature and her beautiful appearance are at odds."

277. *generous* noble.

279. *to blame* at fault (to keep them waiting)—but with another implication for the audience.

281. *upon my forehead* secretly alluding to the "forkèd plague."

282. *watching* lack of sleep—with covert ironic implications.

284. *napkin* handkerchief.

285 Let it alone.   [*He pushes away her hand, and
                                        the handkerchief falls unnoticed.*]
       Come, I'll go in with you.

DESDEMONA

I am very sorry that you are not well.   *Exit* [*with* OTHELLO].

EMILIA

I am glad I have found this napkin:
This was her first remembrance from the Moor.
My wayward husband hath a hundred times
290 Wooed me to steal it; but she so loves the token
(For he so conjured her that she should ever keep it)
That she reserves it evermore about her
To kiss and talk to. I'll ha' the work ta'en out
And give't Iago. What he will do with it
295 Heaven knows, not I;
I nothing but to please his fantasy.
                    [*Re-*]*enter* IAGO.

IAGO

How now? What do you here alone?

EMILIA

Do not you chide; I have a thing for you.

---

285. **S.D.** Rowe (subst.).
286. **S.D.** F has '*Exit*.' after 'you' line 285; Q has '*Ex. Oth. and* Desd.'
        after 'napkin' line 287.
293. **to** Q. F has 'too'. **ha'** Q. F has 'haue'.
294. **he will** F. Q has 'hee'll'.
296. **but to please** F. Q has 'know, but for'.
        S.D. As in F. Q places after 'not I' line 295.

285. *it* i.e. my pained forehead (not the handkerchief).
288. *remembrance* keepsake. A presentation handkerchief was a
common Elizabethan token-gift at troth-plight; cf. lines 290–3.
289. *wayward* oddly-willed, unaccountable—usually in Shakespeare = "capricious."
293. *the work ta'en out* the embroidered pattern copied.
296. *I nothing* We can construe this to mean "I nothing am (to
him)" or (with the Quarto) "I nothing know." *fantasy* here,
evidently, "whim."

IAGO

A thing for me? it is a common thing—

EMILIA

300 Ha?

IAGO

—To have a foolish wife.

EMILIA

O, is that all? What will you give me now
For that same handkerchief?

IAGO

What handkerchief?

EMILIA

What handkerchief!
305 Why, that the Moor first gave to Desdemona,
That which so often you did bid me steal.

IAGO

Hast stole it from her?

EMILIA

No, faith; she let it drop by negligence,
And, to th'advantage, I being here, took't up:
310 Look, here it is.

IAGO

A good wench! give it me.

---

299. **A thing** Q. F has 'You haue a thing'.
300. **wife** F. Q has 'thing'.
303–4. **handkerchief** F. Q has 'handkercher' (as throughout).
307. **stole** Q. F has 'stolne'.
308. **faith** Q. F has 'but'.
309. **th'advantage** F. Q has 'the advantage'.
310. **it is** Q. F has ''tis'.

299. *a common thing* double entendre involving *common* in the sense "existing for the use of the public" and *thing* in the slang meaning "female pudenda."
309. *to th'advantage* as luck would have it, opportunely.
310. *wench* girl—often used familiarly without disagreeable implication.

EMILIA

What will you do with it, that you have been
So earnest to have me filch it?

IAGO

Why, what's that to you?

[*He snatches it.*]

EMILIA

If it be not for some purpose of import,
Give't me again. Poor lady, she'll run mad
315   When she shall lack it.

IAGO

Be not acknown on't; I have use for it.
Go, leave me.   *Exit* EMILIA.
I will in Cassio's lodging lose this napkin,
And let him find it. Trifles light as air
320   Are to the jealous confirmations strong
As proofs of Holy Writ: this may do something.
The Moor already changes with my poison:
Dangerous conceits are in their natures poisons
Which at the first are scarce found to distaste,
325   But, with a little act upon the blood,

311–12. Q. Prose in F.
311. **with it** Q. F has 'with't'.
312. **what's** Q. F has 'what is'. **S. D.** Rowe.
314. **Give't me** F. Q has 'Giue mee't'.
316. **acknown** F. Q has 'you knowne'.
317. **S.D.** F. Q places after 'napkin' line 318.
318. **lose** Q. F has 'loose'.
322. F. Not in Q.
325. **act upon** F. Q has 'art, vpon'.

313. *import* importance.
315. *lack* miss.
316. *Be not acknown on't* Don't confess you know anything about it. The meaning comes close (I think) to: "It'll be best if you just forget you know anything about it."
321. *proofs of Holy Writ* passages adduced from Scripture (to support a moral or theological proposition).
323. *conceits* conceptions, imaginings.
324. *distaste* taste bad.

Burn like the mines of sulphur.

Enter OTHELLO.

I did say so:

Look where he comes! Not poppy, nor mandragora,

Nor all the drowsy syrups of the world

Shall ever medicine thee to that sweet sleep

330   Which thou owedst yesterday.

OTHELLO

Ha! ha! false to me?

IAGO

Why, how now, general! no more of that.

OTHELLO

Avaunt! be gone! thou hast set me on the rack:

I swear 'tis better to be much abused

Than but to know't a little.

IAGO

How now, my lord?

OTHELLO

335   What sense had I of her stol'n hours of lust?

I saw't not, thought it not, it harmed not me:

---

326.   **mines** F.   Q has 'mindes'.
    S.D. Q places after 'blood' line 325, F after 'so' line 326.
330.   **owedst** Q.   F has 'owd'st'.   **to me?** F.   Q has 'to me, to me?'
334.   **know't** F.   Q has 'know'.
335.   **of her** Q.   F has 'in her'.
336.   **not, it** Q.   F has 'not: it'.   **me:** F.   Q has 'me,'.

326. *the mines of sulphur*   alluding to the famed sulphur mines in the Aeolian Islands between Italy and Sicily (Pliny, *Natural History*).

327. *poppy*   opium.   *mandragora*   mandrake, a soporific medicine.

330. *owedst*   didst own, didst enjoy.   *Ha! ha! false to me?*   to himself though, ironically, in Iago's presence—"to be throttled down in the speaking, not rung out clear" (Granville-Barker).

332. *Avaunt*   "exclamation of . . . abhorrence, uttered to drive one away." (Schmidt). It is, ironically, later applied to Desdemona (IV. i. 243).   *the rack*   a torture machine which unbearably stretches the limbs.

333. *much abused*   so well deceived you suspect nothing.

335. *sense*   awareness—literally, "feeling."

I slept the next night well, fed well, was free and merry;
I found not Cassio's kisses on her lips.
He that is robbed, not wanting what is stol'n,
340   Let him not know't, and he's not robbed at all.

IAGO

I am sorry to hear this.

OTHELLO

I had been happy if the general camp,
Pioners and all, had tasted her sweet body,
So I had nothing known. O now, for ever
345   Farewell the tranquil mind, farewell content!
Farewell the plumèd troop, and the big wars
That makes ambition virtue! O, farewell!
Farewell the neighing steed and the shrill trump,
The spirit-stirring drum, th' ear-piercing fife,
350   The royal banner, and all quality,
Pride, pomp, and circumstance of glorious war!
And O ye mortal engines, whose rude throats

---

337.   **fed well** F. Not in Q. **merry;** Q. F has 'merrie.'
346.   **troop** Q. F has 'Troopes'.
349.   **th'ear-piercing** F. Q has 'the eare-peircing'.
352.   **ye** Q. F has 'you'. **rude** F. Q has 'wide'.

342.   *the general camp*   the camp at large.
343.   *Pioners*   pioneers—i.e. sappers, the lowest order of soldier, used merely for manual labor. Pronounced *píoners.*
347.   *That makes ambition virtue*   The Elizabethans often regarded *ambition* a dangerous vice, overweening, unlawful, disordering. Othello is saying that "glorious war" transmutes its meaning.
349.   *spirit-stirring . . . fife*   These instruments here carry the ancient ethical implication of Dorian music, which was supposed to make men disciplined, brave, and martial. *Spirit-stirring* and *ear-piercing* (cf. *Merchant of Venice* V. i. 67–8) are commonplace terms in treatises on music referring to the "penetrative power of music" by which the soul is reached and "drawn": i.e. in Elizabethan physiology, by way of the senses and the intermediary between the senses and the phantasy, the "spirits."
350.   *quality*   the nature (specified in "Pride, pomp, and circumstance").
351.   *circumstance*   magnificent ceremony, pageantry. *glorious* worthy of praise and famous.
352.   *mortal engines*   deadly artillery.

Th' immortal Jove's dread clamors counterfeit,
Farewell! Othello's occupation's gone!

IAGO

355   Is't possible, my lord?

OTHELLO

Villain, be sure thou prove my love a whore!
Be sure of it; give me the ocular proof;
Or, by the worth of mine eternal soul,   [*He seizes him.*]
Thou hadst been better have been born a dog
360   Than answer my waked wrath!

IAGO

Is't come to this?

---

353. **Th'immortal** F. Q has 'The immortall'. **dread clamors** F. Q
       has 'great clamor'.
356. **thou** F and Q corr. (state 3). Q uncorr. (states 1 and 2) has
       'you'.
358. **mine** F. Q has 'mans'.

353. *Th'immortal Jove's dread clamors* God's awful thunders (of
judgment)—literally, those of Jupiter Tonans, the thunder god.
counterfeit imitate. The Elizabethans most often consider war
glorious when it is "justly" waged "in God's name" and for His
cause; (cf. Richmond's prayer in *Richard III* V. iii. 109–14: "Look on
my forces with a gracious eye./ Put in their hands thy bruising irons
of wrath,/ . . . Make us thy ministers of chastisement"). Such an
army's artillery makes a proper likeness of God's judgmental
thunders by being the minister of His will. However, the danger of
erroneously supposing any particular strife to be carried on "in God's
name" is hinted through the other sense of *counterfeit*, "to make a
deceitful imitation, a forgery."
356. *prove* emphatic.
358. *S.D.* Although a few editors demur (e.g. Kittredge), editorial
tradition since Rowe, and stage practice since the eighteenth century
at least, have called for physical gesture to underscore the threats to
Iago issuing from Othello's "waked wrath." It is variously placed—
e.g. at line 357 (Rowe, Capell), line 360 (Kean), or line 365 (Booth).

OTHELLO

Make me to see't, or at the least so prove it
That the probation bear no hinge nor loop
To hang a doubt on—or woe upon thy life!

IAGO

My noble lord—

OTHELLO

365 If thou dost slander her and torture me,
Never pray more; abandon all remorse;
On horror's head horrors accumulate;
Do deeds to make heaven weep, all earth amazed:
For nothing canst thou to damnation add
370 Greater than that!

IAGO

O grace! O heaven forgive me!
Are you a man? have you a soul? or sense?
God buy you! take mine office. —O wretched fool,

---

367. **accumulate** F. Q has 'accumilate'.
370. **forgive** F. Q has 'defend'.
371. **a soul? or sense?** F. Q has 'a soule or sence?'
372. **God buy you** F and Q corr. (states 2 and 3). Q uncorr. (state 1)
has 'God buy, you'. **mine** F and Q corr. (state 3). Q uncorr.
(states 1 and 2) has 'thine'.

362. *probation*   proof.

362–3. *bear . . . on*   The general sense has seemed clearer than
the passion-compressed specific imagery. I think this means Othello
wants a proof solid and complete, bearing no *hinge* to be turned or
moved on, no *loop*-hole by which it could be penetrated—smooth
wholeness, without anything, qualifying addition or built-in insufficiency, to hang a motive for disbelief upon.

366. *Never pray more*   for you have committed so ultimate a sin
that it is incapable of pardon and there could be no further sin to fore-
stall. Cf. *Hamlet* III. iii. 48–50: "And what's in prayer but this two-
fold force,/ To be forestalled ere we come to fall,/ Or pardon'd being
down?"   *remorse*   humane feeling, compassion.

368. *all earth amazed*   all mankind utterly perplexed with horror.

371. *have . . . sense?*   with bitter sarcasm, following upon "Are
you a man?"—"Do you have a rational *soul*, which distinguishes
man? or only *sense*, the sensitive soul of the beast?"

372–4. *O . . . world!*   playing ironically upon the proverb "The
World is so much Knave, that it holds Honesty to be a Vice and
Folly" (Fuller, 4843).

That liv'st to make thine honesty a vice!

O monstrous world! Take note, take note, O world,

375 To be direct and honest is not safe. —

I thank you for this profit, and from hence

I'll love no friend sith love breeds such offense.   [*Going.*]

OTHELLO

Nay, stay; thou shouldst be honest.

IAGO

I should be wise; for honesty's a fool,

380 And loses that it works for.

---

373. **liv'st.** Pope.   Q has 'liuest'; F has 'lou'st'.   **thine** F and Q corr.
    (state 3).   Q uncorr. (states 1 and 2) has 'mine'.
377. **sith** F.   Q has 'since'.

373. *That . . . vice   Vice* can mean "a fault, a dangerous weakness," thus linking it with "To be direct and honest is not safe." But Shakespeare normally uses the word to mean "a sin," a sense demanded by "O heaven forgive me!" Iago's open (and to the audience also covertly ironic) point is that he has lived to make his honesty a vice requiring God's pardon by placing the significance of his directness in the reactions of a brutally irrational, distrustful, and inappreciative Othello. A similar double meaning can be seen in "offense" (line 377).

376. *profit*   profitable lesson—said with the bitter irony of the unrewarded, outraged honest man.

377. *sith*   since.   *offense*   i.e. "injury" to the lover; but the word can also mean "sin." The rhyme with "hence" (line 376) suggests the couplet conventionally used to close a scene ending a sequence of action, as, e.g., at I. ii. 98–9, II. iii. 355–6.

378. That Othello (as Iago goes) hesitates before speaking this is suggested by the metrical shortness of the line.   *shouldst* "used in the peculiar sense in which we sometimes use *ought:* 'You ought to be honest if there is any trust to be put in appearances and reputation'" (Kittredge). As with "Nay, stay" (i.e. in spite of my violent outburst), the tone comes close to grudgingly contrite admission. Iago, however, picks up Othello's *shouldst* as though he had meant "you have a duty to be honest in spite of the risks and dangers."

380. *that it works for*   i.e. trust, and the rewards trust deserves.

OTHELLO

By the world,
I think my wife be honest, and think she is not;
I think that thou art just, and think thou art not.
I'll have some proof! My name, that was as fresh
As Dian's visage, is now begrimed and black
385   As mine own face. If there be cords, or knives,
Poison, or fire, or suffocating streams,
I'll not endure it. Would I were satisfied!

IAGO [*returning*]

I see, sir, you are eaten up with passion.
I do repent me that I put it to you.
390   You would be satisfied?

OTHELLO

Would? Nay, I will!

380–7. **OTHELLO By . . . satisfied.** F. Not in Q.
383. **My** F. Q2 has 'her'.
388. **sir** Q. Not in F.
390. **satisfied?** F. Q has 'satisfied.' **I** Q. F has 'and I'.

380. *By the world* ironic, in view of the Elizabethan Christian and gnomic ideas of the "world": "He that trusts to the World is sure to be deceived." (Tilley, W871) .
381. *honest* chaste. This word and "not" are emphatic.
382. *just* upright, honest—ironic, since the immediate problem is not whether Iago is upright, but whether his insinuation is "just," i.e. right, true, founded in fact.
383. *My name* the QF reading. Many editors emend with that of Q2, "Her"—which makes good, if very different, sense but has no authority. However, Othello's outraged preoccupation is with his own dirtied honor. "As Dian's visage," which goes so easily with "Her" (and may have suggested it), has in dramatic context a complex ironic force with *My*. *fresh* unsullied.
384. *Dian's* of Diana, the maiden goddess of chastity and the moon.
385–6. *cords . . . streams* This catalogue violently brings images suggesting suicidal desperation together with those of torture (to extort truth) and those of revenge and punishment (of proven guilt).
387. *were satisfied* freed from doubt and uncertainty—(one way or the other).
389. *put it* imparted this doubt.

IAGO

And may; but how? how satisfied, my lord?
Would you, the supervisor, grossly gape on—
Behold her topped?

OTHELLO

Death and damnation! O!

IAGO

It were a tedious difficulty, I think,
395 To bring 'em to that prospect. Damn 'em then,
If ever mortal eyes do see them bolster
More than their own! What then? how then?
What shall I say? Where's satisfaction?
It is impossible you should see this,
400 Were they as prime as goats, as hot as monkeys,
As salt as wolves in pride, and fools as gross
As ignorance made drunk. But yet, I say,
If imputation and strong circumstances
Which lead directly to the door of truth
405 Will give you satisfaction, you might have't.

---

392. **you, the supervisor,** Q (superuisor). F has 'you the supervision'.
393. **topped** F (top'd). Q has 'topt.'
395. **'em . . . 'em** Q. F has 'them . . . them'.
396. **do** F. Q has 'did'.
405. **might have't** F. Q has 'may ha't'.

392. *supervisor* spectator. *gape* stare open-mouthed.
396. *bolster* "make a bolster, by lying one under the other"
(Schmidt).
398. *satisfaction* evidence which would free you from doubt. But
given the issue so closely touching Othello's honor, the word already
perhaps tempts the hearer to anticipate the meaning "amends for an
injury."
400–1. *prime . . . hot . . . salt . . . in pride* all synonyms for
"lecherous," "on heat."
403. *imputation and strong circumstances* "opinion founded on
strong circumstantial evidence" (Schmidt)—hendiadys.
404. *the door of truth* where you must cross the threshold by
drawing an inference. Ridley suggests "the slightest of pauses after
door; Othello is led in imagination to stand outside the closed bedroom door."

OTHELLO

Give me a living reason she's disloyal.

IAGO

I do not like the office;
But sith I am entered in this cause so far,
Pricked to't by foolish honesty and love,
410 I will go on. I lay with Cassio lately,
And being troubled with a raging tooth,
I could not sleep.
There are a kind of men so loose of soul
That in their sleeps will mutter their affairs.
415 One of this kind is Cassio.
In sleep I heard him say, "Sweet Desdemona,
Let us be wary, let us hide our loves."
And then, sir, would he gripe and wring my hand,
Cry "O sweet creature!" and then kiss me hard,
420 As if he plucked up kisses by the roots
That grew upon my lips; then laid his leg
Over my thigh, and sighed, and kissed, and then
Cried "Cursèd fate that gave thee to the Moor!"

OTHELLO

O monstrous! monstrous!

IAGO

Nay, this was but his dream.

---

406.   **reason** F. Q has 'reason, that'.
408.   **in** F. Q has 'into'.
417.   **wary** F. Q has 'merry'.
419.   **Cry "O** F (Cry, oh). Q has 'Cry, out,'. **and** Q. Not in F.
421.   **then** Q. Not in F.
422.   **Over** Q. F has 'ore'.
422-3. **sighed . . . kissed . . . Cried** Q.   F has 'sigh . . . kisse
            . . . cry'.

406. *a living reason she's* an evidence drawn from actual living
deeds that she is.
408. *sith*   since.

OTHELLO

425   But this denoted a foregone conclusion!

IAGO

'Tis a shrewd doubt, though it be but a dream;
And this may help to thicken other proofs
That do demonstrate thinly.

OTHELLO

I'll tear her all to pieces!

IAGO

Nay, but be wise: yet we see nothing done;
430   She may be honest yet. Tell me but this:
Have you not sometimes seen a handkerchief
Spotted with strawberries in your wife's hand?

OTHELLO

I gave her such a one: 'twas my first gift.

---

425. **denoted** F. Q has 'deuoted'.
426. **IAGO 'Tis . . . dream;** Q (dreame,). F ('Tis . . . Dreame.)
      gives the line to Othello.
427. Q. F starts Iago's speech here.
429. **but** Q. F has 'yet'.

425. *foregone conclusion* previous consummation (of the affair).
(The phrase has become an idiom in a sense utterly different from
Shakespeare's.)

426. *a shrewd doubt* a telling suspicion, cursedly suspicious. I
think Q correctly assigns this line to Iago, who, at this stage of the
temptation, ironically can afford to raise the reservations and have
Othello be the one to challenge them.

432. *Spotted with strawberries* i.e. embroidered with a pattern of
the fruit, flowers, or leaves of the strawberry plant, a common subject
of Elizabethan domestic embroidery. *Spotted* is an equivoke (cf.
V. i. 36)—not merely "decorated with spots" but *spotted* as Desdemona in Othello's eyes is now "morally stained" (OED). In
commonplace symbolism the strawberry enjoyed an ambivalent
significance. It could be emblematic of an attractive, but only seeming,
good whose real perniciousness is hidden—and thus applied to the
hypocrite, the beautiful but corrupt woman, or the objects of concupiscent desire (see above, p. xi, fig. c). It could also stand for a
genuine good, and be an emblem of the righteous human being who
bears the "fruit of the Spirit" and (like the Virgin, with whom the
strawberry is often associated) brings forth "the fruit of righteousness."

IAGO

I know not that; but such a handkerchief—
435 I am sure it was your wife's—did I today
See Cassio wipe his beard with.

OTHELLO

If't be that—

IAGO

If it be that, or any that was hers,
It speaks against her with the other proofs.

OTHELLO

O that the slave had forty thousand lives!
440 One is too poor, too weak for my revenge.
Now do I see 'tis true. Look here, Iago:
All my fond love thus do I blow to heaven—
'Tis gone.
Arise, black vengeance, from the hollow hell!

---

436. **If't** Q. F has 'If it'.
437. **any that** Malone. QF have 'any, it'.
441. **true** F. Q has 'time'.
444. **the hollow hell** F. Q has 'thy hollow cell'.

434. *I know not that*   I don't know anything about that.

437. *any that*   An argument could be made for the QF reading (with Q's end comma: "any it was hers,") by interpreting: "any something whatever that belongs to her"; but this seems strained in view of the ease with which "y$^{t'}$" (= that) in Elizabethan handwriting can be misread "yt" (= it).

439. *the slave*   i.e. Cassio.

442. *my fond love*   Given his gesture—blowing his love toward the "heavens"—*fond* means not only "foolish," "doting," but also "not worth considering," "insubstantial." For Othello, the phrase dismisses his love because of the unworthiness of its object; but the audience may ironically apply it to his love itself.

442–4. *heaven . . . hell*   The contrast, enforced by gesture, sharply evokes conventional symbolic values of parts of the Elizabethan public theater—the "heavens" over the actor and the "hell" beneath his feet. Othello stages a symbolic drama of the occurrence in his being.

444. *the hollow hell*   the infernal abyss—because vengeance is God's (Deuteronomy 32: 35) and vengeful feelings must be hell-inspired.

445   Yield up, O love, thy crown and hearted throne
       To tyrannous hate! Swell, bosom, with thy fraught,
       For 'tis of aspics' tongues!

IAGO

Yet be content.

OTHELLO

O blood, blood, blood!

IAGO

Patience, I say; your mind perhaps may change.

OTHELLO

450   Never, Iago. Like to the Pontic sea,
       Whose icy current and compulsive course

---

447. **Yet** F. Q has 'Pray'.
448. **O blood, blood, blood!** F (blood.). Q has 'O blood, *Iago*,
      blood.'
449. **perhaps** Q. Not in F.
450. **Never, Iago.** F (Neuer *Iago*.). Q has 'Neuer:'.
450–7. **Like . . . heaven,** F. Not in Q.

445. *hearted throne*   throne in the heart, whose legitimate ruler,
the fulfiller of the divine law, is love. Cf. Leviticus 19: 17, "Thou
shalt not hate thy brother in thy heart." Also, e.g., 1 Thessalonians
3: 12–13.

446. *tyrannous*   This includes the implications: cruel and usurping.
fraught   freight, burden (of poison).

447. *aspics' tongues*   tongues of asps—ironic because conventionally used in descriptions and personifications of slander: "They have
sharpened their tongues like a serpent: Adders poison is under their
lips" (Psalm 140: 3). Cf. *Cymbeline* (III. iv. 31–3) regarding
"Viperous slander": "whose tongue/ Out-venoms all the worms of
Nile."

448. *O blood, blood, blood!*   primarily, an oath and a cry for
blood-vengeance, but alluding as well to Desdemona's supposed "lust
of the blood" and also ironic in the light of the arousal, at Iago's
hands, of "the blood and baseness" of his own nature.

449. *Patience*   be patient—in Iago's reductive use, little more than
"wait, hold on." But if precisely, and therefore ironically, taken, it is
the exact Christian virtue requisite in Othello's presently vengeful
state of mind.   *your . . . change*   To a general this is a temptation
to confirm his decision, not change it.

450. *the Pontic sea*   the Black Sea.

451. *compulsive*   irresistible and headlong.

Ne'er feels retiring ebb, but keeps due on
To the Propontic and the Hellespont,
Even so my bloody thoughts, with violent pace,
455   Shall ne'er look back, ne'er ebb to humble love,
Till that a capable and wide revenge
Swallow them up. (*He kneels*.)   Now, by yond marble heaven,
In the due reverence of a sacred vow,
I here engage my words.

IAGO

Do not rise yet.   IAGO *kneels.*

460   Witness, you ever-burning lights above,
You elements that clip us round about,
Witness that here Iago doth give up
The execution of his wit, hands, heart
To wronged Othello's service! Let him command,
465   And to obey shall be in me remorse,
What bloody business ever.   [*They rise.*]

---

452.   **feels** Q2.   F has 'keepes'.
457.   **S.D.** Q corr. (but placed after 'content' line 447).   Not in F.
459.   **S.D.** Q (but placed after 'about,' line 461).   Not in F.
463.   **execution** F.   Q has 'excellency'.   **hands** F.   Q has 'hand'.
465.   **in me** F.   Not in Q.
466.   **business ever** F.   Q has 'worke so euer'.   **S.D.** Capell (*Rising*).

453. *the Propontic and the Hellespont*   viz. the Sea of Marmora and the Bosporus.

456. *capable*   capacious, comprehensive.

457. *by yond marble heaven*   The immediate reference is to the "radiant roof" of heaven (cf. *Cymbeline* V. iv. 120–1) symbolized by "the heavens" of Shakespeare's theater. For Shakespeare *marble* was emblematic of hardness, wholeness, permanency, and unyielding rigidity—particularly before claims on the emotions. Othello thus lays claim in his vow to a likeness between his resolution and the nature of "heaven." The proverbial connection of *marble* with the obdurate inflexibility of the unforgiving spirit, however, makes the vow dramatically ironic, contrasting the hero's vengeful will both with Heaven's mercy and with its condemnation of private vengeance.

459. *engage*   solemnly pledge.

461. *clip*   embrace.

463. *The execution of*   all that can be done by.   *wit*   intellect.

465. *shall be in me remorse*   shall (implied: as it must) take the place of human compassion in me—heightening the straightfaced parody of Othello's oath.

OTHELLO

I greet thy love,
Not with vain thanks, but with acceptance bounteous,
And will upon the instant put thee to't:
Within these three days let me hear thee say
470 That Cassio's not alive.

IAGO

My friend is dead;
'Tis done at your request. But let her live.

OTHELLO

Damn her, lewd minx! O damn her! damn her!
Come, go with me apart. I will withdraw
To furnish me with some swift means of death
475 For the fair devil. Now art thou my lieutenant.

IAGO

I am your own for ever.   *Exeunt.*

---

471. **at your** F. Q has 'as you'.
472. **O damn her! damn her!** F (her, damne her.). Q has 'O dam
      her,'.

467. *acceptance bounteous* generous, wholehearted acceptance—
i.e. "better than empty thanks is an acceptance which makes immediate use of the gift." (Ridley).

468. *put thee to't* put you to the proof, the test.

476. *I . . . for ever* confirming the dreadful parody of the kneeling "marriage" vow that has been performed (cf. "I greet thy love"
line 466). The "sacred vow" at marriage often was cited as the
definitive example of the "lawful oath"—whereas, of course, "It is a
great sin to swear unto a sin/ . . . Who can be bound by any
solemn vow/ To do a murd'rous deed?" (2 *Henry VI* V. i. 182–5).
The Christian who by infidelity turns back from God to sinfulness is
said to violate the "marriage" between his regenerate soul and the
Spirit of God, and revert to the marriage between his fallen nature
and Sin or the Devil. See, for a basic text, Romans 7: 2–6.

[*Scene iv.*] *Enter* DESDEMONA, EMILIA, *and Clown.*

DESDEMONA

Do you know, sirrah, where the Lieutenant Cassio lies?

CLOWN

I dare not say he lies anywhere.

DESDEMONA

Why, man?

CLOWN

He's a soldier; and for one to say a soldier lies, 'tis stabbing.

DESDEMONA

5   Go to. Where lodges he?

CLOWN

To tell you where he lodges, is to tell you where I lie.

DESDEMONA

Can anything be made of this?

CLOWN

I know not where he lodges; and for me to devise a lodging,
and say he lies here or he lies there, were to lie in mine own
10   throat.

III. iv   1.   **the** Q.   Not in F.
4.   **CLOWN He's** F.   Q has 'He is' without S.P. **one** Q.   F has 'me'.
'tis F.   Q has 'is'.
6–7.   F.   Not in Q.
9.   **here or he** F.   Not in Q. **mine own** F.   Q has 'my'.

III. iv   There is no interval after III. iii: lines 14–15, 18, 27–8
indicate the continuity of time. The scene, as regards locale, is a
so-called "split" one. The place is nowhere specified, only implied
by character and action. Thus, although much of the dialogue seems
to assume an "interior" and private setting, there is no discrepancy
created when Cassio is told to "walk hereabout" (line 156) and Bianca
enters "going to [Cassio's] lodging" (line 163).

1.   *sirrah*   a form of "sir" ordinarily used in addressing inferiors.
lies   lodges.

5.   *Go to*   here an interjectional phrase of protest or impatience.
9–10.   *lie . . . throat*   i.e. tell a deep deliberate lie.

DESDEMONA

Can you inquire him out, and be edified by report?

CLOWN

I will catechize the world for him, that is, make questions, and
by them answer.

DESDEMONA

Seek him, bid him come hither. Tell him I have moved my lord
15   on his behalf, and hope all will be well.

CLOWN

To do this is within the compass of man's wit, and therefore
I'll attempt the doing of it.   *Exit.*

DESDEMONA

Where should I lose that handkerchief, Emilia.

EMILIA

I know not, madam.

DESDEMONA

20   Believe me, I had rather lose my purse
Full of crusadoes; and but my noble Moor
Is true of mind, and made of no such baseness
As jealous creatures are, it were enough
To put him to ill thinking.

EMILIA

Is he not jealous?

12–13.   F.   Divided as though verse in Q.
15.   **on** F.   Q has 'in'.
16.   **man's wit** F.   Q has 'a man'.
17.   **I'll** Q.   F has 'I will'.   **of** Q.   Not in F.
18.   **that** Q.   F has 'the'.
20.   **lose** Q (loose).   F has 'haue lost'.

11.   *edified*   instructed.
14.   *moved*   spoken to, urged—but the audience hears the ironic
undermeaning, "angered."
16.   *compass*   range, scope.
21.   *crusadoes*   Portuguese gold coins, stamped with a cross, current in Elizabethan England at a value of three shillings.

DESDEMONA

25 Who? he! I think the sun where he was born
Drew all such humors from him.

Enter OTHELLO.

EMILIA

Look where he comes.

DESDEMONA

I will not leave him now till Cassio
Be called to him. —How is't with you, my lord?

OTHELLO

Well, my good lady. [*Aside*] O, hardness to dissemble! —
30 How do you, Desdemona?

DESDEMONA

Well, my good lord.

OTHELLO

Give me your hand. This hand is moist, my lady.

DESDEMONA

It yet hath felt no age nor known no sorrow.

---

26. **S.D.** Q. F places after 'comes.'
27. **till** F. Q corr. (states 2 and 3) has 'Let'. Q uncorr. (state 1) has 'Tis'.
28. **is't** F. Q has 'is it'.
29. **S.D.** Hanmer. Not in QF.
32. **yet** Q. Not in F. **hath** F. Q has 'has'.

26. *humors* morbid fluids responsible for such a disposition. In the old physiology, the relative proportions of the principal fluids in the body were believed to determine mental as well as physical qualities. Ironically, Desdemona's supposition about the relation of torrid climate and jealousy directly contradicts general Elizabethan opinion. Yet her view does remind us that Othello is by no means jealous "by nature."

27. *till* Q's reading ("Let"), which appears a command to Emilia, must be a miscorrection of a transcriber's error since she is given no exit. Her silent presence throughout the whole of Desdemona and Othello's long dialogue (lines 28–88) is required by the text (line 89) and crucial to the scene's dramatic effect.

29. *hardness* difficulty—with a glance (remembering I. iii. 230) at the sense "hardship, adversity."

31. *moist* A moist palm was taken to be an indication of eager sexuality, fertility, and youth.

OTHELLO

This argues fruitfulness and liberal heart:
Hot, hot and moist. This hand of yours requires

35   A sequester from liberty, fasting and prayer,
Much castigation, exercise devout;
For here's a young and sweating devil here
That commonly rebels. 'Tis a good hand,
A frank one.

DESDEMONA

You may indeed say so;

40   For 'twas that hand that gave away my heart.

OTHELLO

A liberal hand! The hearts of old gave hands;
But our new heraldry is hands, not hearts.

DESDEMONA

I cannot speak of this. Come now, your promise!

---

34. **Hot, hot** F.   Q has 'Not hot'.
35. **prayer** F.   Q has 'praying'.
43. **now** F.   Q has 'come'.

33. *liberal*   free, but implying the sense "licentious."
34. *hot and moist*   the qualities of "Venus" and a sign of youth.
35–6. *sequester . . . devout*   all of these are means to bring down and mortify the "Flesh."
35. *sequester*   confinement, retirement. The first syllable is accented.
36. *castigation*   severe self-discipline, chastening.   *exercise* in the special religious sense—religious devotion, prayer, and meditation.
37. *devil*   Cupid or the Flesh—i.e. the spirit of sensual lust.
39. *frank*   liberal, bounteous (repeating the point of "liberal," line 33), but perhaps also touching on the sense "candid." Desdemona (lines 39–40) takes it up in the sense "generous."
41. *liberal*   free, again with the punning sense "too free": "Yes, you give your heart away with a free hand."
42. *our . . . hearts*   the heraldic symbol (coat of arms) appropriate to marriage nowadays is joined hands, but without the heart in it. Some commentators see an allusion to the coat of arms of a new order of baronetage instituted by James in 1612—which would make this line a late, and most inartistic, interpolation. But *heraldry* is figurative and hearts-hands symbolism is commonplace. Cf. *Tempest* III. i. 89–90.

OTHELLO

What promise, chuck?

DESDEMONA

45   I have sent to bid Cassio come speak with you.

OTHELLO

I have a salt and sorry rheum offends me;
Lend me thy handkerchief.

DESDEMONA

Here, my lord.

OTHELLO

That which I gave you.

DESDEMONA

I have it not about me.

OTHELLO

Not?

DESDEMONA

No, faith, my lord.

OTHELLO

That's a fault. That handkerchief

50   Did an Egyptian to my mother give.
She was a charmer, and could almost read
The thoughts of people. She told her, while she kept it,

---

46.   **sorry** F.   Q has 'sullen'.
49.   **Not?** F.   Q has 'Not.' **faith** Q.   F has 'indeed'.
       fault F.   Q has 'fauit'.

44. *chuck*   chick, a common term of endearment.
46. *a . . . me*   a wretched running head-cold that pains me.
Salt rheum is a running cold. However, *salt* can mean "lecherous,"
sorry, "exciting sorrow or sadness," and *offends me,* "wrongs me."
Cf. "I have a pain upon my forehead, here" (III. iii. 281). Q's "sullen"
means "dismal."

50. *an Egyptian*   i.e. a gypsy sorceress. The gypsies were supposed to have come from Egypt. Cf. *Antony and Cleopatra* I. i. 10.
Egypt, for the Elizabethans, often was associated with spiritual bondage as well as with mystery.

51. *charmer*   sorceress, a witch who practices with black magical
"charms."

'Twould make her amiable and subdue my father
Entirely to her love; but if she lost it,

55   Or made a gift of it, my father's eye
Should hold her loathly, and his spirits should hunt
After new fancies. She dying gave it me,
And bid me, when my fate would have me wive,
To give it her. I did so; and take heed on't:

60   Make it a darling like your precious eye;
To lose't, or give't away, were such perdition
As nothing else could match.

DESDEMONA

Is't possible?

OTHELLO

'Tis true: there's magic in the web of it.
A sybil that had numbered in the world

65   The sun to course two hundred compasses
In her prophetic fury sewed the work;
The worms were hallowed that did breed the silk;
And it was died in mummy which the skillful
Conserved of maidens' hearts.

DESDEMONA

I' faith, is't true?

---

56.   **loathly** Q (lothely).   F has 'loathed'.
58.   **wive** Q.   F has 'Wiu'd'.
61.   **lose't** F (loose't).   Q has 'loose'.
65.   **course** F.   Q has 'make'.
68.   **which** F.   Q has 'with'.
69.   **Conserved** F.   Q has 'Conserues'.   **I'faith** Q.   F has 'Indeed'.

53.   *amiable*   desirable (stronger than in modern usage).

60.   *your precious eye*   with (I think) a clear *double entendre*; cf. *Measure for Measure* I. ii. 104.

61.   *such perdition*   such a disastrous loss. "As nothing else could match" (line 62) brings the idea of "perdition of the soul" into play.

64.   *sybil*   prophetess.

65.   *compasses*   yearly circuits.

66.   *fury*   afflatus, inspiration.

68.   *mummy*   liquor derived from embalmed bodies and used for magical and medicinal purposes.

69.   *Conserved of*   made into a conserve, a preparation, from.

OTHELLO

70   Most veritable; therefore look to't well.

DESDEMONA

Then would to God that I had never seen it!

OTHELLO

Ha! wherefore?

DESDEMONA

Why do you speak so startingly and rash?

OTHELLO

Is't lost? is't gone? Speak! is't out o' the way?

DESDEMONA

Heaven bless us!

OTHELLO

Say you?

DESDEMONA

75   It is not lost; but what an' if it were?

OTHELLO

How!

DESDEMONA

I say it is not lost.

OTHELLO

Fetch't, let me see't.

DESDEMONA

Why, so I can, sir; but I will not now.
This is a trick to put me from my suit:
80   Pray you let Cassio be received again.

---

71. **God . . . seen it** Q.   F has 'Heauen . . . seene't'.
72. **rash** F.   Q has 'rashly'.
73. **is't out** F.   Q has 'is it out'.   **o' the** Q.   F has 'o'th' '.
74. **Heaven** Q.   Not in F.
75. **an'** Theobald.   QF have 'and'.
76. **How** F.   Q has 'Ha'.
77. **see't** F.   Q has 'see it'.
78. **sir** Q.   Not in F.
80. **Pray you** F.   Q has 'I pray'.

72. *startingly and rash*   abruptly, by starts, and urgently.
75. *an' if*   if indeed.

OTHELLO

Fetch me the handkerchief! my mind misgives.

DESDEMONA

Come, come; you'll never meet a more sufficient man.

OTHELLO

The handkerchief!

DESDEMONA

I pray talk me of Cassio—

OTHELLO

The handkerchief!

DESDEMONA

—A man that all his time

85 Hath founded his good fortunes on your love,
Shared dangers with you—

OTHELLO

The handkerchief!

DESDEMONA

I' faith, you are too blame.

OTHELLO

'Zounds!   *Exit.*

EMILIA

Is not this man jealous?

DESDEMONA

90 I ne'er saw this before.
Sure there's some wonder in this handkerchief;

---

81. **the** F. Q has 'that'.
83–4. **I . . . handkerchief** Q. Not in F.
87. **I'faith** Q. F has 'Insooth'. **too blame** QF.
88. **'Zounds** Q. F has 'Away'.

82. *sufficient* fit, able—a word Othello can hear with a tainted sense.
87. *too blame* blameworthy (for speaking thus to me). But again, as in their last interview (III. iii. 279), the audience is allowed a deeper implication. The QF reading (often emended, "to blame") is a Renaissance idiom in which what was historically a dative infinitive was misconstrued and "blame" taken as an adjective.

I am most unhappy in the loss of it.

> *Enter* IAGO *and* CASSIO, [*at a distance.*]

EMILIA

'Tis not a year or two shows us a man.
They are all but stomachs, and we all but food:
95   They eat us hungerly, and when they are full
They belch us. Look you: Cassio and my husband.

IAGO

There is no other way; 'tis she must do't.
And lo, the happiness! Go and importune her.

DESDEMONA

How now, good Cassio? What's the news with you?

CASSIO

100   Madam, my former suit. I do beseech you
That by your virtuous means I may again
Exist, and be a member of his love
Whom I with all the office of my heart
Entirely honor. I would not be delayed.
105   If my offense be of such mortal kind

---

92. **the loss of it.** F. Q uncorr. has 'this losse.' Q corr. has 'the losse.' **S.D.** as in Q. F places after 'belch us' line 96.
97. **do't** F (doo't). Q has 'doe it'.
103. **office** F. Q has 'duty'.

94. *are all but* are all only (not "are almost").
98. *happiness* good luck. *importune* accented on second syllable.
101. *by your virtuous means* by your powerful (and thus, "efficacious") help. In Cassio's elaborate way of speaking, this could also mean "by means of you, virtuous madam."
101–12. *I . . . alms* Cassio expresses his petition in terms drawn, for emphasis, from the situation of the repentant soul. To "be a member of [God's] love" is to "exist" spiritually in a state of grace; it is God one must "Entirely honor" "with all the office [i.e. duteous devotion] of [the] heart" (cf. Matthew 22: 37); a "mortal offense" is a fatal, i.e. deadly, sin; "present sorrows" and "purposed merit in futurity" are contrition and purposed amendment of life; the insufficiency of these and other "works" ("service past") by themselves to "ransom" the penitent into God's love is Protestant doctrine, as is the abandonment to fortune of the soul deprived of divine grace.

That nor my service past, nor present sorrows,
Nor purposed merit in futurity
Can ransom me into his love again,
But to know so must be my benefit;
110   So shall I clothe me in a forced content,
And shut myself up in some other course
To fortune's alms.

DESDEMONA

Alas, thrice-gentle Cassio!
My advocation is not now in tune;
My lord is not my lord, nor should I know him
115   Were he in favor as in humor altered.
So help me every spirit sanctified
As I have spoken for you all my best,

---

106.   **nor my** F.   Q has 'neither'.
111.   **shut** F.   Q has 'shoote'.

109. *But . . . benefit*   And only to be certain of that must be the favor granted me.

110. *clothe . . . content*   put on a constrained appearance of contentedness.

111–12. *shut . . . alms*   "confine myself to some humbler course of life, in which I shall receive from fortune merely such slight favours as she doles out to the needy" (Kittredge). The verb *shut . . . up* is in this context difficult, and the passage lies under some suspicion.

113. *advocation*   advocacy—Desdemona picks up Cassio's religious diction (as line 116, "So help me every spirit sanctified," and line 119, "be patient," show).   *not now in tune*   Given the religious terms in Cassio's petition and in Desdemona's response, the Elizabethan audience very likely saw here allusion to the orthodox Protestant tenet that Christ alone was repentant man's "Solicitor" and "Advocate" with God. The "advocation" by the Virgin which had been accepted under the "old" religion was *not now in tune* because it was believed "intercession and reconciliation go together" only when Christ is man's Advocate (Genevan-Tomson Bible). Cf. 1 John 2: 1–2 (". . . if any man sin, we have an Advocate with the Father, Jesus Christ, the Just./ And he is the reconciliation for our sins.") Cf. also III. iii. 44–6, above: "Good my lord,/ If I have any grace or power to move you,/ His present reconciliation take."

115. *in favor*   in external appearance and expression (i.e. that by which we recognize a person).

And stood within the blank of his displeasure
For my free speech. You must awhile be patient.
120 What I can do I will; and more I will
Than for myself I dare. Let that suffice you.

IAGO

Is my lord angry?

EMILIA

He went hence but now,
And certainly in strange unquietness.

IAGO

Can he be angry? I have seen the cannon
125 When it hath blown his ranks into the air
And, like the devil, from his very arm
Puffed his own brother . . . and can he be angry!
Something of moment then. I will go meet him;
There's matter in't indeed if he be angry.

DESDEMONA

130 I prithee do so.   *Exit* [IAGO].
              Something sure of state,

---

127. **can he be** Q. F has 'is he'.
130. **S.D.** F. Not in Q.

118. *within the blank* in the direct line of aimed fire. The *blank* is the white at the center of a target.

126. *like the devil* pointing up the passage's dependence on the commonplace Elizabethan use of artillery as a figure for the instruments of man's spiritual enemies—including fortune's accidents and adversities as well as evil tempters and the devil.

127–8. *and . . . then* "[and he stood unmoved;] and can such a man be angry?—It must really be something of importance then." The ellipsis has seemed difficult (to many interpreters if not to all actors), and the repetition in Q and metrically insufficient variant in F have put line 127 under suspicion. Iago's uncompleted anecdote recalls the Othello inured to "hardness" (I. iii. 230)—"the nature/ . . . whose solid virtue/ The shot of accident nor dart of chance/ Could neither graze nor pierce" (IV. i. 248–51). Its relevance depends on the normal Elizabethan opposition of patience (which Othello presumably showed then) and anger. The ellipsis should be said (I think) with covert exultation.

130. *Something sure of state* surely some state business.

Either from Venice or some unhatched practice
Made demonstrable here in Cyprus to him,
Hath puddled his clear spirit; and in such cases
Men's natures wrangle with inferior things,
135   Though great ones are their object.
'Tis even so; for let our finger ache,
And it endues our other, healthful members
Even to that sense of pain. Nay, we must think,
Men are not gods,
140   Nor of them look for such observancy
As fits the bridal. Beshrew me much, Emilia,
I was, unhandsome warrior as I am,
Arraigning his unkindness with my soul;
But now I find I had suborned the witness,
145   And he's indicted falsely.

---

135. **their** F. Q has 'the'.
137. **healthful** F. Q has 'heathfull'.
138. **that** Q. F has 'a'.
140. **observancy** F. Q has 'obseruances'.
142. **unhandsome warrior** Q uncorr. Q corr. has 'vnhandsome, warrior'; F has 'vnhandsome Warrior,'.

131. *some unhatched practice*   some as yet unmatured plot.
132. *Made demonstrable*   disclosed.
133. *puddled* muddied.   *clear*   This retains its Latinate sense of "light," "transparent": here, "serene"—yet the sense "spotless," "irreproachable," "free from guilt" lurks in the background. Cf. *Macbeth* I. v. 68.
137–8. *endues . . . pain*   I.e. it makes them ache too.
140. *of*   from.
141. *Beshrew me*   an expression of lady-like self-blame—literally, "curse me."
142. *unhandsome*   "not living up to my character as" (Ridley)—recalling her wish to share Othello's warrior's life, and "O my fair warrior!" (II. i. 176).
144. *I . . . witness*   I.e. she had induced the witness (her experience of his harshness) to commit perjury (before the judgment seat of her soul).

EMILIA

Pray heaven it be state matters, as you think,
And no conception nor no jealous toy
Concerning you.

DESDEMONA

Alas the day! I never gave him cause.

EMILIA

150   But jealous souls will not be answered so;
They are not ever jealous for the cause,
But jealous for they are jealous: 'tis a monster
Begot upon itself, born on itself.

DESDEMONA

Heaven keep that monster from Othello's mind!

EMILIA

155   Lady, amen.

DESDEMONA

I will go seek him. —Cassio, walk here about:
If I do find him fit, I'll move your suit
And seek to effect it to my uttermost.

CASSIO

I humbly thank your ladyship.   *Exeunt* DESDEMONA *and*
                                                              EMILIA.

Enter BIANCA.

BIANCA

160   Save you, friend Cassio.

CASSIO

What make you from home?

---

152. **they are . . . 'tis** Q.   F has 'they're . . . it is'.
154. **that** Q.   F has 'the'.
159. **S.D.** Q (but placed after 'suit' line 157). F has 'Exit.' after
        'uttermost' line 158.

147. *conception* supposition. *toy* fancy.
151. *for* because of.
160. *Save you* God save you. *make you from* are you doing
away from.

How is't with you, my most fair Bianca?
I' faith, sweet love, I was coming to your house.

BIANCA

And I was going to your lodging, Cassio.
What, keep a week away? seven days and nights?
165 Eightscore eight hours? and lovers' absent hours
More tedious than the dial eightscore times?
O weary reckoning!

CASSIO

Pardon me, Bianca:
I have this while with leaden thoughts been pressed;
But I shall in a more continuate time
170 Strike off this score of absence. Sweet Bianca,
Take me this work out.

[*He gives her* DESDEMONA's *handkerchief.*]

BIANCA

O Cassio, whence came this?
This is some token from a newer friend:
To the felt absence now I feel a cause.
Is't come to this? Well, well.

CASSIO

Go to, woman!

---

161. **is't** F.   Q has 'is it'.
162. **I'faith** Q.   F has 'Indeed'.
167. **O** F (Oh).   Q has 'No'. **reckoning** Q.   F has 'reck ning'.
168. **leaden** F.   Q has 'laden'.
169. **continuate** F.   Q has 'conuenient'.
174. **Well, well.** F.   Not in Q.   **Go to** Q.   F has 'Go too'.

165. *Eightscore eight*   i.e. eight score plus eight.
166. *the dial*   the hands' rounding of the dial.
168. *with . . . pressed*   alluding to the torture known as "pressing with weights."
169. *more continuate*   less interrupted. Q's "conuenient" would mean "fitting."
171. *Take . . . out*   Copy this embroidery for me.
172. *friend*   polite for "paramour."
174. *Go to*   see above, line 5; here, virtually: "O, come on."

175 Throw your vile guesses in the devil's teeth,
From whence you have them. You are jealous now
That this is from some mistress, some remembrance.
No, by my faith, Bianca.

BIANCA
Why, whose is it?

CASSIO
I know not, sweet; I found it in my chamber.
180 I like the work well; ere it be demanded,
As like enough it will, I'd have it copied.
Take't, and do't; and leave me for this time.

BIANCA
Leave you! wherefore?

CASSIO
I do attend here on the general,
185 And think it no addition, nor my wish,
To have him see me womaned.

BIANCA
Why, I pray you?

CASSIO
Not that I love you not.

BIANCA
But that you do not love me.
I pray you, bring me on the way a little,
And say if I shall see you soon at night.

---

175. **vile** Q. F has 'vilde'.
178. **by my faith** Q. F has 'in good troth'.
179. **sweet** Q. F has 'neither'.
181. **I'd** Q. F has 'I would'.
186–7. **BIANCA Why . . . not.** F. Not in Q.

177. *remembrance* keepsake, love-token.
185. *no addition* no credit to me—literally, "no additional title."
186. *womaned* accompanied by a woman.

CASSIO

190   'Tis but a little way that I can bring you,
      For I attend here; but I'll see you soon.

BIANCA

'Tis very good; I must be circumstanced.   *Exeunt.*

[*Act IV, scene i.*] *Enter* OTHELLO *and* IAGO.

IAGO

Will you think so?

OTHELLO

Think so, Iago!

IAGO

What?

To kiss in private—

OTHELLO

An unauthorized kiss.

IAGO

Or to be naked with her friend abed,
An hour or more, not meaning any harm?

OTHELLO

5   Naked abed, Iago, and not mean harm!
     It is hypocrisy against the devil:

IV. i   3, 5.   **abed** Q.   F has 'in bed'.

192. *be circumstanced*   yield to circumstances.

IV. i   Some students of the play's time scheme suppose an interval between Acts III and IV, but none is specified in the text, which (apart from the "long-time" references) in fact gives quite the opposite impression. The locale again is left to the shifting implications of the dialogue in the different segments of the scene. The "here" of lines 75, 79, indicating the place of Othello's "ecstasy" and his eavesdropping on Cassio's conversation with Iago and Bianca, is never further defined.

1. *Will*   Regarding the irony of this emphasis on "will," see above I. iii. 313 ff., III. iii. 390, and below IV. i. 34, IV. ii. 24.

2. *unauthorized*   unjustified, unwarrantable—properly pronounced with main accent on the third syllable.

6. *hypocrisy against the devil*   quite logically: to give every appearance of evil, without "meaning any harm."

They that mean virtuously and yet do so,
The devil their virtue tempts, and they tempt heaven.

IAGO

So they do nothing, 'tis a venial slip.
10   But if I give my wife a handkerchief—

OTHELLO

What then?

IAGO

Why then, 'tis hers, my lord; and being hers,
She may, I think, bestow't on any man.

OTHELLO

She is protectress of her honor too:
15   May she give that?

IAGO

Her honor is an essence that's not seen;
They have it very oft that have it not.
But for the handkerchief—

OTHELLO

By heaven, I would most gladly have forgot it.
20   Thou said'st—O, it comes o'er my memory
As doth the raven o'er the infected house,
Boding to all—he had my handkerchief.

---

9.   **So** Q. F has 'If'.
14.   **too** F. Q has 'to'.
21.   **infected** Q. F has 'infectious'.

8. *they tempt heaven* "they make a wanton trial of heaven's power to keep them from sin." (Kittredge). Cf. "Thou shalt not tempt the Lord thy God" (Deuteronomy 6: 16, Matthew 4: 7, Luke 4: 12); also *Troilus and Cressida* IV. iv. 94–5: "we are devils to ourselves/ When we will tempt the frailty of our powers."
9. *So*   provided that.   *do*   emphatic.
17. I.e.   dishonorable people often are reputed honorable.
21. *raven*   a bird of ill-omen, harbinger of death, and carrier of infection.   *infected house*   house in which the pestilence is raging. F's "infectious" defeats the irony; I think it a sophistication induced by "Boding to all."
22. *Boding*   being ominous.

IAGO

Ay, what of that?

OTHELLO

That's not so good now.

IAGO

What if I had said I had seen him do you wrong?
25   Or heard him say—as knaves be such abroad
Who, having by their own importunate suit,
Or voluntary dotage of some mistress,
Convincèd or supplied them, cannot choose
But they must blab—

OTHELLO

Hath he said anything?

IAGO

30   He hath, my lord; but be you well assured,
No more than he'll unswear.

OTHELLO

What hath he said?

IAGO

Faith, that he did—I know not what he did.

OTHELLO

What? what?

IAGO

Lie—

OTHELLO

With her?

IAGO

With her, on her: what you will.

---

27.   **Or** F.   Q has 'Or by the'.
28.   **Convincèd** F and Q corr.   Q uncorr. reads 'Coniured'.
32.   **Faith** Q.   F has 'Why'.
33.   **What? what?** F.   Q has 'But what?'

25. *as knaves be such abroad*   (as well I might, for) there are such knaves at large.

28. *Convincèd or supplied*   prevailed upon them (by "importunate suit") or satisfied their desires (in their "voluntary dotage").

28–9. *cannot . . . blab*   cannot help blabbing.

OTHELLO

35 Lie with her, lie on her!—We say lie on her when they belie
    her. —Lie with her! 'Zounds, that's fulsome! —Handkerchief
    —confessions—handkerchief! —To confess, and be hanged
    for his labor; first to be hanged, and then to confess! I tremble
    at it. Nature would not invest herself in such shadowing
40 passion without some instruction. It is not words that shakes
    me thus. Pish! noses, ears, and lips! Is't possible? —Confess?
    Handkerchief? —O devil!   [*He*] *falls in a trance.*

IAGO

    Work on, my medicine, work!
    Thus credulous fools are caught;
45 And many worthy and chaste dames even thus,

---

36. **'Zounds** Q. Not in F.
     that's F and Q corr.   Q uncorr. has 'thar's'.
36–7. **Handkerchief—confessions—handkerchief** F. Q has 'hand-
       kerchers, Confession, handkerchers'.
37–42. **To confess . . . devil.** F. Not in Q.
42. **S.D.** F (*Traunce*). Q corr. has '*He fals downe.*' after 'handker-
       chers' line 37. Not in Q uncorr.
43–7. F. As prose in Q.
43. **medicine, work** Q. F has 'Medicine workes'.

36. *fulsome* nauseating.
37. *confess, and be hanged*   an old cynical proverb (Tilley, C587).
39. *it* i.e. these thoughts, or the actuality which stirs them.
39–40. *Nature . . . instruction* simplified in what follows: "It
is not words that shakes me thus." Othello says, in effect: "Lacking
some external stimulus, my normal natural faculties would not so
disguise themselves through such powerful emotion." *Shadowing* I
take to mean not only "overshadowing" and "mind-darkening," but
also "cast by the reality," "image-beset"—even "imitative": his
nature acts out (as an actor clothed in a costume) what some external
prompting instructs.
42. *S.D.* This action evokes "The Image of Prostration" conventional in the underlying morality play to demonstrate the fall of
the once-virtuous beneath the foot of the devil or vice (an obversion
of a symbolic commonplace: Virtue, or an individual personifying
Virtue, triumphant over Vice). Actors of Iago have sometimes nudged
the prostrate Othello contemptuously with the foot—an action
Granville-Barker approved.
43. *medicine* poison. Cf. III. iii. 322.

All guiltless, meet reproach. —What ho! my lord!
My lord, I say! Othello!

Enter CASSIO.

How now, Cassio!

CASSIO

What's the matter?

IAGO

My lord is fall'n into an epilepsy.
50 This is his second fit; he had one yesterday.

CASSIO

Rub him about the temples.

IAGO

No, forbear.

The lethargy must have his quiet course;
If not, he foams at mouth, and by and by
Breaks out to savage madness. Look, he stirs.
55 Do you withdraw yourself a little while.
He will recover straight; when he is gone,
I would on great occasion speak with you. —   [*Exit* CASSIO.]
How is it, general? Have you not hurt your head?

OTHELLO

Dost thou mock me?

---

51. **No, forbear** Q. Not in F.
53. **he** F and Q corr. Q uncorr. has 'he he'.
57. **S.D.** Rowe. Not in QF.

46. *reproach* the foulest shame.
49. *fall'n into an epilepsy* i.e. had a fit of the falling sickness (cf.
Julius Caesar I. ii. 256)—with a play, picking up the implicit motif
from lines 8, 42 S.D., on spiritual "falling."
50. *he had one yesterday* I suppose this to refer to the night scene
in II. iii, but others see in it a "long time" reference.
51. *about the temples* an unintentionally ambiguous expression,
in view of the cuckold's horns which have prostrated Othello (see
line 61).   *forbear* i.e. don't do it, let him alone.
52. *lethargy* coma, insensibility.   *his* its.
53. *by and by* immediately.
56. *straight* in a moment.
59. *mock me* i.e. with my cuckold's horns.

IAGO

I mock you! no, by heaven.

60 Would you would bear your fortune like a man!

OTHELLO

A hornèd man's a monster and a beast.

IAGO

There's many a beast then in a populous city,
And many a civil monster.

OTHELLO

Did he confess it?

IAGO

Good sir, be a man:

65 Think every bearded fellow that's but yoked
May draw with you. There's millions now alive
That nightly lie in those unproper beds
Which they dare swear peculiar. Your case is better.
O, 'tis the spite of hell, the fiend's arch-mock,

70 To lip a wanton in a secure couch,
And to suppose her chaste! No, let me know;
And knowing what I am, I know what she shall be.

---

59. **you! no, by** Q (you? no by). F has 'you not, by'.
60. **fortune** F. Q has 'fortunes'.
64. **it** F. Not in Q. **Good** F and Q corr. Q uncorr. has 'God'.
67. **lie** F. Q has 'lyes'.
70. **couch** Q2. F has 'Cowch'. Q has 'Coach'.

61. *a monster* i.e. disordered in "natural" form. There are, more-over, perennial Renaissance pairings of cuckolds and (those other horned monsters) devils.

63. *civil* among the citizenry.

65. *every . . . yoked* every grown-up man that's bound by matrimony.

65–6. *yoked . . . you* alluding to the proverb, "In time the savage bull doth bear the yoke." (Cf. *Much Ado* I. i. 271). Ironically, the yoke is also a symbol of patience.

67. *unproper* not exclusively their own.

68. *peculiar* all their own, reserved for themselves.

70. *secure* free from suspicion or care. Accented on the first syllable.

72. A cryptic, and tempting, remark, implying: "knowing myself honor-concerned and manly, I know what her fate will surely be."

OTHELLO

O, thou art wise: 'tis certain.

IAGO

Stand you awhile apart;
Confine yourself but in a patient list.
75 Whilst you were here, o'erwhelmèd with your grief—
A passion most unsuiting such a man—
Cassio came hither. I shifted him away,
And laid good 'scuse upon your ecstasy;
Bade him anon return, and here speak with me;
80 The which he promised. Do but encave yourself,
And mark the fleers, the gibes, and notable scorns
That dwell in every region of his face;
For I will make him tell the tale anew—
Where, how, how oft, how long ago, and when
85 He hath and is again to cope your wife.
I say, but mark his gesture. Marry, patience!

---

75. **o'erwhelmèd** F (o're-whelmed). Q has 'ere while, mad'.
76. **unsuiting** Q corr. (vnsuting). Q uncorr. reads 'vnfitting': F has 'resulting'.
78. **'scuse** Q (scuse). F has 'scuses'.
79. **Bade** Johnson. F has 'Bad'. Q has 'Bid'.
     return F. Q has 'retire'.
80. **Do** F. Not in Q.
81. **fleers** F. Q uncorr. has 'geeres,'. Q corr. 'Ieeres'.
85. **hath** F. Q has 'has'.

74. *in a patient list* within the limits set by patience—with a profoundly ironic undermeaning. Cf. line 86 and above, III. iii. 449.

76. Triply ironic—given the speaker.

78. *ecstasy* trance, swoon—literally (and symbolically) "your being out of (or beside) yourself."

80. *encave* conceal, hide. Ironically, the cave as a symbol of error was a commonplace. Cf. the cave of Error in *The Faerie Queene* I. i. 11 ff.

81. *fleers . . . jibes . . . scorns* synonyms for the scornfully sneering looks Othello is asked to observe (*notable*).

85. *cope* have a love encounter, an assignation, with.

86. *gesture* whole behavior, bearing, demeanor. *Marry* Here this interjection virtually means, "Come on, now: come, come!"

Or I shall say y'are all in all in spleen,
And nothing of a man.

OTHELLO

Dost thou hear, Iago?
I will be found most cunning in my patience;
90   But—dost thou hear? —most bloody.

IAGO

That's not amiss;
But yet keep time in all. Will you withdraw?

[OTHELLO *draws back to watch*.]

Now will I question Cassio of Bianca,
A huswife that by selling her desires
Buys herself bread and cloth. It is a creature
95   That dotes on Cassio, as 'tis the strumpet's plague
To beguile many and be beguiled by one.
He, when he hears of her, cannot refrain
From the excess of laughter.

[*Re-*]*enter* CASSIO.

Here he comes.

As he shall smile, Othello shall go mad;
100   And his unbookish jealousy must conster
Poor Cassio's smiles, gestures, and light behaviors
Quite in the wrong. —How do you now, lieutenant?

---

87.   **y'are** F.   Q has 'you are'.
91.   **S.D.** Rowe (*withdraws*).   Not in QF.
94.   **cloth** F (Cloath).   Q has 'cloathes'.
97.   **refrain** Q.   F has 'restrain'.
98.   **S.D.** Q places after 'one' line 96.   F places after 'comes' line 98.
100.   **conster** Q.   F has 'conserue'.
101.   **behaviors** F.   Q has 'behauiour'.
102.   **now** Q .   Not in F.

87. *all . . . spleen*   completely at the mercy of violent emotion—the source of which was supposed the spleen.

91. *keep time*   a figure drawn from music, particularly ironic after the blatant "That's not amiss" (line 90).

93. *huswife*   hussy.   *desires*   appetites.

100. *unbookish*   unlearned,   inexperienced.   *conster*   construe, interpret.

CASSIO

The worser that you give me the addition
Whose want even kills me.

IAGO

105 Ply Desdemona well, and you are sure on't.
Now, if this suit lay in Bianca's power
How quickly should you speed!

CASSIO

               Alas, poor caitiff!

OTHELLO [*in concealment*]

Look how he laughs already!

IAGO

I never knew woman love man so.

CASSIO

110 Alas, poor rogue! I think, i' faith, she loves me.

OTHELLO

Now he denies it faintly, and laughs it out.

IAGO

Do you hear, Cassio?

OTHELLO

               Now he importunes him
To tell it o'er. Go to! well said, well said!

IAGO

She gives it out that you shall marry her.
115 Do you intend it?

---

106. **power** Q. F has 'dowre'.
109. **woman** F. Q has 'a woman'.
110. **i'faith** Q. F has 'indeed'.
113. **o'er** F (o're). Q has 'on'.
     to Q. F has 'too'. **well said, well said** F. Q has 'well said'.

103. *addition* title.
105. *on't* of it.
107. *speed* succeed in it. *caitiff* wretch (with contemptuous pity)—literally, "captive."
112. *importunes* accented on second syllable.
113. *well said* well done.

CASSIO

Ha, ha, ha!

OTHELLO

Do ye triumph, Roman? do you triumph?

CASSIO

I marry her? what, a customer! I prithee bear some charity to
my wit; do not think it so unwholesome. Ha, ha, ha!

OTHELLO

So, so, so, so! Laugh that wins!

IAGO

120 Faith, the cry goes you shall marry her.

CASSIO

Prithee say true.

IAGO

I am a very villain else.

OTHELLO

Have you scored me? Well.

---

116. **Do ye** F. Q has 'Do you'.
117. **marry her?** Q. F has 'marry.'
      what, a customer! F (What? A customer;). Not in Q.
      I prithee Q. F has 'prythee'.
117–18. Prose. Both Q and F try to divide as verse, but differently.
119. **Laugh** Q. F has 'they laugh'.
120. **Faith** Q. F has 'Why'. **you shall** Q. F has 'that you'.
123. **Have** F. Q has 'Ha'. **scored me? Well.** F (scoar'd). Q has
      'stor'd me well.'

116. *Do ye triumph, Roman* an obscure and (given Cassio's
Florentine breeding) even puzzling expression; but does it mean anything more than: "enjoying your triumph like a Roman are you?
well!"

117. *a customer* a courtesan, one who serves the trade.

118. *unwholesome* diseased.

119. *Laugh that wins* Let him laugh who wins—proverbial
(Tilley, L93).

120. *the cry goes* rumor has it that.

123. *Have you scored me* "There seem to be three possible meanings—(1) 'marked me' (with infamy)—as with lashes from a whip;
(2) 'scored me up,' 'posted my name—as a cuckold' . . .; (3)
'added up my score,' 'settled my account,' 'summed me up.' The third
seems to be the best" (Kittredge).

CASSIO

This is the monkey's own giving out. She is persuaded I will
125 marry her out of her own love and flattery, not out of my
promise.

OTHELLO

Iago beckons me: now he begins the story.

CASSIO

She was here even now; she haunts me in every place. I was t'
other day talking on the sea-bank with certain Venetians, and
130 thither comes the bauble, and, by this hand, falls me thus
about my neck—

OTHELLO

Crying "O dear Cassio!" as it were: his gesture imports it.

CASSIO

So hangs, and lolls, and weeps upon me; so hales and pulls me!
Ha, ha, ha!

OTHELLO

135 Now he tells how she plucked him to my chamber. O I see
that nose of yours, but not that dog I shall throw't to.

124–6. Q. As verse in F.
127. **beckons** Q. F has 'becomes'. **me:** F. Q has 'me,'.
128–9. **t'other** Q. F has 'the other'.
130. **the bauble, and** F. Q has 'this bauble'. **by this hand** Q. Not in F.
falls me F. Q has 'she fals'.
133. **hales** Q. F has 'shakes'.
135. **O** F. Not in Q.
136. **throw't** Q. F has 'throw it'.

124. *giving out*   deliberately circulated report.
125. *flattery*   self-flattery: i.e. she flatters herself that he will.
127. *beckons me*   An indication for the actor of Iago to have signaled Othello to pay attention to Cassio's behavior.
129. *sea-bank*   seashore. As some in the original audience would have known, this is where Cyprian girls were reputed to earn their dowries by prostitution.
130. *bauble*   plaything, bit of frippery.   *by this hand*   a common mild oath.
133. *hales*   tugs.
135–6. *I . . . to*   This violent remark appears to mean: "I see that nose of yours that needs cutting off (a common form of physical revenge); but the time isn't ripe as I do not yet see the cur before whom I shall hurl it in the dirt!"

CASSIO

Well, I must leave her company.

Enter BIANCA

IAGO

Before me, look where she comes.

CASSIO

'Tis such another fitchew! marry, a perfumed one. —What do
140 you mean by this haunting of me?

BIANCA

Let the devil and his dam haunt you! What did you mean by
that same handkerchief you gave me even now? I was a fine
fool to take it. I must take out the whole work? A likely piece
of work that you should find it in your chamber and not know
145 who left it there! This is some minx's token, and I must take
out the work? There! give it the hobby-horse, wheresoever
you had it. I'll take out no work on't.

CASSIO

How now, my sweet Bianca? how now? how now?

OTHELLO

By heaven, that should be my handkerchief!

BIANCA

150 An' you'll come to supper tonight, you may; an' you will not,
come when you are next prepared for.   *Exit.*

---

137. **S.D.** As in Q.   F places after 'comes' line 138.
139. **CASSIO.** F. Not in Q.
      fitchew F. Q has 'ficho'. **one.** Q has 'one,'; F has 'one?'
143. **whole** Q. Not in F.
144. **not know** Q. F has 'know not'.
146. **it the** Q. F has 'it your'.
150. **An' . . . an'** Q. F has 'If . . . if'.

138. *Before me* Upon my word. The expression is a euphemistic
form of "Before God."
139. *such another fitchew* such a tart! *Fitchew* (the polecat,
known for its lechery and strong smell) was slang for "prostitute."
a perfumed one i.e. her strong perfume drowns out the polecat
smell.
145. *minx's* whore's.
146. *the hobby-horse* the harlot, your mountable wench.
147. *take . . . on't* copy no embroidered pattern from it.

IAGO

After her, after her!

CASSIO

Faith, I must; she'll rail i' the street else.

IAGO

Will you sup there?

CASSIO

155   Faith, I intend so.

IAGO

Well, I may chance to see you, for I would very fain speak
with you.

CASSIO

Prithee come, will you?

IAGO

Go to; say no more.   *Exit* CASSIO.

OTHELLO [*coming forward*]

160   How shall I murder him, Iago?

IAGO

Did you perceive how he laughed at his vice?

OTHELLO

O Iago!

IAGO

And did you see the handkerchief?

OTHELLO

Was that mine?

---

153. **Faith** Q. Not in F. **i' the street** Q.   F has 'in the streets'.
155. **Faith** Q. F has 'Yes'.
159. **to** Q.   F has 'too'. **S.D.** Q.   Not in F.
160. **S.D.** Collier (*Advancing*).

156. *fain*   gladly.
159. *Go to*   well and good!

IAGO

165 Yours, by this hand! And to see how he prizes the foolish
woman, your wife! She gave it him, and he hath giv'n it to his
whore.

OTHELLO

I would have him nine years a-killing! —A fine woman! a
fair woman! a sweet woman!

IAGO

170 Nay, you must forget.

OTHELLO

Ay, let her rot and perish, and be damned tonight; for she
shall not live. No, my heart is turned to stone: I strike it, and
it hurts my hand. O, the world hath not a sweeter creature!
she might lie by an emperor's side and command him tasks.

IAGO

175 Nay, that's not your way.

OTHELLO

Hang her! I do but say what she is: so delicate with her needle,
an admirable musician—O, she will sing the savageness out of
a bear!—Of so high and plenteous wit and invention—

IAGO

She's the worse for all this.

OTHELLO

180 O, a thousand thousand times—and then, of so gentle a condition!

165–7. **IAGO Yours . . . whore** F. Not in Q (but S.P. 'Iag.' is the
catchword after line 164).
168–9. Q. As verse in F.
170. **forget** Q. F has 'forget that.'
171. **Ay,** F (I,). Q has 'And'.
173. **hath** F. Q has 'has'.
180–1. Q. As verse in F.
180. **O,** F. Not in Q.
       a thousand thousand Q. F has 'a thousand, a thousand'.

165. *prizes* rates, values.
177. *admirable* stronger than our word: "to be wondered at."
178. *bear* The "churlish bear" (*Troilus and Cressida* I. ii. 20) is a
common figure of wrath, violence, and savage cruelty. Othello's description of Desdemona's musicianship evokes the figure of Orpheus.
180–1. *so gentle a condition* so high-born a quality.

IAGO

Ay, too gentle.

OTHELLO

Nay, that's certain. But yet the pity of it, Iago! O Iago, the
pity of it, Iago!

IAGO

185   If you be so fond over her iniquity, give her patent to offend;
for if it touches not you, it comes near nobody.

OTHELLO

I will chop her into messes! —cuckold me!

IAGO

O, 'tis foul in her.

OTHELLO

With mine officer!

IAGO

190   That's fouler.

OTHELLO

Get me some poison, Iago—this night! I'll not expostulate
with her lest her body and beauty unprovide my mind again.
This night, Iago!

IAGO

Do it not with poison. Strangle her in her bed, even the bed
195   she hath contaminated.

183–4. Q. As verse in F.
183. **Nay** F. Q has 'I'.
183–4. **O . . . Iago!** F (Iago.). Q has 'the pitty.'
185. **be** Q. F has 'are'.
186. **touches** Q. F has 'touch'.
191. **night! I'll** F (night.). Q has 'night I'le'.
194–8. Q. As verse in F.

182. *gentle* Iago sourly picks up the word in the sense "yielding."
185. *fond* foolish, doting. *patent* letters patent, a licence—
i.e. "carte blanche."
186. *touches* (1) concerns; (2) hurts.
187. *messes* small pieces, gobbets.
191. *expostulate* reason, argue at length.
192. *body and beauty* bodily beauty—hendiadys. *unprovide*
undo the readiness of.

OTHELLO

Good, good! the justice of it pleases. Very good!

IAGO

And for Cassio, let me be his undertaker: you shall hear more
by midnight.

OTHELLO

Excellent good!   *A trumpet [sounds].*

What trumpet is that same?

IAGO

200   I warrant something from Venice.

Enter LODOVICO, DESDEMONA, *and Attendants.*

'Tis Lodovico:

This comes from the Duke; see, your wife is with him.

LODOVICO

God save the worthy general!

OTHELLO

With all my heart, sir.

LODOVICO

The Duke and senators of Venice greet you.

[Gives him a letter.]

---

196.   **pleases. Very** F (pleases: very). Q has 'pleases very'.

199.   **S.D.** Q (after 'midnight' line 198). Not in F.

200–1.   **I . . . him.** ('this comes' F3). F1 has 'I warrant something
from Venice, / 'Tis *Lodouico*, this, comes from the Duke. /
See, your wife's with him.' Q has 'Something from *Venice*
sure, tis *Lodouico*, / Come from the Duke, and see your
wife is with him.'

200.   **S.D.** QF place after line 198.

202.   **God save the** Q. F has 'Saue you'.

203.   **and** Q. F has 'and the'. **S.D.** Rowe.

197. *be his undertaker*   undertake to dispose of him, take him on.
There may be a grim pun ("put him underground") but not in the
modern sense, unknown to Shakespeare, of "funeral undertaker."

199. S.D. *trumpet*   used to announce the approach of those in
authority. The trumpet is also a commonplace symbol of spiritual
judgment (cf. *Macbeth* I. vii. 19) or of warning to sinners of the
divine justice which will overtake them unless they repent.

202. *With all my heart*   equivalent to an emphatic "Amen!"

OTHELLO

I kiss the instrument of their pleasures.

[*Opens the letter and reads.*]

DESDEMONA

205 And what's the news, good cousin Lodovico?

IAGO

I am very glad to see you, signior.
Welcome to Cyprus.

LODOVICO

I thank you. How does Lieutenant Cassio?

IAGO

Lives, sir.

DESDEMONA

Cousin, there's fall'n between him and my lord
210 An unkind breach; but you shall make all well.

OTHELLO

Are you sure of that?

DESDEMONA

My lord?

OTHELLO [*reads*]

"This fail you not to do, as you will—"

LODOVICO

He did not call; he's busy in the paper.
Is there division 'twixt my lord and Cassio?

---

204. **S.D.** Capell.
211. **lord?** F.   Q has 'Lord.'
212. **S.D.** Theobald.
214. **'twixt my** F.   Q has 'betweene thy'.

204. I.e. "I welcome the document in which their desires are communicated." However, *instrument* frequently means "tool," "organ," and, given Othello's over-wrought state, there may be a wildly inappropriate "unintended" meaning here.

210. *unkind* (1) destitute of benevolence; (2) unnatural—accented on the first syllable.   *shall* will surely.

212. This warning in his orders from a distant superior authority, read aloud by Othello, ironically is pertinent in the immediate situation.

DESDEMONA

215   A most unhappy one. I would do much
       T' atone them, for the love I bear to Cassio.

OTHELLO

Fire and brimstone!

DESDEMONA

My lord?

OTHELLO

Are you wise?

DESDEMONA

What, is he angry?

LODOVICO

May be the letter moved him;
For, as I think, they do command him home,
220   Deputing Cassio in his government.

DESDEMONA

By my troth, I am glad on't.

OTHELLO

Indeed!

DESDEMONA

My lord?

OTHELLO

I am glad to see you mad.

---

216.   **T'atone** F.   Q has 'To attone'.
218.   **the** Q.   F has 'th'.
221.   **By my troth** Q.   F has 'Trust me'.

216. *T'atone them*   to make them at one, reconcile them.
217. *Are you wise?*   i.e. in your right wits to make a public display of your love for Cassio?
221. *By my troth*   Ironically, this literally means "by my plighted faith." All her comments are open to his misconstruction.
222. *glad to see you mad*   An obscure remark, particularly for this climactic moment, and textual corruption has been suspected. I suppose it to be wild sarcasm: "I'm glad to see you so out of your senses with infatuation that you thus leave no doubt of your infidelity in anyone's mind!"

DESDEMONA

Why, sweet Othello! —

OTHELLO

Devil!   [*He strikes her.*]

DESDEMONA

I have not deserved this.

LODOVICO

225   My lord, this would not be believed in Venice,
Though I should swear I saw't. 'Tis very much.
Make her amends; she weeps.

OTHELLO

O devil, devil!

If that the earth could teem with woman's tears,
Each drop she falls would prove a crocodile.—

230   Out of my sight!

DESDEMONA

I will not stay to offend you.   [*Going.*]

LODOVICO

Truly, an obedient lady.
I do beseech your lordship, call her back.

OTHELLO

Mistress!

DESDEMONA

My lord?

---

222.   **Why** F.   Q has 'How'.
223.   **S.D.** Theobald.
228.   **woman's** F.   Q has 'womens'.
230.   **S.D.** Rowe.
231.   **an** Q.   Not in F.

227–9. *O devil . . . crocodile* "If the earth could conceive by
(*teem with*) woman's tears, each drop she lets fall (*falls*) would become a *crocodile* (*prove, OED* II. 9) and thus show her to be one
(*OED* II. 8). The crocodile was fabled to attract victims through their
sympathy for its false tears: "the mournful crocodile/ With sorrow
snares relenting passengers" (*2 Henry VI* III. i. 226–7). As a figure of
pernicious Fraud, it was associated with Lechery and also used, as
here, as an emblem of the Devil (liar, tempter, and devourer). The
weeping crocodile (whose tears are yet proverbial) was commonly
used to represent the insidious false woman.

OTHELLO

What would you with her, sir?

LODOVICO

Who, I, my lord?

OTHELLO

235 Ay! you did wish that I would make her turn.
Sir, she can turn, and turn, and yet go on
And turn again; and she can weep, sir, weep;
And she's obedient, as you say, obedient,
Very obedient. —Proceed you in your tears.—
240 Concerning this, sir—O well-painted passion!—
I am commanded home.—Get you away;
I'll send for you anon. —Sir, I obey the mandate,
And will return to Venice. —Hence, avaunt!

[*Exit* DESDEMONA.]

Cassio shall have my place. And, sir, tonight
245 I do entreat that we may sup together.
You are welcome, sir, to Cyprus. —Goats and monkeys! *Exit.*

LODOVICO

Is this the noble Moor whom our full senate
Call all in all sufficient? Is this the nature
Whom passion could not shake? whose solid virtue
250 The shot of accident nor dart of chance
Could neither graze nor pierce?

---

241. **home** F. Q has 'here'.
243. **S.D.** Rowe.
246. **S.D.** F and Q corr. Not in Q uncorr.
247. **Is this the** F. Q has 'This the'.

236-7. *turn* playing on the senses (1) change direction, (2) alter, (3) be inconstant, and (4) do a (sexual) "turn" (cf. *Antony and Cleopatra* II. v. 59).

239. *Very obedient* submissive to command indeed—she'll obey anybody. Cf. the play on "gentle" line 182.

240. *this* i.e. the letter. *well-painted passion* well-acted grieving—"a true to the life performance of suffering!"

246. *Goats and monkeys* These creatures were types of lasciviousness.

248. *all in all* in every respect, completely. *sufficient* able, fit for office.

IAGO

He is much changed.

LODOVICO

Are his wits safe? is he not light of brain?

IAGO

He's that he is: I may not breathe my censure
What he might be; if what he might he is not,
255   I would to heaven he were!

LODOVICO

What! strike his wife?

IAGO

Faith, that was not so well; yet would I knew
That stroke would prove the worst.

LODOVICO

Is it his use?
Or did the letters work upon his blood,
And new-create this fault?

IAGO

Alas, alas!
260   It is not honesty in me to speak
What I have seen and known. You shall observe him,
And his own courses will denote him so

---

253. **censure** Jennens. Q has 'censure,'; F has 'censure.'
254. **be; if what** F (be:). Q has 'be, if as'.
259. **this** Q. F has 'his'.
262. **denote** Q. F uncorr. has 'deuote'; F erroneously corr. 'deonte'.

252. *safe* sound.
253. *censure* judgment.
254–5. *if . . . were* deliberately cryptic, playing on *might* in the senses "should (be)" and "might (yet be)"—with the private meaning: "If he's not yet as mad as my plot to practise 'upon his peace and quiet' should have made him, would to heaven he were!"
257. *use* habit, custom.
259. *new-create this fault* make him commit this fault for the first time.
260. *honesty* honorable conduct.

That I may save my speech. Do but go after
And mark how he continues.

LODOVICO

265   I am sorry that I am deceived in him.   *Exeunt.*

[*Scene ii.*] *Enter* OTHELLO *and* EMILIA.

OTHELLO

You have seen nothing then?

EMILIA

Nor ever heard, nor ever did suspect.

OTHELLO

Yes, you have seen Cassio and she together.

EMILIA

But then I saw no harm; and then I heard
5   Each syllable that breath made up between 'em.

OTHELLO

What, did they never whisper?

EMILIA

Never, my lord.

OTHELLO

Nor send you out o' th' way?

EMILIA

Never.

IV. ii   3. **Yes** F. Q has 'Yes, and'.
   5. **em'** Q. F has 'them'.
   7. **o'th'** F. Q has 'o'the'.

IV. ii   The continuity of time is unbroken. This is another "split"
scene of unspecified locale. A private, interior setting may be
imagined for the questioning of Emilia, the "Brothel Scene" and its
aftermath, but it is only implied. Thus, no discrepancy need be felt
when Roderigo enters to challenge Iago, though Iago remains where
Desdemona had summoned him to her.

   3. *she*   The nominative for the accusative is common Elizabethan
grammar and not uncommon in Shakespeare.

OTHELLO

To fetch her fan, her gloves, her mask, nor nothing?

EMILIA

10 Never, my lord.

OTHELLO

That's strange.

EMILIA

I durst, my lord, to wager she is honest,
Lay down my soul at stake. If you think other,
Remove your thought; it doth abuse your bosom.
15 If any wretch ha' put this in your head,
Let heaven requite it with the serpent's curse!
For if she be not honest, chaste, and true,
There's no man happy: the purest of her sex
Is foul as slander.

OTHELLO

                Bid her come hither; go.   *Exit* EMILIA.
20 She says enough; yet she's a simple bawd

---

   9. **her gloves, her mask** F. Q has 'her mask, her gloues'.
   15. **ha'** Q. F has 'haue'.
   16. **heaven** F. Q has 'heauens'. **requite** Q. F has 'requit'.
   18. **her sex** Q. F has 'their wiues'.
   19. **S.D.** F. Q places after 'slander.'

9. *mask* Elizabethan ladies often wore masks, particularly in
public places such as the theater. Masks in Renaissance iconography
symbolize deception.
   12. *honest*   chaste.
   13. *other*   otherwise.
   14. *abuse your bosom*   deceive your heart.
   16. *the serpent's curse*   i.e. as a crime equal to that of Satan at the
Fall of Man. The reference is to the curse pronounced upon the serpent in Genesis 3: 14. It was widely explained in Elizabethan sermons
that the name "devil" came from the Greek word for "slanderer."
   18. *purest of her sex*   F's "their Wiues" (which at first may look
right) quite seriously weakens Emilia's emphatic point: she means
"even the purest maiden."
   20. *She*   i.e. Emilia.
   20–1. *she's . . . much*   That's a naive bawd indeed who cannot
cover up as much. Othello takes Emilia to be Desdemona's
accomplice.

That cannot say as much. This is a subtle whore,
A closet lock and key of villainous secrets;
And yet she'll kneel and pray: I ha' seen her do't.

Enter DESDEMONA *and* EMILIA.

DESDEMONA

My lord, what is your will?

OTHELLO

Pray, chuck, come hither.

DESDEMONA

25   What is your pleasure?

OTHELLO

Let me see your eyes:
Look in my face.

DESDEMONA

What horrible fancy's this?

OTHELLO

[*To* EMILIA] Some of your function, mistress:
Leave procreants alone, and shut the door;
Cough or cry hem if anybody come.

30   Your mystery, your mystery! Nay, dispatch!   *Exit* EMILIA.

---

23. **ha'** Q. F has 'haue'.
24. **Pray** Q. F has 'Pray you'.
30. **Nay** Q. F has 'May'.

21. *This* usually taken to refer to Emilia, but "whore" and the kneeling and praying which he next recalls with bemused scornful irony (line 23) fit Desdemona better.

22. *closet* private room.

24–5. *will . . . pleasure* The undermeanings which can be found in her obedient questions feed his growing "horrible fancy" that he is a stranger visiting Desdemona as a whore in a brothel. *Will* can mean "lust," "carnal appetite."

27. *Some . . . mistress* "Do your job, madam bawd."

28. *procreants* would-be copulators.

29. *cry hem* clear your throat.

30. *mystery* trade, office—i.e. as procuress.

DESDEMONA

Upon my knees, what doth your speech import?
I understand a fury in your words,
But not the words.

OTHELLO

Why, what art thou?

DESDEMONA

35 Your wife, my lord, your true and loyal wife.

OTHELLO

Come, swear it, damn thyself;
Lest, being like one of heaven, the devils themselves
Should fear to seize thee. Therefore be double-damned:
Swear thou art honest.

DESDEMONA

Heaven doth truly know it.

OTHELLO

40 Heaven truly knows that thou art false as hell!

DESDEMONA

To whom, my lord? with whom? How am I false?

OTHELLO

Ah, Desdemon! away! away! away!

DESDEMONA

Alas the heavy day! Why do you weep?
Am I the motive of these tears, my lord?
45 If haply you my father do suspect
An instrument of this your calling back,
Lay not your blame on me; if you have lost him,
Why, I have lost him too.

---

31. **knees** Q.   F has 'knee'. **doth** F.   Q has 'does'.
33. Q.   Not in F.
36–9. Q.   As prose in F.
42. **Ah, Desdemon** F.   Q has 'O Desdemona'.
44. **motive** F.   Q has 'occasion'. **these** F.   Q has 'those'.
47. **lost** F.   Q has 'left'.
48. **Why** Q.   Not in F. **lost** F.   Q has 'left'.

43. *heavy*   sorrowful.
45. *haply*   perhaps.
46. *instrument*   agent.
47. *lost him*   i.e. as a friend; cf. I. iii. 127.

OTHELLO

Had it pleased heaven
To try me with affliction, had they rained
50 All kinds of sores and shames on my bare head,
Steeped me in poverty to the very lips,
Given to captivity me and my utmost hopes,
I should have found in some place of my soul
A drop of patience; but alas, to make me
55 The fixèd figure for the time of scorn
To point his slow unmoving finger at!
Yet I could bear that too: well, very well.
But there where I have garnered up my heart,
Where either I must live or bear no life,
60 The fountain from the which my current runs
Or else dries up—to be discarded thence!

---

49. **they rained** F. Q has 'he ram'd'.
50. **kinds** Q. F has 'kind'.
52. **utmost** F. Not in Q.
53. **place** F. Q has 'part'.
55. **The** F. Q has 'A'.
56. **unmoving** Q. F has 'and mouing'.
     finger at! F (at.). Q has 'fingers at--oh, oh,'.

50-1. *sores . . . poverty* details recalling Job, for the Elizabethans a type of patience, suffering God's trials of affliction and hardship.

55-6. A difficult clock figure (spoiled in F by sophistication), gradually developed in *fixèd figure* (in the sense "fixed numeral") and *time*, for Othello's pained image of himself as a supreme object of humiliation.

55. *the time of scorn* the scornful world at large.

56. *his* its. *slow unmoving finger* The finger of the scornful world moves slowly but inexorably to point with steady contempt at the *fixèd figure*, as the hand of a clock points at a figure on the dial, moving so slowly it seems stationary.

58-63. *But . . . in* explaining what he cannot "bear" with patience: to be expelled from the heart's treasure layed up for his very means of life, to be cast out from the spring of his being, the fountain-head of his continued being in live issue—or to have the choice of keeping it a foul place for loathsome engendering. The images of fountain, "living waters," and cistern have important backgrounds in Scripture; cf. Canticles 4: 15; Proverbs 5: 15-18, John 4: 13.

Or keep it as a cistern for foul toads
To knot and gender in! —Turn thy complexion there,
Patience, thou young and rose-lipped cherubin!
65   Ay, here look grim as hell!

DESDEMONA

I hope my noble lord esteems me honest.

OTHELLO

O, ay! as summer flies are in the shambles,
That quicken even with blowing. O thou weed,
Who art so lovely fair, and smell'st so sweet
70   That the sense aches at thee, would thou hadst ne'er been born!

---

64.   **thou** F. Q has 'thy'.
67.   **as summer** F corr. F uncorr. has 'as a Sommer'; Q has 'as summers'.
68.   **weed** F . Q has 'blacke weede'.
69.   **Who . . . fair,** F. Q has 'Why . . . faire?'
        and F. Q has 'Thou'.
70.   **ne'er** Q. F has 'neuer'.

63. *knot and gender*   copulate and breed.

63–5. *Turn . . . hell*   An important crux because of the two abrupt ellipses, ambiguous diction, variants, and the question raised by QF's 'I': it could represent "ay" or the pronoun. In the face of such unbearable adversity (lines 58–63), cherubic Patience itself would alter both temperament and natural color (*turn . . . complexion*) and *look grim* (i.e. "threatening," "ugly," "black") *as hell*. Many editors emend to "Ay, there"—which the rhetorical pattern would seem to require. But the hero ceases to consider his adversity at a distance of mental recognition, and climactically recognizes it embodied in Desdemona who stands before him (*here*). I think *Ay, here* is meant to have double value in the speaking so that what has happened to black Othello's patience in confronting his fountain-turned-cistern ironically is attributed to *rose-lipped* Patience.

64. *cherubin* (Shakespeare's normal singular)—one of the order of angels beneath the Seraphim. An old tradition identified the various virtues with particular ranks of the angelic host.

67. *shambles*   slaughterhouse.

68. *quicken even with blowing*   come to life at the very moment fly eggs and ordure befoul the meat.

70. *aches at thee*   i.e. is pained with the intensity of the pleasure; with an implied distraught undermeaning based on *at* in the sense "for" ("serving to point out a mark aimed at" Schmidt). *would . . . born* echoing (ironically) Matthew 26: 24.

DESDEMONA

Alas, what ignorant sin have I committed?

OTHELLO

Was this fair paper, this most goodly book,
Made to write whore upon? What committed!
Committed! O thou public commoner!
75   I should make very forges of my cheeks,
That would to cinders burn up modesty,
Did I but speak thy deeds. What committed!
Heaven stops the nose at it, and the moon winks;
The bawdy wind, that kisses all it meets,
80   Is hushed within the hollow mine of earth
And will not hear it. What committed!
Impudent strumpet!

DESDEMONA

By heaven, you do me wrong!

OTHELLO

Are not you a strumpet?

---

73.   **upon** F. Q has 'on'.
74-7. **Committed . . . committed!** F. Not in Q.
80.   **hollow** F. Q has 'hallow'.
81.   **hear it** Steevens. QF have 'hear't'.
82.   **Impudent strumpet** Q. Not in F.

72. *this . . . book* i.e. her forehead.

73. *write whore upon* alluding to the Whore of Babylon and the "name" written "upon her forehead" in Revelation 17: 5—"The Mother of harlots and abominations of the Earth." *committed* Othello's outraged iteration depends on Elizabethan use of this word alone specifically to signify "commit adultery." Cf. *King Lear* III. iv. 72, "Commit not with man's sworn spouse."

74. *commoner* prostitute.

75. *forges* with (because of Desdemona's innocence) an ironic undermeaning drawn from the verb in the sense "to frame falsely."

80. *hollow mine of earth* i.e. the interior of the earth whence winds were supposed to issue.

DESDEMONA

No, as I am a Christian!
If to preserve this vessel for my lord
85 From any other's foul unlawful touch
Be not to be a strumpet, I am none.

OTHELLO

What, not a whore?

DESDEMONA

No, as I shall be saved!

OTHELLO

Is't possible?

DESDEMONA

O heaven, forgive us!

OTHELLO

I cry you mercy then.
90 I took you for that cunning whore of Venice
That married with Othello. [*Calling to* EMILIA] You, mistress,
That have the office opposite to Saint Peter
And keeps the gate of hell!

Enter EMILIA.

You, you, ay, you!

---

85. **other's** Wilson conj. F has 'other'; Q has 'hated'.
89. **forgive us** F. Q has 'forgiuenesse'. **then** F. Not in Q.
93. **S.D.** Q places after 'saved' line 87, F after 'mistress' line 91.
keeps QF (keepes). **gate of** F. Q has 'gates in'.
You, you, ay, you. F (you: I). Q has 'I, you, you, you;'.

84–5. With reference to 1 Thessalonians 4: 3–4: " . . . that ye should abstain from fornication: That every one of you should know how to possess his vessel in holiness and honor."

89. *I cry you mercy* a sarcastically elaborate "I beg your pardon."

91–5. Again acting out his "horrible fancy," with Emilia cast as bawd.

92–3. *That . . . hell* I.e., as member of "the hold-door trade" (*Troilus and Cressida* V. x. 50), Emilia is keeper of *the gate of hell* as her opposite number, St. Peter (whose attribute is a key), is that of heaven's. The thought is based on the proverbial idea that the harlot's "house is the way unto the grave, which goeth down to the chambers of death" (Proverbs 7: 27).

We have done our course; there's money for your pains;
95 I pray you turn the key, and keep our counsel.   *Exit.*

EMILIA

Alas, what does this gentleman conceive?
How do you, madam? how do you, my good lady?

DESDEMONA

Faith, half asleep.

EMILIA

Good madam, what's the matter with my lord?

DESDEMONA

100 With who?

EMILIA

Why, with my lord, madam.

DESDEMONA

Who is thy lord?

EMILIA

He that is yours, sweet lady.

DESDEMONA

I have none. Do not talk to me, Emilia;
I cannot weep; nor answer have I none
But what should go by water. Prithee, tonight
105 Lay on my bed my wedding sheets, remember;
And call thy husband hither.

EMILIA

Here's a change indeed!   *Exit.*

---

94. **have** F. Q has 'ha'.
101. F. Not in Q.
102. **have** F. Q has 'ha'.
103. **answer** Q. F has 'answers'.
105. **my** F. Q has 'our'.
106. **Here's** F. Q has 'Here is'.

96. *conceive*   imagine.
104. *go by water*   be conveyed by tears: i.e. since she cannot
weep, she has no answer. *Water* is common in the sense "tears," but
the wordplay here has sometimes been criticized as "a conceit quite
out of place" (Hudson). However, Shakespeare does not aim for a
complete naturalism. Cf. the paranomasia noted at lines 161–2, below.

DESDEMONA

'Tis meet I should be used so, very meet.
How have I been behaved, that he might stick
The small'st opinion on my least misuse?

Enter IAGO *and* EMILIA.

IAGO

110   What is your pleasure, madam? How is't with you?

DESDEMONA

I cannot tell. Those that do teach young babes
Do it with gentle means and easy tasks:
He might ha' chid me so; for, in good faith,
I am a child to chiding.

IAGO

What is the matter, lady?

EMILIA

115   Alas, Iago, my lord hath so bewhored her,
Thrown such despite and heavy terms upon her
As true hearts cannot bear.

---

107. **very meet** F. Q has 'very well'.
109. **small'st . . . least misuse?** F. Q has 'smallest . . . greatest
     abuse.'
113. **ha'** Q. F has 'haue'.
114. **to** F. Q has 'at'.
117. **As . . . bear.** Q. F has 'That . . . beare it.' F uncorr. reads
     'heart'.

107. *meet* ironically used.
108–9. *How . . . misuse* a tiresome crux, beginning with
opinion which does not elsewhere in Shakespeare mean "ill-opinion."
Q's version is the more easily logical, but "abuse" is an impossibly
strong word, for Desdemona is not admitting she has committed an
offense worthy of chastisement. I take F's version to mean: "How
have I behaved that my slightest misconduct could be open in the
least to his construction?"
114. *I . . . chiding* i.e. I respond as well as a child to being
chidden. A father's correction of his child and, analogously, the
merciful Father in Heaven's chastisement of His "children," were
often held up by Elizabethan marriage manuals as the models for
proper husbandly dealing with the faults of the "weaker vessel."
115. Emilia evidently has been listening at the door.
116. *despite* contemptuous abuse. *heavy* unbearable.

DESDEMONA

Am I that name, Iago?

IAGO

What name, fair lady?

DESDEMONA

Such as she says my lord did say I was.

EMILIA

120   He called her whore. A beggar in his drink
Could not have laid such terms upon his callet.

IAGO

Why did he so?

DESDEMONA

I do not know; I am sure I am none such.

IAGO

Do not weep, do not weep. Alas the day!

EMILIA

125   Hath she forsook so many noble matches,
Her father and her country, all her friends,
To be called whore? Would it not make one weep?

DESDEMONA

It is my wretched fortune.

IAGO

Beshrew him for't!

How comes this trick upon him?

---

119.   **says** Q. F has 'said'.
125.   **Hath** F. Q has 'Has'.
126.   **all** Q. F has 'And'.
128.   **for't** F. Q has 'for it'.

121. *callet*   base-born slut.

128. *my wretched fortune*   The name "Desdemona" is Greek for "the unfortunate."   *Beshrew him*   a very mild form of imprecation —but it does literally mean "Curse him," "Woe upon him."

129. *trick*   freakish behavior.   *Nay, heaven doth know*   equivalent to our "God only knows"—but with an important literal sense suggesting she has just used the word "fortune" in the strict meaning frequently defined by Elizabethan writers: "fate or destiny chancing to any man by the will of God, without man's providence" (Becon).

DESDEMONA

Nay, heaven doth know.

EMILIA

130   I'll be hanged if some eternal villain,
Some busy and insinuating rogue,
Some cogging, cozening slave, to get some office,
Have not devised this slander. I'll be hanged else.

IAGO

Fie, there is no such man; it is impossible.

DESDEMONA

135   If any such there be, heaven pardon him.

EMILIA

A halter pardon him! and hell gnaw his bones!
Why should he call her whore? Who keeps her company?
What place? what time? what form? what likelihood?
The Moor's abused by some most villainous knave,
140   Some base, notorious knave, some scurvy fellow.
O heaven, that such companions thou'dst unfold,
And put in every honest hand a whip
To lash the rascals naked through the world,
Even from the east to th' west!

---

138.   **form** F (Forme).   Q has 'for me'.
139.   **most villainous** F.   Q has 'outragious'.
141.   **heaven** Q.   F has 'Heauens'.
143.   **rascals** F.   Q has 'rascall'.
144.   **to th'** F.   Q has 'to the'.

130. *eternal*   a common intensive, used to express abhorrence—but here, ironically (like "villain"), literally apt.

131. *busy*   meddlesome. *insinuating*   worming his way into favor.

132. *cogging, cozening*   cheating, swindling. "To cog" is, literally, to "cheat with loaded dice."

139. *abused*   been deceived.

140. *notorious*   used intensively, i.e. "egregious," "notable"—with its more usual sense, "known to the whole world with evil repute," lurking because so ironically inappropriate. *scurvy*   scabby, vile.

141. *companions*   knaves. *unfold*   disclose, reveal.

IAGO

Speak within door.

EMILIA

145   O, fie upon them! Some such squire he was
      That turned your wit the seamy side without
      And made you to suspect me with the Moor.

IAGO

You are a fool; go to.

DESDEMONA

O good Iago,
What shall I do to win my lord again?
150   Good friend, go to him; for, by this light of heaven,
      I know not how I lost him. Here I kneel: [*She does so.*]
      If e'er my will did trespass 'gainst his love,
      Either in discourse of thought or actual deed,
      Or that mine eyes, mine ears, or any sense
155   Delighted them in any other form,
      Or that I do not yet, and ever did,
      And ever will (though he do shake me off
      To beggarly divorcement) love him dearly,
      Comfort forswear me. Unkindness may do much,
160   And his unkindness may defeat my life,

---

144. **door** F.   Q has 'dores'.
145. **them** F.   Q has 'him'.
148. **to** Q.   F has 'too'.   **O good** Q (Good).   F has 'Alas'.
151–64. **Here . . . me** F.   Not in Q.
155. **them in** Q2.   F has 'them: or'.

144. *Speak within door*   Quiet down, don't speak so loud and wildly.
145. *squire*   fine fellow—with contemptuous sarcasm.
146. *the seamy side without*   wrong side out.
147. See above II. i. 279–80.
148. *go to*   a rebuke: "enough," "go away."
153. *discourse of thought*   process of thinking.
154, 6. *that*   if.
159. *Comfort forswear me*   "May happiness swear by vow to have nothing more to do with me." A powerful phrase since the context—Desdemona's kneeling attestation of innocence "by this light of heaven"—urges the sense "even spiritual comfort from God."
160. *his*   emphatic.   *defeat*   destroy.

But never taint my love. I cannot say "whore":
It does abhor me now I speak the word;
To do the act that might th' addition earn
Not the world's mass of vanity could make me.

IAGO

165　I pray you be content; 'tis but his humor.
The business of the state does him offense,
And he does chide with you.　　　　　　[*She rises.*]

DESDEMONA

　　　　　　If 'twere no other—

IAGO

'Tis but so, I warrant you.　　　　[*Trumpets sound within.*]
Hark how these instruments summon you to supper!
170　The messengers of Venice stay the meat:
Go in, and weep not; all things shall be well.

　　　　　　　　　Exeunt DESDEMONA *and* EMILIA.
　　　　　　　Enter RODERIGO.

How now, Roderigo?

163.　**th'addition** Q2.　F has 'the addition'.
167.　**And . . . you.** Q.　Not in F.
168.　**'Tis . . . warrant you** Q.　F has 'It is . . . warrant'.
　　　S.D. Rowe.
169.　**you** Q.　Not in F.
170.　**The** F.　Q has 'And the great'.
　　　stay Q.　F has 'staies'.　**the meat** F.　Not in Q.
171.　**S.D.** F.　Q has '*Exit women.*'
　　　S.D. *Enter* **RODERIGO** F.　Q places after 'Roderigo?' line 172.

161.　*taint*　injure, impair.
162.　*abhor me*　fill me with abhorrence. (The identical wordplay occurs in the official Elizabethan Homily on adultery: "Hitherto have we heard how grievous sin fornication and whoredom is and how greatly God doth abhor it.")
163.　*addition*　title.
164.　*the world's mass of vanity*　all the enormous sum of vain glories, riches, pleasures offered in temptation by a "world" where "all is vanity" (Ecclesiastes 1: 2). Cf. IV. iii. 62, 66, 76 and Mark 8: 36: "For what shall it profit a man, though he should win the whole world, if he lose his soul."
165.　*be content*　don't be distressed.　*humor*　mood.
170.　*stay the meat*　wait for their food.
171.　*shall*　will surely.

RODERIGO

I do not find that thou deal'st justly with me.

IAGO

What in the contrary?

RODERIGO

175 Every day thou daff'st me with some device, Iago, and rather,
as it seems to me now, keep'st from me all conveniency than
suppliest me with the least advantage of hope. I will indeed
no longer endure it; nor am I yet persuaded to put up in peace
what already I have foolishly suffered.

IAGO

180 Will you hear me, Roderigo?

RODERIGO

Faith, I have heard too much; for your words and performance
are no kin together.

IAGO

You charge me most unjustly.

RODERIGO

With naught but truth. I have wasted myself out of means.
185 The jewels you have had from me to deliver Desdemona would

---

175–82. F. As verse in Q.
175. **daff'st** Collier. F has 'dafts'. Q has 'doffest'. **device** F2.
       QF have 'deuise'.
176. **now, keep'st** F. Q has 'thou keepest'.
181. **Faith** Q. Not in F. **for** Q. F corr. has 'and'. F uncorr. has
       'And hell gnaw his bones,' in place of 'I . . . words and'.
       performance Q. F has 'performances'.
184. **With . . . truth** F. Not in Q. **of** Q. F has 'of my'.
185. **deliver** F. Q has 'deliuer to'.

175. *daff'st me* put me off. *device* trick.
176. *all conveniency* everything suiting my wishes.
177. *advantage of hope* opportunity for achieving my hope.
178. *put up in peace* accept without resentment—"put up" means
to "pocket" a wrong or injury.
185. *deliver Desdemona* F's reading can be understood in Q's
sense ("deliuer to *Desdemona*"), but also precisely with the force of
Falstaff's "I will deliver his wife into your hand" (*Merry Wives of
Windsor* V. i. 26–7).

half have corrupted a votarist. You have told me she hath
received 'em, and returned me expectations and comforts of
sudden respect and acquittance; but I find none.

IAGO

Well, go to; very well.

RODERIGO

190 Very well! go to! I cannot go to, man; nor 'tis not very well.
Nay, I think it is scurvy, and begin to find myself fopped
in it.

IAGO

Very well.

RODERIGO

I tell you 'tis not very well. I will make myself known to
195 Desdemona. If she will return me my jewels, I will give over
my unlawful solicitation; if not, assure yourself I will seek
satisfaction of you.

IAGO

You have said now.

RODERIGO

Ay, and said nothing but what I protest intendment of doing.

---

186. **hath** F. Q has 'has'.
187. **'em** Q. F has 'them'. **expectations** F. Q has 'expectation'.
188. **acquittance** Q. F has 'acquaintance'.
189. **to** Q. F has 'too'. **well** F. Q has 'good'.
190. **nor 'tis** F. Q has 'it is'.
191. **Nay, I think it is** F. Q has 'by this hand, I say tis very'.
194. **tell you 'tis** F (you,). Q has 'say it is'.
195. **Desdemona. If** F. Q has '*Desdemona*, if'.
196. **I will** F. Q has 'I'le'.
199. **said** F. Q has 'I haue said'.

186. *a votarist* one who has taken religious vows, a nun.

187. *comforts* encouraging reports.

188. *sudden respect* immediate consideration. *acquittance* discharge of (her) debt. F's "acquaintance"—perhaps a genteel sophistication or substitution of an ordinary word—must be wrong in view
of I. i. 99, 174 and ii. 68.

191. *scurvy* vile. *fopped* made a fool of.

198. *You have said now* now you've said the whole thing!—with
two possible implications (1) "There's no more to be said"; and (2)
"Now you're talking!"

IAGO

200 Why, now I see there's mettle in thee, and even from this
instant do build on thee a better opinion than ever before. Give
me thy hand, Roderigo. Thou hast taken against me a most
just exception; but yet I protest I have dealt most directly in
thy affair.

RODERIGO

205 It hath not appeared.

IAGO

I grant indeed it hath not appeared, and your suspicion is not
without wit and judgment. But, Roderigo, if thou hast that in
thee indeed which I have greater reason to believe now than
ever—I mean purpose, courage, and valor—this night show it.

210 If thou the next night following enjoy not Desdemona, take me
from this world with treachery and devise engines for my life.

RODERIGO

Well, what is it? Is it within reason and compass?

IAGO

Sir, there is especial commission come from Venice to depute
Cassio in Othello's place.

RODERIGO

215 Is that true? why then, Othello and Desdemona return again
to Venice.

IAGO

O no; he goes into Mauritania, and takes away with him the
fair Desdemona, unless his abode be lingered here by some

---

201. **instant** F.   Q has 'time'.
203. **exception** F.   Q has 'conception'.
204. **affair** F.   Q has 'affaires'.
207. **in** F.   Q has 'within'.
210. **enjoy** F.   Q has 'enioyest'.
212. **what is it?** F.   Not in Q.
213–23. F.   As verse in Q.
213. **commission** F.   Q has 'command'.
217. **takes** Q.   F has 'taketh'.

211. *from this world* with a secondary ironic sense since (for the
Elizabethans) "treachery" was an expected characteristic of the
"world." *engines for* plots against.
212. *compass* range—i.e. capable of being done.

accident: wherein none can be so determinate as the removing
220   of Cassio.

RODERIGO

How do you mean, removing of him?

IAGO

Why, by making him uncapable of Othello's place—knocking
out his brains.

RODERIGO

And that you would have me to do?

IAGO

225   Ay, if you dare do yourself a profit and a right. He sups tonight
with a harlotry, and thither will I go to him. He knows not yet
of his honorable fortune. If you will watch his going thence,
which I will fashion to fall out between twelve and one, you
may take him at your pleasure. I will be near to second your
230   attempt, and he shall fall between us. Come, stand not amazed
at it, but go along with me. I will show you such a necessity in
his death that you shall think yourself bound to put it on him.
It is now high supper time, and the night grows to waste.
About it!

RODERIGO

235   I will hear further reason for this.

---

221. **of him** Q.   F has 'him'.
225. **if** F.   Q has 'and if'. **a right** F.   Q has 'right'.
226. **harlotry** F.   Q has 'harlot'.

219. *determinate*   finally decisive.
222. *uncapable of Othello's place*   unable to succeed to Othello's position as governor.
226. *a harlotry*   harlot—(the abstract used, contemptuously, I think, for the particular).
232. *to put it on him*   a softening circumlocution for "to make sure he suffers it."
233. *high*   quite.
235. *further reason*   As though there could be such to lie in wait to murder—about which he has qualms. This reservation is highly ironic in view of the endlessly iterated Elizabethan distinction between "right reason" (according with God's "natural law") and "carnal reason" (rationalizing the ends of appetite). Cf. 2 Corinthians 1: 12 and Romans 8: 6–7.

IAGO

And you shall be satisfied.   *Exeunt.*

[*Scene iii.*] *Enter* OTHELLO, LODOVICO, DESDEMONA, EMILIA, *and Attendants.*

LODOVICO

I do beseech you, sir, trouble yourself no further.

OTHELLO

O pardon me; 'twill do me good to walk.

LODOVICO

Madame, good night. I humbly thank your ladyship.

DESDEMONA

Your honor is most welcome.

OTHELLO

            Will you walk, sir? —

5 O, Desdemona—

DESDEMONA

My lord?

OTHELLO

Get you to bed on th' instant; I will be returned forthwith.
Dismiss your attendant there: look it be done.

IV. iii **S.D.** F. Q places after 'About it.' ii. 234.
2. **'twill** F. Q has 'it shall'.
3. **Madame** Q. F has 'Madam'.
6. **lord?** Capell. QF have 'Lord.'
7–8. Verse. As prose in QF.
7. **bed on th' instant; I** F (instant,). Q has 'bed, o'the instant I'.
    returned forthwith. F (forthwith:). Q has 'return'd, forthwith,'.
8. **Dismiss** F. Q has 'dispatch'. **look it** Q. F has 'look't'.

IV. iii The scene begins at the conclusion of the entertainment for Lodovico, the emissary from Venice, whom Othello had invited to supper. It is localized by action as in a room of the Governor's residence in the citadel.

1. *trouble yourself no further* in context, with an unintended ironic sense. Literally: "You need not escort me to my lodgings."

DESDEMONA

I will, my lord.   *Exit* [OTHELLO, *with* LODOVICO *and*
                                                   Attendants].

EMILIA

10   How goes it now? He looks gentler than he did.

DESDEMONA

He says he will return incontinent.
He hath commanded me to go to bed,
And bade me to dismiss you.

EMILIA

                    Dismiss me?

DESDEMONA

It was his bidding; therefore, good Emilia,
15   Give me my nightly wearing, and adieu.
We must not now displease him.

EMILIA

I would you had never seen him!

DESDEMONA

So would not I: my love doth so approve him
That even his stubbornness, his checks, his frowns—
20   Prithee unpin me—have grace and favor in them.

EMILIA

I have laid those sheets you bade me on the bed.

----

9. **S.D.** Q (*Exeunt.*) and F (*Exit.*) placed after 'done' line 8.
11–12. **incontinent./He** Q (incontinent:).   F has 'incontinent,/And'.
13. **bade** Q2. Q1 has 'bad'; F has 'bid'.
17. **I would** Q. F has 'I, would'.
19. **checks, his** F. Q has 'checks and'.
20. **in them** Q. Not in F.
21. **those** F. Q has 'these'.

11. *incontinent*   immediately.
19. *stubbornness* roughness. *checks* rebukes.
20. *grace and favor* This is usually interpreted "attractiveness
and charm" (Ridley). But what her words deeply mean, I think, is
that the "checks" and "frowns" of her lord (like those of the Lord to
the soul) *have grace and favor in them* because they show her sufficient in his eyes to be worthy of his correction.

DESDEMONA

All's one. Good Father, how foolish are our minds!
If I do die before thee, prithee shroud me
In one of those same sheets.

EMILIA

Come, come! you talk.

DESDEMONA

25 My mother had a maid called Barbary.
She was in love; and he she loved proved mad
And did forsake her. She had a song of "Willow"—
An old thing 'twas, but it expressed her fortune,
And she died singing it. That song tonight
30 Will not go from my mind. I have much to do
But to go hang my head all at one side
And sing it like poor Barbary. Prithee dispatch.

EMILIA

Shall I go fetch your nightgown?

DESDEMONA

No, unpin me here.
This Lodovico is a proper man.

---

22. **one. Good Father,** F (one:). Q has 'one good faith:'.
23. **thee** Q. Not in F.
24. **those** Q. F has 'these'.
27. **had** F. Q has 'has'.
30–51. **I . . . next.** F. Not in Q.

22. *All's one* It's no matter. *foolish* i.e. full of superstitious folly. The reason the heroine recognizes before her "Good Father" that her superstitious foreboding is *foolish* can be found in Romans 8: 15–16, "For ye have not received the Spirit of bondage, to fear again: but ye have received the Spirit of adoption, whereby we cry, Abba, Father./ The same Spirit beareth witness with our spirit, that we are the children of God."

24. *talk* i.e. idly.

26. *mad* wayward, with probable near-homonymic play on "made" = "false."

30–1. *much . . . head* all I can do to keep myself from hanging my head.

34. *proper* handsome.

EMILIA

35   A very handsome man.

DESDEMONA

He speaks well.

EMILIA

I know a lady in Venice would have walked barefoot to
Palestine for a touch of his nether lip.

DESDEMONA [*sings*]

The poor soul sat sighing by a sycamore tree,
40   Sing all a green willow;
Her hand on her bosom, her head on her knee,
Sing willow, willow, willow.
The fresh streams ran by her and murmered her moans;
Sing willow, willow, willow;
45   Her salt tears fell from her, and softened the stones—

Lay by these—

Sing willow, willow, willow—

Prithee hie thee; he'll come anon—

Sing all a green willow must be my garland.
50   Let nobody blame him; his scorn I approve—

Nay, that's not next. —Hark! who is't that knocks?

---

39.   **soul sat sighing** Q2. F corr. has '*Soule sat singing*'.
      F uncorr. has '*Sonle set sining*'.
48.   **hie** Q2. F has 'high'.
51.   **who is't** F. Q has 'who's'.

35. *handsome*   of attractive external person and manners.
38. *nether*   lower.
39ff. On the text and music of the Willow Song, see App. D,
particularly for the popular model of the lyrics which Shakespeare
meaningfully alters. As Desdemona sings, Emilia "unpins" her
"here" (line 33), localizing the scene by action and indicating the
place to be other than the bedroom in V. ii.
40. *green willow*   a symbol of the forsaken and forlorn lover.
48. *hie thee*   make haste.
50. *approve*   admit the propriety of. Desdemona does not sing
the next, rhyme-completing, line of the song; in the popular model
(where the "false love" is the woman), it goes (as the audience no
doubt knew): "She was born to be false, and I to die for her love."

EMILIA

It's the wind.

DESDEMONA [*sings*]
    I called my love false love; but what said he then?
        Sing willow, willow, willow:
55   If I court moe women, you'll couch with moe men—

So, get thee gone; good night. Mine eyes do itch:
Doth that bode weeping?

EMILIA
                    'Tis neither here nor there.

DESDEMONA

I have heard it said so. O, these men, these men!
Dost thou in conscience think—tell me, Emilia—
60 That there be women do abuse their husbands
In such gross kind?

EMILIA
                There be some such, no question.

DESDEMONA

Wouldst thou do such a deed for all the world?
EMILIA

Why, would not you?

DESDEMONA
            No, by this heavenly light!

---

52. **It's** F. Q has 'It is'.
53–5. F. Not in Q.
56. **So, get** F (So). Q has 'Now get'.
57. **Doth** F. Q has 'Does'.
58–61. **I . . . question.** F. Not in Q.

55. *moe*   more (of number).
57. *neither here nor there*   neither yes nor no—it has no value as a portent.
59. *in conscience think*   believe with real conviction.
60. *abuse*   deceive.
61. *such gross kind*   such a gross way.
62. *for all the world*   see above, IV. ii. 164, note.

EMILIA

Nor I neither by this heavenly light;
65 I might do't as well i' th' dark.

DESDEMONA

Wouldst thou do such a deed for all the world?

EMILIA

The world's a huge thing: it is a great price
For a small vice.

DESDEMONA

Good troth, I think thou wouldst not.

EMILIA

By my troth, I think I should, and undo't when I had done it.
70 Marry, I would not do such a thing for a joint-ring, nor for
measures of lawn, nor for gowns, petticoats, nor caps, nor
any petty exhibition; but for all the whole world—'Ud's pity!

---

65. **do't . . . i' th'** F.   Q has 'doe it . . . in the'.
66. **Wouldst . . . deed** F.   Q has 'Would . . . thing'.
67. **world's** F.   Q has 'world is'.
68. **Good troth** Q.   F has 'Introth'.
69. **By my troth** Q.   F has 'Introth'.   **it** Q.   Not in F.
'70. **nor** F.   Q has 'or'.
71. **petticoats** F.   Q has 'or Petticotes'.
72. **petty** F.   Q has 'such'.   **all** F.   Not in Q.
     'Ud's pity Q.   F has 'why'.

65. *might*   could.

68. *a small vice*   playing on *vice* in the senses "sin" and "fault."
Cf. *Measure for Measure* III. i. 111–13: "Sure it is no sin,/ Or of
the deadly seven it is the least./ Which is the least?"   *Good troth*
in sincere faith.

69. *By my troth*   a mild oath, playfully ironic here since "troth-
plight" and its violation is the subject.

70. *joint-ring*   a ring made of halves that could be separated—
often used as a love token.

71. *lawn*   a kind of fine linen.

72. *petty exhibition   Exhibition* usually means "allowance" and
hence, here, "gratuity." I think *petty* is emphatic.   *'Ud's pity* an
oath—"by God's pity"—ironically called for.

who would not make her husband a cuckold to make him a
monarch? I should venture purgatory for't.

DESDEMONA

75   Beshrew me if I would do such a wrong
      For the whole world.

EMILIA

Why, the wrong is but a wrong i' the world; and having the
world for your labor, 'tis a wrong in your own world, and
you might quickly make it right.

DESDEMONA

80   I do not think there is any such woman.

EMILIA

Yes, a dozen; and as many to th' vantage as would store the
world they played for.
But I do think it is their husbands' faults
If wives do fall. Say that they slack their duties
85   And pour our treasures into foreign laps;
      Or else break out in peevish jealousies,
      Throwing restraint upon us; or say they strike us,
      Or scant our former having in despite—

---

73.   **cuckold** F.   Q has 'Cuckole'.
74.   **for't** F.   Q has 'for it'.
77.   **i' the** Q.   F has 'i' th' '.
81.   **th' vantage** F.   Q has 'the vantage'.
83–100.   F.   Not in Q.

74. *I should venture*   I'd take a chance on going to.   *purgatory*
the place where souls of the dead are purged by fire of carnal im-
purity—an amusingly ironic reference for the original audience since
their religion allowed the existence only of heaven and hell.
81. *to th' vantage*   over and above, to boot.   *store*   populate.
85. With a quite physical *double entendre.   our treasures*   treasures which should be ours.   *foreign*   alien.   *laps*   In Shakespearean usage *lap* is invariably feminine in reference and often more
restricted in sense than in ours: "the seat formed by a female body
in sitting or lying down" (Schmidt). Cf. *Hamlet* III. ii. 108ff.
86. *peevish*   silly, childish.
87. *Throwing*   inflicting.
88. *scant . . . despite*   reduce our former allowances to spite us.

Why, we have galls; and though we have some grace,
90 Yet have we some revenge. Let husbands know
Their wives have sense like them: they see, and smell,
And have their palates both for sweet and sour,
As husbands have. What is it they do
When they change us for others? Is it sport?
95 I think it is. And doth affection breed it?
I think it doth. Is't frailty that thus errs?
It is so too. And have not we affections,
Desires for sport, and frailty, as men have?
Then let them use us well; else let them know,
100 The ills we do, their ills instruct us so.

DESDEMONA

Good night, good night. God me such uses send,
Not to pick bad from bad, but by bad mend!   *Exeunt.*

---

101. **God** Q.   F has 'Heauen'. **uses** F.   Q has 'vsage'.

89. *galls* i.e. to make our resentment bitter.   *some grace* and therefore some virtue.

90. *have we some revenge* in context, with two senses: (1) "we have in our power some revenge we can take"; (2) "we take some revenge."

91. *sense* five senses.

94. *sport* sexual pleasure.

95. *affection* appetitive desire; see above I. iii. 313, note.

101. *uses* habitual ways—i.e. of conducting oneself in the uses of the world and experience. The phrase *such uses* is explained by the next line. I think Q's "usage" a first thought with the same sense, and suspect it replaced because its usual meaning, "treatment," left the passage open to a misinterpreting emphasis on "usage" of Desdemona (i.e. "God send such treatment of me that I won't be caused to learn evil from evil").   *send* optative, as appropriate in a prayer—"may God send." The choice of this verb is predicated on the Anglican article of faith (10) that man has "no power to do good works . . . without the grace of God . . . that we may have a good will, and working with us, when we have that good will."

102. I.e. not to gather, from evils done me, to return evil for evil, but rather by those very evils to become spiritually better—viz. through patience. Cf. James 1: 3–4.

[*Act V, scene i.*] *Enter* IAGO *and* RODERIGO.

IAGO

Here, stand behind this bulk; straight will he come.
Wear thy good rapier bare, and put it home.
Quick, quick! Fear nothing; I'll be at thy elbow.
It makes us or it mars us: think on that,
5   And fix most firm thy resolution.

RODERIGO

Be near at hand; I may miscarry in't.

IAGO

Here at thy hand. Be bold, and take thy stand.   [*Stands aside.*]

RODERIGO [*apart*]

I have no great devotion to the deed;
And yet he hath given me satisfying reasons.
10   'Tis but a man gone. Forth my sword: he dies!

IAGO [*apart*]

I have rubbed this young quat almost to the sense,
And he grows angry. Now, whether he kill Cassio,

V. i   1. **bulk** Q (Bulke). F has 'Barke'.
     4. **on** F.   Q has 'of'.
     7. **stand** F.   Q has 'sword'.   **S.D.** Capell (subst.).
     8. **deed** F.   Q has 'dead'.
     9. **hath** F.   Q has 'has'.
    11. **quat** F.   Q has 'gnat'.
    12. **angry. Now** F.   Q has 'angry now:'.

V. i   The preparations for the ambush of Cassio set the action in a street, which Othello's entrance and Emilia's exit further define as presumably near the citadel. The time, as prepared for at the end of IV. ii, is between twelve and one the same night.

1. *bulk*   a term used for a structure projecting into a street from the wall of a building—e.g. a stall. That it here refers to something physically used for an ambuscade may indicate the presence on the platform stage of a "fit-up booth," extending from the theater façade. The curtained bed of V. ii could have been within, or even served as, such a structure.   *straight*   straightway.

6. *miscarry*   fail to succeed.

7. *stand*   station for waiting and watching—"particularly applied to the station of huntsmen waiting for game" (Schmidt).

11. *quat*   pimple, pustule.   *to the sense*   to the quick—i.e. with irritation.

      Or Cassio him, or each do kill the other,

      Every way makes my game. Live Roderigo,

15   He calls me to a restitution large

      Of gold and jewels that I bobbed from him

      As gifts to Desdemona:

      It must not be. If Cassio do remain,

      He hath a daily beauty in his life

20   That makes me ugly; and besides, the Moor

      May unfold me to him: there stand I in much peril.

      No, he must die.

Enter CASSIO.

Be't so! I hear him coming.

RODERIGO

I know his gait: 'tis he. Villain, thou diest!

[*He makes a thrust at* CASSIO.]

CASSIO

That thrust had been mine enemy indeed,

---

    14. **game** Q. F has 'gaine'.

    16. **Of** F. Q has 'For'.

    19. **hath** F. Q has 'has'.

    21. **much** F. Not in Q.

    22. **S.D.** QF place after 'coming.' **Be't** Q. F has 'But'.

        hear Q. F has 'heard'.

    23, 26. **S.D.s** Hart (adapting Rowe and Theobald). Not in QF.

    24. **mine** F. Q has 'my'.

    14. *makes my game* a gambling term: "gives me the game."
Live Roderigo subjunctive: "If Roderigo survive."

    16. *bobbed from him* swindled out of him.

    21. *unfold* disclose—viz. by telling of my accusation.

    24. *mine enemy* i.e. because it was a palpable hit.

25   But that my coat is better than thou know'st.
      I will make proof of thine! [*He draws, and wounds* RODERIGO.]

RODERIGO

O, I am slain!
[IAGO *rushes forth behind* CASSIO, *wounds his leg, and exit.*]

CASSIO

I am maimed for ever!   [*He falls.*]
      Help, ho! murder! murder!
      Enter OTHELLO.

OTHELLO

The voice of Cassio: Iago keeps his word.

RODERIGO

O villain that I am!

OTHELLO

It is even so.

CASSIO

30   O help, ho! light! a surgeon!

---

25. **know'st** F.   Q has 'think'st'.
27. **maimed** F (maym'd).   Q1 has 'maind';   Q2 has 'maimd'.
     Help F.   Q has 'light'.
29. **It is** F.   Q has 'Harke tis'.

25. *coat*   i.e. a "privy coat" or "jack"—a hidden armor protecting the upper half of the body (like a bullet-proof vest), made of over-lying metal plates and faced with fabric so that it gives no outward impression of the wearer's defense. As Cassio discovers, a "privy coat" does not protect the legs.

26. *make proof*   the technical term for testing the penetrability of armor—ironic because Roderigo actually wears no protection just as Cassio only appears not to. *S.D.s* These directions, first sup-plied by eighteenth-century editors, have sometimes been challenged, but the ironies of the remainder of the scene absolutely require them to be substantially correct.

29. *It is even so*   Othello takes Roderigo's exclamation, a con-fession of villainy justly served, as so appropriate to the guilty "Cassio" that it confirms the "voice" as his. The ironic effect may have been heightened by placing Othello's entrance to overhear the action "above."

OTHELLO

'Tis he. O brave Iago, honest and just,
That hast such noble sense of thy friend's wrong!
Thou teachest me. Minion, your dear lies dead,
And your unblest fate hies. Strumpet, I come!

35 Forth of my heart those charms, thine eyes, are blotted.
Thy bed, lust-stained, shall with lust's blood be spotted.

Exit [OTHELLO].

Enter LODOVICO *and* GRATIANO.

CASSIO

What ho! no watch? no passage? Murder! murder!

GRATIANO

'Tis some mischance; the voice is very direful.

CASSIO

O, help!

LODOVICO

40 Hark!

RODERIGO

O wretched villain!

---

34. **unblest fate hies** F.   Q has 'fate hies apace'.
35. **Forth** Q.   F has 'For'.
38. **voice** F.   Q has 'cry'.

31. *brave* nobly valiant, becomingly gallant. This word, because of its connections with "ostentation," "display," and "threat" was readily capable of ironic use; cf. *Midsummer Night's Dream* III. ii. 70.

33. *Minion* i.e. Desdemona. A word used, often contemptuously, of someone generally loved and flattered; but it can mean "a favorite," "a darling."

35. *of* from.   *charms* objects magically empowered irresistibly to vanquish the affections. *Charm* is a much stronger word in Shakespeare's English than in ours; (cf. *Antony and Cleopatra* IV. xii. 16, where the hero calls her his "charm," i.e. his witch).

37. *no passage?* no one passing by?

LODOVICO

Two or three groan. It is a heavy night;
These may be counterfeits: let's think it unsafe
To come in to the cry without more help.

RODERIGO

45   Nobody come? then shall I bleed to death.

LODOVICO

Hark!

[*Re-*]*enter* IAGO, *with a light.*

GRATIANO

Here's one comes in his shirt, with light and weapons.

IAGO

Who's there? Whose noise is this that cries on murder?

LODOVICO

We do not know.

IAGO

Did not you hear a cry?

CASSIO

50   Here, here! for heaven's sake, help me!

IAGO

What's the matter?

GRATIANO

This is Othello's ancient, as I take it.

---

42. **groan** F.   Q has 'grones'. **It is a** Q.   F has ' 'Tis'.
44. **in to** Capell.   QF have 'into'.
46. **S.D.** *with a light* Q.   Not in F.
47. **light** F.   Q has 'lights'.
49. **We** F.   Q has 'I'. **Did** Q.   F has 'Do'.
50. **heaven's** Q (heauens).   F has 'heauen'.

42. *heavy*   gloomy, cloudy-black and dark.
44. *come in to the cry*   approach where the cries come from. But
I think there is a hunting metaphor: "join the pack of hounds where
the (perhaps dangerous) quarry appears to lie wounded."
46 S.D.–8. Iago's entrance, so described, is deliberately reminiscent
of the turn of "the honest man aroused from lawful slumber by
violence," a cliché of the Elizabethan drama established by the success of Kyd's *The Spanish Tragedy*.
48. *cries on*   cries out.

LODOVICO

The same indeed, a very valiant fellow.

IAGO

What are you here that cry so grievously?

CASSIO

55 Iago? O, I am spoiled, undone by villains!
Give me some help.

IAGO

O me, lieutenant! What villains have done this?

CASSIO

I think the one of them is hereabout,
And cannot make away.

IAGO

O treacherous villains!

60 [*To* LODOVICO *and* GRATIANO] What are you there? Come in
and give some help.

RODERIGO

O help me here!

CASSIO

That's one of 'em!

IAGO

O murd'rous slave! O villain!

[*He stabs* RODERIGO.]

RODERIGO

O damned Iago! O inhuman dog!

IAGO

Kill men i' th' dark! Where be these bloody thieves?
65 How silent is this town! Ho! murder! murder!

---

57. **me,** F. Q has 'my'.
58. **the** Q. F has 'that'.
60. **S.D.** Theobald.
61. **here** Q. F has 'there'.
62. **'em** Q. F has 'them'. **murd'rous** F. Q has 'murderous'.
    S.D. Rowe. Q2 has '*Thrusts him in.*' Not in QF.
63. **dog!** F. Q has 'dog,--o, o, o.'
64. **men i' th'** F. Q has 'him i' the'. **these** F. Q has 'those'.

55. *spoiled* hurt to death, crippled. *undone* ruined.

[LODOVICO *and* GRATIANO *come forward.*]

What may you be? are you of good or evil?

LODOVICO

As you shall prove us, praise us.

IAGO

Signior Lodovico?

LODOVICO

He, sir.

IAGO

I cry you mercy. Here's Cassio hurt by villains.

GRATIANO

70   Cassio?

IAGO

How is't, brother?

CASSIO

My leg is cut in two.

IAGO

Marry, heaven forbid!
Light, gentlemen. I'll bind it with my shirt.
Enter BIANCA.

BIANCA

What is the matter, ho? Who is't that cried?

IAGO

75   Who is't that cried!

---

71. **is't** F. Q has 'is it'.

67. "As you shall find us good or bad, so value (literally, appraise) us." An evasive proverbial saying.

69. *I cry you mercy* I beg your pardon (for not recognizing you).

75. *Who is't that cried!* This repetition of Bianca's question has been suspected of being the result of textual corruption. I think it should be uttered with broadly scornful irony (with the implication: "as if you didn't know!") and that it is meant to display the opportunistic plotter Iago at his most white-hot efficient—conceiving and realizing a plausible dodge almost instantaneously.

BIANCA

O my dear Cassio! my sweet Cassio!
O Cassio, Cassio, Cassio!

IAGO

O notable strumpet! —Cassio, may you suspect
Who they should be that thus have mangled you?

CASSIO

80   No.

GRATIANO

I am sorry to find you thus. I have been to seek you.

IAGO

Lend me a garter. So. O, for a chair
To bear him easily hence!

BIANCA

Alas, he faints! O Cassio, Cassio, Cassio!

IAGO

85   Gentlemen all, I do suspect this trash
To be a party in this injury. —
Patience awhile, good Cassio. —Come, come!
Lend me a light. Know we this face or no?
Alas, my friend and my dear countryman
90   Roderigo? No—yes, sure. O heaven, Roderigo!

GRATIANO

What, of Venice?

IAGO

Even he, sir. Did you know him?

---

76. **my sweet** F. Q has 'O my sweete'.
77. **O Cassio** F. Not in Q.
79. **thus have** Q. F has 'haue thus'.
82–3. **IAGO Lend . . . hence!** F. Not in Q.
86. **be a party in this injury** F. Q has 'beare a part in this'.
87. **Come, come** F. Not in Q.
90. **O heaven** Q. F has 'Yes, 'tis'.

78. *O notable strumpet* sarcastically imitating her mode of apostrophe.

82. *a garter* addressed, of course, to one of the men (who wore garters at this time).

85. *trash* worthless stuff.

GRATIANO

Know him? Ay.

IAGO

Signior Gratiano! I cry you gentle pardon.
These bloody accidents must excuse my manners
95 That so neglected you.

GRATIANO

I am glad to see you.

IAGO

How do you, Cassio? —O, a chair, a chair!

GRATIANO

Roderigo?

IAGO

He, he, 'tis he!   [*A chair is brought in.*]
O, that's well said! the chair.
Some good man bear him carefully from hence.
100 I'll fetch the general's surgeon. [*To* BIANCA] For you, mistress,
Save you your labor. —He that lies slain here, Cassio,
Was my dear friend. What malice was between you?

CASSIO

None in the world; nor do I know the man.

IAGO

[*To* BIANCA] What, look you pale? —O, bear him out o' th' air.
[CASSIO *is borne off, and* RODERIGO's *body removed.*]

---

93.   **you** Q. F has 'your'.
97.   **Roderigo?** F. Q has 'Roderigo.'
98.   **He, he** F. Q has 'He'.
      S.D. Capell (subst.). Not in QF. **the** F. Q has 'a'.
100, 104.   **S.D.s** *To* **BIANCA** Johnson.
102. **between** F. Q has 'betwixt'.
104. **out** Q. Not in F.

93. *I . . . pardon* "I beg you will be so courteous as to pardon
me" (Kittredge).
94. *accidents* happenings.
98. *well said* well done!
100. *For* as for. *mistress* madam (with careful irony).
101. *your labor* Bianca is attempting to tend the wounded
Cassio.
102. *malice* enmity, cause of bloody quarrel.

105   Stay you, good gentlemen. —Look you pale, mistress?—
Do you perceive the gastness of her eye?—
Nay, an' you stare, we shall hear more anon.—
Behold her well; I pray you look upon her:
Do you see, gentlemen? nay, guiltiness will speak
110   Though tongues were out of use.

Enter EMILIA.

EMILIA

'Las, what's the matter, what's the matter, husband?

IAGO

Cassio hath here been set on in the dark
By Roderigo, and fellows that are scaped.
He's almost slain, and Roderigo quite.

EMILIA

115   Alas, good gentleman! alas, good Cassio!

IAGO

This is the fruits of whoring. Pray, Emilia,
Go know of Cassio where he supped tonight. —
[*To* BIANCA] What, do you shake at that?

BIANCA

He supped at my house; but I therefore shake not.

IAGO

120   O, did he so? I charge you go with me.

---

105.   **gentlemen** F. Q has 'Gentlewoman'.
106.   **gastness** F. Q has 'ieastures'.
107.   **an'** Q. F has 'if'. **stare . . . hear** F. Q has 'stirre . . . haue'.
108.   **well; . . . you look** F (well:). Q has 'well . . . you, looke'.
110.   **S.D.** Q. Not in F.
111.   **'Las, what's . . . what's** Q. F has 'Alas, what is . . . /What is'.
112.   **hath** F. Q has 'has'.
114.   **quite.** F has 'quite dead.' Q has 'dead.'
116.   **fruits** F. Q has 'fruite'. **Pray** Q. F has 'Prythe'.

106.   *gastness*   frighted look.
107.   Tantamount to: "If you look so scared (with guilt), we will surely have a confession momentarily."
117.   *know of*   learn from.

EMILIA

Fie, fie upon thee, strumpet!

BIANCA

I am no strumpet, but of life as honest
As you that thus abuse me.

EMILIA

As I? foh! fie upon thee!

IAGO

Kind gentlemen, let's go see poor Cassio dressed.
125   [*To* BIANCA] Come, mistress, you must tell's another tale.—
Emilia, run you to the citadel
And tell my lord and lady what hath happed.   [*Exit* EMILIA.]
Will you go on afore? [*Aside*] This is the night
That either makes me or fordoes me quite.   *Exeunt.*

---

121. **Fie, fie** Q. F has 'Oh fie'.
123. **foh** Q (fough). Not in F.
127. **hath** F. Q has 'has'.
128. **afore?** F. Q has 'I pray,'.
129. **makes** F. Q has 'markes'.

124. *see poor Cassio dressed* i.e. see that poor Cassio's wounds
get dressed.

125. *tell's* tell us.

129. *makes me* i.e. makes my fortunes—picking up the gambling
spirit of "It makes us or it mars us" (line 4) and "Every way makes
my game" (line 14) at the start of the scene.   *fordoes* ruins.

[*Scene ii.*] DESDEMONA [*asleep*] *in her bed. Enter*
OTHELLO *with a light.*

OTHELLO

It is the cause, it is the cause, my soul.

Let me not name it to you, you chaste stars!

It is the cause. Yet I'll not shed her blood,

V. ii   **S.D.** *in her bed* F.   Not in Q.   *with a light* Q.   Not in F.

V. ii.   S.D.   The direction is possibly ambiguous, but it appears
that Desdemona's bed, the central property and symbol of the scene,
was already on-stage at its start (instead of being "thrust on" as such
large properties often were on the Elizabethan stage). See the note on
the staging of V. i. The bed alone localizes the open stage so that, for
the actor of Othello, standing beneath the theater's "heavens," there
is no incongruity in his addressing the "stars" which probably were
represented in its symbolic decoration. Desdemona wears her "nightly
wearing"—the white "smock" noted at line 270. Othello, as he enters,
must have not only the "light" but also (at least on his person, but
perhaps in his hand until line 3) the sword used to threaten Emilia
and later lost to Montano (lines 161, 232 S.D., 237). These properties
have an appropriately ambivalent symbolism. The figure of the "light-
bearer" could represent one who preserves and lives by the "light of
the Lord" (see Proverbs 20: 27, Psalm 18: 28)—i.e. who "walks" as
the "children of light" because he is "light in the Lord" and not
"darkness" (Ephesians 5: 8). However, "He that saith he is in that
light, and hateth his brother, is in darkness . . ." (1 John 2: 9). A
man with fire and sword commonly was used, in fact, to personify
Wrath. The sword is an attribute of Justice (line 17) and also of the
legitimate "magistrate" (which Othello, as governor of Cyprus, is),
responsible not only "to bear" the sword but also to use it on evil-
doers as the minister of God's vengeance (Romans 13: 4), as distinguished from man's private, wrathful revenge.

1. *the cause*   This difficult abstract word, in this charged context, has a wide range of evoked meanings—primarily, "the motive,
or necessary ground for, the (intended) action," and thus "the charge
against the accused," "the case before the law," and "the end in view
for which the deed must be done." *my soul* suggesting the
literary convention of the "dialogue of self and soul."

2. *chaste stars*   so called because they were thought incorruptible
and traditionally symbolized the heavenly host and the state of the
blessed in heaven (cf. 1 Corinthians 15: 41).

Nor scar that whiter skin of hers than snow,

5   And smooth as monumental alabaster;

Yet she must die, else she'll betray more men.

Put out the light, and then put out the light:

If I quench thee, thou flaming minister,

I can again thy former light restore

10   Should I repent me; but once put out thy light,

Thou cunning'st pattern of excelling nature,

---

10.   **thy light** F.   Q has 'thine'.
11.   **cunning'st** F.   Q has 'cunning'.

4. *whiter . . . snow*   In context, this common comparison (the stock sample of "hyperbolic simile" learned by Elizabethan schoolboys) ironically evokes the associations of the whiteness of snow with chastity, innocence, and spiritual purification. Cf. Tilley, S591, Psalm 51: 7, Isaiah 1: 18, and, e.g., *Hamlet* III. iii. 46.

5. *monumental alabaster*   i.e. alabaster carved and polished in a sculptured figure on a tomb, the reference here being specifically to the recumbent figures of the dead often seen on Elizabethan funerary monuments. Cf. *Cymbeline* II. ii. 32. Shakespeare elsewhere thinks of alabaster as a white stone (*Venus and Adonis*, line 363).

7. *Put . . . light*   Cf. particularly John 3: 19, "And this is the condemnation, that light is come into the world, and men loved darkness rather than light, because their deeds were evil." The line depends for its meaning on the crucial duality of "light" in scriptural symbolism. It can signify the "light of the Lord" which the faithful cherish and by which they guide their lives (see above V. ii. S.D., note). It can also represent the "light of the wicked" condemned to be "put out." See Proverbs 13: 9, "The light of the righteous rejoiceth: but the candle of the wicked shall be put out." Also Job 18: 5–6, "Yea, the light of the wicked shall be quenched . . . The light shall be dark in his dwelling, and his candle shall be put out with him." Shakespeare anticipates, in *Lucrece*, lines 190–3, the figure of a man with a light at the bedside of a chaste woman whose more excellent divine light he is about to "darken" by a terrible crime.

8. *flaming minister*   a phrase associated with the greatness and power of God "Who maketh his angels spirits, and his ministers a flaming fire" (Psalm 104: 4, Hebrews 1: 7). *Minister* means "servant."

11. *the cunning'st pattern*   the most skillfully wrought model, or masterpiece.   *excelling nature*   This can be understood to mean "nature when it surpasses its own artistry" or "human nature at its most excellent, surpassing all rivals."

I know not where is that Promethean heat
That can thy light relume. When I have plucked the rose,
I cannot give it vital growth again;
15   It needs must wither: I'll smell thee on the tree.

                                        [*He kisses her.*]

O balmy breath, that dost almost persuade
Justice herself to break her sword once more!
Be thus when thou art dead, and I will kill thee,

---

13. **relume** Malone.   F has 're-Lume';   Q has 'returne'.
     the rose Q.   F has 'thy Rose'.
15. **needs must** F.   Q has 'must needs'.   **thee** F.   Q has 'it'.
     S.D. Q2.   Not in QF.
16. **O balmy . . . dost** F.   Q has 'A balmy . . . doth'.
17. **Justice herself** Q.   F has 'Iustice'.
     sword once more Q.   F has 'Sword. One more, one more'.

12. *Promethean heat*   In the Greek myth, Prometheus stole fire
from heaven with which he animated an image he had made of clay,
and was punished by Jupiter.

13. *relume*   relight.

13–15. *rose . . . wither*   Traditionally, the rose is the type of
beauty (Sonnet 1), the exemplary flower in the earthly lover's
"garden of delights," and a symbol of spiritual beauty as well
(Ecclesiasticus 39: 13–14; Canticles 2:1). The association of the rose
and its withering inevitably recalls the frequent (and often ironic)
Renaissance reminiscence of the advice of the worldly-wise ungodly
in Wisdom 2: 8, "Let us crown ourselves with rosebuds afore they be
withered." See, e.g., *The Faerie Queene* II. iv. 74–5.

16–19. Editorial decision here is most difficult. F's reading (including the variants in line 19) has dramatic simplicity and affective
power; but I think it must be based on simplification or misunder-
standing of, or supposition of error in, that preserved by Q. Justice
broke her sword *once* before at the Expiation of man's sin—a point
found in Renaissance depiction of the Crucifixion. Other allusions in
this scene (e.g. at lines 39, and 99ff.) support the reference. The
repetition of *once more*, ironically in a new sense, appears to me very
Shakespearean.

17. *Justice . . . sword*   When Justice breaks her sword (a principal attribute of the symbolic person), it becomes the pointless sword
of Mercy (technically called the "curtana")—a property familiar in
Elizabethan pageantry; see, e.g. Greene, *Friar Bacon and Friar
Bungay*, V. iii. S.D.

And love thee after. Once more, and this the last:

> *He kisses her.*

20 So sweet was ne'er so fatal. I must weep,
But they are cruel tears. This sorrow's heavenly:
It strikes where it doth love. She wakes.

DESDEMONA

Who's there? Othello?

OTHELLO

Ay, Desdemona.

DESDEMONA

Will you come to bed, my lord?

OTHELLO

25 Have you prayed tonight, Desdemon?

DESDEMONA

Ay, my lord.

OTHELLO

If you bethink yourself of any crime
Unreconciled as yet to heaven and grace,
Solicit for it straight.

DESDEMONA

Alack, my lord, what may you mean by that?

---

19. **Once more, and this** Q.   F has 'One more, and that's'.
     S.D. Q.   Not in F.
22. **where it doth** F.   Q has 'when it does'.
23. **there? Othello?** F.   Q has 'there, Othello?'
25. **Desdemon** F.   Q has *'Desdemona'*.
29. **Alack** F.   Q has 'Alas'.

21. *cruel tears* because they are not those of mercy. *This sorrow's heavenly* i.e., with profound double irony, like the sorrow of God, Who afflicts with the adversity of trial or punishment those souls He loves. Cf. Hebrews 12: 6, "For whom the Lord loveth, he chasteneth; and he scourgeth every son that he receiveth."

22. *where* i.e. "in the very place" and "even though." Q's reading "when"—graphically almost indifferent in Elizabethan handwriting—would mean "at the very time that" or even "just because."

27. *heaven and grace* the mercy of heaven—hendiadys.

28. *Solicit* pray for pardon.

OTHELLO

30 Well, do it, and be brief; I will walk by.
I would not kill thy unprepàrèd spirit;
No, heaven forfend! I would not kill thy soul.

DESDEMONA

Talk you of killing?

OTHELLO

Ay, I do.

DESDEMONA

Then heaven

Have mercy on me!

OTHELLO

Amen, with all my heart!

DESDEMONA

35 If you say so, I hope you will not kill me.

OTHELLO

Hum!

DESDEMONA

And yet I fear you; for you are fatal then
When your eyes roll so. Why I should fear I know not,
Since guiltiness I know not; but yet I feel I fear.

OTHELLO

40 Think on thy sins.

---

32. **heaven** Q. F has 'Heauens'.
35. **so** Q. Not in F.
37. **you are** Q. F has 'you're'.

32. *forfend* forbid.
35. *If . . . me* because to say "Amen" is to join in the prayer
(cf. *Macbeth* II. ii. 31–3), and because the obligation to be merciful in
order to have mercy of God was understood to be a "confirmation"
of "Thou shalt not kill."
40. *Think on thy sins* i.e. because you are about to die and should
make a confession before the execution.

DESDEMONA

They are loves I bear to you!

OTHELLO

Ay, and for that thou diest.

DESDEMONA

That death's unnatural that kills for loving.
Alas, why gnaw you so your nether lip?
Some bloody passion shakes your very frame.
45   These are portents; but yet I hope, I hope,
They do not point on me.

OTHELLO

Peace and be still!

DESDEMONA

I will so. What's the matter?

OTHELLO

That handkerchief which I so loved and gave thee,
Thou gav'st to Cassio.

DESDEMONA

No, by my life and soul!
50   Send for the man and ask him.

---

41.   **Ay** F (I).   Not in Q. **diest** Q.   F has 'dy'st'.
45.   **I hope, I hope,** F.   Q has 'I hope'.
49.   **gav'st** F.   Q has 'gauest'.

40. *They . . . you* "I am conscious of no sin, unless it be the
sin of loving you too much. An allusion to the idea that to idolize a
mortal is a sin against God" (Kittredge).

41. *that* emphatic, and with bitter irony—either referring to
"loves" in the sense "unlawful loves" or to "bear" in the senses
"bring" or "bare." He reacts to her exclamation as though it were
hypocrisy.

45. *portents* ominous signs—with the accent probably upon the
second syllable.

46. *Peace and be still* Ironically, the very words (in all Tudor
bibles) Christ spoke to still the storm on the Sea of Galilee when His
disciples "of little faith" cried "Master, carest thou not that we
perish?" (Mark 4: 37–40).

OTHELLO

Sweet soul, take heed,

Take heed of perjury; thou art on thy deathbed.

DESDEMONA

Ay, but not yet to die.

OTHELLO

Yes, presently.

Therefore confess thee freely of thy sin;

For to deny each article with oath

55   Cannot remove nor choke the strong conception

That I do groan withal. Thou art to die.

DESDEMONA

Then Lord have mercy on me!

OTHELLO

I say amen.

DESDEMONA

And have you mercy too! I never did

Offend you in my life; never loved Cassio

60   But with such general warranty of heaven

As I might love. I never gave him token.

---

52. **Yes** Q. Not in F.
55. **conception** F. Q has 'conceit'.
57. **Then Lord** Q. F has 'O Heauen'.

50. *Sweet soul*   i.e. returning, with increasing irony, and difficulty, to the attempted likeness with the punishing Christian God's solicitude for the soul invoked in lines 21–2.

52. *presently*   right now, immediately.

54. *article*   item or count in the accusation.

55. *conception*   idea, belief—the image of physical conception and birth being picked up by "groan withal" (line 56).

58. *And . . . too*   "Be ye therefore merciful, as your Father also is merciful./ Judge not and ye shall not be judged: condemn not and ye shall not be condemned: forgive, and ye shall be forgiven." (Luke 6: 36–7). Cf. above, line 35 and note.

60–1. *with . . . love*   i.e. with such love as heaven authorizes us all to feel for our fellow man—viz. charity.

OTHELLO

By heaven, I saw my handkerchief in's hand!
O perjured woman! thou dost stone my heart,
And mak'st me call what I intend to do
65   A murder, which I thought a sacrifice.
I saw the handkerchief.

DESDEMONA

He found it then;
I never gave it him. Send for him hither:
Let him confess a truth.

OTHELLO

He hath confessed.

DESDEMONA

What, my lord?

OTHELLO

70   That he hath—used thee.

DESDEMONA

How? unlawfully?

OTHELLO

Ay.

---

62. **in's** F.   Q has 'in his'.
63. **my** F.   Q has 'thy'.
64. **mak'st** Q2 (makst).   Q1 has 'makest'. F has 'makes'.
68. **Let** F.   Q has 'And let'. **hath** F.   Q has 'has'.
70. **hath—used thee.** F has 'hath vs'd thee.' Q has 'hath----vds
     death.'

63. *stone my heart* i.e. your perjury proves an obduracy in evil
which (1) kills my heart by stoning, (2) turns my heart to stone—
making impossible the compassion with which I intended to offer
you, reconciled to heaven, as a sacrifice to offended impersonal
justice. Q's reading, "thy," simply accuses Desdemona of the
"hardening of heart" of the unrepentant confirmed sinner. The line
in F implies this accusation, but it also, by way of this image, locates
the "hardening of heart" with telling irony in the deluded Othello
himself.

70. *used thee* Desdemona's response proves this reading correct,
so we may suspect that Q's reading, the oath " 'ud's death," results
from careless misreading of some original spelling such as "vsde
the."

DESDEMONA

He will not say so.

OTHELLO

No, his mouth is stopped;
Honest Iago hath ta'en order for 't.

DESDEMONA

O, my fear interprets. What, is he dead?

OTHELLO

Had all his hairs been lives, my great revenge
75 Had stomach for 'em all.

DESDEMONA

Alas, he is betrayed, and I undone!

OTHELLO

Out, strumpet! Weep'st thou for him to my face?

DESDEMONA

O banish me, my lord, but kill me not!

OTHELLO

Down, strumpet!

DESDEMONA

80 Kill me tomorrow; let me live tonight!

OTHELLO

Nay, an' you strive—

---

73. **O, my fear interprets.** F. Q has 'My feare interprets then,--'.
75. **'em** Q. F has 'them'.
77. **Out . . . Weep'st** F. Q has 'O . . . weepest'.
81. **an'** Q. F has 'if'.

72. *ta'en order* made arrangements—ironic, given his ignorance of Roderigo's role.
75. *stomach* appetite—cf. III. iii. 456–7.
76. *he . . . undone* Desdemona means Cassio has been delivered by some fraudulent plot into the power of enemies and she is ruined because his death removes the possibility of his testifying to her innocence. But Othello can take her words to mean a confession—"Cassio's guilt has been disclosed and therefore I too am lost."
78. *banish me* reminding us of the extreme response permitted Othello if she were guilty—"beggarly divorcement" (IV. ii. 158).

DESDEMONA

But half an hour!

OTHELLO

Being done, there is no pause.

DESDEMONA

But while I say one prayer!

OTHELLO

It is too late.

[*He*] *smothers her.*

DESDEMONA

O Lord, Lord, Lord!

EMILIA [*calls within*]

85   My lord, my lord! What ho! my lord, my lord!

OTHELLO

What voice is this? Not dead? not yet quite dead?

---

82. **Being . . . pause.** F. Not in Q.
83. **It is** F. Q has 'Tis'. **S.D.** *smothers* F. Q has *'stifles'*.
84. Q. Not in F.
85. **S.D.** Q. F has *'Æmilia at the doore.'*
86. **voice** Q. F has 'noise'.

84–5. *O Lord . . . lord* Desdemona's prayerful iteration of the
divine name ("I am the Lord, this is my Name" Isaiah 42: 8) is
juxtaposed with Emilia's use of "lord" referring to Othello—a
stunning ironic effect prepared for, in this scene, e.g. by "flaming
minister" (line 8), "This sorrow's heavenly" (line 21), "Peace and
be still" (line 46), as well as by his taking God's vengeance into his
own hands ("Vengeance is mine, . . . saith the Lord" Romans 12:
19), and by Desdemona's addressing him, with a propriety stressing
his proper role, as "my lord" (lines 24, 25, 29). The effect is antici-
pated at lines 57–8 (where F replaces "Lord" with "Heaven"). Cf.
particularly Matthew 7: 21, and Luke 13: 25 ("When the good man
of the house is risen up, and hath shut to the door, and ye begin to
stand without, and to knock at the door, saying, Lord, Lord, open to
us, and He shall answer and say unto you, I know you not whence
ye are . . ."). "Lord" is expurgated by the F text again at line 117—
the first of Emilia's twelve uses of the word since line 85 to refer to
God.

86. *voice* F's reading, "noise," I think a sophistication following
upon its expurgation of "O Lord, Lord, Lord."

I that am cruel, am yet merciful;
I would not have thee linger in thy pain.
So, so.

EMILIA [*within*]

What ho! my lord, my lord!

OTHELLO

Who's there?

EMILIA [*within*]

90 O good my lord, I'd speak a word with you!

OTHELLO

Yes, 'tis Emilia. —[*Aloud*] By and by. —She's dead.
'Tis like she comes to speak of Cassio's death:
The noise was here. Ha! no more moving?
Still as the grave. Shall she come in? were't good?
95 I think she stirs again. No. What's best to do?
If she come in, she'll sure speak to my wife.
My wife! my wife! what wife? I have no wife.

---

87. **I that am** Q and F corr. F uncorr. reads 'I am that'.
89. **S.D.** F. Not in Q.
90, 101. **S.D.s** *within* Malone. Not in QF.
90. **I'd** Q. F has 'I would'.
93. **here** Q. F has 'high'.
95. **best to do** F. Q has 'the best'.
97. **what wife? I have** F. Q has 'my wife; I ha'.

87. *cruel, am yet merciful* i.e., and most ironically, the hangman's "mercy."

89. *So, so* A stage tradition starting in the mid-eighteenth century (and occasionally still supposed justified by critics) calls for a cruelly "merciful" *coup de grace* with a dagger at this point. But this is decidedly unsupported both by evidence of earlier staging (where a pillow was used), by the text itself (see lines 3–4, 199), and by both early texts in S.D. calling for "stifling." Othello applies the pillow more firmly.

91. *By and by* in a moment.

93. *The noise was here* I think, given Othello's shifts of attention —between the figure on the bed and Emilia at the door—that this reading has a nicely ambiguous sense, perhaps referring to the noise of the ambush of Cassio, but certainly to the noise of Desdemona's supposed movement, which he then listens for. I consider F's "high" an "explaining" sophistication.

O insupportable! O heavy hour!
Methinks it should be now a huge eclipse
100 Of sun and moon, and that th'affrighted globe
Should yawn at alteration.

EMILIA [*within*]
I do beseech you
That I may speak with you. O, good my lord!

OTHELLO

I had forgot thee. O, come in, Emilia.
Soft, by and by. Let me the curtains draw.
[*He closes the bed-curtains.*]
105 Where art thou?   [*Opens the door.*]
Enter EMILIA.
What's the matter with thee now?

EMILIA

O, my good lord, yonder's foul murders done!

OTHELLO

What! now?

EMILIA

But now, my lord.

---

100. **th'affrighted** F. Q has 'the affrighted'.
101. **Should** Q. F has 'Did'.
102. **That I** F. Q has 'I'. **O** F. Not in Q.
104. **S.D.** Not in QF.
105. **S.D.** *Theobald (Unlocks).*
      S.D. *Enter* **EMILIA** Q places after 'draw' line 104, F after 'now?'
      line 105.
107. **What! now?** F has 'What? now?' Q has 'What, now?'

99–101. *should . . . alteration*   The signs conventionally expected
at a judgment of God—". . . when the prophets denounce unto men
any great and horrible and fearful judgment of God, they commonly
say: that the sun, the moon, and the stars shall lose their brightness . . . and the . . . whole face of the world shall be changed"
(La Primaudaye, *The French Academye*, III, 163). The most notable
such judgment (evoked in this context) was that at the Crucifixion
(see Luke 23: 44–5). Old science did not suppose simultaneous *eclipse
of sun and moon* naturally possible. It did, however, perhaps oddly
assume a relation between eclipses and earthquakes—which cause the
earth to *yawn* in chasms (Pliny).

OTHELLO

It is the very error of the moon:
She comes more nearer earth than she was wont,
110 And makes men mad.

EMILIA

Cassio, my lord, hath killed a young Venetian
Called Roderigo.

OTHELLO

Roderigo killed!
And Cassio killed?

EMILIA

No, Cassio is not killed.

OTHELLO

Not Cassio killed! then murder's out of tune,
115 And sweet revenge grows harsh.

DESDEMONA [*from the curtained bed*]
O, falsely, falsely murdered!

EMILIA

O Lord! what cry is that?

OTHELLO

That? what?

EMILIA

Out and alas! that was my lady's voice.
                    [*She opens the bed-curtains.*]
Help! help, ho! help! O lady, speak again!
120 Sweet Desdemona! O sweet mistress, speak!

---

109. **nearer** F.   Q has 'near the'.
111. **hath** F.   Q has 'has'.
117. **O Lord** Q. F has 'Alas'.
118. **that was** F.   Q has 'it is'.

108. *error*   aberration—i.e. the moon's wandering from her course.
110. *makes men mad*   i.e. with "lunacy"—our word still preserves a trace of this ancient belief.
115. *sweet . . . harsh*   i.e. (continuing the musical image) harmonious revenge (viz. in accord with my purposes) becomes discordant.
118. *Out*   a cry for help and interjection of distress.

DESDEMONA

A guiltless death I die.

EMILIA

O, who hath done this deed?

DESDEMONA

Nobody—I myself. Farewell;
Commend me to my kind lord. O, farewell!   *She dies.*

OTHELLO

125   Why, how should she be murdered?

EMILIA

Alas, who knows?

OTHELLO

You heard her say herself, it was not I.

EMILIA

She said so: I must needs report a truth.

OTHELLO

She's like a liar gone to burning hell!
'Twas I that killed her.

EMILIA

O, the more angel she,
130   And you the blacker devil!

OTHELLO

She turned to folly, and she was a whore.

EMILIA

Thou dost belie her, and thou art a devil.

OTHELLO

She was false as water.

---

122.   **hath** F.   Q has 'has'.
124.   **S.D.** Q.   Not in F.
126.   **heard** Q.   F has 'heare'.
127.   **a** Q.   F has 'the'.

124.   *Commend me to*   remember me to, give my love to.
131.   *folly*   a biblical word for "unchastity"—cf. above, II. i. 136.
133.   *false as water*   a proverbial comparison (Tilley, W86), based
on the idea that water is "unstable" (Genesis 49: 4) and takes any
shape it is put in.

EMILIA

Thou art rash as fire to say
That she was false. O, she was heavenly true!

OTHELLO

135 Cassio did top her. Ask thy husband else.
O, I were damned beneath all depth in hell
But that I did proceed upon just grounds
To this extremity. Thy husband knew it all.

EMILIA

My husband?

OTHELLO

Thy husband.

EMILIA

That she was false to wedlock?

OTHELLO

140 Ay, with Cassio. Nay, had she been true,
If heaven would make me such another world
Of one entire and perfect chrysolite,
I'd not have sold her for it.

EMILIA

My husband?

---

133. **art rash** F. Q has 'as rash'.
140. **Nay** Q. Not in F.

133. *rash as fire*   i.e. hasty—an answering proverbial comparison.
138. *extremity*   ultimate rigor (of justice).
141. *such another world*   This can be doubly construed as referring to the whole world God made for man or to Desdemona as his whole world.
142. *one . . . chrysolite*   The chrysolite is said by Pliny to be the largest of all precious stones; he reports that Ptolemaeus Philadelphus King of Egypt had a statue of his wife made of one. Considered a perfectly hard stone, it was supposed to crack if it had any flaw; thus an *entire and perfect chrysolite* was held to signify the virtues of irrefrangible faith and constancy, and to symbolize the spiritual beauty of innocence of life through the possession of grace and the wisdom of the Spirit. Early lapidaries claim for it the magical power to prevent sin and drive off devils.

OTHELLO

Ay, 'twas he that told me first.

145   An honest man he is, and hates the slime
That sticks on filthy deeds.

EMILIA

My husband!

OTHELLO

What needs this iterance, woman? I say thy husband.

EMILIA

O mistress, villainy hath made mocks with love!
My husband say she was false?

OTHELLO

He, woman:

150   I say thy husband. Dost understand the word?
My friend, thy husband, honest, honest Iago.

EMILIA

If he say so, may his pernicious soul
Rot half a grain a day! he lies to th' heart.
She was too fond of her most filthy bargain.

OTHELLO

155   Ha!

EMILIA

Do thy worst.
This deed of thine is no more worthy heaven
Than thou wast worthy her.

OTHELLO

Peace, you were best.

---

144.   **me first** Q. F has 'me on her first'.
147.   **iterance, woman? I** F. Q has 'iteration? woman I'.
148–51.   **EMILIA O . . . Iago.** F. Not in Q.

147.   *iterance*   iteration.
148.   *made mocks with love*   made love a cause of derision—
after the verbal construction "to mock with" where the prepositional
phrase indicates what the mockery is about, as in "mock us with our
bareness" (*All's Well* IV. ii. 20).
158.   *you were best*   it would be best for you.

EMILIA

Thou hast not half the power to do me harm

160   As I have to be hurt. O gull! O dolt!
As ignorant as dirt! thou hast done a deed—

                                    [*He threatens to draw.*]

I care not for thy sword: I'll make thee known
Though I lost twenty lives.—Help! help! O help!
The Moor hath killed my mistress! Murder! murder!

                Enter MONTANO, GRATIANO, IAGO, *and others.*

MONTANO

165   What is the matter? How now, general?

EMILIA

O, are you come, Iago? You have done well
That men must lay their murders on your neck.

GRATIANO

What is the matter?

EMILIA

Disprove this villain, if thou be'st a man.

170   He says thou told'st him that his wife was false.
I know thou didst not; thou'rt not such a villain.
Speak, for my heart is full.

---

159.   **the** Q. F has 'that'.
161.   **S.D.** Not in QF.
162.   **known** F. Q has 'know'.
163.   **O** Q. F has 'hoa'.
164.   **hath** F. Q has 'has'. **S.D.** *and others* Q. Not in F.
167.   **murders** F (Murthers). Q has 'murder'.
168.   **GRATIANO** F. Q has '*All*'.
171.   **thou'rt** F. Q has 'thou art'.

159–60. *Thou . . . hurt* usually interpreted "I have in this cause more power to endure than thou hast power to inflict" (Johnson). But this (I think) quite misunderstands the play on *to be hurt*, which does not mean what the context seems to invite, "to suffer bodily harm," but rather, "to feel pain," Emilia's new-spirited reference being to her enlarged capacity to feel pain through her anguish over her loved mistress.

160. *gull*   dupe.

IAGO

I told him what I thought, and told no more
Than what he found himself was apt and true.

EMILIA

175   But did you ever tell him she was false?

IAGO

I did.

EMILIA

You told a lie, an odious damnèd lie!
Upon my soul, a lie! a wicked lie!
She false with Cassio! Did you say with Cassio?

IAGO

180   With Cassio, mistress. Go to, charm your tongue.

EMILIA

I will not charm my tongue; I am bound to speak:
My mistress here lies murdered in her bed—

ALL

O heavens forfend!

EMILIA

—And your reports have set the murder on.

OTHELLO

185   Nay, stare not, masters. It is true indeed.

GRATIANO

'Tis a strange truth.

MONTANO

O monstrous act!

EMILIA

Villainy, villainy, villainy!
I think upon't; I think; I smell't: O villainy!

182–90.   **My . . . villainy!** F.   Not in Q.

174. *apt*   probable, readily believed.

180. *charm your tongue*   i.e., literally, silence it as though it were constrained by a magical spell—idiomatic for "shut up."

181. *bound*   i.e. in duty bound—that constraint being set against the one in "charm" and the dutiful obedience to her husband it implies. Cf. lines 192–3.

I thought so then—I'll kill myself for grief—
190   O villainy, villainy!

IAGO

What, are you mad? I charge you, get you home.

EMILIA

Good gentlemen, let me have leave to speak.
'Tis proper I obey him, but not now.—
Perchance, Iago, I will ne'er go home.

OTHELLO *falls on the bed.*

OTHELLO

195   O! O! O!

EMILIA

Nay, lay thee down and roar;
For thou hast killed the sweetest innocent
That e'er did lift up eye.

OTHELLO

O, she was foul!   [*He rises.*]
[*To* GRATIANO] I scarce did know you, uncle. There lies your niece,
Whose breath, indeed, these hands have newly stopped.
200   I know this act shows horrible and grim.

GRATIANO

Poor Desdemon! I am glad thy father's dead.
Thy match was mortal to him, and pure grief
Shore his old thread atwain. Did he live now,

---

194.   **S.D.** Q. Not in F.
197.   **S.D.** Theobald (*Rising*).
200.   **horrible** F. Q has 'terrible'.
201.   **Desdemon** F. Q has '*Desdemona*'.
203.   **atwain** Q. F has 'in twaine'.

189.   *I thought so then*   Emilia means that she thought of villainy then, not that she suspected Iago. See IV. ii. 130–3.
194.   *I will ne'er go home*   not simply "I shall never" but "I won't ever"—her point being that if her suspicion proves true she will refuse to live with him as his wife. Also, of course, preparatively ominous.
200.   *shows*   appears.
203.   *thread*   i.e. of life—severed by "pure grief" instead of the Fate Atropos with her shears.

This sight would make him do a desperate turn,
205   Yea, curse his better angel from his side,
And fall to reprobance.

OTHELLO

'Tis pitiful; but yet Iago knows
That she with Cassio hath the act of shame
A thousand times committed. Cassio confessed it;
210   And she did gratify his amorous works
With that recognizance and pledge of love
Which I first gave her: I saw it in his hand.
It was a handkerchief, an antique token
My father gave my mother.

EMILIA

215   O God! O heavenly God!

IAGO

'Zounds! hold your peace!

---

206.   **reprobance** F.   Q has 'reprobation'.
211.   **that** F. Q has 'the'.
215.   **God . . . God** Q.   F has 'Heauen . . . Powres'.
216.   **'Zounds** Q.   F has 'Come'.

204. *a desperate turn*   some desperate act—i.e. commit suicide out of despair.

206. *reprobance*   a nonce word for "reprobation," the technical theological term for "rejection by God; the state of being so rejected or cast off, and thus ordained to eternal misery" (OED).

210. *gratify*   reward, requite.

211. *recognizance*   bond-token—literally, a law term for a recorded obligation.

214. *My . . . mother*   The inconsistency with the account of the handkerchief at III. iv. 49ff. suggests this may be either a Shakespearean slip or deliberate simplification.

216. *'Zounds*   This tremendous oath (see I. i. 87, note) is the precisely appropriate response to Emilia's cry (in its unexpurgated form) and, ironically, even to its discernible note of challenge to God (cf. *Macbeth* IV. iii. 223–4).

EMILIA

'Twill out, 'twill out! I peace?

No, I will speak as liberal as the north.

Let heaven and men and devils, let 'em all,

All, all cry shame against me, yet I'll speak.

IAGO

220   Be wise, and get you home.

EMILIA

I will not.

[IAGO *draws and threatens her.*]

GRATIANO

Fie!

Your sword upon a woman?

EMILIA

O thou dull Moor! that handkerchief thou speak'st of

I found by fortune, and did give my husband;

For often with a solemn earnestness—

225   More than indeed belonged to such a trifle—

He begged of me to steal't.

---

216. **'Twill . . . peace?** F. Q has ' 'Twill out, 'twill: I hold peace
       sir, no,'.
217. **No . . . north** F. Q has 'I'le be in speaking, liberall as the
       ayre'.
218. **'em** Q. F has 'them'.
220. **S.D.** Rowe (subst.).
222. **of** F. Q has 'on'.
226. **steal't** F. Q has 'steale it'.

217. *liberal as the north* freely as the north wind—"called the
scattering wind, because it driveth away the clouds and purgeth the
air," as a note in the Genevan Bible explains. Cf. Proverbs 25: 23,
"As the Northwind driveth away the rain, so doth an angry counte-
nance the slandering tongue."; also Job 37: 21–2, "And now men see
not the light, which shineth in the clouds, but the wind passeth and
cleanseth them./The brightness cometh out of the North; the praise
thereof is to God, which is terrible." I consider F's version of lines
216–17 due to Shakespearean revision.

IAGO

Villainous whore!

EMILIA

She give it Cassio? No, alas, I found it,
And I did give't my husband.

IAGO

Filth, thou liest!

EMILIA

By heaven, I do not, I do not, gentlemen.
230 [*To* OTHELLO] O murderous coxcomb! what should such a fool
Do with so good a wife?

OTHELLO

Are there no stones in heaven
But what serves for the thunder? —Precious villain!
[OTHELLO *runs at* IAGO, *but* MONTANO *disarms him;*
IAGO *stabs* EMILIA *and bolts.*]

GRATIANO

The woman falls: sure he hath killed his wife.

EMILIA

Ay, ay. O, lay me by my mistress' side.   [*They do so.*]

GRATIANO

235 He's gone, but his wife's killed.

---

227. **give** F. Q has 'gaue'.
230. **murderous** Q. F has 'murd'rous'.
231. **wife** F. Q has 'woman'.
232. **S.D.** Q has '*The Moore runnes at Iago, Iago kils his wife.*' after
       'woman?' line 231, and '*Exit Iago.*' after 'side.' line 234. Not
       in F.
233. **hath** F. Q has 'has'.

230. *coxcomb* fool—after the red crest like the comb of a cock
on the cap of the professional fool or jester.
231–2. *Are . . . thunder* i.e. "are there thunder-bolts only for
storms and not for God's judgments?"—the implication being that
in justice heaven should have struck down such a villain.
232. *Precious* in ironic colloquial use, an intensifier for a word of
abuse.

MONTANO

'Tis a notorious villain. Take you this weapon,
Which I have here recovered from the Moor.
Come, guard the door without; let him not pass,
But kill him rather. I'll after that same villain,
240 For 'tis a damnèd slave.

                          Exit [MONTANO, *with all but* OTHELLO *and* EMILIA.]

OTHELLO

                          I am not valiant neither,
But every puny whipster gets my sword.
But why should honor outlive honesty?
Let it go all.

EMILIA

What did thy song bode, lady?
Hark, canst thou hear me? I will play the swan,
245 And die in music. [*Sings*] "Willow, willow, willow."
Moor, she was chaste. She loved thee, cruel Moor:
So come my soul to bliss as I speak true;
So speaking as I think, I die, I die.   *She dies.*

---

236. **you this** F. Q has 'your'.
237. **here** Q. Not in F.
243–5. **What . . . willow** F. Not in Q.
248. **I die, I die.** Q. F has 'alas, I dye.' **S.D.** Q. Not in F.

236. *notorious*   notable, outrageous, out-and-out.

240. *not valiant neither*   "So my valour is gone—as well as my good conscience" (Kittredge).

241. *puny whipster*   skilless whippersnapper. *Whipster* is a term of contempt, but it is not clear why. A frequent suggestion is that it comes from a boy whipping a top—an activity treated elsewhere by Shakespeare as typically childish (cf. *Love's Labours Lost* V. i. 56). I think *puny* has the force of "puisny" in *As You Like It* III. iv. 39— "having but the skill of a novice."

242. *why . . . honesty*   i.e. "Why should *honor*—my outward reputation for valor and soldiership—outlive my *honesty*—all that made my character honorable?" With the implication, in context, "why should I concern myself that it hasn't?"

244–5. *swan . . . music*   The idea that the swan sings just before its death was used emblematically to signify those who "die well" in pure conscience. The idea is expressed literally in line 247.

OTHELLO

I have another weapon in this chamber:
250 It is a sword of Spain, the Isebrook's temper.
O, here it is. —Uncle, I must come forth.

GRATIANO ([*on guard,*] *within*)
If thou attempt it, it will cost thee dear:
Thou hast no weapon, and perforce must suffer.

OTHELLO

Look in upon me then, and speak with me,
255 Or, naked as I am, I will assault thee.
[*Re-enter* GRATIANO.]

GRATIANO

What is the matter?

OTHELLO

Behold, I have a weapon:
A better never did itself sustain
Upon a soldier's thigh. I have seen the day
That with this little arm and this good sword
260 I have made my way through more impediments
Than twenty times your stop. But O vain boast!
Who can control his fate? 'Tis not so now.

---

250. **is** Q. F has 'was'.
 Isebrook's Q (Isebrookes). F has 'Ice brookes'.
252. **S.D.** *within* Q. Not in F.
254. **with** F. Q has 'to'.
255. **S.D.** Theobald.
261. **your** F. Q has 'you'.

250. *sword . . . temper* i.e. the very best a soldier could ask for (see below, lines 256–8): a sword made by the famous Spanish crafts-men with a blade of the finest military steel available, tempered by a secret process in Innsbruck (for which "Isebrooke" was a con-temporary English spelling). Such Spanish swords with German blades can yet be seen in collections of old weapons. The best-known Spanish swords, however, those from Bilbao and Toledo, had Spanish blades some of the finest of which were tempered in ice-cold water. The vivid, but easier, F reading (which I think a corruption) no doubt owes its existence to this latter fact.

253. *perforce must suffer* of necessity must acquiesce (in my stopping you). But *suffer* can also mean "suffer death."

255. *naked* unarmed.

Be not afraid, though you do see me weaponed;
Here is my journey's end, here is my butt,
265   And very sea-mark of my utmost sail.
Do you go back dismayed? 'Tis a lost fear.
Man but a rush against Othello's breast,
And he retires. Where should Othello go?
Now: how dost thou look now? O ill-starred wench,
270   Pale as thy smock! When we shall meet at compt,
This look of thine will hurl my soul from heaven,
And fiends will snatch at it.   [*He touches her.*]
        Cold, cold, my girl?
Even like thy chastity.
O cursèd, cursèd slave! Whip me, ye devils,
275   From the possession of this heavenly sight!
Blow me about in winds! roast me in sulphur!
Wash me in steep-down gulfs of liquid fire!

263–9. **Be . . . wench** F. Not in Q.
270. **compt** F. Q has 'count'.
274. **cursèd, cursèd** F. Q has 'cursed'. **ye** F. Q has 'you'.
277. **steep-down** F. Q has 'sleep downe'.

264. *butt* The butt is the structure on which the targets are placed in archery, and thus the utter limit of the aimed arrow's flight.

265. *sea-mark* a beacon or other prominent object which tells a sailor he has made landfall at his destination.

266. *a lost fear* a wasted fear—for you need not be afraid I am going to assault you.

267. *Man but a rush* wield but a bullrush as a spear—i.e. the least show of valor with the most forceless weapon would be enough to make Othello retire now.

270. *compt* the Last Judgment—"when the last account 'twixt heaven and earth/ Is to be made" (*King John* IV. ii. 216).

271. *This look of thine* i.e. this look not only of innocence (which will brand him a murderer) but also of love (cf. her attempt with her last breath to protect him with a lie). This is the "heavenly sight" from the possession of which he calls for devils to whip him (lines 274–5).

274. *O cursèd, cursèd slave* The reference is to himself, though of course it links him to the "damnèd" and "cursèd slave" Iago (lines 240, 289).

274–7. Othello calls for and envisions the banishment from heaven and eternal punishment in hell which he despairingly believes such a "cursèd slave" in justice deserves.

O Desdemona! Desdemona dead!

O, O! O!

> *Enter* LODOVICO, MONTANO, IAGO [*as prisoner*],
> *and Officers;* CASSIO [*carried*] *in a chair.*

LODOVICO

280   Where is this rash and most unfortunate man?

OTHELLO

That's he that was Othello. Here I am.

LODOVICO

Where is that viper? Bring the villain forth.

> [IAGO *is brought forward.*]

OTHELLO

I look down towards his feet; but that's a fable.

If that thou be'st a devil, I cannot kill thee.

> [*He wounds* IAGO.]

LODOVICO

285   Wrench his sword from him!   [OTHELLO *is disarmed.*]

IAGO

I bleed, sir, but not killed.

278–9. **O Desdemona . . . dead!/ O, O! O!** Q. (O . . . dead,
O, o, o.). F has 'Oh *Desdemon!* dead *Desdemon:* dead.
oh, oh!'

279. **S.D.** *in a chair* Q. Not in F.

280. **unfortunate** F. Q has 'infortunate'.

282. **that** F. Q has 'this'.

284. **If that** F. Q has 'If'. **S.D.** Rowe.

285. **Wrench** F. Q has 'Wring'.

283. *I . . . feet*   i.e. to see if they are cloven hoofs, as the devils'
feet are supposed to be.

285. *I . . . killed*   tauntingly treating Othello's preceding line and
action as if they had truly been hypothesis and experiment.

OTHELLO

I am not sorry neither: I'd have thee live;
For in my sense 'tis happiness to die.

LODOVICO

O thou Othello that wert once so good,
Fall'n in the practice of a cursèd slave,
290   What shall be said to thee?

OTHELLO

                    Why, anything:
An honorable murderer, if you will;
For naught did I in hate, but all in honor.

LODOVICO

This wretch hath part confessed his villainy.
Did you and he consent in Cassio's death?

OTHELLO

295   Ay.

---

288. **wert** Q. F has 'was'.
289. **cursèd** F. Q has 'damned'.
290. **shall** F. Q has 'should'.
292. **did I** Q. F has 'I did'.

286–7. *I'd . . . die*   i.e. "To live with any consciousness of what
he has done would be punishment enough for Iago if he suffers what
I suffer being alive; to go on living is an agony for me in comparison
with which death would be a happiness too good for him." *In my
sense* means "to one who feels as I" (not "in my meaning"). The
phrase *'tis happiness to die* recalls the reunion in Cyprus (II. i.
183–4) and ironically brings to mind oft-repeated Elizabethan
exhortation about the appropriate "happiness" of the faithful Christian at the prospect of death.

289. *in the practice*   through the machinations.   *cursèd*   I print
F's reading on the assumption that it represents deliberate echoing
of line 274, and not memorial contamination by it.

292. *For . . . honor*   sustaining, although perhaps less con-
sciously, the sardonic paradox in "An honorable murderer." "To do
naught" can mean "to do wickedly" (OED, 8c) as well as "to do
nothing" (cf., for the same wordplay, *Richard III* I. i. 97–100); and of
course his *honor* so countenanced "tyrannous hate" (III. iii. 446)
that he could plot murder (as line 294 stresses) and commit it.

294. *consent in*   agree upon.

CASSIO

Dear general, I never gave you cause.

OTHELLO

I do believe it, and I ask your pardon.
Will you, I pray, demand that demi-devil
Why he hath thus ensnared my soul and body?

IAGO

300   Demand me nothing. What you know, you know;
From this time forth I never will speak word.

LODOVICO

What, not to pray?

GRATIANO

                    Torments will ope your lips.

OTHELLO

Well, thou dost best.

LODOVICO

Sir, you shall understand what hath befall'n,
305   Which, as I think, you know not. Here is a letter

---

296.   **never gave** F. Q has 'did neuer giue'.
297.   **your** F. Q has 'you'.
298.   **Will you, I pray**, F. Q has 'Will you pray,'.

298. *demi-devil*   half-devil, human in shape but diabolic in nature.
(The only other of his characters Shakespeare graces with this title
is Caliban, sired by a demon on a witch—but he, at the end of a
tragicomedy, finally decides to "seek for grace." *Tempest* V. i. 272,
295.)

301. Another withdrawal from humanity, as speech, and society,
were (for the Renaissance) marks distinguishing man from the savage
and the brute (cf. *Tempest* I. ii. 354–7).

302. *What, not to pray?*   indicating a still deeper point in Iago's
tight-lipped obduracy. Lodovico's exasperated shock is at what must
be an evidence of Iago's reprobation, as *not to pray* (here, repentantly
for God's forgiving mercy) signalizes lack of Christian faith requisite
to achieve the reward of the "children of God." Characteristically,
"children of the devil," like their father, lack faith in God's merciful
promises to save those who believe from damnation.

303. *thou dost best*   i.e. since your crime is unspeakable, and un-
pardonable. Cf. "Never pray more . . . / For nothing canst thou to
damnation add/ Greater than that" (III. iii. 366–70).

> Found in the pocket of the slain Roderigo,
> And here another. The one of them imports
> The death of Cassio to be undertook—
> By Roderigo.

OTHELLO

> O villain!

CASSIO

> Most heathenish and most gross!

LODOVICO

310   Now here's another discontented paper
> Found in his pocket too; and this it seems
> Roderigo meant t' have sent this damnèd villain,
> But that, belike, Iago in the nick
> Came in and satisfied him.

OTHELLO

>   O, the pernicious caitiff!—

315   How came you, Cassio, by that handkerchief
> That was my wife's?

CASSIO

>   I found it in my chamber;
> And he himself confessed but even now

308–9. **undertook—/ By Roderigo** Q (vndertooke———by *Roderigo*).
       F has 'vndertooke/By *Rodorigo*'.
312. **t'have** F. Q has 'to haue'.
313. **nick** Q. F has 'interim'.
314. **O, the** Q (O). F has 'O thou'.
315. **that** F. Q has 'a'.
317. **but** Capell. Q has 'it'. F has 'it but'.

308. I preserve the dash in Q: Lodovico offers a surprise to his on-stage audience.

309. *gross* outrageous, monstrous.

313. *belike* probably, in all likelihood. *in the nick* at the right time (to settle the bill). (The idiom's reference is to nicks made on sticks to keep reckonings.) F's "interim" is generally conceded to be that text's most self-evident sophistication.

314. *Came in* interposed. *caitiff* slavish wretch.

315. *that* As Ridley points out, Q's "a" is the logical word for a cross-examining attorney, but Othello is well beyond that, and F's reading is much the more natural.

That there he dropped it for a special purpose
Which wrought to his desire.

OTHELLO

O fool! fool! fool!

CASSIO

320   There is besides in Roderigo's letter
How he upbraids Iago that he made him
Brave me upon the watch, whereon it came
That I was cast; and even but now he spake,
After long seeming dead—Iago hurt him,
325   Iago set him on.

LODOVICO

You must forsake this room, and go with us.
Your power and your command is taken off,
And Cassio rules in Cyprus. For this slave,
If there be any cunning cruelty
330   That can torment him much and hold him long,
It shall be his. You shall close prisoner rest
Till that the nature of your fault be known
To the Venetian state.—Come, bring him away.

OTHELLO

Soft you! a word or two before you go.
335   I have done the state some service, and they know't;
No more of that. I pray you, in your letters,
When you shall these unlucky deeds relate,

---

333.   **bring him** Q. F has 'bring'.
334.   **before you go** F. Not in Q.

319.   *wrought to*   worked to effect.
322.   *Brave*   insolently provoke. *whereon it came*   because of which it came about.
323.   *cast*   cashiered.
331.   *rest*   remain.
332.   *Till that*   until.
334.   *Soft you*   wait a moment. *before you go*   a dry touch, which hints to the audience that he does not intend to go with them. Apparently, the phrase is an addition, sacrificing the "commanding abruptness" (Ridley) of the line in Q.

Speak of me as I am: nothing extenuate,
Nor set down aught in malice. Then must you speak
340   Of one that loved not wisely, but too well;
Of one not easily jealous, but, being wrought,
Perplexed in the extreme; of one whose hand,
Like the base Judean, threw a pearl away

---

338.   **me as I am** F.   Q has 'them as they are'.
343.   **Judean** F (Iudean).   Q has 'Indian'.

338.   *extenuate*   mitigate, tone down (not "excuse").

341.   *not easily jealous*   not without difficulty jealous—i.e. because not prone by natural temperament to suspiciousness.   *wrought* powerfully moved, "wrought up"—with (I think) a secondary sense, "having my emotions wrought to that end."

342.   *Perplexed*   much stronger than our word: not "puzzled," but "distractedly bewildered," "pulled this way and that, confounded in a maze of doubt."   *whose hand*   synecdoche—keeping the terrible deed at a distance.

343.   *Like the base Judean*   a famous and important crux. Neither variant is likely to have been produced by a simple printing error, though either could have resulted from a false start in the reading of copy—a blunder, however, more typical of transcribers than of compositors. Q's reading, "*Indian*," adopted by the later Folios as well as Quartos, would refer to the then widely supposed ignorance of savages regarding the value of precious stones. But the story of a particular Indian would appear to be required, and it has not yet been produced. I think, then, that though Q's reading could be a first thought, it is most likely due to an error of the transcriber responsible for Q's copy, and that it was provoked by the near-proverbial idea about savages and precious stones. F's reading (pronounced, as normally by the Elizabethans, "Júdean") refers, with elaborate dramatic pertinence, to Judas Iscariot, the betrayer to judicial murder of Jesus. The word "tribe" (line 344)—which we connect with Indians but the Elizabethans associated with the "tribes of the world" —supports the F reading: because, as was generally known, only Judas among the disciples was a Judean; because he was supposed representative of the Judeans, "which tribe only fell from Christ" (John Bradford); and because every mortal sinner could be regarded analogically "as" a Judas and Judean ("they crucify unto themselves the son of God afresh" Hebrews 6: 6). "I kissed thee ere I killed thee" (line 354) joins other immediate and also earlier references in confirming the F reading.

343-4.   *pearl . . . tribe*   Pearls were proverbially associated with

Richer than all his tribe; of one whose subdued eyes,
345 Albeit unusèd to the melting mood,
Drops tears as fast as the Arabian trees
Their med'cinable gum. Set you down this;
And say besides that in Aleppo once,
Where a malignant and a turbaned Turk
350 Beat a Venetian and traduced the state,

---

347. **med'cinable** Capell. F has 'Medicinable'; Q has 'medicinall'.

the invaluably precious virtuous woman and wife (e.g. Proverbs 31: 10). The primary reference here, however, linking the loss of Desdemona with the loss Othello spiritually suffers, is "the pearl of great price" (Matthew 13: 46), i.e. faith and hope of eternal life, the "possession of Christ," one's own innocence: that which every Christ-betraying mortal sinner, like Judas, throws away.

346–7. *Drops . . . gum* The "medicinable gum" for which Arabia was famous was myrrh, associated with atonement. However, in view of Shakespeare's associations of tears and balm (e.g. *Richard III* I. ii. 13, *2 Henry IV* IV. v. 115), his probable reference here is to the juice of the balsam tree, or opobalsamum, sometimes called the "tears" of the balsam (OED). According to *Batman upon Bartholomew* "The tree is all medicinible. The chief grace thereof and first, is in the iuyce" which "droppeth out of the holes of the rind" (XVII. 18). Numerous Elizabethan treatments of repentance discuss *med'cinable tears* (those of true contrition), and contrast them with those only apparently so curative because the sinner's remorse is unaccompanied by faith and not followed by amendment of life.

349. *turbaned Turk* the climax of the "Turk" theme, emphasizing the self Othello slays as an infidel. The turban—elsewhere associated by Shakespeare with proud impiety (*Cymbeline* III. iii. 6)—was "the symbol of Mohammedanism, or of those who profess it" (OED); in Renaissance imagery the *turbaned Turk* was the exemplary figure of unchristian infidelity and cruel injustice. The headdress itself was conventional in popular art and drama as a symbol of infidelity to Christian belief and righteousness.

I took by th' throat the circumcisèd dog,
And smote him thus!   *He stabs himself.*

LODOVICO

O bloody period!

GRATIANO

All that's spoke is marred.

---

352. **S.D.** Q. Not in F.
353. **that's** Q. F has 'that is'.

351. *circumcisèd* a term of opprobrium and abuse (used particularly of Turks and Jews), indicating wilful denial of Christian faith
through rejection of the "spiritual circumcision" of Christ—"made
without hands, by putting off the sinful body of the flesh" (Colossians 2: 11).

352. *S.D.* Othello's suicide by means of a secreted knife or
dagger inevitably draws its significance in part from his repeated loss
of a sword earlier in the scene (lines 232 S.D., 285). The substitution
of a knife (suggestive of treachery, private "authority" and vengeance,
and despair) for a sword (suggestive of Justice, true magistracy, and
the Christian's proper "strife") is a commonplace found elsewhere
in Shakespeare (cf. *Merchant of Venice* IV. i. 240, *1 Henry IV* II. iv.
324). The knife (particularly at the breast) was a symbol of self-
destroying wrath and despair; cf. the illustration in the Introduction
p. x, fig. b; *King Lear* V. iii. 218 S.D., and especially *The Faerie
Queene*, I. ix. 51–3, where the spiritually weakened Red Cross Knight
is tempted by Despair to commit suicide with "a dagger."

353. *period* conclusion, full stop—picked up by Gratiano in the
sense, "peroration." *All . . . marred* because his confession,
remorse, contrition, and satisfaction did not end, as repentance
should, with "turning to God" and amendment of life, but with
suicide. Such "false" or "outward repentance" of the deeply sorrow-
ing and remorseful sinner, which gives the appearance of "godly
repentance" but ends in despair (because lacking in faith of God's
mercy), was carefully distinguished in Elizabethan discussion and
labelled "Judas repentance" by the official Homilies.

OTHELLO [*at the bed*]

I kissed thee ere I killed thee. No way but this,

355   Killing myself, to die upon a kiss.   *He* [*kisses her, and*] *dies.*

CASSIO

This did I fear, but thought he had no weapon;
For he was great of heart.

LODOVICO

[*To* IAGO] O Spartan dog,
More fell than anguish, hunger, or the sea!
Look on the tragic lodging of this bed:

---

359.   **lodging** Q. F has 'loading'.

355. *to die upon a kiss*   *Upon* has, besides the temporal sense "on the occasion of" or "following upon"—here combined with the idea of nearness to the beloved object—a causal force ("Indicating the ground, basis, occasion or reason of an action" OED, 11c); Cf. *Midsummer Night's Dream* II. i. 244. The presence of *to die* suggests the idiomatic use of the preposition to indicate a cause of death (OED, 11d). The whole line looks back to "loved not wisely, but too well," and evokes the Elizabethan proverb, "They love too much that die for love" (Tilley, L546).

357. *For . . . heart*   explaining, by way of "homage to his lost hero overriding prescribed disapproval" (Granville-Barker), why he was apprehensive of such an outcome. In Shakespeare's view, greatness of "heart" can go with profoundly wrong and futilely wasteful misuse of powers. Cf. Hal on the dead Hotspur: "Fare thee well, great heart!/Ill-weaved ambition, how much art thou shrunk!" (*1 Henry IV* V. iv. 86–7).   *Spartan dog*   "The allusion seems to be both to the ferocity of the hounds of Sparta . . . and to the traditional stony calmness of the Spartans themselves" (Kittredge).

358. *fell*   fierce.   *anguish*   physical agony.

359. *lodging*   *Lodging* means "the beating down of corn (by wind or rain)." Its unusual use here makes a figure akin to the commonplace horticultural or arboricultural Elizabethan images for untimely death (e.g. line 13 above, or "Cut is the branch that might have grown full straight" in Marlowe's *Faustus*, Epilogue). I consider F's "loading" a sophistication, probably by someone who objected either to this "countryman's" sense of the word (Ridley) or to the wordplay inevitably invited by the presence of "bed." (Cf. "my bosom as a bed shall lodge thee" *Two Gentlemen of Verona* I. ii. 115).

360   This is thy work. The object poisons sight;
       Let it be hid.   [*The bed-curtains are drawn.*]
                    Gratiano, keep the house,
       And seize upon the fortunes of the Moor,
       For they succeed on you. [*To* cassio] To you, lord governor,
       Remains the censure of this hellish villain,
365   The time, the place, the torture: O, enforce it!
       Myself will straight aboard, and to the state
       This heavy act with heavy heart relate.   *Exeunt.*

                          FINIS.

---

363. **on** F.   Q has 'to'.

360. *object*   not the "thing," but "that which presents itself to our eyes."

362. *fortunes of the Moor*   A reminder that the tragedy has struck down a great and wealthy noble public figure.

364. *censure*   judicial condemnation and punishment.

367. *heavy act*   playing on *heavy* in the senses "woeful," "important," and "grievous."

APPENDIX A

A Shakespeare Chronology

Some Important Dates Relating to Shakespeare's Life, and to OTHELLO in Particular

1557   (about). John Shakespeare of Stratford-on-Avon marries Mary Arden. (They are to have four daughters, all but one of whom dies young, and four sons.)

1558   November 17. Queen Elizabeth accedes to the throne.

1564   April 26. William Shakespeare, eldest son and third child of John and Mary Shakespeare, christened.

1565   First publication of Giraldi Cinthio's *De gli Hecatommithi*, a collection of *novelle*, one of which (III, 7) is to be the principal source of *Othello*.

1582   November 27. The license for Shakespeare's marriage to Anne Hathaway of Stratford is issued by the bishop's office in Worcester. (The bishop's register, presumably in error, calls his wife Anne Whately of Temple Grafton.) The marriage may have been legally contracted earlier, but without church ceremony.

1583   May 26. Shakespeare's first child, Susanna, is christened at Stratford.

1585   February 2. Christening of twins, Hamnet and Judith Shakespeare, at Stratford.

1585–1591   No references have been found to this period of Shakespeare's life.

1588   The Armada with which Philip II of Spain attempts to reconquer England for Catholicism is defeated by storms and the English fleet.

1590   Publication of Spenser's *The Faerie Queene*, Books I-III.

1592   First reference to performance of a play written (or at least revised) by Shakespeare: *Henry VI, Part I*.

      Robert Greene, in his *Groats-worth of Wit*, attacks Shakespeare (his rival and successor) as an "upstart crow" who is "in his own conceit the only Shake-scene in a country."

1593   Shakespeare dedicates his first published work, the witty Ovidian narrative poem, *Venus and Adonis*, to the young Earl of Southampton (to whom he will also dedicate his next poem, *The Rape of Lucrece,* in 1594).

Christopher Marlowe, Shakespeare's leading rival as a poetic dramatist, is killed in a tavern fight.

1594   After a period of disorder caused by the plague and frequent bankruptcies among dramatic companies, two principal groups of players emerge: the Lord Admiral's Men, run by "sharers" (or partners) including Philip Henslowe the theatrical entrepreneur and his actor son-in-law Edward Alleyn, and the Lord Chamberlain's Men, run by sharers including Richard Burbage, who will become the premier tragedian of the company, and William Shakespeare.

1595   (about). *Romeo and Juliet,* Shakespeare's early tragedy of love, written.

1596   August 11. Hamnet, Shakespeare's only son, buried in Stratford. October 20. The right to the coat of arms of a gentleman is granted (probably at the solicitation of William) to John Shakespeare by the College of Heralds.

1597   Shakespeare buys New Place, a large house in Stratford.

1598   Francis Meres writes in his book *Palladis Tamia:* "As Plautus and Seneca are accounted the best for comedy and tragedy among the Latins: so Shakespeare among the English is the most excellent in both kinds for the stage . . ."

1599   Opening of the Globe Theatre, built and run by a syndicate of the Lord Chamberlain's Men, with Shakespeare as one of the share-holders.

1599–1600   Shakespeare turns from writing histories and romantic comedies (including, about 1598, *Much Ado About Nothing,* whose plot turns on a slander-of-the-innocent-beloved motif) to tragedies and the "problem" plays (two of which, *Troilus and Cressida* and particularly *Measure for Measure,* have thematic links with *Othello*). Shakespeare's version of *Hamlet* (first performed about 1600) is followed by *Othello, Macbeth,* and *King Lear.*

1601   September 8. Shakespeare's father, John, is buried.

1603   Death of Queen Elizabeth. King James I (already James VI of Scotland) succeeds her. The acting companies are taken under royal patronage. The Lord Chamberlain's Men, Shakespeare's company, become the King's Men (and, technically, officers of the royal household).

1604   November 1. *Othello* performed at Court in the Banqueting House at Whitehall.

1605   January 6. Ben Jonson's *Mask of Blackness* performed at Whitehall, the Queen and other ladies of the Court dancing as Moors, without masks, "their faces, and arms up to the elbows, . . . painted black" (Dudley Carleton).

1606–8   Shakespeare engaged in writing tragedies on classical themes: *Timon of Athens, Antony and Cleopatra,* and *Coriolanus.*

1608–9   Shakespeare's company acquires a roofed, indoor "private" theater, the (Second) Blackfriars, for winter performances. He begins to write tragicomic romances: *Pericles, Cymbeline* and *The Winter's Tale* (both of which involve a jealousy theme), and *The Tempest.*

1609   *Shake-speares Sonnets* published.

1610   (about). Shakespeare moves permanently back to Stratford from London.

1613   June 29. The Globe Theatre burns down during a performance of *Henry VIII,* probably the last play to which Shakespeare contributed.

1616   April 23. Shakespeare dies and is buried in the parish church at Stratford.

1622   The First Quarto of *Othello* is published by Thomas Walkley.

1623   The First Folio collection of Shakespeare's plays, gathered by his fellow actors and sharers, John Heminge and Henry Condell, is registered for publication at the Stationers' Company (November 8), and published late in the year.

APPENDIX B

The Textual Problem in OTHELLO

The difficult textual problem posed by *Othello* has been remarked, and the theory underlying the present edition sketched, in the introduction preceding the version of the play offered above. This theory (it is hoped) accounts more adequately than others currently available for the confusing and contradictory evidence regarding the nature, relationship, and authority of the extant substantive texts. It differs from other recent theorizing principally in positing behind the Folio text a manuscript distinct from (although also based upon) the earlier authorial draft a transcription of which served as copy for the Quarto; in supposing this manuscript a fair copy, anterior to the prompt book, containing Shakespeare's second thoughts and revisions; and in considering this authoritative manuscript in various respects unreliably represented by the Folio version printed from it.

This theory, even if correct, is in its editorial consequences not without its own uncertainties, limitations, and pitfalls. As any such theory, it is grounded in study of the variants, whose causes, where we think they can be discerned, encourage us to build hypotheses regarding the provenance, history, and reliability of the texts. To some degree, therefore, such evidence must (with inevitable peril) be used in a circular manner: study of the readings eventuates in theory which then guides the editor in his choices of variants, conflations, and emendations. Furthermore, evidence which may be sufficient to urge an aspect of the theory may not also by itself be adequate to dictate editorial decision at every crux possibly involved. For example, there is plentiful evidence of expurgation and toning down of oaths in the F text; but an editor dare not therefore assume that every oath not in F owes its absence to expurgation (see III. iii. 152, V. ii. 70).

Although the manuscript underlying the Folio text is here assumed to have been authoritative, the play's editor, lacking it, cannot rely only upon the version printed from it. In fact, whatever his theory, he can depend on neither of the substantive texts alone. There are accidental omissions in both texts (Q: IV. i. 165–7; F: III. iv. 83–4), evident cuts in Q (I. i. 120–36), and possible additions in F; and manifestly erroneous readings are found in Q and F alike. Thus, since neither text is complete an edition must be "synthetic"; and since there is incontrovertible evidence of corruption in both, it must also be "eclectic."

The question an editor confronts, then, is this: can he, with the aid of his theory, adequately distinguish among the kinds of readings encountered, correctly balancing probabilities about causes of variation, so that his editorial eclecticism is based to a greater degree than heretofore on sufficient knowledge rather than mere subjective preference? Such knowledge of course must concern matters like Elizabethan handwriting, characteristics of play-texts, printing house practices, and errors typical of authors, transcribers, editors, and compositors. However, as the notes already will have suggested, evidence of many other kinds—historical, philological, theatrical, critical—often is crucial to editorial judgment. For instance: knowledge of Renaissance armor tells us that Q's "Isebrookes" at V. ii. 250 is not a blunder; a theological commonplace reveals the precise aptness of F's "Good Father" at IV. iii. 22; and we can presume "night" (Q) and not "might" (F) is the correct reading at I. i. 181 because such "special officers of night" are specifically discussed in Contareno's book about Venice which we have reason to suppose Shakespeare knew in Lewkenor's translation.

The following examples illustrate—by no means exhaustively—the variety of readings found in the Quarto and Folio and at least some of the problems they typically raise. (Italics indicate those cited from the corresponding pages of the two texts reproduced here to give the reader some impression of the basic material from which the editor starts; the Q page compares with I. iii. 12–51 in the present edition, the F with I. iii. 13–124.) As will be apparent, the possible sources of inferior and erroneous readings are discouraging in their number and complexity.

A Quarto reading may be what Shakespeare intended; however, the presence of the identical reading in the Folio does not automatically confirm this as there are errors shared by the two texts. Where the texts vary, the Quarto reading may be what Shakespeare wrote and someone else—e.g. actor, book-keeper, editor—later altered. Or it may represent a transcriber's choice of alternative readings in the foul papers; or it could be Shakespeare's first thought which he himself later changed. Finally, Quarto readings can be errors. A number of erroneous readings were carried over from the foul papers, including false starts and slips (note the erroneous inclusion of Desdemona in the S.D. at *I. iii. 46*), unfinished or uncorrected touches of staging (cf. Q and F at *I. iii. 12–13*, II. i. 96), and adjustments of context which had been made in the cutting (e.g. I. ii. 78, and note the awkward "And" at *I. iii. 31* following the omission of lines *24–30*). The remaining errors were introduced during the making of the transcript used as copy for the printed text or through the operations of the printing house itself. A number of printing errors is encountered—foul case, turned and transposed letters, erroneous number (note "galley" and "griefes" *I. iii. 13, 55*), "literals" (e.g. "lacke" for "lackd" at *I. iii. 51*), careless omissions (*I. iii. 118*), mistaken deletions (*I. iii. 63*), and so on. But some errors which could be interpreted as compositor's mistakes may already have stood in the transcript which served as copy—e.g. "resterine" (F: "re-stem") *I. iii. 37*; "youth" (F: "vouch") line *106*; "ere while mad" (F "O're-whelmed") IV. i. 75. Actually, the work of Q's compositors generally was good and certainly no worse than that of F's. The principal source of error in Q was the transcript itself. The transcriber (though I think he may have seen the play performed) was not particularly familiar with the text; he had difficulty reading the foul papers; and he was often careless, satisfied to be approximately right, and sometimes even high-handed. The text displays a whole spectrum of copyist's blunders—such as transposition ("place of sense" [read: "sense of place"] II. iii. 146), anticipation ("good wine [read "wine"] is a good familiar creature" II. iii. 282), wrong take-off (III. iv. 9), and contraction mistaken for a word ("If it be that, or any it, [read: "any that"] was hers" III. iii. 437). Many errors started in the mistaking of single letters ("scorne [F: "storme"] of fortunes" I. iii. 245). But the transcriber also read inattentively

In fearefull fenfe.   *Enter a Meffenger.*

  One within. What ho, what ho, what ho ?

  Sailor. A meffenger from the Galley.

  Du. Now, the bufineffe ?

  Sailor. The *Turkifh* preparation makes for *Rhodes*,
So was I bid report here, to the ftate.

  Du. How fay you by this change ?

  1 Sena. This cannot be by no affay of reafon ---
Tis a Pageant,
To keepe vs in falfe gaze : when we confider
The importancy of *Cypreffe* to the *Turke* :
And let our felues againe, but vnderftand,
That as it more concernes the *Turke* then *Rhodes*,
So may he with more facile queftion beare it.

  Dn. And in all confidence, hee's not for *Rhodes.*

  Officer. Here is more newes.   *Enter a* 2. *Meffenger.*

  Mef. The *Ottamites*, reuerend and gracious,
Steering with due courfe, toward the Ifle of *Rhodes*,
Haue there inioynted with an after fleete
Of 3 0. faile, and now they doe refterine
Their backward courfe, bearing with franke appearance
Their purpofes towards *Cypreffe* : Seignior *Montano*,
Your trufty and moft valiant feruitor,
With his free duty recommends you thus,
And prayes you to beleeue him.

  Du. Tis certaine then for *Cypreffe*,
Marcus Luccicos is not here in Towne.

  1 Sena. Hee's now in *Florence.*

  Du. Write from vs, wifh him poft, poft haft difpatch.

      Enter Brabantio, Othello, Roderigo, Iago, Caffio,
           Defdemona, *and Officers.*

  1 Sena. Here comes *Brabantio* and the valiant *Moore.*

  Du. Valiant *Othello*, we muft ftraite imploy you,
Againft the generall enemy *Ottaman* ;
I did not fee you, welcome gentle Seignior,
We lacke your counfell, and your helpe to night,

Bra

A page from the First Quarto (1622, sig. C^v) above, compared
with a page from the First Folio (1623, sig. [ss5]^r). The passage is I. iii. 12–124 in the present edition.

Officer. A Messenger from the Gallies.
Duke. Now? What's the businesse?
Sailor. The Turkish Preparation makes for Rhodes,
So was I bid report here to the State,
By Signior *Angelo.*
Duke. How say you by this change?
  1. Sen. This cannot be
By no assay of reason. 'Tis a Pageant
To keepe vs in false gaze, when we consider
Th'importancie of Cyprus to the Turke;
And let our selues againe but vnderstand,
That as it more concernes the Turke then Rhodes,
So may he with more facile question beare it,
For that it stands not in such Warrelike brace,
But altogether lackes th'abilities
That Rhodes is dress'd in. If we make thought of this,
We must not thinke the Turke is so vnskillfull,
To leaue that latest, which concernes him first,
Neglecting an attempt of ease, and gaine
To wake, and wage a danger profitlesse.
  Duke. Nay, in all confidence he's not for Rhodes.
  Officer. Here is more Newes.

Enter a Messenger.

Messen. The Ottamites, Reueren'd, and Gracious,
Steering with due course toward the Ile of Rhodes,
Haue there inioynted them with an after Fleete.
  1. Sen. I, so I thought : how many, as you guesse?
Mess. Of thirtie Saile : and now they do re-stem
Their backward course, bearing with frank appearance
Their purposes toward Cyprus. Signior *Montano,*
Your trustie and most Valiant Seruitour,
With his free dutie, recommends you thus,
And prayes you to beleeue him.
  Duke. 'Tis certaine then for Cyprus :
Marcus Luccicos is not he in Towne?
  1. Sen. He's now in Florence.
  Duke. Write from vs,
To him, Post, Post-haste, dispatch.
  1. Sen. Here comes *Brabantio,* and the Valiant Moore.

*Enter Brabantio, Othello, Cassio, Iago, Rodorigo,
and Officers.*

Duke. Valiant *Othello,* we must straight employ you,
Against the generall Enemy Ottoman.
I did not see you : welcome gentle Signior,
We lack't your Counsaile, and your helpe to night.
  Bra. So did I yours · Good your Grace pardon me.
Neither my place, nor ought I heard of businesse
Hath rais'd me from my bed ; nor doth the generall care
Take hold on me. For my perticular griefe
Is of so flood-gate, and ore-bearing Nature,
That it engluts, and swallowes other sorrowes,
And it is still it selfe.
  Duke. Why? What's the matter?
  Bra. My Daughter : oh my Daughter !
  Sen. Dead?
  Bra. I, to me.
She is abus'd, stolne from me, and corrupted
By Spels, and Medicines, bought of Mountebanks;
For Nature, so preposterously to erre,
(Being not deficient, blind, or lame of sense,)
Sans witch-craft could not.
  Duke. Who ere he be, that in this foule proceeding
Hath thus beguil'd your Daughter of her selfe,

And you of her; the bloodie Booke of Law,
You shall your selfe read, in the bitter letter,
After your owne sense : yea, though our proper Son
Stood in your Action.
  Bra. Humbly I thanke your Grace,
Here is the man; this Moore, whom now it seemes
Your speciall Mandate, for the State affaires
Hath hither brought.
  All. We are verie sorry for't.
  Duke. What in your owne part, can you say to this?
  Bra. Nothing, but this is so.
  Othe. Most Potent, Graue, and Reueren'd Signiors,
My very Noble, and approu'd good Masters;
That I haue tane away this old mans Daughter,
It is most true : true I haue married her;
The verie head, and front of my offending,
Hath this extent; no more. Rude am I, in my speech,
And little bless'd with the soft phrase of Peace;
For since these Armes of mine, had seuen yeares pith,
Till now, some nine Moones wasted, they haue vs'd
Their deerest action, in the Tented Field :
And little of this great world can I speake,
More then pertaines to Feats of Broiles, and Battaile,
And therefore little shall I grace my cause,
In speaking for my selfe. Yet, (by your gratious patience)
I will a round vn-varnish'd vTale deliuer,
Of my whole course of Loue.
What Drugges, what Charmes,
What Coniuration, and what mighty Magicke,
(For such proceeding I am charg'd withall)
I won his Daughter.
  Bra. A Maiden, neuer bold :
Of Spirit so still, and quiet, that at her Motion
Blush'd at her selfe, and she, in spight of Nature,
Of Yeares, of Country, Credite, euery thing
To fall in Loue, with what she fear'd to looke on;
It is a iudgement main'd, and most imperfect.
That will confesse Perfection so could erre
Against all rules of Nature, and must be driuen
To find out practises of cunning hell
Why this should be. I therefore vouch againe,
That with some Mixtures, powrefull o're the blood,
Or with some Dram, (coniur'd to this effect)
He wrought vp on her.
  Duke. To vouch this, is no proofe,
Without more wider, and more ouer Test
Then these thin habits, and poore likely-hoods
Of moderne seeming, do prefer against him.
  Sen. But *Othello,* speake,
Did you, by indirect, and forced courses
Subdue, and poyson this yong Maides affections?
Or came it by request, and such faire question
As soule, to soule affordeth?
  Othel. I do beseech you,
Send for the Lady to the Sagitary.
And let her speake of me before her Father;
If you do finde me foule, in her report,
The Trust, the Office, I do hold of you,
Not onely take away, but let your Sentence
Euen fall vpon my life.
  Duke. Fetch *Desdemona* hither.
  Othe. Aunciant, conduct them :
You best know the place.
And tell she come, as truely as to heauen,
I do confesse the vices of my blood,
So iustly to your Graue eares, Ile present

How

("Not [F: "Hot"] hot" III. iv. 34), unthinkingly ("no great devotion
to the dead" [F: "deed"] V. i. 8), approximately ("I have rubbed this
young gnat" [F: "Quat"] V. i. 11), guessingly ("The excellence [F:
"Execution"] of his wit" III. iii. 463), and crudely ("wholesome to my
pate" [F: "place"] I. i. 144). He made context-induced substitutions
("mindes [F: "Mines"] of sulphur" III. iii. 326), and "interpreting"
ones ("with a little art [F: "acte"] upon the blood" III. iii. 325); and
he misconstrued ("Than giue thee cause: away" [F: "thy cause
away"] III. iii. 28), erroneously "corrected" ("his Worships [F:
"Moorships"] ancient" I. i. 33), substituted common for unfamiliar
words ("muttering" [F: "mam'ring"] III. iii. 69; "reprobation" [F:
"reprobance"] V. ii. 206), and vulgarized ("vpon this heate [F:
"hint"] I spake" I. iii. 165).

Folio readings display an even greater variety than the Quarto's.
They may give us what Shakespeare originally wrote or chose from
alternative readings in the foul papers. They may also represent his
second thoughts. Such authorial substitutions need not invariably
have been improvements since a writer can sophisticate his own work
in a revision-transcription. Some passages preserve what was cut or
accidentally omitted in Q; others are possible additions (e.g. *I. iii.
36*, II. iii. 255–6, V. ii. 334), though I think none of the longer F-only
passages can safely be regarded as such. There can be little doubt
that certain passages were revised by the playwright (e.g. I. iii. 256,
264–6, 273–4; V. ii. 216–17), and others carefully retouched (II. i.
230–50).

The corruption in the Folio *Othello* is the more unfortunate since
it stands between us and what must have been the most authoritative
manuscript of the play. It is also more complicated as it derives from
a greater variety of causes than that in Q. The larger the number of
links in the chain of transmission to published text, the greater the
likelihood of error. And the chain for F is long. There probably survive in F a few errors carried over from the foul papers, or made
during the writing of the authorial fair copy. There would seem to
be a few deriving from the Quarto wherever an exemplar of that
publication, "corrected" by collation with Shakespeare's later manuscript, was used as copy by the Folio's printer (e.g. "hope's" for
"hope" II. i. 50, "league" for "leagued" and "deuotement" for
"denotement" II. iii. 197, 289). Some misreadings appear to have
resulted from misunderstood changes in the fair copy ("He's almost
slaine, and *Roderigo* quite dead" [Q: "and *Roderigo* dead"]; read:
"and Roderigo quite" V. i. 114), and from botched or incomplete
corrections ("that your wisedome [omission]" III. iii. 146). For a
substantial number of blunders the F compositors were responsible.
Some of these are manifest printer's errors—note, on the reproduced
page of F: "hor," "yonr," "u Tale," "main'd," "wtought," "ouer,"
"tell" (*I. iii. 54, 74, 90, 99, 106, 107, 122*). Others are difficult to dis-

tinguish from copyist's mistakes—e.g. accidental omission (note the missing speech prefix at *I. iii. 106*), transposition ("Who they should be, that haue thus [Q: "thus haue"] mangled you" V. i. 79), and careless, memorially contaminated, and vulgarizing substitutions ("And knowes all Quantities [Q: "qualities"] with a learn'd Spirit" III. iii. 256; "And his vnbookish Ielousie must conserue [Q: "conster"]/ Poore *Cassio's* smiles" IV. i. 100; "She gaue me for my paines a world of kisses" [Q: "sighes"] I. iii. 158); still others could be the kind of misreadings an editor might introduce (e.g. the possibly "correcting" substitution at I. iii. 154—"Whereof by parcels she had something heard,/ But not instinctiuely" [Q: "intentiuely"]).

There can be little doubt that the text did suffer various kinds of editorial tampering before being printed in F. Most obviously, it underwent an expurgation which was extraordinarily intent, thorough, and disregarding of dramatic purposes. Indeed, if we except *2 Henry IV, Othello* is the most completely (if rather oddly) expurgated text in the Folio. Oaths and references to God are cut, sometimes with (I. i. 4), sometimes without (I. i. 33), adjustment of context; some objectionable expressions are weakened ("O God, O heauenly God" V. ii. 215 becomes "Oh Heauen! oh heauenly Powres!"), and others replaced with innocuous ones ("Godswill Gentlemen" becomes "Alas Gentlemen" II. iii. 137). The concerned attentiveness of the expurgator is readily illustrated. From her entrance at V. ii. 85 Emilia uses the word "lord" twelve times in her first nine speeches; only the one referring to God was altered ("Alas" for "O Lord," line 117). In another remarkable instance the expurgator evidently purged a reading in the copy which he mistakenly thought was "profanity" ("Alas *Iago*" IV. ii. 148, where Q reads "O Good *Iago*").

The various other kinds of "editing" found in the F text have a decidedly "literary" cast. Whereas (according to our theory) the underlying manuscript had been designed as basis for a prompt book, the printed text itself shows many signs of having been prepared for readers. Of these, the careful act and scene division, list of characters, and heavy punctuation are only the most noticeable. Although the editor little bothered about the manuscript's missing and defective stage directions, he did shift a number of those he found with a reader, not Elizabethan staging, in view (I. ii. 28 S.D., *I. iii. 46 S.D.*). When he cut "with his Trunchen" (II. i. 258–9), I think he was balking at a tiny seeming-inconsistency only a reader, remembering ahead, could see as such. When he cut the repeated "hand" in Cassio's "this is my right hand; and this is my left hand" (II. iii. 98), he was thinking of good style, not of the over-careful articulation of a tipsy man attempting to show himself sober. He filled out contractions (every "em" in Q appears as "them"), and sometimes with absurdly pedantic effect ("Alas, what is the matter?/ What is the matter, Husband?" V. i. 111; "All that is spoke, is marr'd" V. ii. 353). With a reader's eye rather than a dramatist's ear, he changed colloquial constructions ("they laugh, [Q: "laugh"] that winnes" IV. i. 119) and spoken forms ("on shore" [Q: "ashore"] II. i. 28, "in bed" [Q: "abed"] IV. i. 3). At points he tried to regularize meter (I. iii. 144), or worried about tenses (III. iii. 422–3, III. iv. 20); and he fiddled with pronouns even to the extent of disturbing meter "Haue there inioynted them with [Q: "inioynted with"] an after Fleete" *I. iii. 35*), naturalness ("I pray you Sir, [Q: "pray sir"] hold your hand" II. iii. 133), and sometimes dramatic point ("Good name in Man, & woman (deere my Lord)/ Is the immediate Iewell of their [Q: "our"] Soules" III. iii. 154; "O thou [Q: "the"] pernitious caitiffe" V. ii. 314). In this sort of tampering he could be remarkably obtuse ("Dost thou heare me, mine [Q: "heare my"] honest Friend" III. i. 20) and heavy-handed "(You haue a thing for me?" III. iii. 299). The editor was also responsible for many sophistications of diction. He changed unusual words ("provulgate" [F: "promulgate"] I. ii. 21), and others that might be regarded difficult ("banning [F: "foaming"] shore" II. i. 11), too colloquial ("in the nick" [F: "in the interim"] V. ii. 313), or countryman-like ("Lodging [F: "loading"] of this bed" V. ii. 359). And he also made context-induced "corrections" ("it comes ore my memorie,/ As doth the Rauen o're the infectious [Q: "infected"] house:/ Boading to all" IV. i. 21), "interpreting" substitutions ("when these mutabilities [Q: "mutualities"] so marshall the way" II. i. 248), seemingly "logical" alterations ("in the bitter letter,/ After your [Q: "its"] owne sense" *I. iii. 69*; "slow, and mouing [Q: "vnmouing"] finger" IV. ii. 56; "The purest of their Wiues" [Q: "her sex"] IV. ii. 18), and careful misconstructions of sense ("not bound to that: All slaues are free:" [Q: "that all slaues are free to"] III. iii. 133).

When all is said and done, it must be admitted that the attempt to establish a theory of the texts, discern their characteristic kinds of corruption, and delicately weigh the probabilities in every instance of variation has only shrunk, not eliminated, the penumbral area in which taste questionably guides editorial decision. Major uncertainties and difficulties bar the way to a securely authoritative text, among them the following. First, there are irrecoverable readings. Where Q omits or corrupts, we may have lost an original reading more authoritative than that in F (? "enscerped" II. i. 70). When F corrupts we occasionally may be able to reconstruct plausibly the fair copy reading ("grounds/ Christen [F: "Christen'd"], and Heathen" I. i. 30; "From any other's [F: "other"; Q: "hated"] foul unlawful touch" IV. ii. 85). In other cases we may have lost a reading more authoritative than that found in either text and not even be aware of it. Again, in some instances where both Q and F corrupt a passage, a plausible conflation is possible ("feats [F] of broil [Q] and battle" *I. iii. 87*); but in the case of a single word like that at II. i. 287 (Q: "crush"; F: "trace"), we probably have lost the reading(s) of both manuscripts.

Another important problem arises from the likelihood that not all of Shakespeare's second thoughts were improvements. This means we cannot reject F readings merely because we are pleased to regard them as "inferior"; the circumstances oblige us to distinguish between authorial and editorial sophistication. However, our attempts to do so are bound to be on grounds of widely varying solidity. Inappropriate connotation, facile reduction of poetic point, discrepancy with previous action, and gross weakening of sense cue us to the probability that F's "promulgate" (I. ii. 21), "foaming" (II. i. 11), "acquaintance" (IV. ii. 188) and "write from vs,/ To him" (*I. iii. 46*) probably are all erroneous. But consider Q's "acerbe as the Coloquintida" (I. iii. 338–9). It is almost certainly Shakespearean in view of the unusual adjective, particularly as the playwright presumably had encountered it in the Italian of Cinthio's source story (*in acerbissimo odio*). But we are in no position to assert positively that it was, beyond doubt, an actor or editor, and not Shakespeare, who finally preferred the blunt simplicity of F's "bitter as Coloquintida." Of course, the greater the degree of indeterminacy as to cause or agency of variation, or even locus of error, the less confident must be our choice. Graphically indifferent variants (like "Doues"/ "Dawes" I. i. 66), both of which make textually adequate sense, readily illustrate the point. Where neither gains advantage in our judgment on some other basis (as I believe should be the case with "toged"/ "tongued" I. i. 25), we are obliged, as in the case of "indifferent" variants (e.g. "soft"/ "set" *I. iii. 82*), to give weight to the fact that our theory in general allows F more presumptive authority than Q. In any individual instance, however, we may be quite wrong to do this.

Given the present scope of our ignorance, then, an editor can realistically hope only that most of his operations will be grounded on sufficient knowledge. His problem, generally, is to get at least that part of the truth about a variation essential to decision. I believe that in a very large number of cases this is possible. For example (to take a famous crux): I do not see that we can assuredly determine whether Q's *"Indian"* at V. ii. 343 was an error or a first thought, or whether F's "Iudean" was the original reading or an authorial second thought. The crucial point, I think, is that there are very substantial historical and critical grounds for supposing it most unlikely for F's reading to have been either an error or an unauthoritative sophistication.

Readers interested in further pursuing this fascinating textual problem should consider the important discussions by M. R. Ridley (Arden edition, Cambridge [Mass.], 1958), W. W. Greg (in *The Shakespeare First Folio*, Oxford, 1955), and Alice Walker (*Textual Problems in the First Folio*, Cambridge, 1953). The best facsimile of the Folio is the Norton prepared by Charlton Hinman (New York, 1968); there is no comparable one of the Quarto, but the Praetorius (Berlin, 1885), though untrustworthy, can serve most elementary purposes. Valuable background can be found in E. K. Chambers, *William Shakespeare: A Survey of Facts and Problems* (Oxford, 1930), W. W. Greg, *The Editorial Problem in Shakespeare* (Oxford, 1942), Fredson Bowers, *On Editing Shakespeare* (Charlottesville, Va., 1966) and *Textual and Literary Criticism* (Cambridge, 1959). A monograph by the present writer, *On the Text of Shakespeare's* OTHELLO, is forthcoming.

APPENDIX C

Sources for OTHELLO

Apart from the dramatic tradition, which (among so much else) supplied Shakespeare with the stock types upon which to base the characterizations of Iago, Brabantio, and Roderigo, a variety of sources contributed to the making of the play. Historical facts about the Turkish menace in the Mediterranean earlier in the sixteenth century were suggestive to the dramatist; and his reading in various books provided him with detail. For example: from Cardinal Contareno's book, translated by Sir Lewes Lewkenor as *The Commonwealth and Government of Venice* (1599), came useful information about Venice and items of diction; from Ariosto's *Orlando Furioso* (in the original Italian) seems to have been drawn the fateful handkerchief's "sibyl" and her "prophetic fury"; and Pliny's *Natural History* probably was the starting point not only for much of the exotic imagery associated with the Moor (e.g. chrysolite, Arabian balm, Propontic and Hellespont), but also for the charge of witchcraft against Othello, and his ironic response to it ("This only is the witchcraft I have used"), during his trial in I. iii. Shakespeare also depended upon commonplace wonders of geographic and travel literature ("The Anthropophagi, and men whose heads/ Do grow beneath their shoulders" I. iii. 143–4); familiar charges in anti-feminine satire (Iago's extempore verses in II. i.); iconographic tradition and proverbial lore; and, very importantly, Holy Scripture and theological and demonological concepts and associated imagery.

The principal narrative source was the seventh *novella* of the third "Decade" (or group of ten stories—in this case devoted to the theme of marital infidelity) in Giambattista Giraldi Cinthio's *Hecatommithi* (1565). Shakespeare clearly had detailed knowledge of this story. Since no early English translation is known, and the available French translation (by Gabriel Chappuys, 1575) seems less close to Shakespeare in verbal detail, it has generally been assumed that he read

❧ TABVLA ASIAE VIII·

Detail of a map of Asia, showing "The Anthropophagi, and men whose heads/ Do grow beneath their shoulders," from Claudius Ptolemaeus, *Geographia vniversalis* (Basle, 1540).

the story in Italian. As this source affords a remarkable opportunity to watch the dramatist at work, the bulk of it is offered below. The translation is a new one by the present editor.

HECATOMMITHI, *Decade Three, Story Seven*

"There was in Venice once a Moor most valiant, who for his personal courage and for the proofs he had given of great judgment and lively skill in matters of war was highly esteemed by the Signiory, which in rewarding manly acts surpassed all republics that ever were. It happened that a virtuous lady of marvellous beauty called Disdemona, drawn not by feminine appetite, but by the *virtù* of the Moor, fell in love with him. And he, conquered by the beauty of the lady, and the nobility of her mind, likewise became enamored of her. And they enjoyed so mutual a love that they united in matrimony, although the lady's relatives did all they could to get her to take for her husband someone other than him. And they lived together in such harmony and peace, while they were in Venice, that no word passed between them that was not loving.

"It happened that the Venetian Signiory determined a change of the troops which they used to maintain in Cyprus, and they appointed the Moor Captain of the soldiers dispatched there. Although he was joyful at the honor offered to him, since so high a dignity was conferred only on men noble, brave, and faithful who had shown themselves capable of great valor, yet his happiness diminished when he considered the length and difficulty of the voyage, worrying that Disdemona might be harmed. The lady, who had no other good in the world than the Moor, and rejoiced at the testimony of her husband's *virtù* received from so powerful and noble a Republic, could scarce await the time that he with his troops would set forth, and she accompany him to so honorable a post. But seeing the Moor troubled deeply disturbed her, and not knowing the cause, one day at dinner she said to him: 'How is it, Moor, that since the Signiory conferred so honored a rank upon you, you have been so melancholy?' The Moor answered Disdemona: 'The love that I bear you itself disturbs my pleasure at this honor, for I see that of necessity one of two things must happen—either I take you with me into the perils of the sea, or, to spare you that, leave you here in Venice. The first could not be other than serious to me since every hardship you would have to bear and every danger that might befall you would grieve me extremely. The second possibility, leaving you behind, would make me hateful to myself, because in parting from you I should be parting from my own life.'

"Seeing it was thus, Disdemona replied, 'Come, tell me my husband, what thoughts are these that come into your mind? why let such things disturb you? I want to come with you wherever you go, even were it to pass through fire in my smock, as now to sail with you in a safe and well-furnished ship; and if indeed there be trials and dangers, I want to be with you at your side. And I should fear myself little loved by you if, not to have me accompany you on the sea, you should think to leave me in Venice or could suppose I would rather stay in safety here than share the same danger with you. I want you to prepare for the voyage with all that happiness that the dignity of rank you hold deserves.' The Moor then with all joy threw his arms about his wife's neck, and with an affectionate kiss told her, 'May God keep you long in this love, my dear wife!' And soon, donning his armor, having put all in order for the journey, he embarked with his wife and with all the company in the galley, and, sails to the wind, they set on their way and upon a perfectly tranquil sea sailed safely to Cyprus.

"The Moor had in his company an ensign of very fine appearance, but with the most wicked nature of any man in the world. This man was very dear to the Moor, who had no inkling of his wickedness. For although he had the vilest soul, he so hid with lofty and proud words, and with his specious presence, the evil that was in his heart that outwardly he appeared a Hector or an Achilles. This scoundrel had likewise taken his wife, who was a beautiful and honorable young woman, with him to Cyprus. And since she was Italian, she was much loved by the Moor's wife, and they were together the greater part of every day. In the same company there was also a captain, most dear to the Moor, who used very frequently to go to the Moor's home, and often dined with him and his wife. As the lady knew him to be so well esteemed by her husband, she showed him the greatest kindness. This pleased the Moor very much. The wicked ensign, caring nothing for the faith pledged to his wife, or for the friendship, loyalty, and duty he owed the Moor, fell passionately in love with Disdemona, and turned all his thoughts to seeing whether he might enjoy her. But he dared not declare himself, fearing he might meet sudden death if the Moor should perceive it. Instead he sought in various ways, as secretly as he could, to put the lady wise that he loved her. But she, who had only the Moor in her thoughts, gave no thought at all to the ensign or anyone else. Everything he did to kindle in her a love for him did no more good than if he had not tried it. Whereupon he imagined that the reason was that she had fallen in love with the captain; and so he pondered how to put him out of the way. To this did he bend his mind, but not alone: for he changed the love he bore the lady into the bitterest hatred, and he pondered deeply how, once the captain was killed, he might bring it about, if he could not enjoy the lady, that the Moor also might not enjoy her. And revolving in his mind various schemes, all wicked and dastardly, he finally decided to accuse her of adultery to her husband, and to make him think the captain was her partner in guilt. But knowing the singular love the Moor bore Disdemona, and the friendship which he had for the captain, he knew full well that unless he deceived the Moor with a clever fraud it was impossible to make either accusation credible to him. For this reason he decided to wait until time and place should open the way for him to set about his villainous plot.

"It was not long after, that the Moor deprived the captain of his rank for having, on guard duty, drawn his sword against a soldier and wounded him. This grieved Disdemona; and many times she tried to make peace again between her husband and him. Meanwhile, the Moor told the wicked ensign that his wife was pestering him so much about the captain that he feared he would finally be compelled to reinstate him. This gave the evil man occasion to put in motion his deceitful plot, and he said, 'Perhaps Disdemona has reason to look kindly on him.' 'And why?' said the Moor. 'I do not wish,' replied the ensign, 'to interfere between man and wife; but, if you'd keep your eyes open, you'd see it for yourself.' By nothing the Moor did would the ensign be pressed to say more. But these words left such a stinging thorn in the mind of the Moor that he gave himself over

completely to thinking what they could mean, and became quite
melancholy.

"One day, when his wife was trying to soften his anger against
the captain, praying him not, for one small fault, to be forgetful of
the service and friendship of so many years—especially since peace
was now made between the wounded soldier and the captain—the
Moor became angry and said to her: 'How extraordinary it is, Disdemona, that you are so anxiously concerned about this man; yet he
is neither a brother nor a relative that he should be so much at your
heart.' The lady, all courteous and humble, replied, 'I would not want
to make you angry with me; nothing moves me to speak but that I
grieve to see you deprived of so dear a friend, as you yourself have
said the captain has been to you; and he has not committed so serious
a fault that you should bear him so much hatred. But you Moors are
of so hot a nature that any little thing moves you to wrath and to
vengeance.' To these words the Moor replied more angrily, 'A certain
someone could experience it who doesn't expect it. I will see such
vengeance for the injuries which have been done me that I shall be
satisfied!' The lady was quite frightened at these words, and having
seen her husband angered with her as was never his wont, she humbly
said, 'In speaking to you of this I had none but good intent; since I
would not have you angry with me more, I will not say another word
about it.'

"The Moor, having observed the insistence with which his wife
had again pleaded for the captain, supposed that the ensign's words
must have meant that Disdemona was enamored of him, and full of
melancholy he went to that villain to try to get him to speak more
openly of it. The ensign, intent on harming this poor lady, after
feigning reluctance to speak of anything that might displease the
Moor, pretended to be overcome by his entreaties, and said: 'I
cannot deny that it pains me beyond belief to have to tell you something that is bound to be to you a grief greater than any other; but,
since you indeed wish that I speak to you of it, and since the care
which I have of your honor, as my lord, compels me to tell you, I
wish no longer to fail your request or my duty. You must know, then,
that to see the captain in your disfavor is distressing to your Lady
for no reason other than the pleasure she has with him when he
comes to your house, for this blackness of yours already has come to
displease her.' These words pierced the Moor's heart to the roots.
However, to know still more (now that he believed true all the ensign
had told him because of the suspicion that had been born in his
mind), he said with a fierce look, 'I know not what keeps me from
tearing out of you that tongue, so bold, that has dared to put such
infamy upon my lady!' Then the ensign said, 'Captain, I expected
for this my loving service no other reward. But since my duty has
carried me thus far, as well as my concern for your honor, I reply

to you that the matter stands just as you have had it from me. And if your lady, with a show of loving you, has so closed your eyes that you have not seen what you should, that is no argument at all that I have not told you the truth. Indeed, the captain himself has told me of it, like one whose happiness seems incomplete unless someone else shares in the knowledge of it.' And he went on, 'And had I not feared your anger, I should, when he told me this, have given him the reward he deserved by killing him. But, since making you know what concerns you more than anyone else has brought me so unsuitable a recompense, I wish I had kept quiet, for, being silent, I should not have incurred your disfavor.' Then the Moor in utter rage said, 'Live assured I'll make you know it would have been better for you to have been born dumb if you do not make me see with these eyes what you have told me!' 'That would have been easy for me,' the villain responded, 'when he used to come to your home; but now that you have sent him packing, not for what really is deserving of it, but rather for something trivial, it cannot but be difficult for me, though I assume he still enjoys Disdemona whenever you give him the opportunity. However, now that he has become hateful to you, he must act much more cautiously than he did before. Still, I do not lose hope of being able to make you see what you do not want to credit from my tongue.' And with these words they parted.

"The wretched Moor, as though struck by the sharpest dart, went home to await the coming of the day when the ensign would show him what would make him miserable forever. But the accursed ensign was no less troubled by the chastity which, as he was aware, the lady kept inviolate, for it appeared to him there was no way to make the Moor believe what he had falsely told him. But, having turned various ways over in his mind, the rascal hit upon a new evil device. The wife of the Moor often went, as I have said, to the home of the ensign's wife, and stayed with her a good part of the day. One day, seeing that she carried about with her a handkerchief which he knew the Moor had given her—a handkerchief, worked in the most subtle Moorish fashion, which was most precious to the lady and the Moor alike—he got the idea of taking it from her secretly, and with it to work her final ruin. He had a little daughter three years of age who was much loved by Disdemona, and one day when the unhappy lady had gone to visit at that villain's home, he took the little girl up in his arms and held her to the lady; she took the child and pressed her to her breast, and that trickster, surpassingly dexterous of hand, so cunningly lifted the handkerchief from her waistband that she noticed not at all. And then, quite happy, he took his leave of her.

"Disdemona, unaware of this, went home, and busy with other thoughts took no notice of the missing handkerchief. But, a few days later, looking for it and not finding it, she was afraid that the Moor might ask her about it as he often did. The wicked ensign, having found a fitting moment, went to the captain and with cunning malice left the handkerchief at the head of his bed. The captain did not notice it until the following morning when, arising from bed, and the handkerchief having fallen on the floor, he set his foot on it. He could not imagine how it had come to be in his house. Knowing it to belong to Disdemona, he decided to return it to her; and waiting until the Moor had left the house, he went to the back door and knocked. It seems that fortune was in league with the ensign to bring about the death of the poor woman, for just at that moment the Moor returned home, and hearing the knocking at the door, went to the window and, very angry, called 'Who knocks there?' The captain heard the voice of the Moor, and fearing he would come down and harm him, took to flight without answering a word. The Moor went downstairs, opened the door and went out in the street; and, looking about for him, found no one. Then he reentered the house and demanded of his wife who it was that had knocked. The lady answered the truth, which was that she did not know. But the Moor said, 'It looked like the captain.' 'I don't know,' she said, 'whether it was he or another.' The Moor held back his rage, however much it burned with wrath. He did not wish to do anything until he first spoke with the ensign, to whom he went at once and told what had happened, and begged him to learn from the captain all that he could about it. He, delighted at this turn of events, promised to do so.

"So one day he spoke to the captain when the Moor was placed where he could see them talking together. And speaking to him of everything but the lady, he laughed uproariously and, putting on a show of being astonished, made many gestures with his head and hands as one who heard marvelous things. The Moor, as soon as he saw them part, went up to the ensign to know what the other had said to him. After having himself entreated for a long while, the ensign at last told him, 'He has hidden nothing from me; and he told me that he has enjoyed your wife every time that you by being away have given him opportunity; and that the last time he was with her, she gave to him that handkerchief you presented her when you married.'

"The Moor thanked the ensign, and it seemed to him that if he should find that the lady did not have the handkerchief, it would be clear that things were just as the ensign had told him. Therefore, one day after dinner, during conversation on various matters with his wife, he asked her for the handkerchief. The unhappy lady, who had greatly feared such a request, became all red in the face, and to hide her blushing, which the Moor had very well noted, she ran to her chest and pretended to look for it. After searching for it a long while, she said, 'I don't know how it is I do not find it just now—may you perhaps have had it?' 'If I had had it,' he said, 'why should I ask you for it? But you will look for it more unhurriedly another time.'

"And when he left, he began to think how he might put the lady to death, and the captain with her, in such a way that he would not be supposed guilty of their slaying. And having this in his thoughts night and day, he could not prevent his wife's observing that he was not the same toward her as he used to be before. And she said to him over and over, 'What is the matter? What is disturbing you, that you who used to be the merriest man in the world are now the most melancholy one alive?' The Moor found various ways of answering the lady, but she was left no whit satisfied. And though she knew that for no misdeed of hers should the Moor be so troubled, nevertheless she feared that by their being too much with one another she had become a bother to him. And sometimes she would say to the ensign's wife, 'I don't know what to say of the Moor; he used to be all love towards me, but now, for the last few days, for what reason I know not, he has become another man. And I greatly fear that I may prove an example to young people not to marry against the wishes of their parents, and that Italian ladies may learn of me not to go with a man whom nature, heaven, and way of life separate from us. But, as I know he is a great friend of your husband and confides his affairs to him, I beg of you, if you have heard anything from him of which you could inform me, that you fail not to help me.' And all the while she was saying this, she wept unrestrainedly. The wife of the ensign, who knew everything (for it was she whom her husband wished to use as a means in the death of the lady, but she would never consent to it), fearing her husband, did not dare tell anything. She only said, 'Be careful not to give your husband any suspicion of you, and seek in every way to make him aware of the love and loyalty in you.' 'That I am doing,' she said, 'but nothing helps!'

"The Moor meanwhile was seeking in every way further to confirm what he did not want to find; and he asked the ensign to contrive a way for him to be able to see the handkerchief in the captain's possession. And though this was difficult for the villain, he promised nonetheless to make every effort in order that the Moor might satisfy himself about that. Now the captain had a woman at his house who did marvellous embroidery on linen of Rheims; she, seeing the handkerchief and knowing it belonged to the Moor's lady and was to be returned to her, set herself to making one like it before it was restored. And while she worked on it, the ensign noticed that she was standing by a window and could be seen by anyone who passed in the street. He then had the Moor get a view of this, and the Moor was utterly convinced that his most chaste lady was in fact an adulteress.

"So he planned with the ensign to kill her and the captain, the two of them discussing together how it should be done. The Moor asked him to be the one to kill the captain, promising to be forever in debt to him for it. He tried to refuse, being unwilling to attempt such a deed, as difficult as greatly dangerous, for the captain was as cunning as he was valorous. However, the Moor, having much entreated him and given him a large sum of money, induced him to say that he would try his luck.

"Having made this resolve, the ensign, one evening when the captain was leaving the house of a prostitute with whom he had been solacing himself, the night being dark, accosted him and aimed a blow at his legs to make him fall. By chance it slashed him across the right thigh, whereat the poor fellow fell, and the ensign was upon him to finish him off. But the captain, who was brave and used to blood and death, having drawn his sword, as wounded as he was maintained his defense, crying out in a loud voice, 'I am assassinated!' As a result, the ensign, hearing people come running, along with a good many soldiers who were billeted nearby, took to flight so as not to be caught. Then turning about, he pretended to be among those running toward the noise. And mingling amongst the others, having seen the captain's leg cut off, he judged that even if he was not yet dead, he must in any event die from that blow. And as utterly delighted as he was about this, he nevertheless grieved with the captain as if he had been his brother.

"By the morning, news of the affair had spread all about the town and also reached the ears of Disdemona, who, being of a kindly nature, and not thinking that evil would thence befall her, showed the greatest sorrow that such a thing had happened—a fact upon which the Moor put the worst construction. And he went to find the ensign, and told him, 'Do you know that ass of a wife of mine is so upset at what happened to the captain, that she is nearly off her mind?' 'And how could you think otherwise,' replied the ensign, 'he being for her her very soul itself.' 'Her soul, eh?' responded the Moor, 'I'll draw out the very soul from her body; call me no man if I do not rid the world of this wicked wretch!' After discussing together whether the lady should be put to death by poison or by dagger, and finding neither method acceptable, the ensign said, 'One way has come into my mind which will satisfy you and raise no suspicion. It is this: the house where you live is very old, and the ceiling of your bedroom has many cracks. I propose we beat Disdemona, so much she dies of it, with a stocking full of sand—that way no mark of a beating will show on her. When she's dead, we will make part of the ceiling fall, and break the lady's head, making it seem a rotten timber fell and killed her. That way no one will suspect you, supposing that her death happened by accident.' This cruel counsel pleased the Moor."

From this point Shakespeare used so little of Cinthio's story that summary can suffice. The brutal murder is executed as planned, the lady, as she succumbs to the villain's blows and her husband's accusation, calling upon divine justice to witness her fidelity. Heaven does not leave her innocence unavenged. The Moor, "who had loved the lady more than his eyes," becomes distracted with grief at her loss and grows to hate the ensign so much he would kill him but for his fear of "the inviolable justice of the Venetian Signiory." Instead, he cashiers him, making the deadly hatred mutual. The villain now plots the Moor's ruin. He gets the captain to return with him to Venice, and there tells him that it was the Moor who cut off his leg and that Disdemona had been murdered by her husband. The captain denounces the Moor, supported by the ensign as witness, and the Signiory, moved at "the cruelty used by a barbarian on a lady of their city," have the Moor arrested. Torture secures no confession from him, but the Signiory banish him, and Disdemona's kinsmen later kill him. The ensign, still up to his old villainous ways, falls afoul of the law in another case of false accusation and after torture dies miserably. After his death, his wife reveals the whole story.

In view of the great amount Shakespeare derived from this story, it is remarkable how much he altered it in fundamentals and detail. A great deal is new, including the storm, arrival in Cyprus, Cassio's appeal to Desdemona, the report of his "dream," Othello's "ecstasy" and recall, the Brothel and Willow Song scenes, and much else; a quite different catastrophe is substituted for the sordid crime and ill-connected conclusion of the *novella*; and a fresh beginning emphasizes altered premises for the action. Little of Act I depends on Cinthio: Roderigo and Brabantio, the elopement (which eliminates the harmonious early married life in Venice), the ensuing near-brawl and trial, the tale of Othello's wooing and his past, and the urgent context of the Turkish menace—all these are "inventions." And what Shakespeare took from the remainder of the story, he markedly changed. For instance, all three central scenes "evidencing" Disdemona's guilt—the appearance of the captain at the Moor's house, the observed conversation between the ensign and the captain, and the view of the woman in the captain's house copying the handkerchief—Shakespeare recast, effectively combining the point of the latter two by creating a new character, Bianca, out of the embroideress and the prostitute mentioned in the *novella*.

But the most striking changes are those affecting the principal characters. Cinthio's colorless heroine is newly conceived; the "supposed lover" figure (Cassio) is fleshed out according to the evolved expectations of his part; and the villain's wife undergoes complete transformation of character and function. Her relation to the heroine is differently imagined, and she passes from knowing non-participant in the ensign's plot to unaware contributor to it. The villain himself, melodramatic in Cinthio, is given disturbing substance and complexity. The Moor's ruin rather than the wife's now becomes the primary target of his envious revengeful hate; and his motivation, changed in occasion and emphasis, is developed for searching implication. Tightened coherence results, too, from Shakespeare's making him, much more than his prototype, an opportunistic manipulator of events: the cashiering of the *capo* through an incident on the watch and the intercession of the heroine in his behalf are now due directly to his plotting. It is typical that he now procures the handkerchief both before it is needed in the deception, and by means of another. The most important changes, however, are those wrought on the Moor to give him the dimensions of a tragic hero. Romantically ennobled into the hardship-tested "worthy governor," the "free and open nature" "that passion could not shake," the Moor also is transformed by a much more terrible passion so that he can become the deluded and suffering "honorable murderer" of the catastrophe. Unlike his prototype in the source, this Moor himself commits the murder; he attempts to make it appear a sacrifice, not an accident; he shows concern for his wife's soul, learns of her innocence, and confesses; and he tries to slay the villain and, finally, to expiate his terrible error by executing judgment on himself.

Certain ideas for developing a greater significance in the hero's and heroine's marital trials than could be found in the *novella* were readily available to the playwright (e.g. in Chaucer's *The Clerkes Tale*) in the tradition of one of Desdemona's literary forbears, the patient Griselda. But the most important hints for his alterations of Cinthio probably came from several other stories of falsely accused ladies and jealousy. Two of these share with the main source of *Much Ado About Nothing* (Bandello, *Novelle*, I, 22) an ultimate common ancestor in the ancient Greek romance, *Chaereas and Callirrhoë*, by Chariton (ca. late fourth century); these are the versions of the Ginevra story found in the Fifth Canto of Ariosto's *Orlando Furioso* (translated by Sir John Harington, 1591) and in Book Two, Canto IV, of *The Faerie Queene*. Another such subsidiary narrative source may have been a history of "A lady falsely accused of adultery" (derived from Bandello, I, 24, by way of Belleforest's *Histoires Tragiques*, 8) in William Painter's *The Palace of Pleasure* (1566)—a common mine of the Elizabethan dramatists. Still another minor source of inspiration was the story of a jealous Albanoys captain in Geoffrey Fenton's *Certain Tragical Discourses* (1567), again derived from Bandello (I, 51) through Belleforest (10). The briefest summary of Shakespeare's possible indebtedness to these speculative ancillary sources must suffice here.

The story of the slandered Ginevra, told by Ariosto and recast by Spenser, Shakespeare had already used in developing the main plot of *Much Ado*, and he may have been stimulated by it again in writing *Othello*. In Ariosto's narrative he could have found hints for placing the love relations of the hero and villain in parallel and contrast, and also for making the villain's woman an unwitting participant in his plot and, later, an object of his vengeance. Spenser's condensed "tragic" version of the story, altered to stress the jealous hero, Phedon, and the moral interpretation of his unhappy fate, offered the dramatist still more direction. The poet's primary concern is with the theme of misfortune as a test of human love, fidelity, and, above all, temperate "government" of the passions; and he underscores from the start the uselessness of mere might (physical valor and the sword) to overcome such spiritual enemies as have victimized Phedon—the personified irrational "Furor" and his "mother" and inciter, "Occasion." Other points also may have been provocative. Spenser already exploits the ironic possibilities in the jealous figure's substituting a bond with the villainous "friend" for that vowed to the slandered lady. Interesting too, the motive of Spenser's villain is no longer (as in Ariosto, as well as in Cinthio and Painter) frustrated love of the heroine, but rather, more simply, either envy of the hero's "toward good" or an unexplained disposition to treason. Finally, Shakespeare's most likely indebtedness becomes apparent as soon as we compare the new catastrophe he evolved for Cinthio's story with the events (if not their sequence) in Spenser's poem after the "ocular proof" of the lady's guilt has been proffered. The hero slays his lady with his own hand; after he has learned the truth from her handmaid (the unwitting accessory in the villain's plot), he has a despairing wish to turn his vengeful wrath upon himself; but he decides first to murder the villain and afterwards makes an attempt on the life of the handmaid.

In the analogous story in Painter's *Palace of Pleasure* (I, 41), the supposed lover's being where the lady may be compromised by his presence is due, as in Shakespeare, directly to the villain's "devilish counsel." This narrative also may have provided the suggestion, in a prayer by the falsely accused wife (a rather matronly and sermonizing Griselda), for the kneeling Desdemona's protestation of her innocence in IV. ii (lines 151–64), which has no counterpart in Cinthio. But it is most interesting for its treatment of the noble husband figure, who in his deluded self-righteousness comes perilously close to proving an "honorable murderer" like Othello. Deceived by the circumstantial evidence of his wife's infidelity, he is so aggrieved and "vanquished with the choler" that he angrily refuses to hear any defence of her innocency either from her or anyone else, and sends word that she should provide for her soul's health as he has condemned her to death. A romantic miraculous deliverance of the innocent lady according with "God's just judgment" saves him from the consequences of his error, but not from the shame of having proved "that maladies and infections of mind be far more dangerous than outward passions which torment the body"; for his story has illustrated the terrible potency of the "venom" of slanderous "Serpents," "that seizing by little and little, the heart of him disposed to receive it in fury, maketh it to be in effect like the nature of poison and drugs corrupt" (cf. II. iii. 325; III. iii. 322 ff.; 446–7; IV. i. 43).

The last of these conjectured ancillary sources, Fenton's "Tragical Discourse" IV, stands apart from the others; though it also concerns a jealous husband who murders his patient and innocent wife, it lacks a villain and deception plot and is, rather, a tale of morbid fixation bred of intemperate love. Apart from a number of details, Shakespeare seems to have been mainly interested in the beginning and end of this story of the disastrous second marriage of a lady endowed with "wonderful perfection" in beauty and virtues. It begins with her first husband who, as an image of valor and fortitude resisting the temptations of fortune, functions (like the Othello of the past) as a contrast to the second, jealous husband. He has stoically suffered the malice of much misfortune as an exile "wandering in woods and desert places unknown . . . with expectation to fall eftsoons into the hands of his enemies" (implicitly, the Turks); but now his "government," "prudent behavior," and "exploits of arms" ("arguing th'unfained nobleness of his mind") have won him entertainment by the authorities of Mantua and generalship of a "whole army." Unhappily, he dies in his prime, and his beautiful widow is at last successfully urged (despite her misgivings) to take as her second husband a noble Albanoys captain who has fallen in love with her. This captain, who has charge of troops of cavalry "for the credit of his virtue and valiantness in arms," has "hitherto reserved the maidenhead of . . . [his] affection"; but the lady's beauty has made his "heart more assaultable and apt to admit parley than either the noise of the cannon or terror of the enemy," and he eagerly yields his "former liberty." Within the very month of his marriage his indulgence of his passion transforms him; "the extreme and superfluity of hot love of this fond husband towards his wife" converts to "a jealous loathing." "What sudden change and alteration of fortune seems now t'assail this valiant captain, who erst loved loyally within the compass of reason, and now, doting without discretion, thinketh himself one of the forked ministers of Cornwall!" Despite every effort by his patient, obedient, and loving wife to dispel his "frantic jealousy," the "fury and rage of his perverse fancy" dangerously deepen. In the murder and suicide which sensationally conclude the captain's desperate passion, Shakespeare found a number of useful details for his imagination characteristically to transmute. Before the captain, in "extreme frenzy" and prompted by "the terrible suggestion of the devil," slays his innocent wife in their marriage bed, he kisses her "in such sort as Judas kissed our Lord the same night he betrayed him"; a second reference to Judas occurs when the once-valiant captain, "wholly possessed with the devil" and desperately unrepentant, kills himself with a dagger.

For discussion of Cinthio and the miscellaneous sources of the play,

and for further references, see Kenneth Muir, *Shakespeare's Sources*,
I (London, 1957). The speculative ancillary narrative sources, first
treated by the present writer in a dissertation ("The Shakespearean
Othello" [Princeton, 1957], Vol. III, App. II), are discussed in a
forthcoming study. Further consideration of the play's sources can
be found in Geoffrey Bullough, *Narrative and Dramatic Sources of
Shakespeare*, Vol. VII (London and New York, 1973).

APPENDIX D

Music in Othello

The Willow Song passage in IV. iii (lines 30–51, 53–5) is found in the
Folio text only. In view of the careful integration of Desdemona's
singing into the dramatic context, these lines are most unlikely to have
been additions. The Quarto text's evidently deliberate omission of
Emilia's later reference to the song (V. ii. 243–5) suggests that its
lack of the earlier passage is due to theatrical cutting. It has been suggested that these cuts may have been occasioned at some revival involving a boy-actor of the heroine's part who could not (or could no
longer) sing; but it should be noted that two other passages later in
the same scene (lines 58–61 and 83–100) also appear in the Folio only.

In the Willow Song Shakespeare adapts a popular ballad known
from other sources. Extensive texts of it are found in the *Roxburghe
Ballads* and in Percy's *Reliques*, and three contemporary musical
versions are known. One of these, a setting for lute and voice, is
preserved in a British Museum manuscript (Add. MS. 15117) accompanied by a text of the original ballad sufficient to illuminate Shakespeare's dramatically significant variations on the popular model
(and even to guide emendation of the Folio text at IV. iii. 39).

   I The poor soul sat sighing by a sycamore tree
       With his hand in his bosom and his head upon his knee

  II He sighed in his singing, and made a great moan, sing etc.
       I am dead to all pleasure, my true love she is gone, etc.

 III The mute bird sat by him was made tame by his moans, etc.
       The true tears fell from him, would have melted the stones, sing
       etc.

  IV Come all you forsaken and mourn you with me,
       Who speaks of a false love, mine's falser than she, sing etc.

   V Let love no more boast her in palace nor bower,
       It buds, but it blasteth ere it be a flower, sing etc.

Willow Song

Shakespeare's text

(first stanza)

Folger Shakespeare
Library MS.

1. The poor soul sat sigh-ing by a sy-ca-more tree, Sing all a green wil-low: Her hand on her bo-som, her head on her knee, Sing vil-low, wil-low, wil-low, Sing all a green wil-low must be my gar-land.

(second stanza)

Shakespeare's text

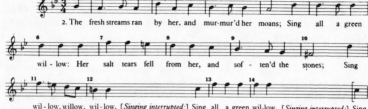

2. The fresh streams ran by her, and mur-mur'd her moans; Sing all a green wil-low: Her salt tears fell from her, and sof-ten'd the stones; Sing wil-low, willow, wil-low, [*Singing interrupted:*] Sing all a green wil-low, [*Singing interrupted:*] Sing
(DESDEMONA) Lay by these (DESDEMONA) Prithee, hie
thee, he'll come anon.

all a green wil-low must be my gar-land.

Desdemona interrupts herself at bar 14, then starts singing again. For the second start, it is necessary to insert six notes. For this editorial insertion the bars, which are not numbered, are enclosed in square brackets.

(third and fourth stanzas)

Shakespeare's text

3. Let no - bo-dy blame him, his scorn I ap - prove
[*Singing stops.*]
(DESDEMONA) Nay, that's not next. Hark! who is't that knocks?
(EMILIA) It is the wind.

4. I call'd my love false love; but what said he? then? Sing all a green wil-low: If I court moe wo-men, you'll couch with moe men
[*Singing stops.*]
(DESDEMONA) So get thee gone; good night. Mine eyes do itch. Doth that bode weeping?

Courtesy of Routledge & Kegan Paul, and Dover Publications.

VI Though fair and more false, I die with thy wound,
  Thou hast lost the truest lover that goes upon the ground,
    sing etc.

VII Let nobody chide her, her scorns I approve,
  She was born to be false, and I to die for her love, sing etc.

VIII Take this for my farewell and latest adieu
  Write this on my tomb, that in love I was true, sing etc.

Which (if any) of the extant contemporary tunes for the Willow
Song may have been used by Shakespeare's company is not known.
However, in view of the fact that Desdemona sings unaccompanied,
and refers to Barbary's ballad as "An old thing," the best contender
may be the version which appears both the oldest and the one most
typical of simple balladry. This is preserved in a purely instrumental
setting in a part of a manuscript dating from the 1570's (Folger
Shakespeare Library MS. V. a. 159). A modern transcription for unaccompanied voice, with the Shakespearean text including asides, has
been prepared for performance by Professor Frederick W. Sternfeld,
and is here reproduced by permission of Kegan Paul and Dover Press,
publishers of his *Music in Shakespearean Tragedy* (rev. ed., London
and New York, 1967).

Contemporary music for the play's other songs, sung by Iago in II.
iii, has not survived. For further discussion of them and the Willow
Song, see Sternfeld, Peter Seng, *The Vocal Songs in the Plays of
Shakespeare* (Cambridge, Mass., 1967), and Richmond Noble, *Shakespeare's Use of Song* (Oxford, 1923). The instrumental wind music at
the start of Act III, and its relation to the play's symbolic motif of
music, is discussed in the present writer's "Shakespeare's 'Dull
Clown' and Symbolic Music," *Shakespeare Quarterly* 17 (1966):
107–28.

APPENDIX E

A Note on Shakespeare's English

Elizabethan English proved close enough to the modern language that
evolved from it for Shakespeare's works to have remained, for the
most part, readily accessible to later generations. At the same time,
it was an English yet in ferment, unregularized and full of eccentric-
ity—a language clearly undergoing an intense and turbulent period
of development. Under the increasingly powerful influence of printed
books, which tended to regularize usage and inhibit linguistic change,
English became largely standardized by the beginning of the

eighteenth century. In 1600, however, it was the spoken language through which most of Shakespeare's audience got its news, entertainment and instruction; and this was an English fluid and erratic, vivid and ebullient, as experimental as it was unsettled. This vernacular, impatient of fixed rules and formal correctness, and permissive of much greater freedom than has been enjoyed since, was the English Shakespeare used and exploited.

Grammar

Among the features of Elizabethan English which immediately mark it as different for the modern reader are its archaisms, irregularities, and tendency to both ellipsis and redundancy. Archaic forms that can be illustrated from this play include, most obviously, the second person inflections ("thou hast") and third singular in -*th* ("hath"); quite primitive "impersonal" verbs ("it *dislikes* me" II. iii. 39) and the old plural "be" ("there *be* souls must be saved" II. iii. 88–9); the use of "his" for the genitive singular of "it" ("The lethargy must have *his* quiet course" IV. i. 52)—where we would use "its," a made-up word, rare in Shakespeare's time, introduced to distinguish the neuter from the masculine possessive; and the third plural indicative inflection in -*s*—although many apparent instances of this must remain doubtful because of the Elizabethan readiness to allow subjects we regard as plural to take singular verbs ("whose subdued eyes,/ Albeit unusèd to the melting mood,/ *Drops* tears" V. ii. 344–6). Elizabethan writers indulge in many irregularities no longer permissible, for example the use of the nominative for the accusative ("you have seen Cassio and *she* together" IV. ii. 3); this frequently is seen with the interrogative "who" even after a preposition ("To who?" I. ii. 52). Notable too among constructions no longer allowable are redundancies used for rhetorical emphasis. Double and even triple negatives are common ("This *cannot* be/By *no* assay of reason" I. iii. 17–18; "It yet hath felt *no* age *nor* known *no* sorrow" III. iv. 32). And we often encounter rhetorical intensification of the comparative and superlative by addition of the redundant "more" and "most" ("*more safer* voice" I. iii. 222–3; "She comes *more nearer* earth" V. ii. 109). But the most striking irregularity, no doubt, is the very frequent false concord, where verb and subject disagree. Some cases result from the Elizabethans' having a sense of the number of the particular noun different from ours. To them, *news* was plural (i.e. "new things"), as at I. iii. 1; and even a word like *kind* could be thought to bear a plural sense ("There *are* a *kind* of men . . . / One of this kind is Cassio." III. iii. 413–15). On the other hand, *riches* was singular, according with its derivation from French "richesse" ("*Riches* fineless *is* as poor as winter" III. iii. 170). However, the false concord also occurs frequently with "there is," after the relative, with two singular nouns as subject, with a subject that could be thought a single entity, and "by attraction" to the nearest noun instead of the proper subject. Consider the following examples: "*Is* there not *charms?*" (I. i. 170); "the big *wars/* That *makes* ambition virtue" (III. iii. 346–7); "With such *things* else of quality and respect/ As *doth* import you" (I. iii. 278–9); "Your *power and your command is* taken off" (V. ii. 327).

Elizabethan writers, in fact, not only tend to be more casual than we about syntax but readily sacrifice exact construction and formal correctness for vivid and condensed effect. There is a marked tendency to omit almost any part of a construction that might be supplied from context. We find the nominative omitted with "has" ("*H'as* had most happy speed" II. i. 67); with "who" as the emphatic relative ("*Who* steals my purse, [he] steals trash" III. iii. 155); and in second person questions ("Didst [thou] not mark that?" II. i. 243). Expressions with "please" often are condensed ("So please [it] your grace, my ancient" I. iii. 279). And verbal elements frequently are abridged ("heaven defend your good souls that you [should] think/ I will your serious and great business scant" I. iii. 262–3). This last ellipsis sometimes includes the repeated pronoun in the latter of two clauses connected by a relative or conjunction ("knave/ That . . . / Wears out his time . . . / For naught but provender; and when he's old, [he is = his reward is to be] cashiered" I. i. 45–8). Even the preposition sometimes is omitted in adverbial phrases ("[by] what drugs, what charms,/ What conjurations, and what mighty magic/ . . . I won his daughter." I. iii. 91–4).

Elizabethan writers felt remarkably free to convert one part of speech into another. Thus verbal forms become nouns without benefit of the suffixes we require ("He hath a person and a smooth *dispose*" I. iii. 381); proper names are turned to adjectival use without alteration ("the *Cyprus* wars" I. i. 149); and adjectives commonly replace adverbs without addition of -*ly* ("*Certain,* men should be what they seem" III. iii. 126). In their use of adjectives, Elizabethans often compound two, with the first in adverbial relation to the second (*wondrous pitiful* I. iii. 160). Frequently, adjectives signifying an effect are made to designate the power to cause it ("*drowsy* syrups" III. iii. 328). Elizabethans also often use an adjective and a noun with the effect of transferred epithet where we would now require a noun and a genitive phrase ("a *secure couch*" IV. i. 70). Finally, the position of adjectives frequently is different from that normal in modern usage. They often appear after the noun ("anters *vast* and deserts *idle*" I. iii. 139); the unemphatic possessive adjective is sometimes transposed ("*dear* my lord" III. iii. 153); and the adjective could be placed before a whole compound consisting of two nouns connected by "of" instead of before the one noun it strictly modifies ("My *thrice-driven* bed of down" I. iii. 228). Adverbs too are often transposed; "almost," for example, often follows the word it qualifies ("his trespass . . . / is not *almost* a fault/ T'incur a private check" III. iii. 63–6—where we would say "is scarcely fault enough to"). Among special adverbial uses, we might note *much* to mean "very" ("I take it *much* unkindly" (I. i. 1); *something* where we would say "somewhat" ("While I spare speech which *something* now offends me" II. iii. 178); verbal nouns with the prefix *a-* in the sense "in the act of" ("I would have him nine years *a-killing*" IV. i. 168); and *nothing* with the meaning "not at all" ("to speak the truth/ Shall *nothing* wrong him" II. iii. 202–3).

Articles, both definite and indefinite, frequently are omitted where we would expect them. This often occurs where the noun carries the force of a class ("I never found man that knew how to love himself" I. iii. 308), and also after the preposition in adverbial phrases ("he foams at mouth" IV. i. 53). Special uses of articles are the indefinite "a" in the sense "one" or "some" in certain expressions ("You or any man living may be drunk at *a* time" II. iii. 286), and the definite "the" before a verbal followed by an object ("I'll attempt *the* doing of it" III. iv. 17).

Conjunctions are used with an Elizabethan looseness, matching their syntax, that can be confusing to the modern reader; and they often have an unfamiliar force. "And" can be emphatically interrogative in a question ("*And*, good lieutenant, I think you think I love you" II. iii. 283–4); and it can have the sense "you are right," "exactly so," in answers ("*And* so she did." III. iii. 205). The same word (*and, an'*) can mean "if," and *and if*, "if indeed" ("It is not lost but what *an' if* it were?" III. iv. 75). *But* in the sense "except" frequently follows negative comparatives where we would say "than" ("no worse nor better guard/ *But* with a knave of common hire" I. i. 123–4). The same conjunction can have a "preventive" meaning ("I have much to do/ *But* to go hang [= to prevent myself from hanging] my head all at one side" IV. iii. 30–1). "As" served a wider variety of purposes than at present, including a nearly redundant use before participles to denote cause ("But he, *as* loving his own pride and purposes" I. i. 12), and a use in result clauses where we would say "that" ("Yet throw such changes of vexation on't/ *As* it may lose some color" I. i. 73–4).

The prepositions in Elizabethan English involve remarkable differences from modern usage, particularly because they were less restricted in meaning, and less precise. Thus we find *in* used where we would say "at" ("*In* this time of the night" I. ii. 94), "of" ("'tis foul *in* her" IV. i. 188) "on" ("What *in* your own part can you say to this?" I. iii. 74), and even "to" ("Tying her duty, beauty, wit, and fortunes/

In an extravagant and wheeling stranger" I. i. 134–5). *Of* often serves for "for" ("I humbly do beseech you *of* your pardon" III. iii. 209), and *on* for "of" or "about" ("Be not acknown *on*'t" III. iii. 316). There are numerous odd usages no longer encountered, such as *upon* in the sense "for the purpose of" ("*Upon* malicious bravery dost thou come" I. i. 101) and *from* in the sense "apart from," "different from" ("Do not believe/ That, *from* the sense of all civility,/ I thus would play and trifle with your reverence" I. i. 129–31). Finally, prepositions often are omitted where we would require them, for example, after certain verbs ("Her father . . . / questioned me the story of my life" I. iii. 127–8), and even (as already noted above) in adverbial phrases (I. iii. 91).

In the personal pronouns of Elizabethan English there is much irregularity, archaism, and special usage. The nominative often is used for the accusative, and vice versa; "his" is the normal genitive of "it"; and there is much use of the unemphatic "mine" and "thine" before vowels. "Your," "our," and "their" are found in an old genitive sense ("An instrument of this *your* calling back" IV. ii. 46); and there is an old dative sense of "me," "thee," "him"—called the ethical dative, or dative of interest—where (in many cases) we would say "for me," "by me," etc. ("Judge *me* the world" I. ii. 72). A related colloquial generalizing use of "your" appears to appropriate an object to the person addressed ("he drinks you with facility *your* Dane dead drunk" II. iii. 70). We also find the old nominative "ye" used in entreaties, prayers, and rhetorical appeals ("And O ye mortal engines" III. iii. 352); "we" used in the royal style by a single speaker in authority ("And though *we* have there a substitute" I. iii. 221); and the construction "this of yours" commonly used without the conception of one out of a class ("that whiter skin of hers" V. ii. 4).

The Elizabethan distinction between "thou" and "you" is full of dramatic significance, but it is much too complex to be treated in detail here. In general, the second person singular form "thou" expressed intimacy to friends, easy superiority to inferiors, and contempt or anger to strangers or others in public. Thus, in I. i, Brabantio, before he knows with whom he is dealing, asks Roderigo "What are *you*?" (line 95). When the rejected suitor identifies himself, Desdemona's fulminating father turns to "thee" and "thou" ("I have charged *thee* not to haunt about my doors" line 97). Our consciousness of the significance of this distinction is heightened when Brabantio challenges the foul-mouthed stranger beneath his windows:

Bra. What profane wretch art *thou*?

Iago. I am one, sir, that comes to tell *you* your daughter and the Moor are now making the beast with two backs.

Bra. *Thou* art a villain.

Iago.   *You* are a senator.

Bra. This *thou* shalt answer.—I know *thee,* Roderigo.

　　　　　　　　　　　　　　　　　　(lines 114–18)

But later, when Brabantio needs Roderigo to locate the runaway couple, he ingratiatingly reverts to "you" forms: "Are they married, think *you?*" (line 166). The "thou"-"you" distinction is extremely important in this play from the very first speeches because it serves to mark the speakers' sense of just those relationships (of service, marriage, and friendship) on which the drama turns. As that sense can be deluded or pretended, the distinction is capable of generating powerful ironic clashes of supposition and reality. Consider, for example:

Iago. How is it, general? Have *you* not hurt *your* head?
Oth. Dost *thou* mock me?
Iago. 　　　　　　　　　I mock *you!* no, by heaven.

　　　　　　　　　　　　　　　　　　(IV. i. 58-9)

Elizabethan relatives too are quite idiosyncratic. They often are omitted with resultant ambiguity for the modern reader ("I am not bound to that [which = in regard to which] all slaves are free to" III. iii. 133). We often drop the objective relative, but not (as the Elizabethans) the nominative ("there be souls [that] must be saved" II. iii. 88–9). The relative (with the verb) also is omitted between a pronominal antecedent and a prepositional phrase predicating locale ("Three else [who are] of Cyprus" II. iii. 47). "Who," more definite than "which" and "that," generally is used to introduce a fact about the antecedent ("knaves be such abroad/ *Who,* having by their own importunate suit,/ Or voluntary dotage of some mistress,/ Convincèd or supplied them" IV. i. 25–8). But this relative is not, as with us, necessarily used after personal pronouns; "that" normally is used for this purpose ("O thou Othello *that* wert once so good" V. ii. 288). "Which," generally more definite than "that," is used where the antecedent is preceded by "that" ("With that recognizance and pledge of love/*Which* I first gave her" V. ii. 211–12); in the form "the which" to expressly distinguish the antecedent ("there where I have garnered up my heart,/ . . . The fountain from *the which* my current runs" IV. ii. 58–60); and where "which" means "a circumstance which" ("If you will watch his going thence,/ *which* I will fashion to fall out between twelve and one" IV. ii. 227–8).

The Elizabethans are adventurously free in making verbs from adjectives ("I do not so *secure* me in the error" I. iii. 10) and nouns ("that *paragons* description" II. i. 62; "see them *bolster*" III. iii. 396); and Shakespeare is much given to vivid created compounds (*Off-capped* I. i. 10; *Non-suits* I. i. 16; *out-tongue* I. ii. 19). Passive verbs, mostly found in the participle, were freely formed from nouns (thus

"To have him see me *womaned*" and "I must be *circumstanced*" III. iv. 186; 192). Another license is the transitive use of intransitive verbs ("Each drop she *falls* [= lets fall] would prove a crocodile" IV. i. 229). Some verbs now used transitively Shakespeare used reflexively ("I do *repent me* that I put it to you" III. iii. 389). With intransitive verbs "is" serves as the auxiliary more commonly than with us, particularly with verbs of motion ("Michael Cassio/ . . . *Is* come ashore" II. i. 26–8) and of happening ("fellows that *are* scaped" V. i. 113). No established rules as yet governed the auxiliaries "do" and "did," but "did" evidently is emphatic in excited narration ("That I *did* love the Moor to live with him" I. iii. 244). The differentiation between "shall" and "will" is more forceful than with us. "Shall" is used to denote inevitable futurity without reference to desire; hence the bite in Iago's straight-faced twitting of Cassio: "She gives it out that you *shall* marry her" (IV. i. 114). Thus, "shall" implies compulsion to a person addressed ("You *shall* close prisoner rest" V. ii. 331). In the first person "will" invariably implies wish, desire, determination ("*I'll* not have it so." I. iii. 237; "Would? Nay, I *will!*" III. iii. 390). Otherwise it signifies, according to context, sometimes purpose, sometimes mere futurity. The auxiliaries "would" and "should" have various special Elizabethan uses. "Would" often means "was accustomed" ("But still the house affairs *would* draw her thence" I. iii. 146). Where we use "should" in a conditional clause and "would" in the consequent one, Shakespeare uses "should" in both ("*Should* you do so, my lord,/ My speech *should* fall into such vile success" III. iii. 218–19). And "should" appears in direct questions about the past in a manner to emphasize the interrogation ("Why, how *should* she be murdered?" V. ii. 125). "Be" is used in questions implying doubt ("Where *be* these bloody thieves?" V. i. 64), and also after verbs of thinking to express greater doubt than "is" ("I think my wife *be* honest, and think she is not" III. iii. 381). After verbs of command we find the subjunctive used ("She . . ./ bade me . . ./ I *should* but teach him" I. iii. 162–4). More frequently than in modern usage, the same mood is used optatively without "let" or "may" ("God me such uses *send*" IV. iii. 101). Sometimes the subjunctive is indicated by the transposed position of the verb before the subject ("*Live* Roderigo [= if Roderigo live],/ He calls me to a restitution large" V. i. 14–15). And occasionally we find the future used for the subjunctive ("That you *shall* surely *find* him,/ Lead to the Sagittary" I. i. 156–7). The participles of verbs in Elizabethan English show much irregularity. The older curtailed forms of the past participles are common (" 'I have already *chose* my officer' " I. i. 17; "Hast *stole* it from her?" III. iii. 307). Where these could be confused with the infinitive (e.g., "shake" for "shaken"), the past tense or an -*ed* form appears for the participle (thus "The wind-*shaked* surge" II. i. 13). Finally, the infinitive often is encountered without the "to" ("You were best go in" I. ii. 30; "You were wont be civil" II. iii. 169).

Diction

Elizabethan times saw an enormous growth in the vocabulary of English which is nowhere more evident than in the astonishing scope and richness of Shakespeare's diction. Elizabethan writers drew on every resource, from learned terms to the colloquialisms and slang of colorful everyday speech. They coined new words with adventurous freedom—Shakespeare's boldness and originality in this respect could be illustrated from his vivid compounds alone: e.g., *counter-caster* (I. i. 31); *steep-down* (V. ii. 277); *self-charity* (II. iii. 181); *swag-bellied* (II. iii. 67); *finder-out* (II. i. 232); *light-winged* (I. iii. 264); *thrice-driven* (I. iii. 228); *knee-crooking* (I. i. 45). Finally, they imported vast numbers of words from other languages, and built many new ones on foreign roots (e.g., *provulgate* I. ii. 21; *exsufflicate* III. iii. 179). Latin was heavily levied upon, and there are many borrowings too from the continental languages: thus, e.g., *anters* (I. iii. 139) and *horologe* (II. iii. 114) from French, *magnifico* (I. ii. 12) from Italian, *crusadoes* (III. iv. 21) from Portuguese, *carroused* (II. iii. 45) from German. It is important to note that many of these borrowings in their Elizabethan meaning remain close to the etymological sense. Thus, "My *letters*" (I. iii. 3) means "the dispatch I received" (Latin "litterae"); "our *proper* son" (I. iii. 69) means "my own son" ("proprius"); and "comply" in "to *comply* with heat the young affects" (I. iii. 259) means "fulfill" ("complere").

For the modern reader the most serious problems raised by Elizabethan English probably are those involving diction. Much of the new Renaissance vocabulary did not survive into modern times: to cite a few words from this play, *theoric* (I. i. 24), *indign* (I. iii. 269), *arrivance* (II. i. 42), *slipper* (II. i. 232), *moraller* (II. iii. 273), *mamm'ring* (III. iii. 69), *continuate* (III. iv. 169). Furthermore, many of the words that have remained in use have undergone serious alteration of force or meaning. The older meanings of many common Elizabethan words have become obsolete. For example, *presently* (V. ii. 52) and *straight* (V. ii. 366) in Elizabethan English mean "immediately," "at once." Some words were narrower in meaning than they are now (*extravagant*, at I. i. 135, means "wandering from one's own country"); others were wider in sense (*success*, at III. iii. 219, means "result" with no implication of "good result"). Again, some words had a much stronger sense in Elizabethan use, for instance, *amazed* (III. iii. 368) and *Perplexed* (V. ii. 342); and still others had a different point of view: thus, at IV. i. 117, *customer* (= "prostitute") denotes the one who serves the trade, not the buyer. The modern reader needs to be particularly cautious where the present meaning of a word would be plausible but wrong: in Elizabethan English *jealousy*, as at III. iii. 145, often means "suspicion," "mistrust"; *mere* (II. ii. 2) means "utter," "absolute"; *sadly* (II. i. 32) means "gravely"; *fond* (I. iii. 311) means "foolish"; *modern* (I. iii. 109) means "commonplace," "ordinary"; and *still* (I. iii. 146) means "ever" or "always." There are many more such words than might at first appear. A modestly lengthened list may serve to suggest the dimensions of the problem: *accidents* (= "events" V. i. 94), *peculiar* (= "personal" III. iii. 78), *quality* (= "profession" I. iii. 247), *conveniences* (= "points of fitness" II. i. 223), *commoner* (= "harlot" IV. ii. 74), *notorious* (= "notable" V. ii. 236), *naked* (= "unarmed" V. ii. 255), *entertainment* (= "maintaining in, or taking into, service" III. iii. 247), *napkin* (= "handkerchief" III. iii. 287), *nightgown* (= "dressing gown" I. i. 158 S. D.), and *closet* (= "private room" IV. ii. 22).

The explanatory notes in this edition attempt to help the modern reader with the above problems raised by Shakespeare's diction and also with two others worthy of note. As they repeatedly illustrate, the multiple meanings or nuances of Elizabethan words are crucial to consider in a dramatic poetry given, as Shakespeare's is, to the serious exploitation of various kinds of wordplay. Again, the connotative force or conceptual burden of many Elizabethan words, particularly those which have survived shorn of such implication, require annotation. Consider, for example, *blood, patience, will, repent*. The point is readily illustrated by the powerful oaths in this play, such as *'Zounds* and *'Sblood* (= "by God's wounds" and "by God's blood"); these can have, even though softened by their slurred form, a more distinct theological sense than analogous modern blasphemies.

Pronunciation, Spelling, and Punctuation

Shakespeare's English as pronounced in his time would be strange to our ears yet still quite comprehensible; researches suggest it sounded remarkably like an Irish brogue. Consonants generally were pronounced as at present, but *r* was trilled and some consonants which are now silent were still voiced, like the *g* in *gnaw* (V. ii. 43). Certain vowel sounds were different: the open *e* was distinguished from the closed *e* (so *meet* II. i. 175 was pronounced differently from *meat* IV. ii. 170); and in diphthongs like *ea* (as in *dear* II. iii. 231) both vowels were heard. The suffix *-ion* was pronounced as two syllables; thus *destruction* in "*Destruction* on my head if my bad blame" (I. iii.

175) was a four-syllable word. Meter shows that in some words the *e* that originally preceded the final syllable also is meant to be sounded; thus *monstrous* in " 'Tis *monstrous*. Iago, who began't?" (II. iii. 196) should be pronounced *mon ste rous*. On the other hand, there was much elision of vowels, as for example in *y'are* (III. iii. 221), *i'th' dark* (IV. iii. 65), *for't* (IV. iii. 74), *th'addition* (IV. ii. 163). Probably the most important point for the modern reader is that many words were accented on a different syllable from that now usual, as for example, *por ténts* (V. ii. 45), *un au thó rized* (IV. i. 2). Moreover, the stress in some words is variable; in particular, disyllabic adjectives are accented on the first syllable when the first syllable of the next word is accented; thus "no *con' trived* murder (I. ii. 3), "the *di' vine* Desdemona" (II. i. 73).

Elizabethan spelling, which is highly phonetic, often is a useful guide to pronunciation, though by no means a reliable one. Spelling was unstandardized, highly irregular and erratic. As Shakespeare's own signatures evidence, it was not uncommon for an Elizabethan to spell even his own name in a variety of ways. In the printing house, compositors freely altered authorial spellings and even departed from their own orthographic habits as circumstances (e.g. the width of a column) required. Elizabethan punctuation is rather more orderly than the spelling, and it often suggests the spoken phrasing of lines since it tends to be rhetorical rather than syntactical. The comma, semicolon, colon, and period mark increasing degrees of pause in speech rather than different grammatical constructions. It is most unlikely, however, that the earliest printed texts of this play preserve with any consistency the Shakespearean pointing in the manuscripts underlying them. Some idiosyncratic usages may be worth noting to clarify punctuation in the textual notes: the question mark sometimes serves for the exclamation point, and (particularly in the Folio) parentheses are used for appositions (where we would point with commas) and for abrupt breaks or intrusions (where we might use a dash). A typographical oddity in the Quarto is the use of successive hyphens (usually three, as ---) for a variety of purposes: parentheses, interruptions of speech, change of subject, and even as an indication of hypermetrical syllables at the ends of lines.

For further discussion of Elizabethan English, see A. C. Baugh, *A History of the English Language* (New York, 1935). A full and authoritative discussion of Shakespeare's grammar is given in E. A. Abbott, *A Shakespearian Grammar* (London, 1905; first edition, 1869). The great authority on the diction is *The Oxford English Dictionary (OED)*, from which Shakespearean usages have been compiled in C. T. Onions, *A Shakespeare Glossary* (London, 1911). Also very useful is Alexander Schmidt's *Shakespeare-Lexicon*, revised by Gregor Sarrazin (Berlin, 1902; first edition, 1874). Speeches from

Shakespeare read in an Elizabethan accent can be heard on the record *Beowulf, Chaucer, Shakespeare and the Gettysburg Address* (National Council of Teachers of English, RL 20–7).

APPENDIX F

OTHELLO *in the Theater*

From the beginning, the play enjoyed marked success on the stage. If we can judge from the allusions, it may well have been the most popular of Shakespeare's tragedies during the seventeenth century. Leonard Digges, in commendatory verses possibly intended for the First Folio but first published in 1640, thus invidiously compared audience reactions won by *Julius Caesar* and *Othello* with those suffered by Ben Jonson's tragedies:

> . . . O how the audience
> Were ravished, with what wonder they went thence,
> When some new day they would not brook a line
> Of tedious (though well labored) Catiline's.
> Sejanus too was irksome; they prized more
> Honest Iago, or the jealous Moor.

Surviving records suggest how well *Othello* held the stage. The earliest recorded performance was at Court, November 1, 1604, but the play presumably had been successfully presented publicly before this. Certainly by 1622 (as the title page of the First Quarto attests) the play had been "acted divers times" at both the Globe and the King's Men's "private" theater, the Blackfriars, and elsewhere. A foreign visitor noted seeing "the history of the Moor of Venice" at the Globe in April 1610; and in September the same year, during a King's Men tour of the Provinces, a performance at Oxford was vividly remarked in a Latin letter by Henry Jackson, a prominent member of Corpus Christi College. By way of illustrating how the "fitly" performed tragedies "not only by the speaking but also by the acting moved [the audience] to tears," he recalled "that Desdemona slain amongst us by her husband" pleading in the murder scene—"when lying in the bed she implored the tears of the spectators by the expression of the face itself." The play was again at Court in 1612–13, during festivities at Whitehall honoring the marriage of Princess Elizabeth and the Elector Palatinate. Later records indicate revivals of the tragedy at the Blackfriars in 1629 and 1635, and at Hampton Court in 1636.

The great early Othello was the gifted Richard Burbage who

doubtless first created the role and was thoroughly identified with it still, as in this anonymous elegy, at his widely mourned death in 1618:

> . . . he's gone, and with him what a world are dead
> Which he revived, to be revivèd so
> No more: young Hamlet, old Hieronimo,
> Kind Lear, the grievèd Moor, and more beside
> That lived in him have now for ever died.

In point of fact, the tradition of such notable roles was continuous with the King's Men until their dissolution at the Closing of the Theaters in 1642. John Lowin (who probably had been in the original cast of *Othello*) and Joseph Taylor (a subsequent Iago) became its later depositaries—a fact perhaps significant for revivals after the Restoration. John Downes, a prompter in London theaters from 1662 to 1706 wrote (1708) that Thomas Betterton was instructed in the role of Henry VIII by Sir John Davenant, "who had it from old Mr. Lowin, that had his instructions from Shakespeare himself." And Betterton (who first played the Moor in 1682) was the finest of late seventeenth-century Othellos. His impersonation in the part later was to be celebrated by Sir Richard Steele (*Tatler*, No. 167), who particularly admired Betterton's "wonderful agony" of mixed emotion that had made the handkerchief scene—one that, in an unimaginative reader's view, might seem made of "dry, incoherent, and broken sentences"—unforgettably natural and convincingly complete.

Othello was the second of Shakespeare's plays to be produced after the Restoration. The diarist Samuel Pepys recorded seeing it at the Cockpit, with Burt as the Moor, 11 October 1660. It was probably in the next performance, December 8 at the competing Theatre on Vere Street, that the play gained the distinction of being the first on the English stage in which an actress performed. This innovation (as the Prologue explained) partly suggested itself as remedy for the absurdities consequent upon the decay of the boy-actor tradition.

> . . . men act that are between
> Forty and fifty, wenches of fifteen;
> With bone so large, and nerve so incompliant,
> When you call Desdemona, enter Giant.

The revived tragedy, though it was cut, fortunately escaped the gross alteration and adaptation suffered by other Shakespearean plays in this period. What we know of the cutting suggests refinement to remove touches thought too vulgar, weak, or savage to accord with the dignity of Othello's heroic role, and matter associated with Desdemona thought too domestic for a heroine's. The play was widely admired, Thomas Rymer (confident it was worthy of ridicule)

Illustration of the Murder Scene, from Nicholas Rowe, ed., *The Works of Shakespeare* (London, 1709). This engraving probably reflects stage practice in the very early eighteenth century. Notable features are the black make-up and contemporary costuming of the Moor, the extinguished candle on the night-table, the elaborate bed, and the pillow used for the murder. (Observe the absence of a dagger and see the note above at V. ii. 89). The sensual undress of the heroine exploits the actress in a manner characteristic of the permissive late seventeenth-century theater.

contemptuously observing, "From all the tragedies on our English stage, *Othello* is said to bear the bell away."

In every year but seven during the eighteenth century the play was produced on the London stage. Early productions (including the impressively cast 1707, with Verbruggen as Iago, Barton Booth as Cassio, and Mrs. Bracegirdle as Desdemona) were headed by Betterton's noble hero of restrained power. His successors in the role were Booth ("his masterpiece" thought Colley Cibber, himself a frequent Iago), and Thomas Quin—a massively imposing figure as the Moor in white wig, white British officer's uniform, and white gloves which he slowly drew off to emphasize the black make-up. But Quin's ponderous stolidity was insufficient for the role and his "hoarse monotony" incapable of its emotional range.

> Heavy and phlegmatic he trod the stage,
> Too proud for tenderness, too dull for rage. (Churchill)

The reaction to such conventional heroics was soon daringly attempted in the new "natural" style by the greatest actor of the century, David Garrick, who presented a busily passionate and violently tortured Othello. It was a failure. Garrick seemed unable to sustain the monumentality of the character, and the passion appeared to most auditors fitful sensation that fretfully dissipated the tragic hero's dignity. The really great Othello of the age, who may have achieved what Garrick only partly conceived, was Spranger Barry, an actor (wrote Francis Gentleman) "born for the Moor." He had the physique, a voice capable of melody, "silver cadence," and contradictory extremes of emotion, and he could project both the immense human dignity of the part and its enormous passion and disturbingly powerful grief. From 1746 to 1774 he dominated the role in over twenty revivals. By contrast, the principal end-of-century Othello, John Philip Kemble, was lordly, Roman-austere, and decorously formal; he emphasized majesty and mystery in the part and completely mantled its ardency. His sister, Mrs. Siddons (a moving Desdemona as well as a great Lady Macbeth), thought he lacked passion for it.

Toward the end of the eighteenth century the play suffered much new deletion. Certain severe cuts of "indecorous" matter were by this time traditional. Garrick had ventured—to some applause and much disgusted criticism—to restore the trance scene; but more than a century passed before it was again staged. Increasingly now, however, the play's language itself was cleansed by deletion of indelicate frankness. That even the carefully purged Kemble version could be assailed in 1808 as "committing such a violence on the modesty and decency of the house as is altogether intolerable" (*Monthly Mirror*) presaged the still more stringent Bowdlerizing of the text in the nineteenth century, when (as the Lacy standard acting version shows) Othello and Iago were not suffered to utter such shocking words as "whore," "cuckold," or even "beds."

Other factors importantly affecting nineteenth-century presentation of the play were the vast size of the curtained proscenium arch theaters and (starting particularly with the regimes of Macready and Charles Kean) their heavy emphasis on increasingly elaborate, and interruptive, representational scenery. It was partly in the spirit of the "realism" and historicism of such scene-setting (though partly also to expunge the idea—"monstrous to conceive"—that a beautiful Venetian girl like Desdemona could fall in love "with a veritable negro") that actors, beginning with Kean and Macready, broke with tradition and (with Coleridge's blessing) first presented Othello "correctly" as a tawny Moor. The distortive importance placed on the spectacular painted scenes is amusingly reflected in the space and enthusiasm devoted to them in playbills.

Theatre Royal, Drury Lane
This Evening, Wednesday, May 16, 1838
Her Majesty's Servants will revive Shakespeare's Tragedy of
OTHELLO
The Following is the order of the New, and extensive Scenery,
Painted by
Mr. Grieve, Mr. T. Grieve, and Mr. W. Grieve
The Grand Canal
A Street in Venice
Council Chamber
Sea Port of Cyprus!
Exterior of Guard House
Chamber in the Palace of Cyprus
Apartment in the Palace
The Bed Chamber!

But the big drawing card of *Othello* revivals (and a main determinant of their character) was the striking succession of actors vying in performance of the major roles. This began with the passionate Othello of Edmund Kean, which epitomized the stunning emotionalism of the new Romantic style of acting.

After Kemble's formalism, Kean's sudden emotional appeals, startling transitions, and emphatic moments of spasmodically violent passion seemed almost shockingly "natural." Although diminutive like Garrick, Kean, unlike him, never seemed to audiences small of stature as the Moor. In the part he exploited both a voice of remarkable range—from the musically delicate to the savagely inarticulate—and (though this could be only for those near the stage in so immense a house) a face of extraordinary expressive power. "His face" wrote

MR KEAN,

as OTHELLO.

Iago. *O, beware my lord of jealousy.*

Edmund Kean as Othello. After a painting by E. F. Lambert.

Hazlitt, "is the running comment on his acting which reconciles the audience to it." There clearly was much to be reconciled to in this great performance. Kean's starts and violences—his rage at the Moor's "waked wrath" (III. iii. 360), we are told, "was nothing less than convulsion"—were powerfully convincing in his representation of Othello's fury, pathos, and desolation in Act III; but where his imagination was less engaged, he was capable of distorting speeches by lunging for a sudden emotional appeal or mannered abruptness of tonal change.

All the great actors of the century were seen in the play, some of the more versatile in both the hero's and the villain's roles. After Kean, the most notable Othellos were, perhaps, the great American tragedian Edwin Forrest, who gave the Moor's jealousy a powerful personal force; the tremendously exciting if "abominably un-Shakespearean" Salvini, who played the part with shocking animal ferocity; and Edwin Booth, who painstakingly intellectualized the Moor into a painfully troubled soul. Macready was weak as the Moor and Irving so abysmal a failure that (as producer) he abandoned the play (thus unhappily sacrificing the celebrated tender yet strongly spirited Desdemona of Ellen Terry); but both were interesting as Iago, Irving's portrayal, the richer, being a typical character-actor's, full of idiosyncratic detail and business. Probably the finest Iago of the age, however, was that of Booth, who in his own way solved the old actor's problem of the degree of disguise appropriate for the ensign's villainy. Especially in his later manner, Booth gave the character firm plausibility and his evil a disturbing profundity. The actor's valuable notes on the play (contributed to the *Othello Variorum*, 1885) are full of such insightful response to problems raised for actors as the following advice to the player of Iago,

"Do not smile, or sneer, or glower,—try to impress even *the audience* with your sincerity. 'Tis better, however, always to ignore the audience; if you can forget that you are a 'shew' you will be natural. The more sincere your manner, the more devilish your deceit. I think the 'light comedian' should play the villain's part, not the 'heavy man'; I mean the Shakespearian villains. Iago should appear to be what all but the audience believe he is. Even when alone, there is little need to remove the mask entirely. Shakespeare spares you that trouble."

A number of intrenched practices of nineteenth-century Shakespearean production were fundamentally deleterious. Among these were the subordination of the action to the star actor, the ruthless cutting of the texts and scenic division of the action, the displacing emphasis on localizing scenery and impertinent spectacle, and the concentration on actors' "points," proliferated business, and "strong" curtains. But the radical evil was the imposition on the plays of the inappropriate conditions of the "picture-frame" stage itself. Starting in the 'nineties, reforms destined to be highly influential were initiated under experimental directors such as William Poel and Granville-Barker, who were concerned to reclaim for productions the Shakespearean dramaturgical values based on the open-stage theaters for which the plays had been intended. All the same, Shakespeare production in the twentieth century (no less than in any other) also has been variously affected, and frequently distorted, by new trends in the contemporary theatrical scene (e.g. naturalistic acting methods) and by the shifting preoccupations and taste of the times.

The tragedy, often revived, has been a standard offering of the many Shakespearean repertory companies, and almost all the important Shakespearean actors have appeared in it. It may be doubted whether anyone in this century has yet emerged to claim the stature in the play of Burbage, Betterton, Barry, Kean, or Booth. Among the more provocative productions was that in 1930 by the black American performer Paul Robeson, who (much more than his nineteenth-century counterpart, Ira Aldrich) brought to the play an openly controversial emphasis on the hero's racial identity. A later Robeson production in 1943 enjoyed a near-record run in New York (where the play probably had had the first of its innumerable New World revivals in 1755). The best-known recent production, which (by way of the motion picture screen) brought a version of the play before a very wide audience, unhappily featured Sir Laurence Olivier's often grotesquely mannered, narrowly sensational, and radically untragic portrayal of the hero.

For further reading, see Arthur Colby Sprague, *Shakespeare and the Actors* (New York, 1963; first published 1944) and *Shakespearian Players and Performances* (Cambridge, Mass., 1953); Marvin Rosenberg, *The Masks of Othello* (Berkeley and Los Angeles, 1961); George C. Odell, *Shakespeare from Betterton to Irving* (2 vols.; New York, 1966; first published, 1920); A. C. Ward, ed., *Specimens of English Dramatic Criticism* (London, 1945); the *Variorum* edition; and the stage history by C. B. Young in Wilson and Walker's edition.

APPENDIX G

Bibliography

Shakespeare has been the subject of an immense amount of writing of widely varying usefulness and significance. The range of the literature is suggested in *The Cambridge Bibliography of English Literature,* edited by F. W. Bateson (New York, 1941) and its *Supple-*

ment, edited by George Watson (1957). More detailed bibliographies are those by Walther Ebisch and Levin L. Schücking, *A Shakespeare Bibliography* (Oxford, 1931), with its *Supplement for the Years 1930–1935* (1937), and Gordon Ross Smith, *A Classified Shakespeare Bibliography, 1936–1958* (University Park, Pa., 1963). Annual Shakespeare bibliographies can be found in *Shakespeare Quarterly* (before 1950, *Shakespeare Association Bulletin*), *Studies in Philology, Publications of the Modern Language Association*, and the yearly volume of the Modern Humanities Research Association. Brief commentaries on each year's Shakespeare studies appear in *Shakespeare Survey* and *The Year's Work in English Studies*, and appraisals of the more important items in *Shakespeare Studies* (since 1965). A helpful annotated introduction to a good number of books and articles on the plays is *A Reader's Guide to Shakespeare's Plays* by Ronald Berman (Chicago, 1965). Bibliographies on *Othello* in particular are S. A. Tannenbaum, *Shakespeare's Othello: A Concise Bibliography* (New York, 1943) and *Othello: A Supplementary Bibliography, 1886–1964* by Louis Marder (New York, 1965).

For the historical and social background of Shakespeare's age, see especially the well-illustrated *Shakespeare's England*, edited by Sidney Lee and C. T. Onions (Oxford, 1917). Some of the Folger Shakespeare Library's useful pamphlets on Elizabethan civilization have been collected in *Life and Letters in Tudor and Stuart England*, edited by Louis B. Wright and Virginia A. LaMar (Ithaca, N.Y., 1962); and a collection of essays on *Shakespeare in His Own Age* comprises *Shakespeare Survey 17* (Cambridge, 1964), edited by Allardyce Nicoll. There is a delightful and informative collection of Elizabethan prose called *Life in Shakespeare's England*, compiled by John Dover Wilson (London: Pelican, 1944). For a readable history of the period, see S. T. Bindoff, *Tudor England* (London: Pelican, 1950); the standard work is a volume in the Oxford History of England by J. B. Black, *The Reign of Elizabeth, 1558–1603* (Oxford, 1959). For an introduction to the Elizabethan intellectual background, see Hardin Craig, *The Enchanted Glass* (New York, 1936), E. M. W. Tillyard, *The Elizabethan World Picture* (New York, 1944), and Theodore Spencer, *Shakespeare and the Nature of Man* (New York, 1942). Some important aspects of Shakespeare's relation to this background are discussed in Virgil K. Whitaker, *Shakespeare's Use of Learning* (San Marino, Calif., 1953) and Walter Clyde Curry, *Shakespeare's Philosophic Patterns* (Baton Rouge, 1937).

The standard reference work on the history of the theater is E. K. Chambers, *The Elizabethan Stage*, 4 vols. (Oxford, 1923), continued in Gerald Eades Bentley, *The Jacobean and Caroline Stage*, 7 vols. (Oxford, 1941–68). Two more accessible studies are G. B. Harrison's *Elizabethan Plays and Players* (Ann Arbor, 1956) and Alfred Harbage's *Shakespeare's Audience* (New York, 1941). A good short account of *Shakespeare's Stage* is that by A. M. Nagler (New Haven, 1958). See also C. Walter Hodges, *The Globe Restored* (New York, 1954), Bernard Beckerman, *Shakespeare at the Globe, 1599–1609* (New York, 1962), and Gerald Eades Bentley, *Shakespeare and His Theatre* (Lincoln, Neb., 1964). A more speculative study is Glynne Wickham's *Early English Stages, 1300 to 1600,* 2 vols. (London, 1959–63). An important discussion of *Elizabethan Playhouse Stages* by Richard Hosley, developing his scholarly work already in print, has been announced for publication.

The authoritative investigation of Shakespeare's life and career, with documentation, is E. K. Chambers, *William Shakespeare: A Study of the Facts and Problems,* 2 vols. (Oxford, 1930); see also Edgar I. Fripp, *Shakespeare, Man and Artist,* 2 vols. (Oxford, 1938). A more recent valuable work is *Shakespeare: A Biographical Handbook* (New Haven, 1961) by Gerald Eades Bentley. For a readable popular account, see Marchette Chute, *Shakespeare of London* (New York, 1949). Ten excellent pamphlets on Shakespeare, with illustrations and bibliographies, have been published by the British Council in their Writers and Their Work Series; and a useful collection of essays on various aspects of Shakespeare, entitled *A Companion to Shakespeare Studies,* has been edited by Harley Granville-Barker and G. B. Harrison (Garden City, N.Y., 1960). Two general accounts of Shakespeare's work, with a main emphasis on style, are D. A. Traversi, *An Approach to Shakespeare,* 2nd ed. (Garden City, N.Y., 1956), and Mark Van Doren, *Shakespeare* (Garden City, N.Y., 1953). For an important brief essay on Shakespeare's later work, see Maynard Mack, "The Jacobean Shakespeare," in *Jacobean Theatre,* ed. J. R. Brown and B. Harris (London, 1960). Several paper-back anthologies make it convenient to obtain some sense of the range and richness of modern Shakespearean criticism: *Shakespeare: Modern Essays in Criticism,* ed. Leonard F. Dean (New York, 1957); *Modern Shakespearean Criticism,* ed. Alvin B. Kernan (New York, etc., 1970); *Essays in Shakespearean Criticism,* ed. J. L. Calderwood and H. E. Tolliver (Englewood Cliffs, N.J., 1970).

Valuable background on ideas and conventions of tragedy in Shakespeare and his age can be found in Madeleine Doran, *Endeavors of Art* (Madison, 1954), Muriel Bradbrook, *Themes and Conventions of Elizabethan Tragedy* (Cambridge, 1935), and Willard Farnham, *The Medieval Heritage of Elizabethan Tragedy* (reprinted, Oxford, 1956). See also Fredson Bowers, *Elizabethan Revenge Tragedy, 1587–1642* (Princeton, 1940), and for Iago's ancestry in the Vice of the morality play, Bernard Spivack, *Shakespeare and the Allegory of Evil* (New York, 1958).

The most fully annotated among the many editions of *Othello* is the *New Variorum,* edited by Horace Howard Furness (Philadelphia, 1886); though still useful, this is now very badly out of date. Later editions with particularly valuable notes are the old Arden edition by H. C. Hart (London, 1903), the edition by George Lyman Kittredge (Boston, 1941), and the new Arden by M. R. Ridley (London, 1958).

Early criticism of the play from Thomas Rymer's neo-classic attack on it (1693), through Johnson's and Coleridge's important comments, to the Victorians can readily be sampled in the *Variorum*. Twentieth-century *Othello* criticism has recently been briefly surveyed by Helen Gardner in *Shakespeare Survey 21* (1968), an issue which has *Othello* as its theme; some representative critical essays are reprinted by Leonard F. Dean in *A Casebook on Othello* (Binghamton, N.Y., 1961). A many-faceted long essay valuable for introductory study of the play is that by Harley Granville-Barker in his *Prefaces to Shakespeare*, Vol. II (Princeton, 1947). Two important (and diametrically opposed) early studies which are basic to much later controversy are A. C. Bradley, *Shakespearean Tragedy* (London, 1904) and Elmer Edgar Stoll, *Othello: An Historical and Comparative Study* (Minneapolis, 1915). Bradley's is the classic realistic analysis of the play's characters and situation; Stoll's view, reasserted in numerous later studies such as *Art and Artifice in Shakespeare* (New York, 1933) and "An *Othello* All-too Modern," *ELH* 13 (1946): 46–58, is that the play is an artificial structure of conventional paradoxes of character and situation which sacrifices probability and psychology in the interest of stunning theatrical effect. For an interesting critique of both Bradley and Stoll, see J. I. M. Stewart, *Character and Motive in Shakespeare* (London, 1949).

Much modern critical controversy has centered on the character of the hero, views of which are very divergent. This issue can be explored in, among others, T. S. Eliot, *Selected Essays 1917–1932* (New York, 1932); F. R. Leavis, "Diabolic Intellect and the Noble Hero," *Scrutiny* 6 (1937): 259–83; Derek Traversi, *An Approach to Shakespeare*, 1st ed. (New York, 1938); Theodore Spencer, *Shakespeare and the Nature of Man* (New York, 1942); Brents Stirling, "Psychology in *Othello*," *Shakespeare Association Bulletin* 19 (1944): 135–44; Leo Kirschbaum, "The Modern Othello," *ELH* 11 (1944): 283–96; H. B. Charlton, *Shakespearian Tragedy* (Cambridge, 1948); Richard Flatter, *The Moor of Venice* (London, 1950); G. R. Elliott, *Flaming Minister: A Study of Othello* (Durham, N.C., 1953); Helen Gardner, "The Noble Moor," *Proceedings of the British Academy* 41 (1955): 189–205; Albert Gérard, " 'Egregiously an Ass': The Dark Side of the Moor. A View of Othello's Mind," *Shakespeare Survey 10* (1957): 98–106; G. K. Walton, "Strength's Abundance," *Review of English Studies* 9 (1960): 8–17; Barbara Everett, "Reflections on the Sentimentalist's Othello," *Critical Quarterly* 3 (1960): 127–39; and John Holloway, *The Story of the Night: Studies in Shakespeare's Major Tragedies* (Lincoln, Neb., 1961). Iago too has been the subject of much fascinated recent study. See, besides Spivack's basic work (cited above, App. C), Theodore Spencer, "The Elizabethan Malcontent," in *J. Q. Adams Memorial Studies* (Washington, 1948); Samuel A. Tannebaum, "The Wronged Iago," *Shakespeare Association Bulletin* 12 (1937): 57–62; John W. Draper, "The Jealousy of Iago," *Neophilologus* 25 (1939): 50–60; J. C. McCloskey, "The Motivation of Iago," *College English* 3 (1941): 25–30; J. R. Moore, "The Character of Iago," *Studies in Honor of A. H. R. Fairchild* (Columbia, Mo., 1949); Kenneth Muir, "The Jealousy of Iago," *English Miscellany* 2 (1952): 65–83; Marvin Rosenberg, "In Defense of Iago," *Shakespeare Quarterly* 6 (1955): 145–58; James A. S. McPeek, "The 'Arts Inhibited' and the Meaning of *Othello*," *Boston University Studies in English* 1 (1956): 129–47.

A controversial issue of major importance in contemporary criticism, though unhappily restricted all too often merely to the question of the hero's damnation, fundamentally turns on the relation of Christianity and tragedy in this play. See particularly Kenneth O. Myrick, "Damnation in Shakespearean Tragedy," *Studies in Philology* 38 (1941): 221–45; Clifford Leech, *Shakespeare's Tragedies and other Studies in Seventeenth Century Drama* (London, 1950); J. V. Cunningham, *Woe or Wonder: The Emotional Effect of Shakespearean Tragedy* (University of Denver Press, 1951); Arthur Sewell, *Character and Society in Shakespeare* (Oxford, 1951); Paul N. Siegel, "The Damnation of Othello," *Publications of the Modern Language Association* 68 (1953): 1063–78; Sylvan Barnet, "Some Limitations of a Christian Approach to Shakespeare," *ELH* 22 (1955): 81–92; H. S. Wilson, *On the Design of Shakespearian Tragedy* (Toronto, 1957); Edward Hubler, "The Damnation of Othello: Some Limitations on the Christian View of the Play," *Shakespeare Quarterly* 9 (1958): 295–300; Irving Ribner, *Patterns in Shakespearean Tragedy* (New York, 1960); J. A. Bryant, Jr., *Hippolyta's View: Some Christian Aspects of Shakespeare's Plays* (University of Kentucky Press, 1961); R. M. Frye, *Shakespeare and Christian Doctrine* (Princeton, 1963); Robert H. West, "The Christianness of *Othello*," *Shakespeare Quarterly* 15 (1964): 333–43. Of course, various special kinds of inquiry, for instance those concerned with the play's imagery, directly impinge on this issue: see, for example, S. L. Bethell, "Shakespeare's Imagery: the Diabolic Images in *Othello*," *Shakespeare Survey* 5 (1952): 62–80; Lawrence J. Ross, " 'Marble,' 'Crocodile,' and 'Turban'd Turk' in *Othello*," *Philological Quarterly*, 40 (1961): 476–84, "World and Chrysolite in *Othello*," *Modern Language Notes* 76 (1961): 683–92, and "The Ship, Pilot, and Storm Motif in *Othello*," *Shakespeare Quarterly*: in press.

Criticism in this century has heavily emphasized study of character, action, and theme through analysis of language and imagery. Pioneer studies are G. Wilson Knight's famous essay "The *Othello* Music" in *The Wheel of Fire* (London, 1930), and Caroline Spurgeon's *Shake-*

speare's *Imagery and What It Tells Us* (Cambridge, 1952). Valuable introductions to this sort of inquiry are Wolfgang H. Clemen, *The Development of Shakespeare's Imagery* (Cambridge, Mass., 1951) and an important book devoted to it by Robert B. Heilman, *Magic in the Web: Action and Language in Othello* (Lexington, Ky., 1956). See also Mikhail M. Morozov, "The Individualization of Shakespeare's Characters through Imagery," *Shakespeare Survey* 2 (1949): 102–6; Paul A. Jorgensen, "Honesty in *Othello*," *Studies in Philology* 47 (1950): 557–67; William Empson, *The Structure of Complex Words* (London, 1951); Bethell's essay on the diabolic imagery (1952); B. Ifor Evans, *The Language of Shakespeare's Plays* (Indiana University Press, 1952); Winifred M. T. Nowottny, "Justice and Love in *Othello*," *University of Toronto Quarterly* 21 (1952): 33–44; J. E. Hankins, *Shakespeare's Derived Imagery* (University of Kansas Press, 1953); Brents Stirling, *Unity in Shakespearean Tragedy* (Columbia University Press, 1956); M. M. Mahood, *Shakespeare's Wordplay* (London, 1957); Hilda M. Hulme, *Explorations in Shakespeare's Language* (New York and London, 1964).

Further selected reading, in backgrounds and in criticism, might include: Lily Bess Campbell, *Shakespeare's Tragic Heroes* (Cambridge, 1930); Richmond Noble, *Shakespeare's Biblical Knowledge* (London, 1935); Moody E. Prior, "Character in Relation to Action in *Othello*," *Modern Philology* 44 (1947): 225–37; Sister Miriam Joseph Rauh, *Shakespeare's Use of the Arts of Language* (Columbia University Press, 1947); Caroll Camden, "Iago on Women," *Journal of English and Germanic Philology* 48 (1949): 57–71; Georges Bonnard, "Are Othello and Desdemona Innocent or Guilty?" *English Studies* (Amsterdam) 30 (1949): 175–86; Derek Traversi, "Othello," *The Wind and the Rain* 6 (1950): 248–68; Kenneth Burke, "Othello: An Essay to Illustrate a Method," *Hudson Review* 4 (1951): 165–203; J. R. Moore, "Othello, Iago, and Cassio as Soldiers," *Philological Quarterly* 31 (1952): 189–94; John Money, "Othello's 'It is the cause . . .': An Analysis," *Shakespeare Survey* 6 (1953): 94–105; Franklin M. Dickey, *Not Wisely But Too Well* (San Marino, Cal., 1957); Lawrence J. Ross, "The Meaning of Strawberries in Shakespeare," *Studies in the Renaissance* 7 (1960): 225–40; C. B. Watson, *Shakespeare and the Renaissance Concept of Honor* (Princeton, 1960); John Lawlor, *The Tragic Sense in Shakespeare* (New York, 1960); John Bayley, *The Characters of Love* (London, 1960); A. P. Rossiter, "Othello: A Moral Essay" in *Angel with Horns: and Other Shakespeare Lectures* (New York, 1961); Terence Hawkes, "Iago's Use of Reason," *Studies in Philology* 58 (1961): 160–9; Maynard Mack, "Engagement and Detachment in Shakespeare's Plays," in *Essays on Shakespeare . . . in Honor of Hardin Craig* (Columbia, Mo., 1962); David Kula, "Othello Possessed: Notes on Shakespeare's Use of Magic and Witchcraft," *Shakespeare Studies* 2

(1966): 112–32; Madeleine Doran, "Good Name in 'Othello'," *Studies in English Literature* 7 (1967): 195–217; G. K. Hunter, "Othello and Colour Prejudice," *Proceedings of the British Academy* 53 (1967): 139–63.

Additional bibliographical references on special topics can be found above in Appendixes B (the text), C (sources), D (music), E (Shakespeare's English), and F (theatrical history).

The Marlowe Society of Cambridge University, under the direction of George Rylands, has recorded the uncut text of the New Cambridge Shakespeare *Othello* (Lon. A-4414). Another available phonographic recording (Vic. LDM-100) features Sir Laurence Olivier as the Moor.

APPENDIX H

Abbreviations, References, and Editions

Batman upon Bartholomew	Stephen Batman, *Batman vppon Bartholome, his booke De proprietatibus rervm* (London, 1582).
Becon	Thomas Becon, *Early Works,* ed. Rev. John Ayre, Parker Society (Cambridge, 1843).
Bersuire	Petrus Berchorius, *Opera omnia,* 6 vols. (Cologne, 1731).
Bible	References are to the Geneva-Tomson Bible (London, 1603), unless otherwise indicated.
Book of Common Prayer	*The Book of Common Prayer, 1559.* In *Liturgies and Occasional Forms of Prayer set forth in the Reign of Queen Elizabeth,* ed. Rev. William Keatinge Clay, Parker Society (Cambridge, 1847).
Bradford	John Bradford, *Writings,* ed. Rev. Aubrey Townsend, Parker Society, 2 vols. (Cambridge, 1848–53).
Bullinger	Henry Bullinger, *Decades,* trans. H. I., ed. Rev. Thomas Harding, Parker Society, 4 vols. (Cambridge, 1849–52).

Capell · *Mr. William Shakespeare, His Comedies, Histories and Tragedies,* ed. E. Capell, 10 vols. (London, 1767–8).

Collier · *The Works of William Shakespeare,* ed. J. P. Collier, 8 vols. (London, 1842–4).

conj. · conjecture.

corr. · corrected.

Delius · Shakespeare, *Werke,* ed. Nicholaus Delius, 3rd ed., 2 vols. (Elberfeld, 1872).

Elze · Theodor Elze, in *Shakespeare Jahrbuch,* XIV (1879): 176.

F, F2, F3, F4 · The first four collected editions of Shakespeare's plays, published in folio in 1623, 1632, 1663–4, and 1685.

Fuller · Thomas Fuller, *Gnomologia: Adagies and Proverbs* (London, 1732).

Granville-Barker · Harley Granville-Barker, *Prefaces to Shakespeare,* 2 vols. (Princeton, 1947).

Greene · *The Life and Complete Works . . . of Robert Greene,* ed. Alexander B. Grosart, 15 vols. (London, 1881–6).

Hanmer · *The Works of Shakespeare,* ed. Sir Thomas Hanmer, 6 vols. (London, 1744–6).

Hart · *The Tragedy of Othello,* ed. H. C. Hart, the Arden Shakespeare (London, 1903).

Henley · *The Plays of Shakespeare,* ed. Samuel Johnson and George Steevens (with notes contributed by Samuel Henley), 10 vols. (London, 1773).

Homilies · *Certaine sermons, or homilies, appoynted by the Queenes Maiestie . . .* (London, 1595).

Hooker · Richard Hooker, *The Works,* ed. John Keble, 7th edition rev. R. Church and F. Paget, 3 vols. (Oxford, 1888).

Hudson   *The Complete Works of Shakespeare*,
                          ed. H. N. Hudson, Harvard Edition, 20
                          vols. (Boston, 1880–1).

Jennens   *Othello*, ed. Charles Jennens (London,
                          1773).

Johnson   *The Plays of William Shakespeare*, ed.
                          Dr. Samuel Johnson, 8 vols. (London,
                          1765).

Jonson   Ben Jonson, *Works*, ed. C. H. Herford,
                          Percy and Evelyn Simpson, 11 vols.
                          (Oxford, 1925–52).

Kittredge   *The Tragedy of Othello*, ed. George
                          Lyman Kittredge (New York, 1941).

Knight   *The Works of Shakespeare*, ed.
                          C. Knight, Pictorial Edition, 7 vols.
                          (London, 1839–42).

Kyd   *The Works of Thomas Kyd*, ed. F. S.
                          Boas (Oxford, 1901).

La Primaudaye   Pierre de La Primaudaye, *The French
                          Academye*, 3 vols. (London, 1602–5).

Lyly   John Lyly, *The Complete Works*, ed.
                          R. Warwick Bond, 3 vols. (Oxford,
                          1902).

Malone   *The Plays and Poems of William
                          Shakespeare*, ed. E. Malone, 10 vols.
                          (London, 1790).

Marlowe   *The Works of Christopher Marlowe*,
                          ed. C. F. Tucker Brooke (Oxford,
                          1929).

OED   *A New English Dictionary*, ed. J. A. H.
                          Murray *et al.*, 13 vols. (Oxford, 1884–
                          1928).

Pliny   *The Historie of the World. Commonly
                          called the Naturall Historie of C.
                          Plinivs Secvndus*, trans. Philemon Hol-
                          land (London, 1601).

Plutarch	*Plutarch's Moralia,* VI, with trans. by W. C. Helmbold, Loeb Classical Library (London and Cambridge, Mass., 1939).
Pope	*The Works of Shakespeare,* ed. Alexander Pope, 6 vols. (London, 1723–25).
Q, Q1	The First Quarto edition of *Othello* (1622).
Q2	The Second Quarto edition of *Othello* (1630).
Quintilian	Quintilian, *Institutio oratoria,* with translation by H. E. Butler, 4 vols., Loeb Classical Library (New York, 1933–6).
Ridley	*Othello,* ed. M. R. Ridley, the Arden Edition (London, 1958).
Rowe	*The Works of Mr. William Shakespeare,* ed. Nicholas Rowe, 7 vols. (London, 1709).
S.D.	Stage direction.
S.P.	Speech prefix.
Schmidt	Alexander Schmidt, *Shakespeare-Lexicon,* rev. Gregor Sarrazin (Berlin, 1902).
Shakespeare	References to other works of Shakespeare are to the Tudor Edition by Peter Alexander, except for plays already published in this series.
Shakespeare's England	*Shakespeare's England,* ed. Sidney Lee and C. T. Onions, 2 vols. (Oxford, 1917).
Staunton	*The Plays of Shakespeare,* ed. Howard Staunton, 3 vols. (London, 1858–60).
Steevens	*The Plays of William Shakespeare,* ed. I. Reed (with notes by George Steevens), 15 vols. (London, 1793).

subst.	substantively.
Theobald	*The Works of Shakespeare*, ed. Lewis Theobald, 7 vols. (London, 1733).
Tilley	Morris Palmer Tilley, *A Dictionary of Proverbs in England in the Sixteenth and Seventeeth Centuries* (Ann Arbor, 1950).
uncorr.	uncorrected.
Upton	John Upton, *Critical Observations on Shakespeare* (London, 1746).
Variorum	*Othello*, ed. Horace Howard Furness, A New Variorum Edition of Shakespeare, 2nd ed. (Philadelphia, 1886).
Warburton	*The Works of Shakespeare*, ed. W. Warburton, 8 vols. (London, 1747).
Wilson and Walker	*Othello*, ed. Alice Walker and John Dover Wilson, The New [Cambridge] Shakespeare (New York, 1957).